SOCIAL SCIENCE AS MORAL INQUIRY

SOCIAL SCIENCE AS MORAL INQUIRY

Edited by

Norma Haan
Robert N. Bellah
Paul Rabinow
William M. Sullivan

Columbia University Press
New York   1983

Library of Congress Cataloging in Publication Data
Main entry under title:

Social science as moral inquiry.

Includes bibliographical references and index.
1. Social sciences—Moral and ethical aspects—
Addresses, essays, lectures. I. Haan, Norma.
H61.S58994 1983 174′.9301   82-19840
ISBN 0-231-05648-6
ISBN 0-231-05649-4(pbk.)

Clothbound editions of Columbia University Press books are Smyth-
sewn and printed on permanent and durable acid-free paper.

Columbia University Press
New York Guildford, Surrey

To the memory of
MICHELLE ROSALDO

CONTENTS

CONTRIBUTORS

Robert N. Bellah is Ford Professor of Sociology and Comparative Studies at the University of California, Berkeley. His published works include (with Philip E. Hammond) *Varieties of Civil Religion* (New York: Harper & Row, 1980) and (with Charles Y. Glock) *The New Religious Consciousness* (Berkeley: University of California Press, 1976).

Michel de Certeau, Professor of Comparative and French Literature at the University of California, San Diego, is the author of *L'Ecriture de l'Histoire* (Paris: Gallimard, 1978); *L'Invention du quotidien. Arts de faire,* No. 1 (Paris: Union Générale D'Editions, 1980); and *La Fable mystique (XVIe–XVIIe siècle)* (Paris: Gallimard, 1982).

Richard Flacks is Professor of Sociology, University of California, Santa Barbara, and has published "Making History vs. Making Life: Dilemmas of an American Left," *Sociological Inquiry* (1976), 46(3–4):263–80; (with Jack Whalen) "The Isla Vista 'Bank Burners' Ten Years Later: Notes on the Fate of Student Activists," *Sociological Focus* (1980), vol. 63; and "Socialists as Socializers: Notes on the Purposes of Organizations," *Socialist Review* (1979), 42.

Carol Gilligan is Associate Professor, Laboratory of Human Development, Harvard Graduate School of Education. Her recent publications include *In a Different Voice: Psychological Theory and Women's Development* (Cambridge: Harvard University Press, 1982); "Development from Adolescence to Adulthood: The Philosopher and the 'Dilemma of the Fact,'" in Judith Gardner, ed., *Readings in Developmental Psychology,* 2d ed. (Boston: Little, Brown, 1982); and "Moral Development in the College Years," in A. Chickering, ed., *The American College* (San Francisco: Jossey-Bass, 1981).

Norma Haan, Research Scientist at the Institute of Human Development of the University of California at Berkeley, is the author of "Hypothetical and Actual Moral Reasoning in a Situation of Civil Disobedience," *Journal of Personality and Social Psychology* (1975), 32:255–70; "Two Moralities: Action, Development and Ego Regulation," *Journal of Personality and Social Psychology* (1978),

36:286–305; and (with Richard Weiss and Vicky Johnson), "The Role of Logic in Moral Reasoning and Development," *Developmental Psychology* (1982), 18:205–16.

Jürgen Habermas is presently at the University of Frankfurt, West Germany. Among his major works are *Knowledge and Human Interests* (Boston: Beacon Press, 1979); *Communication and the Evolution of Society* (Boston: Beacon Press, 1979); and *Theorie des Kommunikativen Handelns* (Frankurt am Main: Suhrkamp Verlag, 1981).

Albert O. Hirschman is Professor of Social Science at the Institute for Advanced Study, Princeton, New Jersey, and author of *The Strategy of Economic Development* (New Haven, Conn.: Yale University Press, Norton Library, 1978); *Exit, Voice, and Loyalty* (Cambridge: Harvard University Press, 1970); and *Private and Public Happiness: Pursuits and Disappointments* (Princeton, N.J.: Princeton University Press, 1982).

Michael S. McPherson, Associate Professor of Economics at Williams College and a Member (1981–82) of the Institute of Advanced Study, Princeton, New Jersey, has written "Mill's Moral Theory and the Problem of Preference Change," *Ethics* (1981), 92; "Imperfect Democracy and the Moral Responsibilities of Policy Advisers," in Daniel Callahan and Bruce Jennings, eds., *Ethics, Social Science, and Policy Analysis* (New York: Plenum Press, 1982); and "Value Conflicts in American Higher Education: A Survey," *Journal of Higher Education* (forthcoming).

Wolf-Dieter Narr is Professor of Political Theory at the Free University of Berlin. He is the author of (with F. Naschold) *Theorie der Demokratie* (Stuttgart: Kohlhamer, 1971). "Hin zu einer Gesellschaft bedingter Reflexe," in Jürgen Habermas, ed., *Stichworte zur 'Geistigen Situation der Zeit'* (Frankfurt am Main: Suhrkamp 1979); and *Zur Kritik politischer Soziologie am Beispiel von Max Weber* (forthcoming).

Paul Rabinow is Associate Professor of Anthropology, University of California at Berkeley. His published works include *Symbolic Domination: Cultural Form and Historical Change in Morocco* (Chicago: University of Chicago Press, 1975); *Reflections on Fieldwork in Morocco* (Berkeley: University of California Press, 1977); and (with Hubert Dreyfus) *Michel Foucault: Beyond Structuralism and Hermeneutics* (Chicago: University of Chicago Press, 1982).

Richard Rorty is Kenan Professor of Humanities at the University of Virginia, editor of *The Linguistic Turn* (Chicago: University of Chicago Press, 1967), and author of *Philosophy and the Mirror of Nature* (Princeton: Princeton University Press, 1979) and *Consequences of Pragmatism* (Minneapolis: University of Minnesota Press, 1982).

Michelle Z. Rosaldo was Associate Professor of Anthropology, Stanford University, Stanford, California. Her published works include *Knowledge and Passion: Ilongot Notions of Self and Social Life* (Cambridge: Cambridge University Press, 1980); (ed., with Louise Lamphere) *Woman, Culture and Society* (Stanford, Calif.: Stanford University Press, 1974); and "The Use and Abuse of Anthropology: Reflections on Feminism and Cross-Cultural Understanding," *Signs,* Spring 1980.

Stephen G. Salkever, Professor of Political Science, Bryn Mawr College, Bryn Mawr, Pennsylvania, is the author of "Virtue, Obligation, and Politics," *American Political Science Review* (1974), 68:78–92; " 'Cool Reflexion' and the Criticism of Values: Is, Ought, and Objectivity in Hume's Social Science," *American Political Science Review* (1980), 74:70–77; and "Aristotle's Social Science," *Political Theory* (November 1981), 9(4):479–508.

Reiner Schürmann is Associate Professor and Department Chairman, Graduate Faculty, New School for Social Research, New York, New York. Among his publications are *Le Principe d'anarchie. Heidegger et la question de l'agir* (Paris: Seuil, 1982); "Political Thinking in Heidegger," *Social Research* (1978), 45(1):191–221; and "Anti-Humanism. Reflections on the Turn Towards the Post-Modern Epoch," *Man and World* (1979), 12(2):160–77.

Bruce R. Sievers, Executive Director of the California Council for the Humanities, San Francisco, California, is the writer of "Knowledge, Mind, and Action: Cassirer, Pyle, Habermas and the Epistemological Approach to Contemporary Political Theory" (Ph. D. diss., Stanford University, 1973) and "Civil Disobedience in Political Theory: The Classical Model Revisited," *Humanities in Society* (1979), 2:61–68.

William M. Sullivan is Associate Professor of Philosophy at La Salle College in Philadelphia, Pennsylvania. His recent works include (with Paul Rabinow) *Interpretive Social Science: A Reader* (Berkeley: University of California Press, 1979) and *Reconstructing Public Philosophy* (Berkeley: University of California Press, 1982).

PREFACE

A small interdisciplinary conference to discuss morality as a problem for the social sciences was held on the Berkeley Campus of the University of California in March of 1980. The participants were five philosophers, one historian, and ten social scientists, two each from the disciplines of anthropology, economics, political science, psychology, and sociology. The problem posed for the participants in preparing papers for the conference was the growing recognition that value neutrality in the social sciences is impossible but that we do not yet have an adequate alternative understanding of the place of morality in social science or of social science in practical life. The conference itself was devoted to comment on and discussion of the previously prepared papers. Afterwards the participants revised their papers in the light of the discussion, and these revised statements became the chapters of this volume.

Concern for the moral implications of social science and its effect on public policy has been growing for a number of years. For example, Stuart Hampshire, an Oxford philosopher, recently wrote about the U.S. involvement in the Vietnam War:

An illusory image of rationality distorted the moral judgment of the American policy-makers. They thought that their opponents in the U.S.A. were sentimental and guided only by their unreflective emotions, while they, the policy-makers, were computing consequences with precision and objectivity, using quasi-quantitative methods. They ignored, and remained insensitive to, the full nature and quality of their acts in waging the war, and of the shame and odium attached to some particular acts. . . . Under the influence of bad social science, and the bad moral philosophy that usually goes with it, they over-simplified the moral issues and provided an example of false rationality.[1]

Others have pointed out that social science has ethical and political implications, often unrecognized by the social scientists themselves, in such fields as behavior modification, intelligence testing, "technical" treatment of unemployment in economics, and third world development research. Among those who have thought most carefully about the place of social science in society and the place of morality in social science is Jürgen Habermas. His presence at Berkeley in the winter quarter of 1980 provided the stimulus to organize the conference from which this book eventuated.

Norma Haan's name is listed first because of the major contribution she made to organizing the conference and preparing papers for publication. However, all the editors participated equally in conceptualizing the issues and choosing who was to be invited.

For their interest and generous financial support, we thank the California Council for the Humanities, the Luke Hancock Foundation, and the National Endowment for the Humanities. Norma Haan's work on the conference and the volume was supported by a Research Scientist Career Award from the National Institute of Mental Health. Dr. Estelle Jelinek did a superb job of editing. Robert Meyer, who was granted an internship award from the California Council for the Humanities, helped with the conference arrangements and wrote an excellent summary of the proceedings. Candy Reynolds, Sheila Hard, Katherine Wooten, Emma Low, and Anita Brown handled many details that made both the conference and the preparation of the book possible. Professor David Schneider of the University of Chicago, who attended the conference as a lively observer, contributed significantly to the deliberations. Finally, we thank the participants, who turned the conference into a very "spirited exchange," and at times a heated argument.

Just as this book was being submitted for publication we received word of the untimely death of our friend and collaborator Michelle Rosaldo. The dedication of the book is a small expression of our sense of her loss not only to her family and friends but also to anthropology and feminism.

Norma Haan
Robert N. Bellah
Paul Rabinow
William M. Sullivan

NOTE

1. Stuart Hampshire, ed., *Public and Private Morality* (Cambridge: Cambridge University Press, 1978), p. 51.

INTRODUCTION

Robert N. Bellah
Norma Haan
Paul Rabinow
William M. Sullivan

The papers in this volume arise out of a sense of unease shared in greater or lesser degree by all the contributors. The unease concerns first of all the relation of social science as presently practiced to the realm of ethics. "Value neutrality," itself a term far from clear, now seems without foundation as a guide in this area, but no forceful alternative has yet gathered a consensus. But the unease, among a number of the contributors, goes deeper than a worry about the moral meaning of social science. It includes a worry about the moral meaning of modern society itself. Social science and modern society were born together and their fates are deeply intertwined.

SOCIAL SCIENCE AS AN ASPECT OF MODERNITY

One of the earliest clear indications that a new kind of society was emerging was the appearance in the seventeenth century of the new natural science, not only as a mode of inquiry, but as an ideology. There was a euphoria about the possibilities inherent in the new science, not only among the scientists themselves, but even more among philosophers such as Bacon and Hobbes. The new science would change the world and make it more amenable to human desires and purposes. The idea that the new method could be applied to human beings emerged almost simultaneously with natural science. Spinoza attempted to develop an ethics that would have the same deductive rigor as geometry. Hobbes attempted to develop a psychology and a sociology that would explain the complex in terms of the simple as the new physics was doing in the natural realm. The new science promised an expansion of human power and freedom. A new society would be based on the new knowledge, one freed from the dogmatism of traditional religion and the arbitrariness of traditional political authority. Modern science became a central part of the ideology of modern society, a promise to liberate the individual from dependence on the whims of nature or powerful men. In time science would help to legitimate both the capitalist economy and the democratic politics that came to characterize distinctively modern societies. Modern science has maintained that emancipatory enthusiasm, despite its attenuation, even into the late twentieth century.

Yet from quite early on there were warnings that all was not going entirely as promised. The process of modernization quickly proved more ambiguous than its early enthusiasts imagined. By the end of the eighteenth century William Blake found the world of "Newton and Bacon and Locke" more destructive than liberating. He saw the "dark Satanic mills" of nascent capitalism destroying a more human rural England. In the mid-nineteenth century Karl Marx argued that capitalism's liberation of productive forces led to new forms of human slavery and oppression. Marx invoked once again the ideology of science, now as "scientific socialism," to construct an alternative to capitalist oppression, but in the twentieth century it became clear that Marxism itself could be used to legitimate extraordinarily oppressive regimes.

Because science itself was so deeply implicated in the structure and texture of modern society, it could not remain aloof from the contradictions and ambiguities of modern life. Technology, which at first seemed to be a straightforward means of freeing human beings from grinding toil and natural catastrophe, developed in directions often more frightening than encouraging. This is particularly true of military technology, which threatens us today with devastation greater than any natural catastrophe. By the late twentieth century we have experienced the irony that the greatest triumph of science and technology, the discovery of how to unleash the power locked in the atom, threatens to end all life on the planet.

Nor has the enormous growth of scientific and quasi-scientific knowledge proved as socially benign as the Enlightenment imagined. Mass public education including a heavy dose of scientific rationality has not rendered the populace at large invulnerable to irrational ideological and religious movements. Nor has it successfully eliminated the use of propaganda and manipulation. Neither did scientific knowledge prove amenable to democratic distribution. On the contrary, scientific knowledge and technological expertise grew ever more specialized. Scientific experts emerged as a new elite in all modern societies, often able to wield power and authority through their monopolization of esoteric knowledge and even more through the prestige which this knowledge has in the modern world. Already in the early twentieth century Max Weber saw that the inexorable advance in scientific accuracy and technological efficiency in field after field—what he called "rationalization"—led not to freedom but to an iron cage in which the human spirit would be finally crushed.

In the name of human emancipation modern society and its ethos of scientific rationality have consistently undermined and eroded the particular, the local, the implicit, and the traditional. The Enlightenment saw this change as an advance from the darkness of unreason to the light of universality and explicit rationality. But here again critics have questioned whether modernity is an unmixed good. Alexis de Tocqueville in the early nineteenth century observed that America, that most modern of societies, nonetheless rested on certain unquestioned moral and religious beliefs and that only the firmness of that foundation of belief allowed endless economic and political experimentation. Tocqueville believed that if rational calculation ever completely replaced these deeply embedded "mores"—the implicit practices of American daily life—the very freedom which was the society's greatest good would be undermined. The romantic reaction against modernity in Germany and elsewhere concentrated precisely on this issue. It attempted with varying success to defend the preconceptual and nonrational aspects of human life in the face of universality and rationalization. It reasserted primordial loyalties of soil, language, and ethnic group. Under modern circumstances the return of this premodern repressed romanticism could become hideously destructive, as fascism was. Nevertheless the problem of overrationalization which the romantics addressed remains serious and unsolved.

Modern society and its accompanying ideology have emphasized nothing so much as the individual, and individual freedom has been its highest value. Yet it is just here that the ambiguities become especially clear. Modern individuals, at least affluent modern individuals in affluent modern societies, have a range of choice unknown in any previous form of society. And yet the meaning and validity of those choices is called into question by the rise of technological, economic, and political structures that seem to have their own autonomy. These structures, which lie beyond the power of the individual, often seem to determine all the really important choices. Further, the worth of the freedom to choose is called into question when all traditional standards of choice fall into oblivion and the self is left alone with its own feelings. Standardless, arbitrary choice among a multitude of possible goods is finally no choice at all.

These criticisms and anxieties have become sufficiently widespread that many social scientists now doubt the earlier Enlightenment thesis that the growth of scientific knowledge per se is an unmixed good. It has become clear that an uncritical pursuit of social scientific knowledge will almost certainly work to reinforce the existing powers in society that fund that research. Thereby the social scientist easily becomes, wittingly or unwittingly, a servant of established power. In a period when unrestrained nuclear war or even permanent universal tyranny is a possibility, such a role has the most ominous ethical implication.

Yet once the social scientist begins to ask the question "knowledge for what?" the ways in which most of us think, as inheritors of modern Enlightenment culture, begin to fail. If we would attempt a more integral relation between social scientific inquiry and the pursuit of the human good, it is not at all clear how we are to go about it. Elements of romantic, Marxist, and Christian critique survive on the margins of social science today, but none is widely persuasive. The problem lies not only with social science itself but within its philosophical basis. Philosophic liberalism, with its ideology of individual emancipation, is that basis today, as it has been for three centuries. Even the critics of modernity have most often produced only variants of that pervasive philosophy of individualism. But how to find an alternative public philosophy and link it to an ethically sensitive social science remains to be discovered.

The contributors to this volume share in varying degrees the foregoing analysis of the background to our present situation in social science. We vary, as will be sketched below, in how we feel this background affects our present condition and where we go from here.

PROBLEMS FACING SOCIAL SCIENCE TODAY

The immediate starting point for many of us is the extraordinary optimism of American social science in the 1950s and the collapse of its utopian expectations without replacement since the 1960s. The "modernization theory" (which seems synonymous with the thought that this was to be an "American Century") assumed that if the secret of "economic development" could only be shared with the "underdeveloped" countries most problems would be solved. This situation seemed an almost perfect instance of the supposition of Enlightenment theory that science serves human progress. It was assumed that in following the natural implications of their theories and methods social scientists were automatically contributing to human betterment. Undoubtedly the experience of the Second World War, when natural and social science were mobilized against the worst tyranny heretofore known, reinforced this understanding. But by the mid-1960s our understanding of the role and meaning of social science as summed up in the idea of modernization theory had begun to unravel, for a variety of reasons.

For one thing, empirical regularities failed to materialize on schedule. The underdeveloped nations failed to develop. The developed nations showed severe and unexpected signs of strain. Even that most advanced of the social sciences, economics, was unable to predict what would happen next, not only from year to year but even from month to month. Doubts about the model of the empirical natural sciences as applicable to social science began to grow.

Even more distressing was the growing recognition that social science usually, readily, and uncritically serves the interests of those who pay for it. The Vietnam War confirmed what many had come to suspect, namely that modernization and its theory served the interests of some nations, classes, and institutions much more effectively than those of others. In the 1960s, the heyday of social science's self-criticism, it was sometimes argued that anthropology had been nothing but a tool of imperialism, sociology an instrument for control of the working class and minorities, psychology a device for social discipline and the increase of productivity. While these arguments were too extreme, they nonetheless made the point that social science is easily prostituted to power and that not to see that fact is naive indeed. A number of papers in this volume stress this recognition, in particular those of Paul Rabinow, Michelle Rosaldo, Michel de Certeau, and Wolf-Dieter Narr.

One obvious response to the growing awareness of the ideological uses of social science was to argue for a heightened self-criticism and ideological awareness. This was sometimes referred to as reflexive social science, that is, one aware of the ideological situation and temptations of the social scientist. Nonetheless the standards for reflexive analysis, other than the conventionally Marxist ones that had already also become suspect, were not clear. There was a sense that uncritical empiricism, or positivism, which was still, as it is today, the actual mainstream practice of social science, would not do. But again no clear idea of where to turn presented itself. Nor was there any certainty that quantification and empirical testing were bad in themselves. There was rather a feeling that quantitative methods needed to be set in a different context or applied with a different sensibility. How this was to be done was far from clear.

One type of social science that has a long and respected lineage and has recently acquired a new lease on life is interpretive, or symbolic, or hermeneutic social science, as it is variously called. Its tradition is attractive because it seems more modest in its claims than the now deflated empiricist or positivist approaches. The interpretive approach starts not with an investigator's grand theory but with the lived reality of those under study. In this respect it profoundly respects the texture of actual life where more scientistic approaches are quick to reduce what is observed to instances of preformulated categories. In the face of the prevailing compulsion to quantify such preformulated data, the revivification of the interpretive approach is undoubtedly a major correction and one that still needs encouragement. But the interpretive approach has no answer to the insistent questions about the relation between social science and ethics. It has frequently been as dedicated to an illusory value neutrality as have other kinds of social science. A desire to interpret a culture from within its own categories gives us no standard for evaluation. When pressed to the extreme the interpretive enterprise can become as closed and self-satisfied as any scientific one. Our insistent problem of the relation of social science to ethics is not solved, then, by replacing one method with another. A hermeneutic method does not render any better answer to the question "knowledge for what?" than do positivistic methods.

If neither positivistic nor hermeneutic social science contains its own ethical justification, perhaps what is missing has to be sought on another level: the level of the philosophical basis of social science. This is a painful recognition for social scientists, for two reasons. On one hand, in its infancy social science went through a long and at times embittered struggle to free itself from the philosophic mother. Such precious autonomy is not to be lightly abandoned. But on the other hand, as social scientists search for philosophical grounding they are in for new disappointments. Philosophy as an academic discipline has shown many of the same tendencies as social science. Unsure of their own metaphysical and moral groundings, philosophers, like social scientists, have engaged in the apotheosis of method and proceeded to an intensive specialization. Furthermore, most philosophy in England and America has accepted, almost without argument, the basic assumptions of the liberal individualism that has proven an inadequate philosophical basis for social science.

It became clear that there are no ready-made philosophical answers to the questions raised by the social scientists. Thus, the problems of the ethical orientation of social science cannot be solved by an "interdisciplinary" conversation between sociologists and philosophers. Only philosophers willing to delve deeply into social science and social scientists willing to become in part philosophers are likely to help. Thus, many of the contributors to this volume view our efforts not as "interdisciplinary" but as "transdisciplinary." Indeed, many of us believe that current disciplinary boundaries are historical products that are more the cause of our intellectual and ethical problems than useful limits of specialization within which to search for their solution.

The work of Jürgen Habermas is exemplary in part because it is transdisciplinary.[1] Habermas is concerned with the fundamental issues of modern society and modern thought. He ranges easily across the social sciences, perceptively discerning what work is most revealing about the present state of culture and society. But he always uses particular studies to help formulate the deeper issues: what is the nature of this modern society in which we live and what must we do to make it more habitable? His work is philosophical because it has to be. He is concerned not just with "facts" but with how we know facts, with the realms of experience in terms of which they make sense, and with how we can evaluate them. The normative dimension is not an afterthought unconnected with the effort to understand. Understanding, evaluating, and criticizing are not finally separable from the totality of human life that includes them. In many of the areas that concern us most it is the work of Jürgen Habermas that has opened the way and suggested to us where we might focus our efforts.

THE ORGANIZATION OF THIS VOLUME

Whatever may be the case for social scientists or philosophers generally, the writers of the papers collected in this volume agree that value commitment in some form or other is inevitable in doing social science. Rather than argue the case against value neutrality, most of the writers are concerned with the consequences of the fact that ethical orientations are present, disguised or not, everywhere in the enterprise of social science. Some of the papers take up the question of the responsibility of social scientists both to those whom they study and to the larger society. Most, however, are mainly concerned with elucidating the implications of the very idea of a social science once its ethical dimension is taken seriously.

The papers focus on three such implications of an ethical social science. The first is the question of what happens to the character of the various disciplines and, to some extent, to the idea of disciplines. The second implication is that recognition of the ethical dimension of social inquiry necessarily alters the underlying assumptions of a science no longer securely based on a natural science model and raises the question of whether social science is still science once it is viewed as also being moral inquiry. Finally, the third implication covers a host of issues surrounding the role of social science in social policy raised by this way of thinking. Most of the papers are involved in some way or other with all three of these issues. Nonetheless, different authors tend to emphasize one or another of them, and it is in terms of these foci that we have organized the book.

The first section deals with disciplinary critiques, analyses of what might be called "paradigm crises," in economics, psychology, anthropology, and history. The papers in this section consider how the failure to deal adequately with the ethical dimension of these disciplines has precipitated questioning and doubt and stimulated the beginning of new formulations. The same kind of ferment described in these illustrative chapters can also be found in sociology, political science, and philosophy itself, as some later papers in the book suggest.

The second section is concerned less with particular disciplines and more with issues that underlie all the social sciences. These are issues of what might be called "philosophical foundations." We prefer to speak of "foundational issues," because we believe that they emerge within social science and force themselves on the attention of social scientists whether or not the latter are versed in philosophy. Moreover, these issues are not adequately dealt with in contemporary philosophy and raise as many questions for it as for social science. Nonetheless, in the broadest sense these are indeed philosophical issues. Perhaps their presence will force us to reconsider the existing division of labor between philosophy and the social sciences.

In the third section the boundary between social science and social practice is called into question. If the model of an initially value-free positivist social science which is subsequently applied by policy experts is rejected, then what are the alternative ways in which social science does and should affect social life? The papers in this section, like those in the others, are both critical of present practice and constructive with respect to possible alternative solutions.

While the papers speak for themselves in a variety of tones, it seems fair to say that on the whole they are modest in their claims and offer no grandiose solutions. All of the writers realize the magnitude and seriousness of our problems. If old verities have proven inadequate no new answers of simple clarity are in sight. The papers move forward tentatively and prefer to open dialogues rather than to dictate answers. That a critical, self-reflective dialogue about these matters is now urgent is the premise on which the book is based.

ALTERNATIVE STRATEGIES

It does seem possible, however, to discern several major alternative strategies that the papers adopt, strategies that have their roots in traditions out of which the writers work. A brief outline of these different strategies and traditions may help the reader to discern the major options that the book offers.

The first alternative, and the one represented by the largest number of papers, is situated squarely in the tradition of the Enlightenment, of modern thought, and of science itself. The tradition that is involved here is critical, but it seeks to criticize the weaknesses of modern thought from within its own assumptions. Major philosophical figures such as Rousseau, Kant, Hegel, and Marx, as well as many of the formative figures in the emergence of the several social sciences, represent this tradition. What seems to characterize the group of papers that fall into this category is an effort to make significant substantive criticisms of modern philosophy and social science without challenging the fundamental idea of social science as science.

The two economists, Albert Hirschman and Michael McPherson, challenge the adequacy of the model of strategic action, the calculating behavior of the self-interested person, so central in the received tradition of modern social science and ideology. They do this first of all in the citadel of the strategic model, economics itself, by suggesting that an economics that overlooks moral commitments which cannot be reduced to expressions of self-interest is bad economics. This criticism has broad implications not only for economics but for all the social sciences, which have of late become enamored of the theoretical power and simplicity of the strategic model. Yet neither Hirschman nor McPherson believes that the existing conception of economics as a science must be challenged. They urge economists, and indirectly social scientists in general, to overcome their present blindness, to become aware of a range of empirical realities that have been too little attended to and give them a central place in social scientific inquiry. That done, our overall enterprise, which they see as being in reasonably good health, may proceed apace.

Norma Haan's position is in some ways comparable. Rather than challenging the assumptions of psychology as an empirical science, she proposes the extension of empirical inquiry into the heartland of everyday morality itself. She suggests that an adequate empirical understanding of how people actually behave as moral actors and the moral beliefs they cherish in everyday life would give us at the least the beginnings of a "thin" theory of morality that might then gather a degree of social consensus. Here a strongly reformist proposal, namely that empirical social science may contribute directly to moral consensus, combines with a conception of empirical social science close to the concerns of the Enlightenment.

What these papers and others in this section suggest is that our problems do not come from the modern Enlightenment conception of rational empirical reflection but rather come from errors and omissions that have crept into it. This view, if it is correct, is encouraging, for it suggests that what we need is a major reform of our present enterprise—a reform that will involve major new subject matter, more adequate theory, and new forms of application—but not a fundamental rejection or recasting of the rational scientific enterprise itself.

Several other papers which can perhaps be classed in this first group push these optimistic assumptions almost to the limit. Stephen Salkever wishes to infuse a chastened and purified sociobiology, often viewed as a form of reductionist scientism, with an Aristotelian sensitivity to the relation between the empirical and the moral. He chooses the well-accepted social scientific conception of "function" to make this link. Salkever seems to say that a careful reading of contemporary social science would find that much of it carries ethical implications not usually discerned.

Carol Gilligan, working out of her own research, argues that the rational individualistic theory of moral development put forth by Kohlberg, emphasizing moral reasoning about justice, needs to be supplemented by attending to the neglected ethics of caring that grows out of the experience of social connectedness. She suggests, however, that taking this kind of moral experience seriously comes close to challenging some of the central norms of our present theory and method. She too, finally, wishes to improve present social science by enriching it and developing theories and methods complementary to existing ones, though her suggestions seem at times to challenge the basic enterprise.

Michelle Rosaldo presses a vigorous critique of some of the central assumptions of Enlightenment social science, particularly its individualism and its tendency to biological reductionism. She even uses the term "deconstruct" to describe her analysis of existing categories of analysis in the field of gender. Yet her suggested alternative approach emphasizes the social and political construction of cultural reality, including what is considered "natural," a line of thinking close to the interpretive strand of Enlightenment social science. She almost but not quite breaks out of the first position into the more radically deconstructionist position that will be described below.

Richard Flacks is another whose suggestions for new directions have radical implications which he does not choose to push. Flacks is concerned above all with eliminating or decreasing the distinction between social scientists and those they study. A democratized social science would serve its historic purpose of human liberation by helping ordinary people to cope with the social and political problems of their lives. It would replace an elitist social science that often serves existing structures of power. But the fundamental rational-empirical structure of modern social science would not be altered by this transformation. Flacks is reviving in contemporary form the democratic and emancipatory aims of Enlightenment figures such as Thomas Jefferson.

Finally, Jürgen Habermas' paper must also be placed in this first category. On the one hand, he shows how hermeneutic analysis, as a process of rational reconstruction, is necessary for social science; on the other hand, he underscores hermeneutics' limits on achieving objectivity. His solution is to forge a model of "mutually fitting" between psychology and philosophy to show how philosophical reconstruction of moral intuitions complements psychological explanations of how people actually acquire moral intuitions. He illustrates, with Kohlberg's theory of moral development, how testing the truth or falsity of empirical propositions can function to check the normative validity of hypothetically reconstructed moral intuitions; at the same time he observes that empiricism can never justify what morally ought to be. Thus, Habermas agrees with the Enlightenment's endorsement of science as a rational, viable method, but he chastens it: it can serve as a check on rational reconstructions, but it cannot tell us what morality ought to be.

Habermas, Flacks, and others in this first group wish to return the tradition of modern Enlightenment social thought to its democratic origins. They view the development of a technological social science in the service of manipulation and control as a fundamental perversion rather than a logical fulfillment of that tradition. They see the dangers for theory and practice of the radical individualism that has been at the heart of modern social thought and much of social science. They insist on taking account of the social dimension of human experience so often excluded by concentration on the isolated individual. Yet those in the second and third categories described below would argue that this Enlightenment position remains inextricably tied to modern individualism and the primacy of individual subjectivity. The social, however seriously it is taken, is in this tradition, its critics say, always derived from the individual as the primary reality. Defenders of the Enlightenment position would counter that the commitment to individual subjectivity, together with the commitment to rationality, is of the essence of the modern intellectual and moral enterprise. They warn us that any tampering with these assumptions contains the danger of regression into fundamentally irrational and undemocratic ideologies.

The second and third positions, otherwise quite different, share the view that the Enlightenment position is untenable. Their proponents find the perversions to which the tradition of modern social thought, including social science, are prone to be intrinsic, not accidental. They see the extensive theoretical and empirical corrections which members of our first group wish to introduce into contemporary social science as being so serious that the Enlightenment enterprise is called into question, and argue that social science as we know it cannot be reformed but must be radically transformed.

With respect to the shape of that transformation the adherents of the next two positions are in strong disagreement. The second, or classical, position seeks a reformulation of social science in terms of the tradition of Aristotelian social and moral thought, a tradition eclipsed quite abruptly in the seventeenth century after many centuries of development. By contrast, the third, or deconstructionist, position argues for the futility of all traditional positions, modern or premodern, and the necessity of a new and unprecedented stance toward social and moral reality.

The papers representing the classical position assume the primacy of moral practice and view ethical theory, together with social science, as ancillary and secondary. To this extent there is a certain resonance of this position with that of Richard Rorty's paper, which resolutely undercuts the pretensions of theory. It is the emphasis on practice that provides a touchstone for the second position, for its defenders see the classical tradition of political and moral discourse surviving in actual practices long after the intellectual triumph of Enlightenment modernity. Republican political practices and the religious practices of biblically based communities have survived in what Tocqueville called the "mores" in modern societies, including the United States. Defenders of the classical position are concerned with giving these mores a theoretical defense against the pervasive individualism of the Enlightenment tradition, which has penetrated so deeply into American and, more generally, modern life. The papers of William Sullivan, Robert Bellah, and Bruce Sievers belong in this category.

Sullivan and Sievers both take the tradition of civic republican politics in America as their primary reference point. They show how that tradition is incompatible with the assumptions of social science and modern ideology that have led to a manipulative attitude toward human action. Sievers shows how the apparently neutral use of polling of political attitudes has actually undercut the functioning of the democratic process as conceived in republican terms. Sullivan shows how openings toward a renewal of that tradition have developed at the very time an applied technical social policy in the service of a facile view of modernization was about to celebrate its triumph. They both call for a revivification of a democratic mode of life rooted in shared conceptions of character and society and in the practices of mutual discussion and mutual responsibility. Social inquiry in this conception would become a part of practical reason, reflecting on the major moral and political problems facing society in the light of a continuing public discussion.

Robert Bellah suggests that this classical conception of practical reason has been evident through most of the history of Western social thought, even modern social science, which has consciously rejected such a self-conception. If social science is not really an abstract, timeless set of scientific propositions but rather a continuing reflection on urgent social issues with which the social scientist is ethically involved, then we would do better, Bellah argues, to accept explicitly this version of what we are about instead of imagining we are in the early stages of creating a "true science" devoid of ethical implications.

The classical position has, as Bellah suggests, a long continuity, even though it has, so to speak, gone underground and lost touch to some extent with its own vocabulary. That situation is clearly changing.[2]

The deconstructionist position quite resolutely rejects both of the others. It regards the Enlightenment notions of individuality and rationality, which are constitutive for modern thought and much of social science, as transient cultural epiphenomena rather than as eternal verities. It sees them, like the notions of objective moral truths in the classical position, as forms of domination that have developed in various historical epochs. Reiner Schürmann's tracing of the genealogy of what he calls "archic domination," the different allegedly fundamental truths that have been imposed on human beings through history, is the fullest exposition of the deconstructionist position contained in this volume.

Paul Rabinow and Michel de Certeau provide more limited examples of such genealogy within the disciplines of anthropology and history. Rabinow's critique of the relativist implications of classical and contemporary anthropology does not lead him, as it might, to a classical alternative. Rather, he places his hope on the cleansing effects of the genealogical approach itself to eventually produce some viable alternative. De Certeau takes a comparable stance. His deconstruction of history as a discipline consists of historicizing historiography itself. By showing that the "past" is a construct designed to hide the process whereby it is produced he proposes to bring the history of the production of history into history itself. This would remove the arrogant assertion that the "present" is superior to all pasts and make possible an ethical rather than a dogmatic role for the historian. But like others in the third category, de Certeau does not tell us concretely what this ethical historiography would be like.

Wolf-Dieter Narr broadens the intensive critique characteristic of the deconstructionist position to examine the institutional basis of present intellectual life, as do Schürmann in passing and de Certeau in substantial degree. Narr suggests that intellectual critique must be combined with political struggle to be either meaningful or effective. In general those in the deconstructionist position view power and knowledge as so closely related that one cannot deal with one without dealing with the other.

What is least clear in the deconstructionist position is the alternative being offered. Here Schürmann comes closest to being explicit. The reality being affirmed is open, multiple—flux itself—"anarchic," that is, not "archic" or principle dominated. What this reality would look like in concrete form remains to be seen. Those in the classical position might fear it would be finally an apocalyptic parody of the Enlightenment position, the liberation of impulse without persons, the play of images without patterns. But the defenders of the deconstructionist position would view such criticism as itself an expression of the implicitly authoritarian direction of the classical position. Both the Enlightenment and the classical positions, on the other hand, would fear that the third position, in spite of its critique of relativism, has itself no defense against a radical relativism and historicism. To which those who hold this genealogical position could answer that it is only in a field opened up by history and anthropology that such a claim could be made to have any pretense to be more than a nostalgic assertion.[3]

Richard Rorty's paper is something of an anomaly and could for different reasons be placed in each of the three categories. Rorty's paper, while challenging almost all our existing preconceptions about what we are doing, at the same time with a magisterial permissiveness leaves things pretty much as they are. It is the effort to use method as a form to legislate what must be done that he rejects. It is unsettling that this refreshing paper leaves us uncertain whether in the end everything is wrong or everything is right. It is perhaps a warning that there are no simple answers presently of help to us.

THE CONTINUING DIALOGUE

This sketch of three positions, which we have designated the Enlightenment, classical, and deconstructionist positions, is an attempt to provide some guidelines for approaching the papers in this book. The assignment of papers to the various positions is based on the papers themselves but also on discussions at the conference. The discussions made it clear that several rather different positions, by no means identical with disciplines, were represented.

Nonetheless, the positions we attribute to individual authors are only tentative, and none of the writers fits easily into any one category.

The common thread in almost all the papers is the idea that social science has an intrinsic connection with the moral and political life of society. All agree on the obligation of the social scientist to view reality as dispassionately as possible. But all also agree that that reality, our perceptions of it, and our assumptions about it, are inescapably moral. We agree that there is no neutral platform of pure science utterly free from value commitments and, further, that social science is a product of the development of a particular kind of society. We believe that we will be not only more ethically responsible if we recognize that fact but also more realistic and better able to understand cognitively the reality that we confront.

One implication of this view is that social science makes its greatest contribution by providing a kind of self-interpretation to society.

In the end it is research which attempts to be part of the conversation among citizens that is most valuable. Even particular solutions to technical problems will be more likely to be helpful if they arise in the course of a continuing discussion between social scientists and public-minded citizens. This conception of social science is offered in deliberate opposition to a scientistic conception that makes social science a mode of technical control in the service of power.

While most of us seek to return social science to its social and historical context as the appropriate situation for our on-going reflection, we are not unanimous about the role of social science nor about how best to make that role effective in society. In the conversation, indeed the argument, among our alternative visions of what is to be done lies a contribution of this volume as important as the agreements we share. In these papers we have clearly taken only one step. There are still many steps ahead before we develop a clear understanding of social science as moral inquiry among social scientists and the public at large. These papers are an invitation to others to join the dialogue.

One important step that most of us were hesitant to take is to address the question, "What is the morality that should guide social science?" even though that question is implied in much of what we have written. Because most of us were schooled in the tradition of value neutrality, there was even a feeling of discomfort and uncertainty whenever we attempted to discuss morality more than descriptively. At stake is the issue of how empirically described life and ethical vision can be brought into relation. The three positions sketched in this introduction each seem to have rather different implications as to how to go about solving that problem, though none of the writers here makes more than a bare beginning. But they do suggest the importance of civil and dispassionate dialogue about the substance of morality if we are to develop a social science adequate to the needs of our common life.

NOTES

1. A particularly useful introduction to the work of Jürgen Habermas is Thomas McCarthy, *The Critical Theory of Jürgen Habermas* (Cambridge: MIT Press, 1978).
2. Since the papers in this volume were written, a distinguished book, Alasdair MacIntyre's *After Virtue* (South Bend, Ind.: Notre Dame University Press, 1981), has

appeared which gives the most complete and compelling exposition of the classical position to appear in a long time.

3. A helpful introduction to the work of Michel Foucault and his genealogy of modern society and philosophy is Hubert Dreyfus and Paul Rabinow, *Michel Foucault: Beyond Structuralism and Hermeneutics* (Chicago: University of Chicago Press, 1982).

PART I

DISCIPLINARY CRITIQUES

One

MORALITY AND THE SOCIAL SCIENCES: A DURABLE TENSION

Albert O. Hirschman

What is the role of moral considerations and concerns in economics? More generally, what can be said about the "problem of morality in the social sciences"? In commenting on these questions, I shall first give some reasons why this sort of topic does not come easily to the social scientist; only later shall I show why there is today an increased concern with moral values, *even* in economics—that rock of positivist solidity. In conclusion, I shall suggest some ways of reconciling the traditional posture of the economist as a "detached scientist" with a role as a morally concerned person.

To deal usefully with the relationship between morality and the social sciences, one must first understand that modern social science arose to a considerable extent in the process of emancipating itself from traditional moral teachings. Right at the onset of the modern age, Machiavelli proclaimed that he would deal with political institutions as they really exist and not with "imaginary republics and monarchies" governed in accordance with the religious precepts and moralistic pieties that have been handed down from one generation to the next by well-meaning persons. Modern political science owes a great deal to Machiavelli's shocking claim that ordinary notions of moral behavior for individuals may not be suitable as rules of conduct for states. More generally, it appeared as a result of the wealth of insights discovered by Machiavelli that the traditional concentration on the "ought," on the manner in which princes and statesmen ought

Originally presented as a lecture on September 25, 1980, when the author received the Frank E. Seidman Distinguished Award in Political Economy in Memphis, Tennessee; also published in Albert O. Hirschman, *Essays in Trespassing: Economics to Politics and Beyond* (Cambridge: Cambridge University Press, 1981), pp. 194–306.

to behave, interferes with the fuller understanding of the "is" that can be achieved when attention is closely and coldly riveted on the ways in which statecraft is, in fact, carried on. The need to separate political science from morality was later openly proclaimed by Montesquieu, another principal founding father of social science, when he wrote: "It is useless to attack politics directly by showing how much its practices are in conflict with morality and reason. This sort of discourse makes everybody nod in agreement, but changes nobody."[1]

A similar move from the "ought" to the "is" was soon to be made in economics. As the actual workings of trade and markets were examined in some detail from the seventeenth century on, a number of discoveries as shocking and instructive as those of Machiavelli were made by writers on economic topics. I am not referring just to Mandeville's famous paradox about private vices leading, via the stimulation of the luxury trades, to public benefits. Quite a bit earlier, in the middle of the seventeenth century, a number of deeply religious French thinkers, the most prominent of whom was Pascal, realized that an ordered society could exist and endure without being based on love or "charity." Another principle, so they found, could do the job of making the social world go round: the principle of self-interest. This ability to do without love came to them as an uneasy surprise and as a worrisome puzzle: a society that is not held together by love is clearly sinful; how could it then be not only workable but so intricately and admirably constructed that Divine Providence seems to have had a hand in it?

A century later, such worries had given way to outright celebration. Adam Smith evinced no religious qualms when he bestowed praise on the Invisible Hand for enlisting self-interested behavior on behalf of social order and economic progress. Yet the idea of morality supplying an alternative way of ordering economy and society still lurks somewhere in the background as Smith mocks it in one of the most striking formulations of his doctrine: "It is not from the benevolence of the butcher, the brewer, or the baker, that we expect our dinner but from their regard to their own interest."[2] Smith fairly bubbles over here with excitement about the possibility of discarding moral discourse and exhortation, thanks to the discovery of a social mechanism that, if properly unshackled, is far less demanding of human nature and therefore infinitely more reliable. And, once again, the refusal to be satisfied with the traditional "ought" created a space within which scientific knowledge could unfold.

Marx remained strictly in the Machiavelli-Montesquieu-Smith tradition when, in his attempt to interpret and, above all, to change the prevailing social and political order, he consistently refused to appeal to moral argument. He scoffed at the "utopian socialists" precisely for doing so in their critique of capitalist society and for resorting to moral exhortation in putting forth their proposed remedies. In spite of the ever-present moralistic undertone of his work, Marx's proudest claim was to be the father of *"scientific* socialism." To be truly scientific, he obviously felt that he had to shun moral argument. True science does not preach; it proves and predicts. So he proves the existence of exploitation through the labor theory of value and predicts the eventual demise of capitalism through the law of the falling rate of profit. In effect, Marx mixed uncannily these "cold" scientific propositions with "hot" moral outrage; and it was perhaps this odd amalgam, with all of its inner tensions unresolved, that was (and is) responsible for the extraordinary appeal of his work in an age both addicted to science and starved of moral values.

The tension between the "warm" heart and the "cold" or, at best, "cool" head is a well-known theme in Western culture, especially since the Romantic age. But I am speaking here not only of tension but of an existential incompatibility between morality and moralizing, on the one hand, and analytical-scientific activity, on the other. This incompatibility is simply a fact of experience. Our analytical performance becomes automatically suspect if it is openly pressed into the service of moral conviction; conversely, moral conviction is not dependent on analytical argument and can actually be weakened by it, just as religious belief has on balance been undermined rather than bolstered by the proofs of God and the intellectual prowess of those who set forth those proofs. The matter has been best expressed by the great German poet Hölderlin in a wonderfully pithy, if rather plaintive, epigram. Entitled "Guter Rat" (Good Advice), it dates from about 1800 and, in my free translation, reads:

> If you have brains and a heart, show only one or the other,
> You will not get credit for either should you show both at once.[3]

The mutual exclusiveness of moralizing and analytical understanding may be nothing but a happenstance, reflecting the particular historical conditions under which scientific progress in various domains was achieved in the West. These conditions have, of course, left strong marks on cultural attitudes, marks so well identified by Hölderlin.

But hostility to morality is more than the hallmark of modern science. With regard to the social sciences in particular, there are some more specific reasons to think that antimoralist petulance will frequently recur because of the very nature of the social scientific enterprise and discourse. Let me briefly explain.

In all sciences fundamental discovery often takes the form of paradox. This is true for some of the principal theorems of physics, such as the Copernican proposition about the earth moving around the sun rather than vice versa. But it can be argued that social science is peculiarly subject to the compulsion to produce paradox.

The reason is that we all know so much about society already without ever having taken a single social science course. We live in society; we often contribute to social, political, and economic processes as actors; and we think—often mistakenly, of course—that we know roughly what goes on not only in our own minds but also in those of others. As a result, we have considerable intuitive, commonsense understanding of social science "problems" such as crime in the streets, corruption in high places, and even inflation, and everyone stands forever ready to come forward with his or her own "solution" or nostrum. Consequently, for social science to *enhance* our considerable, untutored knowledge of the social world, it must come up with something that has not been apparent or transparent before or, better still, with something that shows how badly commonsense understanding has led us astray.[4] Important social science discoveries are, therefore, typically counterintuitive, shocking, and concerned with *unintended* and unexpected consequences of human action.

With the commonsense understanding of social science problems having usually a strong moral component (again, much more so than in the natural sciences), the immoralist vocation of the social sciences can in good measure be attributed to this compulsion to produce shock and paradox. Just as one of social science's favorite pastimes is to affirm the hidden rationality of the seemingly irrational or the coherence of the seemingly incoherent, so does it often defend as moral, or useful, or at least innocent, social behavior that is widely considered to be reprehensible. In economics, examples of this sort of quest for the morally shocking come easily to mind. Following the early lead of Mandeville and his rehabilitation of luxury, many an economist has carved out a reputation by extolling the economic efficiency functions of such illegal or unsavory activities as smuggling, black marketeering, or even corruption in government.

Lately this taste for the morally shocking has been particularly evident in the "imperialist" expeditions of economists into areas of social life outside the traditional domain of economics. Activities such as crime, marriage, procreation, bureaucracy, voting, and participation in public affairs in general have all been subjected to a so-called economic approach with the predictable result that, like the consumer or producer of the economics textbook, the actors involved, be they criminals, lovers, parents, bureaucrats, or voters, were all found to be busily "maximizing under constraints." Such people had, of course, long been thought to be moved and buffeted by complex passions, both noble and ignoble, such as revolt against society, love, craving for immortality, and devotion to the public interest or the betrayal thereof, among many others. In comparison with this traditional image of man's noneconomic pursuits, their analysis at the hands of the imperialist economist, with the emphasis on grubby cost/benefit calculus, was bound to produce moral shock; and, once again, the analysis drew strength from having this shock value.

In a book review, my colleague Clifford Geertz recently wrote a marvelous first paragraph that is eminently applicable to the writings to which I have just been referring:

> This is a book about the "primary male-female differences in sexuality among humans," in which the following things are not discussed: guilt, wonder, loss, self-regard, death, metaphor, justice, purity, intentionality, cowardice, hope, judgment, ideology, humor, obligation, despair, trust, malice, ritual, madness, forgiveness, sublimation, pity, ecstasy, obsession, discourse, and sentimentality. It could be only one thing, and it is. Sociobiology.[5]

To most of us, this sounds like a scathing indictment, but partisans of the book under review may well feel that its author deserves praise precisely for having cut through all those "surface phenomena" listed by Geertz to the *fundamental* mechanism which lays bare the very essence of whatever the book is about. In the same way, practitioners of the "economic approach" to human behavior probably take pride in their "parsimonious" theory, and whatever success they achieve is in fact largely grounded in the reductionist outrageousness of their enterprise.

One cannot help feeling, nevertheless, that this particular way of achieving notoriety and fame for the economist is running into diminishing returns. First, the paradigm about self-interest leading to a workable and perhaps even optimal social order without any admixture of "benevolence" has now been around so long that it has become intellectually challenging to rediscover the need for morality. To affirm this need has today almost the same surprise value and air of paradox which the Smithian farewell to benevolence had in its own time. Second, and more important, it has become increasingly clear that in a number of important areas the economy is in fact liable to perform poorly without a minimum of "benevolence."

The resurgence and rehabilitation of benevolence got started in microeconomics. One of the conditions for the proper functioning of competitive markets is "perfect" information about the goods and services that are being bought and sold. We all know, of course, that this condition is frequently far from being met, but imperfect information might not be too damaging to the market system if it were limited and widely shared among all citizens, be they sellers or buyers. What happens, however, if, as is often the case, the knowledge of the buyers about a certain commodity is far inferior to that of the suppliers and sellers? In that case, the stage is set for exploitation of the buyers by the sellers unless the latter are somehow restrained from taking advantage of their superiority. Government could be and has been entrusted with that task, with varying success; we all know by now that government will not necessarily succeed where the market fails. An ingenious solution would be for the sellers to subject themselves voluntarily to a discipline that keeps them from exploiting their superior knowledge. For example, surgeons could take on the obligation, as a condition for the exercise of their profession, never to prescribe an operation when none is needed. This is the case, pointed out some time ago by Kenneth Arrow, where adherence to a code of professional ethics can remedy one specific form of market failure.[6] So we are back to benevolence. In a somewhat institutionalized form it is here invoked as an input essential for the functioning of a market economy in which sellers have more information than buyers.

The fact that there is a need for ethical behavior in certain situations in which the market system and self-interest, left to their own devices, will result in undesirable outcomes does not mean, of course, that such behavior will automatically materialize. Perhaps it tends to do so when the need is particularly imperious, as it is in the case of surgeons and surgery. In any event, we worry quite a bit more about "being had" when we buy a secondhand car than when we consult a doctor about the need for an operation. Economists have recently identified a number of areas, from the market for "lemons" to day-care services and psychotherapeutic advice, where the performance of the market could be much improved by an infusion of benevolence, sometimes in the modest form of cooperation and exchange of information between suppliers and customers.

The need for ethical norms and behavior to supplement and, on occasion, to supplant self-interest appears with great clarity and urgency in the just noted situations of market failure. But this need is actually always there to some degree; if only because of the time element contained in most transactions, economic efficiency and enterprise are premised on the existence of trust between contracting parties, and this trust must be autonomous, that is, it must not be tied narrowly to self-interest. To quote a recent sweeping statement of this point, "Elemental personal values of honesty, truthfulness, trust, restraint and obligation are all necessary inputs to an efficient (as well as pleasant) contractual society. . . ."[7] If all these needed personal values are added up, the amounts of benevolence and morality required for the functioning of the market turn out to be quite impressive!

So much for microeconomics. But the really giant, if unacknowledged, strides in the rehabilitation of morality as an essential "input" into a functioning economy have taken place in the macro area, as a result of the contemporary experience with, and concern over, inflation. In spite of all the noise caused by certain technical debates (demand-pull vs. cost-push, monetarist vs. Keynesian or post-Keynesian views), there is, in fact, wide agreement—because it is so self-evident—that the understanding *and* control of contemporary inflation require probing deeply into the social and political underlay of the economy. For example, suppose it is correct that increasing public expenditures must be blamed for the inflation; then the question surely is, Why is the modern state subject to ever-increasing pressures for dispensing an evermore comprehensive set of public services to newly assertive interest groups? Similarly, if it is true that wage and price restraint could do much to hold back inflation, then why is it that such restraint is so difficult to come by? A British so-

ciologist has written, in answer to such questions, that "conflict between social groups and strata has become more intense and also to
some extent more equally matched, with these two tendencies interacting in a mutually reinforcing way."[8] Here is a well articulated
expression of the widespread view that primarily inflation reflects increasing combativeness, or in colorful British parlance, "bloody-mindedness," on the part of various social groups that have heretofore been
viewed in our textbooks as "cooperating" in the generation and distribution of the social product. The result of this sort of sociological
analysis of inflation is then to plead for a "new social contract" which
would hopefully result in inhibiting and reducing "bloody-mindedness" all around.[9]

The observation that is in order at this point will already have occurred to the reader: this nasty attribute, "bloody-mindedness," which
it is so important to restrain, is nothing but the obverse of benevolence, which it is therefore essential to foster. Hence, getting on top
of our major current macroeconomic problem turns out to require the
generation and diffusion of benevolence among various social groups!
So it definitely seems time for economists to renounce the amoral
stance affected, at least in the *Wealth of Nations,* by the illustrious
founder of our science. For the solution of both micro- and macroeconomic problems, the pursuit of pure self-interest on the part of
each individual member of society is clearly inadequate.

So far so good. But have we gotten very far? We have learned that
we should not scoff at benevolence and at moral values in general.
We can also appreciate that Malthus had a point when, in endorsing
the Smithian rule according to which everyone should be left free to
pursue his self-interest, he systematically added the reservation "while
he adheres to the rules of justice."[10]

But this sort of addition of a qualifying, moralizing afterthought is
not really much of a contribution. Granted the important place of
moral thought and values in economics, how should we map out the
new terrain and become aware of all the insights we have missed
because of our previous exclusive concentration on self-interest? One
way to proceed is to attempt a head-on attack. The opposite of self-
interest is interest in others, action on behalf of others. So the obvious way of making amends for their previous disregard of moral
values and "generous impulses" is for economists to study altruism.
Indeed, a number of works on this topic have appeared in recent

years.[11] They are instructive and useful but suffer perhaps from the attempt to make up for lost time in too much of a hurry.

In my opinion, the damage wrought by the "economic approach," the one based on the traditional self-interest model, is not just the neglect of altruistic behavior. It extends to wide areas of traditional analysis and is due to the use of far too simplistic a model of human behavior *in general*. What is needed is for economists to incorporate into their analyses, whenever that is pertinent, such basic traits and emotions as the desire for power and for sacrifice, the fear of boredom, pleasure in both commitment and unpredictability, the search for meaning and community, and so on. Clearly, this is a task that cannot be accomplished once and for all by a research project on the injection of moral values into economics. Any attempt of this kind is likely to yield disappointing results and would thus invite an extension to economics of the French saying that "with beautiful sentiments one makes bad literature."

An effective integration of moral argument into economic analysis can be expected to proceed rather painstakingly, on a case-to-case basis, because the relevant moral consideration or neglected aspect of human nature will vary considerably from topic to topic. The task requires a conjunction of talents that is difficult to come by: first, familiarity with the technical apparatus of economics and second, openness to the heretofore neglected moral dimension whose introduction modifies traditional results.

A fine example of such a conjunction—and also of its difficulty— is Robert Solow's recent presidential address to the American Economic Association on the topic of labor markets and unemployment. In explaining why the labor market is not smoothly self-clearing, he stressed the fact that workers pay a great deal of attention to "principles of appropriate behavior whose source is not entirely individualistic," such as the reluctance of those who are out of work to undercut those who hold jobs. "Wouldn't you be surprised," he asked, "if you learned that someone of roughly your status in the profession, but teaching in a less desirable department, had written to your department chairman offering to teach your courses for less money?"[12] Here is an important recognition of how certain moral-social norms profoundly affect the working of a most important market: they make it less perfect from the point of view of self-clearing but certainly more perfect from almost any other conceivable point of view!

I now turn to the difficulty of coming up with such an observation. Note that its vehicle was Solow's presidential address. Is there perhaps a tendency in our profession to wait until one has reached the pinnacle before coming forward with such, after all, only mildly moralistic and heretical views? Now, I am quite sure (at least in the case of Solow) that it is not pusillanimity and the desire for advancement that are responsible for such *late* blooming of moral emphasis; rather, the explanation lies in that mutual exclusiveness of heart and head, of moralizing and analytical understanding, on which I dwelt at the beginning of this paper. When one has been groomed as a "scientist," it takes a great deal of wrestling with oneself before one will admit that moral considerations of human solidarity can effectively interfere with those hieratic, impersonal forces of supply and demand.

There is a notable instance here of what Veblen called a "trained incapacity." It is so strong, in fact, that we will often not avow to ourselves the moral source of our scientific thought processes and discoveries. As a result, quite a few of us are *unconscious* moralists in our professional work. I have a personal story to illustrate this point, and here is how I told it in the special preface I wrote—for reasons that will be apparent—for the German edition of *Exit, Voice, and Loyalty:*

> As is related in my book, its [the book's] intellectual origin lies in an observation I made some years ago in Nigeria. But quite a while after the book had been published in the United States, it dawned on me that my absorption with its theme may have deeper roots. A large part of the book centers on the concern that exit of the potentially most powerful carriers of voice prevents the more forceful stand against decline that might otherwise be possible. This situation is not altogether unrelated to the fate of the Jews who were still in Germany after 1939. Most of the young and vigorous ones, like myself, got out in the early years after Hitler took over, leaving a gravely weakened community behind. Of course, the possibilities of any effective voice were zero in the circumstances of those years no matter who left and who stayed. Nevertheless, the real fountainhead of the book may well lie in some carefully repressed guilt feelings that, even though absurd from the point of view of any rational calculus, are simply there.[13]

At this point, a further afterthought suggests itself: it was probably fortunate that I was *not* aware of those deeper moral stirrings when I wrote the book; otherwise, the presentation of my argument might have been less general, less balanced between the respective merits of exit and voice, and less scientifically persuasive. My excursion into autobiography thus points to an odd conclusion: one perhaps peculiarly effective way for social scientists to bring moral concerns into their work is to do so unconsciously. This bit of advice is actually not quite as unhelpful as it sounds. For the reasons given, it seems to me impractical and possibly even counterproductive to issue guidelines to social scientists on how to incorporate morality into their scientific pursuits and how to be on guard against immoral "side effects" of their work. Morality is not something like pollution abatement that can be secured by slightly modifying the design of a policy proposal. Rather, it belongs in the center of our work; and it can get there only if the social scientists are morally alive and make themselves vulnerable to moral concerns—then they will produce morally significant works, consciously or otherwise.

I have a further, more ambitious, and probably utopian thought. Once we have gone through the historical account and associated reasoning of this paper, once we have become fully aware of our intellectual tradition with its deep split between head and heart and the not always beneficial consequences, the first step toward overcoming that tradition and toward healing that split has already been taken. It is then possible to visualize down the road a kind of social science that would be very different from the one most of us have been practicing: a moral-social science where moral considerations are not repressed or kept apart but are systematically commingled with analytic argument without guilt feelings over any lack of integration; where the transition from preaching to proving and back again is performed frequently and with ease; and where moral considerations need no longer be smuggled in surreptitiously nor expressed unconsciously but are displayed openly and disarmingly. Such would be, in part, my dream for a "social science for our grandchildren."

NOTES

1. Montesquieu, *Oeuvres completes*, Roger Caillois, ed. (Paris: Pleiade, NRF, 1949), 1:112 (my translation).

2. Adam Smith, *Wealth of Nations* (New York: Modern Library, 1937), p. 14.

3. "Hast Du Verstand und ein Herz, so zeige nur eines von beiden / Beides verdammen sie Dir, zeigest Du beides zugleich," Friedrich Hölderlin, *Werke und Briefe*, Friedrich Beissner and Joehen Schmidt, eds. (Frankfurt: Inselverlay, 1969), 1:35. Hölderlin's distinction between *Verstand* ("reason") and *Herz* ("heart") reflects the rehabilitation of the passions in the eighteenth century that led to the heart's standing

for the many generous moral feelings, impulses, and beneficent passions man was now credited with while reason was becoming downgraded; at an earlier time, the contrast not between the heart and the head but between the passions and reason or the passions and the interests carried a very different value connotation. I have dealt with these matters in *The Passions and the Interests: Political Arguments for Capitalism Before Its Triumph* (Princeton, N.J.: Princeton University Press, 1977), pp. 27–28, 43–44, 63–66.

4. See Gilles Gaston Granger, "L'explication dans les sciences sociales," *Social Science Information* (1971), 10:38.

5. Clifford Geertz, review of Donald Symons, *The Evolution of Human Sexuality,* in *The New York Review of Books,* January 24, 1980, p. 3.

6. Kenneth Arrow, "Social Responsibility and Economic Efficiency," *Public Policy* (Summer 1973), 21:303–318.

7. Fred Hirsch, "The Ideological Underlay of Inflation," in Fred Hirsch and John H. Goldthorpe, eds., *The Political Economy of Inflation* (Cambridge: Harvard University Press, 1978), p. 274.

8. John H. Goldthorpe, "The Current Inflation: Toward a Sociological Account," in Hirsch and Goldthorpe, eds., *The Political Economy of Inflation,* p. 196.

9. An alternative solution is to fight fire with fire and to apply what might be called "countervailing bloody-mindedness." The recently much-discussed idea of making it expensive for management to increase wages through a special tax levied on payroll increases beyond a certain norm has the avowed purpose of "stiffening the back" of management as it faces militant labor. The monetarist injunctions can also be regarded as a proposal to counter the bloody-mindedness of various social groups with that of the central bank (something that in a number of countries turns out to require strong-arm regimes, as well as *real* bloodletting). For a more extended examination of the sociological aspects of inflation, see "The Social and Political Matrix of Inflation" in my book, *Essays in Trespassing: Economics to Politics and Beyond* (Cambridge: Cambridge University Press, 1981), ch. 8.

10. Malthus, *Principles of Political Economy* (London: John Murray, 1820), pp. 3, 518. This qualifying clause was brought to my attention by Alexander Field; in his paper "Malthus, Method, and Macroeconomics" (May 1980), Field points out that in the numerous expositions of the same principle with which *The Wealth of Nations* is studded, Adam Smith added the similar phrase "as long as he does not violate the laws of justice" only once (see p. 651).

11. For example, Kenneth E. Boulding, *The Economy of Love and Fear: A Preface to Grant Economics* (Belmont, Calif.: Wadsworth, 1973); Edmund S. Phelps, ed., *Altruism, Morality, and Economic Theory* (New York: Russell Sage Foundation, 1975); and David Collard, *Altruism and Economy: A Study in Non-Selfish Economics* (Oxford: Martin Robertson, 1978).

12. Robert M. Solow, "On Theories of Unemployment," *American Economic Review* (March 1980), 70:3–4.

13. Original English text of preface to German edition in Albert O. Hirschman, *Abwanderung und Widerspruch* (Tübingen: J. C. B. Mohr, 1974), p. vii.

Two

DO THE SOCIAL SCIENCES HAVE AN ADEQUATE THEORY OF MORAL DEVELOPMENT?

Carol Gilligan

When Joan Didion was asked by *The American Scholar* to think "in some abstract way about 'morality,'" she found her mind veering instead "inflexibly toward the particular."[1] The particulars about which she thought were the actions of two people who saw a car veer off the highway at midnight. The driver, a young boy, was instantly killed, and his girlfriend was in shock from internal bleeding. The woman, a nurse, drove the girl to the nearest doctor, 185 miles across the floor of Death Valley and over three ranges of lethal mountain road, while her husband, a talc miner, stayed with the boy's body to protect it from coyotes until the coroner could get over the mountains at dawn. In the nurse's statement that "you can't just leave a body on the highway; it's immoral," Didion heard a use of the word "morality" in whose specificity of meaning she could trust: the promise to try not to abandon each other, to try to retrieve our casualties.

This moral code, graphically illuminated for Didion by the litanies of grief awaiting those, like the Donner party, snowbound in the Sierra, who failed in their loyalties to each other, had as its point "only survival, not the attainment of an ideal good."[2] Survival, however, was seen as contingent on a network of human relationship, "a network kept alive by people whose instincts tell them that if they do not keep moving at night on the desert, they will lose all reason." Thus, reason, contingent on human relationship, is sustained by a morality that protects relationship—a morality whose essence lies in not abdicating responsibility, in not breaching primary loyalties, in not giving way to acrimony, in not deserting one another.

The same ethic is articulated by a woman in her thirties who spoke during an interview for a research project of a dream which led her to discover the moral absolute in her life:

When Tom was very little, I had a dream about the house being on fire and what would happen, and in the dream I was anxious and I woke up. It was a nightmare, and I woke up in the middle of the night in terror. I realized that there was no question in my mind but that I would save the baby at cost of myself, and felt this great sort of peaceful feeling—as if that had been the dilemma (which it wasn't in the dream at all). But lying there in the dark, I realized that there was an absolute in my life, this unquestionable absolute in my life, and it made me feel very relaxed, and I remember feeling very calm; why yes, there is something that I would put far, far higher than anything to do with myself, and I feel that it wasn't something I had thought about beforehand. I didn't give a whole lot of thought to getting pregnant— well, I thought, it's probably time for me to have a child now—but after the fact, I do feel that by consenting, really—and it is consent now, because abortion is available, birth control is available, to bring a child into the world, you are, or you ought to be, undertaking to commit yourself to that kind of dedication. At least until such time as society may organize itself better, to take over from parents some responsibility for the next generation.[3]

For her, as for Didion, safety from terror lay in connection to others; civilization, she said, depended on doing certain things for other people regardless.

An incipient version of this ethic is evident in the response of a six-year-old girl to the question posed by Lawrence Kohlberg as to whether a man named Heinz should steal a drug he couldn't afford to buy in order to save the life of his wife. Like most six-year-olds, she said that Heinz shouldn't steal because he would go to jail, adding, however, that this would be bad because then "he couldn't take care of his wife." The primacy of relationship and the activity of care in the narrative that she constructs of Heinz apprehended with the drug and then in jail while his wife is dying alone at home are apparent in the contrast between her response and that of a boy the same age. The boy also says that Heinz shouldn't steal because he would go to jail, but he sees this as bad because in jail Heinz would "starve to death."

I have begun with the voices of women as they articulate a morality of care because both these voices and this ethic have been missing from our theories of moral development. In their absence, a morality of justice prevails in the psychological and educational domain, supporting the growth of individual freedom by fostering the development of a democratic society but ignoring the relationships that engender and sustain the activity of care. As the image of citizen has overshadowed the persona of parent in the conception of maturity, an ethic of fairness and rights has eclipsed a morality of responsibility and care.

This eclipse is the substance of my present concern and the subject of my ongoing research, which traces the developing understanding of responsibility that delineates the growth of an ethic of care. In suggesting that the inclusion of women's thinking in research on moral development calls attention to the absence of an ethic of care and the failure to represent the world of relationships which this ethic refracts, I do not mean to imply that this ethic lies solely in the feminine domain. In the past as well as in the present, a morality of responsibility and care has been articulated by members of both sexes and speaks to a series of concerns shared by both. This ethic provides a necessary complement, however, to the prevalent justice approach by focusing on connection and interdependence rather than on separation and autonomy.

Thus, if asked whether the social sciences have an adequate theory of moral development or whether existing theories are an adequate reflection of moral experience, I will answer in the negative by arguing for the complexity of moral truth. Although I do not advocate pluralism per se or urge a return to value relativism, I claim that morality is fundamentally dialectical in the sense of containing an ongoing tension between justice and care and that half of this dialectic is currently missing from most psychological accounts.

Consequently, I attempt a "movement of return, retracing our steps in order to see how a certain position was reached,"[4] a position which Iris Murdoch identifies in current moral philosophy and which prevails as well in current moral psychology. As Murdoch points out, this position ignores certain facts of human experience while at the same time it imposes a single theory which admits of no communication or escape into rival theories. What psychologists and philosophers have "forgotten or 'theorized away' is the fact that an unexamined life can be virtuous, and the fact that love is a central concept in morals."[5] Psychologists, like contemporary philosophers, "frequently connect consciousness with virtue and although they constantly talk of freedom, they rarely talk of love."[6]

Thus, when Jean Piaget set out to construct a scaffolding for a psychology of moral development, he built his edifice on the foundation of the child's understanding and practice of rules. Conceiving morality as a system of rules for equilibrating social behavior, he saw the essence of morality in "the respect which the individual acquires for these rules." Asking the psychologist's question of how the mind comes to acquire respect for rules, he considered the conception of rules to reveal the logic of social understanding in the same way as the concept of constancy signaled the equilibration of children's thought with physical reality, so did the concept of equality emerge as the key to children's social adaptation. In the strength of these related concepts lies the power of Piaget's vision but also the limitation of the lens through which he has viewed social reality.

Piaget's account of moral development begins by addressing the problem of inequality inherent in the cycle of human life. Seeing the egocentrism of childhood thought as a blinding reflection of adult constraint, Piaget sought to discover how children develop the capacity for cooperation. Tracing this development through the experience of equality in the microcosm of children's play, Piaget described a major transformation in the child's understanding and practice of rules from a heteronomous conception of rules as constraining to an autonomous conception of rules as the outcome of mutual agreement and respect. In the magnificent sweep of his architectural vision, Piaget saw the experience of equality as the critical juncture in moral development, giving rise to the notion of justice that reflects and sustains cooperation and reciprocity. To Piaget, the rule of justice appeared as an "immanent condition of social relationships or a law governing their equilibrium," and the logic of justice was discovered when the child saw that "so as not to be always quarreling you must have rules and then play properly."[7]

As the idea of justice develops in children, the notion of reciprocity extends from a "brutal equalitarianism" to an ideal that can be sustained through time. Thus, Piaget posits a three-stage progression in the child's moral understanding whereby constraint is followed by cooperation, which in turn gives rise to generosity. Generosity is seen by Piaget as a refinement of justice, a development of equalitarianism in the direction of relativity, manifest in the concept of equity, which Piaget considers a fusion of justice and love. Within this unitary conception of moral development, the logic of justice reflected in the

operations of equality and reciprocity leads to the equilibration of social understanding that sustains cooperative play. As the egocentrism
of constraint is overcome by the experience of cooperation, the child
becomes able to see the other as not only equal but different from
self—and to respond with the generosity of a contextual relativism to
the inequities to which such differences give rise.

And yet there is a subtext present in the narrative of this account
that runs under the compelling logic of justice and suggests a different path of moral development. Pointing out that "the notion of good
which generally speaking appears later than the notion of pure duty,
particularly in the case of the child, is perhaps the final conscious
realization of something that is the primary condition of moral life—
the need for reciprocal affection," Piaget notes that altruism, empathy, and sharing all are evident in the behavior of the very young
child.[8] Considering these affective components of morality to elude
his methodology of interrogation, he chooses to ignore their development, following instead the developing logic of justice as the most
rational of moral ideas.

Yet this group of children who remained at the edge of Piaget's
investigation, when glimpsed, appear to be developing in an alternate
mode. In the four brief entries devoted to girls in *The Moral Judgment of the Child*, Piaget attests that "the most superficial observation is sufficient to show that in the main the legal sense is far less
developed in little girls than in boys,"[9] though girls, by contrast, show
a greater capacity for tolerance and innovation in their play. Girls,
Piaget thought, "rather complicated our interrogatory in relation to
what we know about boys," since the inception of cooperation in their
play coincides with rather than precedes the shift from a heteronomous to an autonomous understanding of rules.[10] Similarly, the rigid
equalitarianism that develops among boys, leading them to modulate
the numbers of blows given to match those received, contrasts with
the tendency of girls, who, once they no longer consider it naughty
to hit back at all, say that one should give back fewer blows than one
has received.[11]

A possible interpretation of such differences arises from the observation that side by side with Piaget's insistence that the equilibrium
of true equality and reciprocity rests on a "collective rule which is the
sui generis product of life lived in common" is his statement that "the
need to communicate *prevents* the self from taking advantage of oth-

ers." [12] Thus, the suggestion emerges that girls *avoid* conflict rather than develop rules for limiting its extent, that their social interaction proceeds through modes of communication that reduce the incidence of violence and obviate the need for systems of rules based on the "consciousness of a necessary equilibrium binding upon and limiting both alter and ego."

These suggestions, however, are only hints in a text which takes the development of boys as the pattern for moral growth. The focus on the experience of equality that leads to the idea of justice and the elaboration of rules overshadows the evidence of greater tolerance and less violence in the development of girls. Instead, the girls' greater empathy and tendency toward forgiveness are seen by Piaget as signs of weakness, and social relationships stabilized by the need for communication and connection are considered capricious in contrast to the order of a society equilibrated by rules.

Since the intimations of another path of social development and moral growth are limited to Piaget's scattered observations of girls and arise from the fact that they did not exhibit what he considered to be the dominant mode, the disappearance of this subtext in Kohlberg's work can be explained by his selection of an all-male sample. Whereas Piaget gathers Kant and Durkheim around him to proclaim morality a system of rules, Kohlberg lines himself up with Socrates to claim that virtue is one and its name is justice, adding only that by justice he means equality in a democratic society. [13] Although Kohlberg conceived his work as an extension into adolescence of Piaget's study of the moral judgment of the child, he takes the study of morality out of the context of naturalistic observation of social behavior, relying solely on interrogation about hypothetical dilemmas and, perhaps as a result, fusing the distinctions between equality and equity, cognition and affect, and justice and love, which are sustained in Piaget's text.

Whether because Kohlberg studied adolescent males eager to justify separation and independence, whether because his study was conducted in the context of American society, where the Bill of Rights attests the historical importance of independence, freedom, and equality, or whether because he was influenced by the lesson of the Holocaust, which showed the dangers of collaboration, Kohlberg built a theory of moral development on a unitary moral conception of justice as fairness. This conception equated moral development with the

refinement of the idea of justice from its initial confusion with obedience to authority, through its equation with conformity to social
roles and rules, to the recognition of its ideal form in the logic of
equality and reciprocity. Thus, the social context of moral decision
was replaced by the structures of formal thought, which provided a
rational system for decision that was autonomous and independent of
time and place. In Kohlberg's system, the rational individual standing
alone is the ideal moral agent, entering with rights into fair contracts
with others to protect the rights of both from interference.

Kohlberg's work thus delineates in its purest form a rational morality of justice and rights. While the power of this ethic lies in the
respect accorded to the individual, its limitation lies in its failure to
see a world of relationship, compassion, and care. Focusing on the
individual as primary in his construction of the moral domain, Kohlberg derives the connections between people first from the constraint
of authority and subsequently through deals of even exchange, ster-
eotypic norms of relationship, societal systems of roles and rules, fair
and equal contracts, and finally rational agreement. The aim of moral
development is to free individuals from societal constraint, to make
them "independent of civil society"[14] by protecting their rights and
limiting their duties to the granting of reciprocal respect. In this sense,
if Piaget's perspective reflects the position of children caught in a
situation of inequality and through cooperation overcoming its constraint, Kohlberg's reflects the concern of adolescents struggling to
free initiative from guilt, justifying by reason their separation from
those to whom formerly they were bound. The educational lesson
inherent in the development that Piaget and Kohlberg trace lies in its
demonstration that although the experiences of equality and of freedom disrupt a social order based on constraint, they generate the more
stable and adaptive social order of cooperation and mutual respect.

Yet, given that justice is deliberately blinded to ensure the impartial weighing of claims; given that equality is achieved by judging
behind a "veil of ignorance"[15] that obscures the inequities of life; and
given that rational decision is reached by a solitary game of "moral
musical chairs,"[16] in which one assumes one is taking the other's
position by putting oneself in his place—all this is an ethic whose
limitation lies precisely in what is not seen. Thus, the shift from a
morality of justice and rights to an ethic of responsibility and care is
marked by a striking change in imagery from that of blindness to that

of sight. Suddenly, the other appears reembodied in personal and social history, as different from the self but connected by living in a common social world. In the Didion story with which I began, morality is premised on the ability to see the connection between self and stranger by understanding the narrative through which it extends. Thus, in the move from rights to responsibilities, the fundamental premise of moral judgment shifts from balancing separate individuals in a social system equilibrated by the logic of equality and reciprocity to seeing individuals as interdependent in a network of social relationship. As the mother sees her life-giving connection to her child as life-sustaining for her as well, so the little girl sees the fracture of relationship as the moral problem in Kohlberg's dilemma. Whereas justice emphasizes the autonomy of the person, care underlies the primacy of relationship. Thus, justice gives rise to an ethic of rights, and care engenders an ethic of responsibility.

The implications for social science theory and research of the dualistic conception of morality that I propose emanate from the suggestion that moral development proceeds along two different but intersecting paths that run through different modes of experience and give rise to different forms of thought. Whereas the analytic logic of justice is consonant with rational social and ethical theories and can be traced through the resolution of hypothetical dilemmas, the ethic of care depends on the contextual understanding of relationship. Since the experiential basis for this understanding and the forms of thought through which it develops have never been systematically traced in psychological research, its manifestations have been described as personality traits or situational effects rather than seen as part of a developmental process.

To trace the interaction of thought and experience through which the understanding of care and responsibility develops requires a different moral theory and a different strategy of research. The analytic logic of justice is manifest in the deductive resolution of hypothetical dilemmas and informs the understanding of rules. In contrast, the ethic of care relies on the understanding of relationships and is manifest most clearly in the consideration of actual dilemmas of moral conflicts and choice. A language of responsibility and care that cannot be assimilated to the logic of justice was discovered empirically through a study of pregnant women who were considering abortion decisions.[17] Although abortion can be construed as a dilemma of rights, in which case the moral problem turns on whether or not the fetus is thought to have rights, the women who participated in the abortion study did not construe the problem this way. Rather, they tended to place the dilemma of abortion in the context of the relationships in which it arises, to see the decision poised at the juncture between two connections—of man and woman and of parent and child. Seen in this context, the pregnancy posed a problem of responsibility, and the women's different understandings of responsibility suggested a sequence in the development of care. This sequence appeared in the texts of in-depth clinical interviews with twenty-nine women of diverse age, race, and class who were facing in common the actual choice of whether to continue or abort a pregnancy. I will describe three modes in the understanding of responsibility and the two transitional phases between them, which indicate the development of the understanding of relationships and chart the growth of an ethic of care.

The language of responsibility begins by delineating connection to others as a way of ensuring survival by providing access to the things one is powerless to get for oneself. In children this understanding of relationship is manifest in the contrast between people they like and people they don't like or people who do and do not meet their needs, and this contrast in turn guides the decision about whom they should care. The moral problem of inclusion, which lies at the center of the ethic of care, is played out through the consideration of who is and who is not my friend. In the context of the abortion dilemma, the choice at this level centers on whether the woman sees the baby as a potential friend, as in the wish to have a baby in order not "to feel lonely and stuff." Similarly, having a baby may provide a way to leave home or, conversely, may interfere with a wish to continue in school. Thus, relationships are seen either as a source of personal gratification or as an impediment to gratification, in which case they are experienced as threatening or disappointing.

In the first transition, the concern with self, which was initially egocentric and thus unreflective, comes to be reconstructed as "selfish" as the experience of relationship extends the understanding of responsibility. A pregnancy can initiate this transition by demonstrating on a physical level the connection between self and other and by indicating how through that connection the actions of self affect the other and the other affects the self. Given the incipient awareness of responsibility for conceiving a child and of the responsibility entailed in raising a child, the exercise of responsibility with respect to the abortion decision can be seen as a way of entering the world of adult relationships. The transitional nature of this understanding is evident, however, as the concept of responsibility repeatedly turns back toward the self, although now with a focus on assessing the self's capacity to care for another.

When the concern with responsibility shifts to consideration of the needs of the other, the second mode is achieved. Now the self is seen as more powerful, since the capacity to give to others provides a means of establishing and maintaining relationships of mutual dependence and care. Relationships become an anchor of personal security by signifying membership in a social world where inclusion is premised on the ability to care and promises care and protection in return. Concern now shifts from the direct satisfaction of needs to maintaining interpersonal connection, and this shift is manifest in a change in perspective toward others from liking and not liking to hurting and not hurting. As the wish to sustain relationships develops, the injunction not to hurt others is seen as the way to ensure continuing connection with others by avoiding conflict with them. The avoidance of hurt to others, however, depends on understanding their feelings and discerning their needs, and the contextual nature of this psychological understanding differs from the logic of justice viewed as fairness. The concept of equity, which Piaget illustrates through the response of an eleven-year-old girl to the dilemma of whether or not to give a second roll to a younger child who had carelessly dropped his first in the water, indicates how a more differentiated interpersonal understanding underlies an ethic of care. Focusing on the issue of care, the girl says that "the little boy ought to have taken care, but then he was a little boy, so they might give him a little more," explaining that older children should understand "that when you are little you don't understand what you are doing."[18]

In the abortion decision, concern for others is expressed at the second mode as a wish not to hurt them. This concern with not hurting may extend to the fetus, the woman's family, her lover, or even to people to whom her lover is connected, such as his wife and children. Decision making in a world that extends along connecting lines of interrelationship differs from the balancing of separate individual claims, since the logic of choice changes from that of rights to a consideration of responsibility in relationships. This distinction was evident in the responses of two lawyers to the dilemma of whether or not to tell the opposing counsel about a document that would support the "meritorious claim" of the other's client.[19] A female lawyer approached the dilemma by considering in turn her responsibility and relationship to everyone involved, whereas a male attorney saw the adversary system of justice as ensuring equal protection for everyone's rights. For the woman, respect for others entailed trying to see the situation through their eyes; for the man, it was manifest in the assumption that the others were capable of protecting their rights.

In the second mode of understanding of responsibility, the needs of others are fused with those of the self, and the focus on the position of the other is so strong that the other's views are experienced as one's own beliefs. Desiring above all not to be selfish and thus in danger of losing a relationship, a woman may confuse self with other, holding herself responsible for the actions of others and considering others responsible for the choices she makes. Since responsibility is directed toward others, choice itself is construed as response to them, and submission to others is considered to be a manifestation of care and concern.

If the egocentrism of the first mode leads to disappointing and unstable relationships, which ultimately do not meet individual needs, the construction of responsibility in the second mode creates in relationships problems of a sort manifest when the attempt to avoid hurt does not succeed in sustaining connection. The focus on not hurting others as the substance of a morality of care then gives way gradually to the realization that basing decisions on the wishes of others and holding them accountable for one's own choice constitutes an evasion of responsibility that erodes the fabric of relationship. Thus, in the second transition, concern for self reemerges to guide a new understanding of relationship as a dynamic process of interaction rather than a bond of mutual dependence. This reassessment centers on a new and more active understanding of care that includes both self and other in the realization of their interdependence. Certainly the decision to have an abortion spurs this kind of reconsideration, since the clear and irrevocable choice brings into focus the issue of responsibility at the same time as the pregnancy highlights the reality of interconnection.

Thus, the discovery through experience of the greater complexity of psychological and social reality, of the ambivalence of feelings, and of the constraints of choice spurs a process of self-reflection and a reexamination of relationships. The transitional features of this process are apparent when the turning back of responsibility toward the other leads the woman to deem as selfish her consideration of herself. This consideration, however, centers on a new understanding of her participation in choice. Through this reexamination, the woman comes to see how decisions made in a context of relationship not only affect both self and other but change the dynamic of their interaction. Thus, the understanding of relationship changes from a static balance maintained by not hurting to a dynamic interaction that arises and is sustained through the activity of care.

Whereas in the second mode care is defined as not hurting others who are the focus of concern, in the third mode care is tied to seeing the connections between everyone involved and thus to a new understanding of what is going on. This expansion of vision widens the conception of responsibility, including both self and other in the world of relationships that care protects, which is affected by what happens to everyone involved. As the injunction against hurting comes to be elevated to an ideal of nonviolence in human relationships, the focus of care shifts from the other to the relationship itself. Given that conflicts will inevitably arise, since the experiences and perspectives of people diverge, modes of dealing with conflict are sought that strengthen rather than sever connection. The moral problem of inclusion that hinges on the capacity to assume responsibility for care is now seen within an expanded network of relationship and with a broader understanding of what responsibility entails.

With this expansion of vision and the commitment to see the network of interrelationship comes a heightened sense of responsibility, tempered, however, by the realization that in dilemmas of responsibility conflict will always remain. A woman working as a counselor in an abortion clinic described the inner turmoil that led her to decide that she "really had to face what was going on." Witnessing a late abortion, she saw the fetus clearly as a developing human life, yet at the same time she realized that the development of that life was contingent on responsible care. Realizing that rights could be universally extended, while the capacity for care was bound by personal and social constraints, she concluded that abortion could be the lesser of two evils in a situation which admitted no absolute good. Morality, then, was contingent on sustaining the connections that revealed the consequences of action, minimizing the occurrence of violence by generating an awareness of responsibility for hurt.

Thus, the ethic of care is dependent on sight, or the ability to discern what is going on, widening the lens on social reality to reveal the connections obscured by the justice approach. The commitment to seeing the other entails a responsiveness to the other's point of view, not as mirroring of one's own but as refracting a different psychological and social reality. Beginning with the assumption that relationship is the fundamental condition of social reality, the ethic of care is contextual in its insistence on seeing connections. Moral judgment thus cannot be abstracted from the context of individual and social history, and decision making relies on a process of communication to discover the other's position and to discern the chain of connections through which the consequences of action extend. Thus, dialogue replaces logical deduction as the mode of moral discovery, and the activity of moral understanding returns to the social domain.

By tracing the ethic of care through a sequence of three modes and delineating the transitions between them, I have indicated how this ethic develops through the changing experience and understanding of relationship. As the understanding of relationship is reflected in the conception of responsibility, the language of responsibility guides the decision about whom to include in the compass of care. The moral problem of inclusion then comes to be reconstructed as the universe of care expands through an elaboration of the network of relationship and the increasing awareness of interdependence.

Since the development of an ethic of care depends on the experience and understanding of relationship, it is not bound by the same cognitive constraints that apply to the understanding of justice and rights. No longer would only moral philosophers or analytic thinkers reach moral maturity but also people who have come through the experience of relationship to understand the dynamics of interdependence. Thus, the ethic of care restores the concept of love to the moral domain, uniting cognition and affect by tying reflection to the experience of relationship.

If the concept of morality contains a fundamental tension between the ethics of justice and of care, then the delineation of moral development requires a more complex rendering of social experience. The development of the idea of justice, as traced through the work of Piaget and Kohlberg, depends on the experience of equality and autonomy that generates and in turn is sustained by the logic of fairness and rights. In the life cycle, adolescence brings issues of equality to the fore, and the development of formal thought at that time can extend the understanding of fairness from a logic of rules to a principled conception of rights, which then provides a justification for freedom, individual respect, and separation from others. Thus, we would expect, as Kohlberg found, that the logic of justice flourishes during adolescence, especially in times of social change, when the sense of possibility expands. The flourishing of justice would be fostered by the development of analytic modes of thought and by the experience of equal participation in democratic social institutions.

In contrast, the ethic of care develops through relationships that give rise to an understanding of interdependence and is sustained by the ability to discern connection. The experiences that foster its growth are connections that extend through time, revealing the changing dynamic of interaction and making it possible to see the consequences of choice. Whereas the experience of relationship that underlies the capacity for care begins early in life, the experience of responsibility reaches its fullest extension only in the adult years. Since care depends on understanding the narrative through which human experience extends, its development is supported by the growth of contextual modes of understanding and by involvement in a world of coherent and continuing relationship.

From this description, it is easy to see how the development of the social sciences toward increasingly formal and analytic modes of thought, reflected in the separation of subject and object in the design of experimental research and manifest in the claim of value neutrality and objective truth, would foster the understanding of an ethic of justice and the elaboration of systems of rules at the expense of an ethic of care and an understanding of the narrative of social relationship. Thus, psychologists trace the development in children of the capacity to perform the reversible operations of equality and reciprocity and to understand the logic of justice that underlies citizenship in a democratic state but ignore their ability to discern the inequities manifest in human society or to respond with care to the inequalities inherent in the cycle of life. Piaget observes that perhaps it is in the relationship of parent and child that "one realizes most keenly how immoral it can be to believe too much in morality and how much more precious is a little humanity than all the rules in the world."[20] And yet his equation of morality with respect for rules sustains the division of cognition and affect and provides little basis for tracing the understanding that reflects and informs the growth of the capacity for care.

Although I have suggested that moral development proceeds along two different paths and have indicated the tension between two different modes of ethical thought, I do not mean to imply that these ethics remain separate or that their development is unconnected. Instead, through the tension between the universality of rights and the particularity of responsibility, between the abstract concept of justice as fairness and the more contextual understanding of care in relationships, these ethics keep one another alive and inform each other at critical points. In this sense, the concept of morality sustains a dialectical tension between justice and care, aspiring always toward the ideal of a world more caring and more just. Conceived of in this way, the dialectic of moral development can be seen to emerge from the cycle of human life, to be embedded in human experience, and thus to be present in both of the sexes. Its tension is manifest in people's responses to actual dilemmas of moral conflict and choice as well as in the current debate about the theory and practice of psychological research.

The age-old dialogue between justice and love, reason and compassion, fairness and forgiveness, reflects not just two opposing or complementary conceptions of the moral domain but the fundamental tension in human psychology between the experience of separation and the experience of connection. As the experiences of attachment and separation run through the cycle of human life, they give rise to the paradoxical truths that describe our social experience: that we know ourselves as individual and separate only insofar as we live in connection with others, and that we experience relationship only insofar as we differentiate other from self. Despite their underlying interconnection, however, the experiences of self and relationship are discrete, and these discrete experiences in turn give rise to two different moral languages: the language of rights that justifies separation and thus fosters and protects autonomy, and the language of responsibilities that sustains relationships and informs the activity of care.

Although these languages are manifest in different vocabularies (rights in the more analytic concepts of fairness, equality, balance, equilibrium, reciprocity, truth, and deceit; responsibility in the more contextual concepts of harmony, relationship, care, love, hurt, friendship, and betrayal) and although the ethics they reflect address different problems (rights, the conflict of self vs. other; responsibilities, the relationship between self and other), they remain in tension with one another. A move toward separation and rights leaves a problem of relationship and care, whereas a move toward connection and responsibility leaves a problem of personal integrity and choice. In the texts of interviews with people about their experiences of actual moral conflict and choice, the intersection of these two languages is marked by references to "terrible ambiguity" or by the awareness of a fundamental contradiction that then leads to confusion and difficulty with choice. This confusion is apparent when problems of relationship are cast in the language of rights, as when a problem of deceit in sexual triangles is formulated as a conflict between one person's "right to truth" and another's "right to sanity," a formulation which defies resolution by logical deduction. Then the apparent impasse of judgment tends to spur the conclusion either that moral judgment itself is relative or that problems of human relationships do not belong in the moral domain. Conversely, when conflicts of rights are construed in the language of responsibility so that opposing claims are formulated as a "balance of selfishnesses," then no resolution can be seen as moral, and integrity of autonomous choice appears uncaring and selfish, a manifestation of indifference.

Through their dialogue, however, these languages address the moral problem of how we can live at once as separate individuals and in continuing relationship with one another. This dialectic of separation and attachment informs an understanding of moral maturity that encompasses both relationships of equality, sustained by the logic of justice, and relationships of interdependence, relying on an ethic of care. The ability to see and respond to differences without abandoning moral judgment to relativism underlies the capacity to understand and protect another person's integrity and vulnerability. Since we know that violence breeds violence in the cycle of human relationships and that differences are embedded in the cycle of life, the moral balance of equality requires as its complement an ethic of care. Seeing the potential for violence to eventuate in the catastrophic destruction of nuclear war, Erikson warned that "in our time, man must decide whether he can afford to continue the exploitation of childhood as an arsenal of irrational fears or whether the relationship between adult and child, like other inequalities, can be raised to a position of partnership in a more reasonable order of things."[21]

The absence of care in the social sciences is evident not only in the conception of morality as solely a problem of justice but also in the relationship between experimenter and subject in social science research. The use of deceit in experimentation, although considered one of the rules of the game, affects the experimenter as well as the victim and colors the results that are thereby obtained. As social scientists have begun to question the separation of experimenter and subject and to pay more attention to the context of research, they have begun to generate a series of findings that point to the contextual nature of psychological truth. The studies by Rosenthal and Jacobson on the effects of teachers' expectations on children's intelligence indicate that the dynamic of relationship operates in ways that challenge basic assumptions about individual behavior.[22] Recent evidence on adaptation to life[23] as well as on survival in old age[24] demonstrates the life-sustaining power of relationships and the importance throughout life of continuing connection.

The moral problem in psychology is reflected as well in the language of its discourse, wherein people are referred to as research "subjects" and love "objects" rather than seen as partners in a shared interaction or pursuit. This language maintains a distance, mistaken for objectivity, which obscures the dynamic of interrelationship and the socially constructed and provisional nature of truth. Then a moral problem arises to compromise the integrity of psychological treatment and research, and the absence of care opens the way to manipulation, exploitation, and the rationalization of hurt. If the ethical potential of the social sciences lies in their ability to discover the social processes that sustain life, then the realization of this potential may depend on a shift not only in the locus of power and truth but also in the substance of concern. As an ethic of individual integrity comes to be seen as necessarily joined to an ethic of nonviolence, social understanding may expand its current focus on self and society to illuminate more fully the network of relationship that reveals the interdependence of life.

NOTES

1. Joan Didion, *Slouching Towards Bethlehem* (New York: Dell, 1969), p. 157.
2. *Ibid.*, p. 159.
3. Confidential source.
4. Iris Murdoch, *The Sovereignty of Good* (New York: Schocken Books, 1971), p. 1.
5. *Ibid.*, pp. 1–2.
6. *Ibid.*, p. 2.
7. Jean Piaget, *The Moral Judgment of the Child* (1932; rpt., New York: Free Press, 1965), p. 171.
8. *Ibid.*, p. 176.
9. *Ibid.*, p. 177.
10. *Ibid.*, p. 180.
11. *Ibid.*, p. 302.
12. *Ibid.*, p. 318; emphasis mine.
13. Lawrence Kohlberg, "Education for Justice: A Modern Statement of the Platonic View," in Nancy Sizer and Theodore Sizer, eds., *Moral Education: Five Lectures* (Cambridge: Harvard University Press, 1970), p. 58.
14. Lawrence Kohlberg, "From Is to Ought: How to Commit the Naturalistic Fallacy and Get Away with It in the Study of Moral Development," in Theodore Mischel, ed., *Cognitive Development and Epistemology* (New York: Academic Press, 1971).
15. John Rawls, *A Theory of Justice* (Cambridge: Harvard University Press, 1971).
16. Lawrence Kohlberg, "Moral Stages and Moralization: The Cognitive-Developmental Approach," in T. Lickona, ed., *Moral Development and Behavior: Theory, Research, and Social Issues* (New York: Holt, Rinehart and Winston, 1976).
17. Carol Gilligan, "In a Different Voice: Women's Conceptions of Self and Morality," *Harvard Educational Review* (November 1977), 47:481–517. I have benefited from David Shawver's discussion of this work in his essay, "Alternative Principles: There's More Than Justice as Fairness." For further description of the abortion decision study, see Carol Gilligan and Mary Belenky, "A Naturalistic Study of Abortion Decisions," in Robert Selman and Regina Yando, eds., *Clinical-Developmental Psychology* (San Francisco: Jossey-Bass Inc., 1980); and Carol Gilligan, *In a Different Voice: Psychological Theory and Women's Development* (Cambridge: Harvard University Press, 1982).
18. Piaget, *Moral Judgment*, pp. 272–73.
19. Sharry Langdale and Carol Gilligan, "The Contribution of Women's Thought to Developmental Theory: The Elimination of Sex Bias in Moral Development Research and Education," interim report submitted to the National Institute of Education, 1980; see also Carol Gilligan, Sharry Langdale, Nona Lyons, and J. Michael Murphy, Final Report to the National Institute of Education, 1982.
20. Piaget, *Moral Judgment*, p. 191.
21. Erik Erikson, *Childhood and Society* (1950; rpt., New York: W. W. Norton, 1963).

22. Robert Rosenthal and Leonore Jacobson, *Pygmalion in the Classroom* (New York: Holt, Rinehart and Winston, 1968).

23. George Vaillant, *Adaptation to Life* (Boston: Little, Brown, 1977).

24. Ellen Langer, "Old Age: An Artifact?" in James McGaugh and Sara Keisler, eds., *Aging: Biology and Behavior* (New York: Academic Press, 1980).

Three

HUMANISM AS NIHILISM:
THE BRACKETING OF TRUTH
AND SERIOUSNESS IN AMERICAN
CULTURAL ANTHROPOLOGY

Paul Rabinow

There has never been a document of culture which was not at one and the same time a document of barbarism.—Walter Benjamin

Those who fancy themselves free of nihilism perhaps push forward its development most fundamentally.—Martin Heidegger

Nihilism is a modern term and a modern problem. Its rise as an issue in society and in reflections on society is roughly coincident with the rise of modern social sciences. If, following Nietzsche, we see nihilism as the equating of all beings, the leveling of meaningful differentiation, the transvaluation of all values, then it might appear logical that anthropology should have escaped this cultural process. A field whose very foundations rest on the existence of an Other—different ways of being human—ought to be the locus of the preservation of difference. I will argue in this paper that, despite itself, American cultural anthropology has had the opposite effect.

It has frequently been pointed out that the numerous attempts to treat man as an object or a thing are potentially dangerous, dehumanizing, and insidious. In this paper I will examine the lineage of anthropological theorists who have developed the concept of "culture" and argue that their attempts to construct a science of culture have also led—despite their intent—to a form of nihilism, a reduction of the Other to the Same.

Schematizing broadly, I argue that modern anthropology has taken two major steps in this direction. The first, associated with Franz Boas, was the articulation of the concept of culture as a replacement for and attack on the racist, hierarchical views of nineteenth-century anthropology. Politically admirable, Boas' attack on racism transformed American anthropology into a science concerned with cultures as wholes, one concerned with diversity and pluralism. The price Boas and his students paid for the construction of cultural relativism was the bracketing of truth. Each culture could not be taken at face value. Earlier anthropologists had ethnocentrically ranked all peoples in relation to the values of the West. For Boas and his students, there were underlying universal boundary conditions of what it meant to be human. All cultures dealt with these in their own way. There was a common human condition with diverse solutions. All Otherness (these diverse solutions) could be understood as really being the Same (the universal boundary conditions).

The second step, located in the Parsonian tradition and its offshoots, seeks to limit the overly broad culture concept by rooting it in underlying but changing biosocial evolutionary processes and in the concept of "symbol," which gives historical specificity to different cultures. The focus is on experience and action as a way of articulating these dimensions. The task of anthropology becomes not just the appreciation of different cultures as "ways of life." Rather, cultures are seen as clusters of symbols. These symbols are analyzed as a group's commentary—its discourse—on experience. The role of the anthropologist is to imaginatively translate their frames of meaning into our frame of meaning. By so doing, the anthropologist enters into a fictive conversation with the other culture. The only price to be paid is the bracketing of the seriousness of the speech acts of the Other. All cultures are brought into the universal conversation of humanity, but what each has to say is only one more text to be translated into Western discourse.

Both moments of American cultural anthropology have major achievements of analysis, cross-cultural description, and convincing intent which are undeniable. I am not questioning motives here, as moralism will get us nowhere. But what is worth examining is how this type of inquiry, by a dogged and at times even heroic championing of anthropology as science, has undermined the deeper intent of its own project, resistance to the iron cage of modernity.

THE BRACKETING OF TRUTH: CULTURAL RELATIVISM

The successful reconstitution of anthropology as a nonracist, non-hierarchical, and relativist science of culture is usually associated (quite correctly) with the name of Franz Boas. Boas led the assault within anthropology both on racism (and the centrality of race in general) and on the unified schemes of cultural evolution which had so dominated both right- and left-wing thinkers throughout the nineteenth century. Boas used the science of culture which he was building as the weapon with which to attack the concept of race. The unity of a people was cultural and had nothing to do with biology. The scientific framework of explanation and the ethical framework of differential evaluation were brought under siege by Boas and his students in the name of cultures—in the plural.

The modern anthropological concept of culture turned on a clustering of terms: historicity, plurality, behavioral determinism, integration, and relativism. Each has its own genealogy—Boas was hardly the first to posit any of them—but their confluence in the culture concept was an event of major significance. According to Stocking, "Once the one grand scheme of evolutionism was rejected, the multiplicity of cultures which took the place of the cultural stages of savagery, barbarism and civilization were no more easily brought within one standard of evaluation than they were within one system of explanation."[1]

Boas is best known for his rigorous particularism, his zealous emphasis on the ethnographic specificity of each culture. Culture traits might be found in different milieus, but culture was more than just disparate traits; it was an organized way of life. So Boas' particularism lay on the level of cultural wholes. Boas was a crusading nominalist, reacting vigorously to the damage done to truth and morality by the premature and false schematizations of his immediate predecessors in anthropology. The result of this particularism of cultural wholes was to establish a trend of relativism and antitheoretical description which were to be the twin marks of American cultural anthropology since his time. By knocking down the universal standards of comparison Boas opened the door for cultural relativism. The shattering of the vertical order of evolutionary schemes left, so to speak, a horizontal plane on which each culture had a place which was as valuable as any other.

Boas from the earliest days of his scientific career opposed both the analysis of separate elements taken out of their historical and cultural context and the universal classification of wholes which predetermined the place of particular facts. Commonly, Boas used each of these two poles to attack (today we might say deconstruct) the other. He refused to admit, for example, that like causes always had like effects—which horrified Durkheim—because, for Boas, the integrative whole always had a primacy over the place of the parts. Conversely, however, he demanded an almost fanatical and literal attention to the facts—literal transcription of texts was a mode for a while—which ultimately made the classification of the whole almost impossible.

According to Boas: "In ethnology, all is individuality."[2] But that individuality resided on the level of the integration of a particular group—the "genius" of a tribe. Meaning was the concept that mediated relations of elements and wholes. Insofar as it implied a causal direction the movement was from whole to element: "From a collection of string instruments, or drums of savage tribes and the modern orchestra, we cannot derive any conclusion but that similar means have been applied by all peoples to make music. The character of their music, the only object worth studying, which determines the form of the instruments, cannot be understood from the single instrument, but requires a complete collection from the single tribe."[3]

Thus, the seeds of the distinctively American variant of holistic analysis—the transformation of the German historicists' conception of *Geist* and *Volk*—emerged in a preliminary manner in Boas' work. The main difference from the Germans, however, is that Boas and his students doggedly called this type of activity science. He refused the de rigueur distinction between *naturwissenschaften* and *geisteswissenschaften*. Boas wanted to study culture scientifically with methods that were universal. Seawater and Eskimos, to cite two of Boas' interests, could be brought within the same purview. The advances of cultural science would go hand in hand with those of the physical sciences. In both, the critique of tradition, the progressive liberating power of reason would be an instrument of humanity in its fight against the realms of unreason. This was Boas' faith.

This position must be situated in the context of its formation: the reaction against universalizing, hierarchical, and racist evolutionary schemes on the one hand, and scientific analysis, in a causal/

functional frame, of the distribution of traits (meaningless in themselves, Boas thought) on the other. Somewhere uneasily situated
between the debris of these two currents, Boas and his followers
attempted to construct a hybrid science of culture that has both defined and bedeviled the mainstream of American anthropology
throughout the twentieth century.

For Boas, "On the one hand, culture was simply an accidental ac-
cretion of individual elements. On the other hand, culture—despite
Boas' renunciation of organic growth—was at the same time an integrated spiritual totality that somehow conditions the form of its elements."[4] The "somehow" became a central concern for Boas and particularly for his students. Boas placed the emphasis on an integration
which was psychological, one of ideas, so as to avoid resorting to any
external condition as the basis of a culture's way of life.

So, in an important sense, the result of the Boasian revolution was
to successfully displace the evaluative procedures of earlier modern
attempts to comprehend other peoples. Each culture was seen as distinctive, each people had its own genius—there was no way to rank
them. One had to respect their individuality and their autonomy and
to promote a general tolerance for human difference. Implicitly, a
purification of all ethnocentrism was at the heart of the matter. Paradoxically, perhaps, the natives under study would not be able to do
much themselves but "express" the underlying holistic way of life
which shaped their smallest movements. This meaningful pattern of
culture could only be articulated, grasped, and discussed by the anthropologist. Hence the seriousness, absurdity, joy, or horror of a particular people's way of life was both given heightened importance and
dramatically relativized at the same time. The daily activities of a people were displayed in their full dignity as worthy of respect and tolerance. But only the anthropologists—not the people themselves—
could understand, describe, and analyze this cultural whole. They
live it, we think it.

The full implications of this cultural relativity and new science of
anthropology emerged with Boas' students. By 1926 they controlled
all the major departments of anthropology in America.

Perhaps the best place to look for a concise statement of the cultural relativist position which Boas' students developed is in Melville
Herskovits' textbook *Man and His Works*,[5] published shortly after
the Second World War. Although other Boasians would put these

points in different ways, Herskovits' formulation touches all the crucial bases in a direct and unblushing fashion.

Herskovits opens his chapter entitled "The Problem of Cultural Relativism" by claiming that it is a human universal to make evaluations of ways of life other than one's own. All groups do it. Scholars and scientists in our culture have laboriously catalogued and organized these judgments into schemata and charts. The initial hope was that we would thereby reveal universals of evaluation, but the result has not been one of consensus. Herskovits says, "It has become increasingly evident, however, that evaluations of this kind stand or fall with the acceptance of the premises from which they derive."[6] Many of these criteria are in conflict and there is no obvious way to decide between them. Many other human groups understand this and have developed an attitude of tolerance towards diversity. Our civilization, however, has lost its tolerance and feels the need for consistency and uniformity. This has bred intolerance. A central task of anthropology is to combat this attitude.

Herskovits gives the example of marriage. There are many different ways in which people marry, although not an infinite number. They all seem, almost by definition, to perform the basic task of marriage, otherwise these societies would have ceased to exist. So, on a simple functional and utilitarian scale we have no way to choose between different arrangements. Further, if we examine these various systems from the inside, from the point of view of the people who practice them, not only do these customs work, but they seem desirable: "Evaluations are relative to the cultural background out of which they arise."[7] Utility of a functionalist sort and contextualization of attitude are the first two criteria Herskovits puts forward.

Each of the societies which anthropologists study, Herskovits continues, has an underlying value system. Reality for each group, and ultimately for each individual, is shaped and experienced in terms of this underlying value system. Hence, it follows that reality is variable and plural. In social life "the very definition of what is normal and abnormal is relative to the cultural frame of reference."[8] It is the job of the anthropologists to penetrate these value systems and to make them available to others.

This leads us directly to the question of cultural relativism. We must evaluate value systems in their own frame—otherwise we are being ethnocentric. Ethnocentrism, however, is really only a danger when it is linked with power. For, as Herskovits admits, most groups evaluate others in generally negative terms—the well-known ethnographic truism that many societies call themselves "humans," implying that other groups are something lower and less fully human. But Herskovits argues that this has been overread and discourse mistaken for reality. The truth is that these groups denigrate other groups verbally but are tolerant in their actions. "It is when, as in Euro-American culture, ethnocentrism is rationalized and made the basis of programs of action detrimental to the well-being of other peoples that it gives rise to serious problems."[9]

We should learn from other cultures that a recognition of difference and tolerance can go hand in hand. "For cultural relativism is a philosophy which, in recognizing the values set up by every society to guide its own life, lays stress on the dignity inherent in every body of custom and on the need for tolerance of conventions though they may differ from one's own."[10] Such a position, Herskovits argues, should lead us to see "the validity of every set of norms for the people whose lives are guided by them, and the values they represent." This sentence was written after the Nazi experience without any qualifications added.

Herskovits closes his chapter on relativism by claiming triumphantly that cultural relativism is a position which opposes absolutism—the existence of any fixed standard. It is, however, not opposed to universals, "those least common denominators to be extracted, inductively from comprehension of the range of variation which all phenomena of the natural or cultural world manifest."[11] There are universal forms which are found as human imperatives in all cultures, but there are no fixed contents to be found in any of these forms. "Morality is a universal, and so is enjoyment of beauty, and some standard of truth." Morality is both universal and relative to the particular value system which gives it content. Anthropology will be a tolerant science of particulars founded on the universals of human existence. Respect for difference is its guiding principle, relativism its norm.

Every culture is worthy of respect; from the outside no judgment of the truth or goodness of another culture is possible; function ensures respect; conformity to the group's standards is the imperative of all social life; there are universals of human existence which are empty; contents vary but are all founded in a value system which

underlies attitudes and behavior; the scientific function of anthropology is to describe this value system; the political function of anthropology is to fight ethnocentrism and promote tolerance.

Cultural relativism marks a major stage in the reduction of the
Other to the Same. All differences are preserved and denied at the
same time. All are treated equally. Previously, cultures had been
ranked on a Eurocentric scale. But the critical assault of cultural anthropology was successful in exposing the ethnocentric bias implicit
in all the hierarchies of evaluation and classification previously constructed. The motto, echoing Husserl, might well be "to the cultures'
underlying value systems themselves."

All that is necessary for the cultural relativist to achieve this aim is
to bracket the truth claims or beauty claims or morality claims of the
culture under consideration. In this act of anthropological purification—ridding ourselves of ethnocentrism—we take *no* culture at its
word. We start by bracketing the truth claims or value positions of
our own culture and then we do the same for the culture we are
attempting to comprehend.

According to this position, on the one side there are the boundary
conditions of what it means to be human, the basic conditions of life
which all human beings must make some sense of. On the other
side, there is the cultural interpretation of a particular people, which
gives one reading of these basic conditions: this is their value system.
Since all of the value systems which function are equally plausible
ways of making sense, none of them can be taken as any truer or
better than any other. So, for example, Margaret Mead can take a
category like sexuality as a universal. She can then show that there
is a spectrum of possible variation in the ways a culture shapes the
sexuality of its people. No one style is the true way to do things.
Anthropology shows us the diversity of sexual practices, that's all.
Sexuality itself has no content, it is just a human universal.

Of course, each of the cultures that the anthropologist studies thinks
that its way of being human is the best way. This is their only mistake. The anthropologist, seeing that any way is only one possibility
among others, brackets the truth of their claim. By the bracketing of
the literal seriousness of a culture's claims, a kind of truth is preserved in each culture. Each is a plausible way of filling in the general conditions of being human.

By so doing, however, all cultural differences have been both preserved and destroyed. First, difference is emphasized, the uniqueness of each culture; then it is reduced to the Same. They are all doing the same thing. All these value systems are the same insofar as they are world views, or ethoses; their content differs but there is no way to choose between them as long as they survive. The role of anthropology is to describe the plurality of these meaningful life worlds. Each way of life is worthy of respect because ultimately each is equally untrue. The being of man is all that we can affirm. This is everywhere the same. Ultimately difference (although praised) is suppressed: the Same is triumphant.

THE BRACKETING OF SERIOUSNESS: SYMBOLIC ANTHROPOLOGY

The triumph of Boas' students both institutionally, in shaping the profession of anthropology, and intellectually, in establishing the absolute primacy of culture over race, is truly an important turning point in modern thought. Many brilliant monographs appeared (one thinks particularly of Ruth Benedict's work at a distance on the Japanese), but little systematic theory.

A subtle but significant shift began to take place as the students of Boas' students began to come of age in the profession during the 1950s and 1960s. Dissatisfaction was expressed about the lack of analytic sophistication in the culture concept. A crisis point of sorts was reached with the publication of Kroeber and Kluckhohn's book on culture,[12] which listed the great profusion of fuzzy definitions which were currently in use. To give a complex movement yet another simplifying tag, we can say that "symbolic anthropology" emerged in reaction to what was perceived as an overly broad and analytically weak emphasis on cultures as wholes. The locus of this work was Harvard, where Talcott Parsons and his colleagues and students sought to build a general theory of action. One of the components of this theory would be a specifying of the place and function of the culture concept.

As with the Boasians, this was no single-minded, coherent school. Disparate interests and approaches abounded even within the Parsonian lair. Much empirical work of distinction emerged even if the promises of a comprehensive theory today seem somewhat over-optimistic. For the sake of convenience, I will concentrate here on the work of Clifford Geertz. This will be convenient because I am most familiar with his work, having studied with him, but also because the scope and depth of Geertz's work encompasses most of the main problems to be considered. Further, the second stage of this new problematic, which I want to chronicle briefly, is currently associated with Geertz and his students.

I will argue that just as the cultural relativists reduced Difference to Sameness by bracketing the truth claims of cultural statements, so the symbolic anthropologists have taken a further step in the advancement of nihilism by bracketing the seriousness of cultural statements. Their position argues strenuously against the underlying universal boundary conditions of the relativists. They are seen as vacuous and unspecifiable. In their place a natural evolutionist picture in which culture has an active role in human evolution is juxtaposed with a view of meaning as historically produced and located. These two poles are brought together in the analysis of experience and action. But the bringing together has turned out to be an exceedingly difficult enterprise. Without these common parameters and without any formally statable propositions culture becomes commentary. This commentary is taken up by the anthropologists and translated back into our own discourse. Ultimately, all seriousness is reduced to a common denominator, our frame of meaning. The proposed "conversation of mankind" takes place not in many tongues but in only one.

Geertz begins by assuming that (at least within anthropology) the battle Boas waged has been won. He begins a reverse cycle in which he claims that the problem is no longer to establish the primacy of culture over race but to begin to whittle down the imperialistic reach of the culture concept. For if culture is everything, then it loses its explanatory value. The problem, Geertz argues, is, rather, to arrive at a conception of culture which limits it. What is needed is a more circumscribed and therefore an analytically more powerful formulation.

This limiting, specifying, situating, rethinking of the culture concept begins with Geertz's attempt to place the concept of culture within a framework of human evolution. As he puts it in his article "The Growth of Culture and the Evolution of Mind": "Recent research in anthropology suggests that the prevailing view that the mental dispositions of man are genetically prior to culture and that his actual capabilities represent the amplification or extension of these pre-existent dispositions by cultural means is incorrect. The apparent fact that the initial stages of the growth of culture implies that 'basic', 'pure', or 'unconditioned' human nature, in the sense of the innate constitution of man, is so functionally incomplete as to be unworkable."[13] The evolution of the human body is inseparable from that of human culture, "Rather than culture acting only to supplement, develop and extend organically based capacities themselves. A cultureless human being would probably turn out to be not an intrinsically talented though unfulfilled ape, but a wholly mindless and consequently unworkable monstrosity. Like the cabbage it so much resembles, the *Homo Sapiens* brain, having arisen within the framework of human culture, would not be viable outside of it."[14]

By situating culture as an essential internal component of human evolution, Geertz roots it within a biological and evolutionary context. If his argument carries, then it has several important consequences. The first is that there is no way to strip culture away in order to get at a more essential human nature. Culture, in Geertz's view, is in no way epiphenomenal or accidental; it has literally shaped us. But this lesson has been largely ignored in anthropology. The two main ways that the irreducibly important place of culture have been negated are described by Geertz as the rationalist approach and the lowest common denominator approach. The beginnings of the first Geertz locates in the French Enlightenment view that underneath the artificiality of custom and the false pandering and passions of social life can be found natural man. Natural man is either the noble savage living untroubled beyond and before the hypocrisies of social life, or natural man as rational and universal man. This view holds, as we have seen, that under the swirling diversity of human custom all are— or at least could be—capable of the same reason, the same full humanity. Not only are they capable of logic and reason, but reason is everywhere the same.

The second evasion of the irreducibility of the particularities of culture Geertz labels the *consensus gentium*—a consensus of all humankind—approach. He says, "At the level of concrete research and specific analysis this grand strategy comes down, first to a hunt for universals in culture, for empirical uniformities that, in the face of the diversity of customs around the world and over time, could be found everywhere in about the same form, and second to an effort to relate such universals, once found, to the established constants of human biology, psychology and social organization."[15]

The reason that this approach has failed to provide substantial categories and not empty ones, specific groundings and not vague underlying realities, is that it can never achieve the ends it proposes for itself. "There is a logical conflict between asserting that, say, 'religion,' 'marriage' or 'property' are empirical universals and giving them much in the way of specific content, for to say that they are empirical universals is to say that they have the same content, and to say that they have the same content is to fly in the face of the undeniable fact that they do not."[16]

But even if some such universals could be found (and the search both in America and on the continent goes on) the question remains what one would have if one found them. There has always been a conflict (or at least an implicit tension) within anthropology between the particularities of the peoples we go out to study and the theories we use to describe them. If the theory was not general enough, then the risk of mere descriptivism, naive empiricism, was present. The other side of the coin, however, is that if the theory is general enough then we tend to get a rather washed out, thin soup of "behind these seemingly bizarre customs lies John Doe just like you and me." The more general the theory the less it could do justice to the particulars under consideration. So, culture, for Geertz, is irreducible to underlying universals; it is resolutely particular. There is no culture in general. Culture is not some superorganic realm. It is rooted in the evolution of the species.

Having, at least in principle, reestablished the interconnection of biology and culture which had been deconstructed by Boas, Geertz clearly must go on to specify the characteristics of culture in a way different from his predecessors. The concept which enables him to do this is "symbol." He takes it directly from Suzanne Langer. Just as culture has been used too broadly, Geertz argues, so too has symbol. Its meaning must be restricted if it is to be a useful analytic tool. Symbol "is used for any object, act, event, quality or relation which serves as a vehicle for a conception—the conception is the symbol's meaning. . . . concrete embodiments of ideas, attitudes, judgments, longings, or beliefs."[17] They are not qualities of mind or mysterious entities but public objects like any others.

Culture is a system of these symbols, these embodiments of conceptions. Its generic trait is that these complexes of symbols are "extrinsic sources of information."[18] They give form to processes external to themselves in a public world. Just as the order of bases in DNA forms a coded program, so culture "patterns provide such programs for the institution of the social and psychological processes which shape public behavior." Geertz emphasizes that this is meant not as some strained analogy but quite literally. "But, unlike genes and other nonsymbolic information sources, which are only models for, not models of, culture patterns have an intrinsic double aspect: they give meaning, that is objective conceptual form, to social and psychological reality both by shaping themselves to it and by shaping it to themselves. . . . The intertransposability of models for and models of which symbolic formulation makes possible is the distinctive characteristic of our mentality."[19]

So the publicly shared and shaped cultural world in which *Homo sapiens* has been literally formed will be the object of Geertz's analysis. It is here that, to use Foucault's phrase, experience "provides a means of communication between the space of the body and the time of culture, between the determinations of nature and the weight of history."

Culture is constituted of clusters of symbols. It is public. It is this publicness which renders the meaning embodied in symbols accessible to analysis, both by the natives and by the anthropologists. Culture is public because meaning is. It takes place on the street, in the marketplace, in mosques, offices, and battlefields. Our lives take place—to paraphrase Geertz's paraphrase of Weber—in webs of signification we ourselves have spun.

But culture, for Geertz, cannot be analyzed in its own terms. It is neither the somehow holistic expression of a people's way of life (à la Benedict) nor a sealed realm of symbols with internal logical or syntactic interconnections (à la Lévi-Strauss). Geertz has strong words of condemnation for those who attempt to treat culture as a closed domain of signifiers. Rather, Geertz has always set these symbols over against something nonsymbolic. At the deepest level, as we have seen, he situates culture in the frame of those "enduring natural processes which underlie" social life. But of equal import, culture is contrasted with society. Culture is the meaningful dimension and society is the behavioral. Just as Geertz has tried out a string of metaphors for the natural processes (genetic code, computer model, etc.), so too there are a string of metaphors for the cultural vs. the social (the logico-meaningful vs. the causal-functional, meaning vs. behavior, significance vs. structure). But they are all attempts to make the same point. Culture is not sui generis. It is only through social action that culture finds its articulation. As Foucault puts it, this focus on experience seeks to "articulate the possible history of a culture upon the semantic density which is both hidden and revealed in actual experience."

What we are after, then, and this is where "interpretive anthropology" splits off from the more hermetic analyses of "symbolic anthropology," is the informal logic of social life. We seek to describe and interpret the taken-for-granted assumptions of an Other's world which makes what at first seems terribly exotic, seem normal, everyday, usual to those who are accustomed to living in it. As that life is shaped publicly by embodied conceptions which are linked together into a whole and articulated in experience, we can describe it. There is a fundamental underlying commonality and a fundamental surface of historical and cultural difference. It is that difference we seek to describe.

We do this by trying to understand the actor's point of view—that is to say, by piecing together the symbols and institutions which constitute the social life of the people we study. We cast our interpretations in terms in which we imagine the natives themselves conceive their own experiences, in terms of the symbols which formulate that experience. But this certainly does not mean that we are trying to be native, or, more important, that such interpretations are the ones the natives use. After all, we are the anthropologists. The object of study is one thing and the study of it another. Geertz says, "We begin with our own interpretations of what our informants are up to or think thay are up to, and then systematize these."[20]

What we do as anthropologists is construct interpretations of what we take to be other peoples' realities. The writing of ethnography is what makes us anthropologists. We create fictions. These ethnographic fictions are constructs of other people's constructs. As Geertz puts it, "Anthropologists have not always been as aware as they might be of this fact: that although culture exists in the trading post, the hill fort, or the sheep run, anthropology exists in the book, the article, the lecture, the museum display, or sometimes nowadays the film. To become aware of it is to realize that the line between mode of representation and substantive content is as undrawable in cultural analysis as it is in painting."[21]

What is the aim of this interpretive anthropological enterprise?

Geertz is extremely reserved about the goals of his enterprise. Here he contrasts with the proselytizing stance of the Boasians, who were actively involved in spreading the good word. A leitmotif in his work is a call to science. However, this "science" contains no laws, is not capable of prediction, is not formulizable, is not falsifiable, and contains no generalizations. The tag is important not because anything resembling what is commonly accepted as science has been produced but as a rhetorical device to ennoble the project and to maintain a strict neutrality.

The aim of interpretive anthropology for Geertz is to bring us "in touch with the lives of strangers . . . [and] in some extended sense of the term to converse with them."[22] That is all. Geertz juxtaposes this intercultural conversation with other, more grandiose ends. "The essential vocation of interpretive anthropology is not to answer our deepest questions but to make available to us answers that others, guarding other sheep, in other valleys, have given and thus to include them in the consultable record of what man has said."[23] This does *not* mean that other people's answers are in some way truer, more penetrating, more moral, more authentic, or more real than ours. We will learn no specific truths from the Balinese or the Moroccans. The task of the anthropologist is to report observations, not to answer questions—the truth does not lie elsewhere any more than it is hidden at home.

The point is to enter into the imaginative universes of others, to construct fictions about these cultures and thereby extend the range of human discourse. The task of anthropology is to go out to other peoples' valleys and watch them watch their sheep, to return home and construct an account, to preserve their culture for the historical record. Ethics, science, and truth all become aesthetic.

In a preface to a recent book, *Language and Art in the Navajo Universe* by Gary Witherspoon, Geertz poses the task of interpretive anthropology in a slightly different way. He sees it as "the comprehension of the frames of meaning in which other people move and the communication of that comprehension to others."[24] In this instance it is the Navajo frame of reference which is being explored. Geertz explains, "Witherspoon approaches his material with the eye of a man seeking to grasp a deep and difficult idea, not that of one trying to describe an exotic project or a curious practice. The effort is to bring Navajo thought within the range of Western discourse, so that we might have some conception of its nature and some appreciation of its power."[25]

Cultures differ in their frames of meaning. These frames can be brought into a common discourse. For the relativists this discourse was nominally the Western discourse of science. But since what was being described was grounded in a common human condition and was cast in a universal language of science, its claims, albeit naive, were nonetheless consistent. But when we move entirely into discourse, the discourse we engage in can only be Western. The claim is that by making the Navajo's frame of reference accessible to us, the "long strangeness between us will finally begin to end."

In this stance, there is no longer a necessity to ground discourse in underlying boundary conditions. As we saw, in the cultural relativist position the anthropologist bracketed the truth claims of various cultures as a way of affirming the universal ground which made all cultures equal expressions of an underlying common humanity. There was still a referent. In the interpretive position, there is a second bracketing. The anthropologist not only remains neutral as to the truth claims of a particular culture but now brackets the seriousness (in the traditional sense of Western philosophy) of the truth claims themselves. Not that there is any failure to understand the statements encountered as being a series of meaningful speech acts; the anthropologist is not bracketing meaning, like a structuralist or behaviorist. Rather, what is bracketed is precisely the claims of serious speech acts to serious meaningfulness. What is suspended is not only the claim to context-free truth but the claim that such a claim is intelligible. The interpretive anthropologist will treat both reference and sense as mere phenomena.

The possibility of pure description of another culture from the outside is now possible. What Geertz once referred to as "a scientific phenomenology of cultural forms" has found its method. We observe what the natives think is true, i.e., what they take seriously. We construct an account of their universe, their frames of meaning, and then we converse with it. We bring it into our conversation. The anthropologist thus succeeds in studying what is serious and truthful to Others without it being serious or truthful to him. As we have been told, there are no truths to be brought back from faraway places.

There is nothing specific to be learned from other cultures; they have nothing to teach us, any more than presumably we have to teach them.

Ultimately, when this new purified phenomenological anthropology has come of age, we will all understand that culture is discourse, that there are many variants of it, that a heightened conversation is our goal. We will be able to bring this project to fruition when not only a small number of Westerners have become anthropologists but presumably everyone else as well. When the Navajo comes of age, and learns to translate his frame of reference into what can *only* be our frame of reference, then the long strangeness between us will have ended—and so will all difference as well.

CONCLUSION: TRUTH AND POWER

To say that the discipline of anthropology emerged in a highly charged political world, during a century in which most of the peoples anthropology has taken as its object of study have been either destroyed or radically transformed by their contact with Western (and other) civilizations, is to restate a truism. All the same, we should not forget that just because something is obvious its importance does not decrease. Several questions still remain: how have anthropologists understood the situation, and more specifically, how have they sought to situate their own developing understanding of anthropology as an intellectual discipline within their diverse interpretations of the political realities of the time? How has the development of the science of culture been related to the political commitments of its founders?

In order to consider (or simply to pose) these questions, let me briefly suggest a convenient schematization of relations of truth and power, not because I think it exhausts the possibilities or adequately accounts for a complex and less coherent history, nor to moralize about our anthropological ancestors, but rather as a means of opening up a debate about how we might proceed from here.

In the first position, that represented by Boas, the role of the anthropologist as scientist was to speak truth to power. Boas was a profoundly political man: a typically secular, emancipated, German, Jewish liberal with a strong faith in the force of reason as a fundamental tool of political emancipation and as an absolute value in its own right. The calling of the intellectual, for Boas, consisted of the advancement of reason through science and the conquest of tradition, irrationality, and injustice. Not unlike Freud, Boas had a faith in reason which never wavered, although his faith in human beings withered rather dramatically.

Born in 1858, Boas came of age in a Bismarckian Germany in which the values he held were put in question by the rise of nationalist and anti-Semitic movements. Boas himself embodied a fundamental contradiction which was to characterize American anthropology: Confronted with a situation of strong destructive political mobilization around national symbols, Boas reacted (and here he is typical of anthropologists) neither by adopting a strong national identity himself nor by choosing to join a political movement which directly confronted the problem. Rather, he emigrated to America and redoubled his faith in the necessity for a science of anthropology which would do battle with biological racism and cultural chauvinism by undercutting their scientific rationale.

Boas arrived in America in the late 1880's during a period of nationalist fervor, racial prejudice (including anti-Semitism), and anti-immigrant frenzy, which were more than once turned on him. The virulent anti-German propaganda in America and the intense patriotism "even in our Eastern universities" during the First World War forced Boas to recognize the weight of tradition and passion even among the elite. This led Boas to redouble his commitment to anthropology, even if it weakened his faith in the progress of humanity. As Stocking says, "He clearly assumed that the anthropological world view might, if appropriately propagated, override forces of economic or diplomatic self-interest."[26] At the same time, there were moral and political limits for the discipline. Boas became the first—and still the only—person ever to be expelled from the American Anthropological Association (for publicly exposing and denouncing the use of anthropologists as spies during the war). Reinstated after the war, Boas successfully placed his students (Mead, Kroeber, etc.) in leading departments, which they eventually took over.

In his last years, coincident with the rise of the Nazis, Boas never doubted in his humanist faith that cultural values were primordial and that reason was the guiding beacon to resist Fascism and nihilism. For him, it was tradition, self-interest, and power that were the enemies, while rationality remained untainted. Between the authentic local expressions of culture and the ideal of a pure critical reason lay a dangerous and polluted realm of political strife, emotions, social domination, economic exploitation, and myriad forms of petty interest. While anthropology could not ignore these dimensions of human existence, Boas considered them to be external to anthropology in a fundamental sense. Both the political and the biological were extrinsic to his understanding of reason and culture. The anthropologists' credo remained: speak truth to power, focus truth on prejudice, separate truth from passion.

The dignity and achievements of Boas and his students are not in question—they were centrally responsible for making antiracism an accepted part of the American academic agenda—but neither are their limits and contradictions. The position of speaking truth to power, opposing humanism to nihilism, is still with us; and it is by no means the worst alternative. But ultimately this position has not proved sufficiently hardy, either intellectually or politically, to have spawned a science or a politics which lives up to the standards of coherence and efficacy by which these individuals wished to be judged. Viewed from some distance, the heroic and stubborn insistence on the externality of humanism and nihilism has, despite itself, contributed to the spread of that which it was constructed to oppose. As the truth of anthropology became increasingly empty of content, and as world circumstances changed, the reformist zeal has come to sound increasingly like American moralizing and less like universal reason.

In an important sense, the second position, that represented by Geertz, has no politics at all. The ascetic imperative of Boas or Weber, who sought to separate truth and politics, still entailed an active vigilance lest these two realms fuse. It never occurred to these European intellectuals that political concerns were not central to the life of an intellectual—they saw them as so central that they had to be kept in check. The sacrifice demanded of the scientist was not the loss of political passions but only that they be kept clearly distinct from scientific activities qua science. Over the time of two generations, the tension between these two callings, and hence the potential threat they posed for each other's autonomy, was gradually dissipated. In its place an ethics of scientific comportment became a code of civility. As this code took center stage, the more directly political concerns were weakened. In a not entirely self-conscious way, the fundamental commitment to academic civility became a model—text and conversation—for all human activity. Those who refused the dialogue (or were never invited to join), even those who tried to expand its terms, ran the risk of being cast outside the pale of science and humanism.

Of course, there are political implications in a model which poses civility and conversation (between colleagues, between cultures) as the norm. Edward Shils, for example, clearly articulated these issues. He defended the university first against the attacks of Senator Mc-Carthy in the 1950s and later against the critiques and disruptions of student radicals in the 1960s and 1970s. But the defense posed the ideal of a university setting outside the political fray. The bulk of writing about how the larger political contexts affect scholars concerned the disruption of civility within the university and refused to place the breakdown (temporary and partial as it was) within a larger political context of war and massive government intervention in the financing and functioning of the university. This must be seen as a retreat from the breadth of Boas' understanding and commitments. Civility and passionate political commitment were too often posed as being contraries—sadly self-validating contraries, as both critics and defenders of the university too frequently insisted on their mutual incompatibility. As Geertz says in the preface to his collection of essays, *The Interpretation of Cultures*, written in 1973, "At a time when the American university system is under attack as irrelevant or worse, I can only say that it has been for me a redemptive gift."[27]

Once again, politics is bracketed to save science. But, as we have argued, no real science emerged from this bracketing. This humanist effort to avoid what is perceived as the threat of barbarism has retreated to a restrictive civility in which the university becomes the institutional and ethical model for all humanity. But it is a university not easily recognizable. It is as if the endless petty squabbling, the massive involvement in social and political affairs, and the workaday bureaucratic environment were not noble enough to be included. But these "hard surfaces" are exactly what we were supposed to focus on in our analyses of other cultures, not so as to reduce culture or meaning or reason to them, but as a means of avoiding the "danger that cultural analysis will [turn] into a kind of sociological aestheticism."[28] The university and science are somehow exempted from the hard analysis to which other cultures are subjected. For the life of the mind to be "redemptive," it must be not of this world.

Short of redemption, where do we go from here?

I am *not* advocating that we jettison the moral and intellectual achievements of the aggressively antiracist anthropology of Boas, nor that we discard what has been constructed and made to function of a civility which allows for dispute within a community of shared discourse. The main conclusion I draw from the analysis presented in this paper is that it is the dogged separation of truth and power in order to construct a science which has had the most deleterious effects on anthropology; it is the conception of humanist activity which has unwittingly pushed these anthropologists into a kind of nihilism which is the exact opposite of their intent.

So where do we go with this? First, to a genealogy of the problem: asking how we have gotten where we are. This paper itself offers little more than a preface to such a project, which would have to extend farther into the past and include a sustained analysis of the institutional arrangements within which anthropology was formed, as well as an analysis of the emergence of other disciplines and the uses to which these disciplines were put. Second, to a rethinking of humanism, nihilism, and the relations of truth and power. Although many people are currently working in that direction, it will come as no surprise that I think the work of Michel Foucault offers us the most developed and powerful approach currently available. Obviously this is not the place to rehearse all of Foucault's project. Let me touch only on his analysis of intellectuals.

At least since the Enlightenment (and, in a different form, since the origins of Christianity), the figure of the intellectual has been defined by its relationship to a universal message. The intellectual has been a master of truth and justice. Whether Voltaire or Marx, the intellectual claimed a special right to speak for all of humanity—or at least that part of humanity which embodies a universal message—whether of the law, of reason, or of history. The intellectual has been that one who, as Foucault puts it, opposed power, despotism, and injustice in the name of justice and reason. "The universal intellectual derives from the jurist/notable and finds his fullest expression in the writer, the bearer of values and significations in which all can recognize themselves."[29] Because he speaks the truth, the intellectual has always seen himself as outside of power. Foucault calls this the "speaker's benefit." As long as truth is external to power, those who speak the truth are in an enviable position. In fact, Foucault argues, one of the main reasons truth and power have been posed as externals is to guarantee the authority of those who proclaim this separation. "What sustains our eagerness to speak of sex [power] in terms of repression is doubtless this opportunity to speak out against the powers that be, to utter truths and promise bliss, to link enlightenment, liberation, and manifold pleasures; to pronounce a discourse that combines the fervor of knowledge, the determination to change the laws, and the longing for the garden of earthly delights."[30]

The anthropologist as a cultural figure easily adopted this position. Clearly, as we have seen, the role of the anthropologist has been to stake out the claims of all humanity; to speak the truth of science; to show us a more fulfilling life which others have led. We should have little trouble recognizing Boas in this portrait. We need only think of Boas' most famous student, Margaret Mead, and her unabashed crusading, her radically confident pronouncements on everything from sex to war in all available media, to see a modern version of the anthropologist as humanist intellectual.

Because of a complex set of technological and economic changes in Western society (analyzed in a similiar fashion with different conclusions by Habermas), Foucault thinks that the universal intellectual is disappearing as a cultural figure. Its last gasp was the figure of the "writer." "All the fevered theorization of writing which we witnessed during the sixties was no doubt only a swan song; the writer was desperately struggling for the maintenance of his historical privilege. But the fact that it should have been precisely a question of theory, that the writer should have needed scientific guarantees, based on linguistics, semiology, psychoanalysis, . . . all this goes to show that the activity of the writer was no longer the active center."[31]

Except that in France such intellectuals were de rigueur on the left, we should have no trouble locating Geertz in this sketch of the writer. If there exists a more "writerly" anthropologist, he is not publishing his work. The problem of authority is somewhat different here, however, in that Geertz no longer claims to be speaking for humanity—which he denies exists—nor for any particular groups, nor out of a defined scientific consensus. Hence his claim to authority—one which he has certainly well established—must stem from the authority of his prose. Clearly, what Foucault calls "writing as the sacralizing mark of the intellectual" is well represented here.

But this turn is not so surprising. Foucault claims that the universal intellectual has been replaced by the "specific" intellectual; the jurist/notable has been replaced as a cultural figure by the savant/intellectual. No longer the crusading voice of humanity and justice, the specific intellectual is a scientist (usually in biology or physics), "the figure who possesses—along with a few others, and either in the service of the state or against it—certain abilities, which can favor life or destroy it definitively."[32] Because these technocrats possess specific and vital information a certain generality and urgency is granted to their statements. It is not that they are in a position to give us universal truths, but they are in control of information whose implications affect everyone. In a certain sense they gain power because of their specific abilities, on which our civilization has grown increasingly dependent.

Perhaps because anthropology does not generate this kind of vital information, only a parody of this figure exists within the discipline. Marvin Harris has unquestionably replaced Margaret Mead as the official media spokesman on all issues about which anthropology presumably has answers to give. Harris is a kind of Sesame Street version of the expert who pronounces truths whenever he is asked on the true meaning of all customs. His answers always reveal that behind culture and diversity lies that which is the really real—techno-economic structures (calories and self-interest), as he calls them. Surely this stance (and its wide acceptance) also reflects the desperate claim that anthropology must possess some vital technical specializations which its unemployed doctorates can sell to the hospitals, forestry services, and military departments of the government. After asserting a claim of utilitarian importance, the ultimate relevance of anthropology, needless to say, is always presented by these technocrats as its unique ability to bring a humanist concern to the problem at hand, be it the delivery of health care to minority communities or the ethnic identification of skeletal remains in Vietnam.

As we all know, narratives are supposed to have endings. This paper does not have one. We have had, in my opinion, too many narrative endings which have deceptively claimed to represent a solution which does not exist except as a literary device. Perhaps it is appropriate, to borrow a phrase from Geertz, to blur our genres. By stopping abruptly, I leave the reader in the same position as the writer—midstream.

NOTES

1. George Stocking, *Race, Culture and Evolution* (New York: Free Press, 1968), p. 229.

2. George Stocking, *The Shaping of American Anthropology 1883–1911: A Franz Boas Reader* (New York: Basic Books, 1974), p. 4.

3. *Ibid.*, p. 5.

4. *Ibid.*, p. 6.

5. Melville Herskovits, *Man and His Works* (New York: Alfred Knopf, 1947).

6. *Ibid.*, p. 61.

7. *Ibid.*, p. 63.

8. *Ibid.*, p. 66.

9. *Ibid.*, p. 68.

10. *Ibid.*, p. 76.

11. *Ibid.*, p. 76.

12. Alfred Kroeber and Clyde Kluckhohn, *Culture* (Cambridge: Papers of the Peabody Museum of American Archaeology and Ethnology, Harvard University, XLVII, No. 1, 1952).

13. Clifford Geertz, *The Interpretation of Cultures* (New York: Basic Books, 1973), pp. 82–3.

14. *Ibid.*, p. 68.

15. *Ibid.*, p. 38.

16. *Ibid.*, pp. 39–40.

17. *Ibid.*, p. 91.

18. *Ibid.*, p. 92.

19. *Ibid.*, pp. 93–4.

20. *Ibid.*, p. 15.

21. *Ibid.*, p. 16.

22. *Ibid.*, p. 24.

23. *Ibid.*, p. 30.

24. Clifford Geertz, preface to Gary Witherspoon, *Language and Art in the Navajo Universe* (Ann Arbor: University of Michigan Press, 1977), p. vii.

25. *Ibid.*, p. x.

26. George Stocking, "Anthropology as Kulturkampf: Science and Politics in the Career of Franz Boas," in *The Uses of Anthropology*, American Anthropological Association, Special Publication 11, 1979, p. 37.

27. Geertz, *The Interpretation of Cultures*, p. ix.

28. *Ibid.*, p. 30.

29. Michel Foucault, "Truth and Power," *Power/Knowledge, Selected Interviews & Other Writings, 1972–77* (New York: Pantheon Books, 1981), p. 128.

30. Michel Foucault, *The History of Sexuality* (New York: Pantheon Books, 1978), p. 7.

31. Michel Foucault, "Truth and Power," p. 127.

32. *Ibid.*, p. 129.

Four

MORAL/ANALYTIC DILEMMAS POSED BY THE INTERSECTION OF FEMINISM AND SOCIAL SCIENCE

Michelle Z. Rosaldo

Our questions are inevitably bound up with our politics. The character, constraint, and promise of our scholarship are informed as much by moral ends and choices as they are by the "objective" postures necessary to research. For feminists, especially, intellectual insight thrives in a complex relation with contemporary moral and political demands.[1]

Few social scientists writing today would deny the fact that feminists have changed our intellectual horizons. At a minimum, we have "discovered" women. More important, we have argued that certain categories and descriptions that at one time made good sense must be reformulated if we are to grasp the shape and meaning of *both* men's and women's lives.[2] That women have—at different times and in quite different ways—impressed their wills on not just "domestic" but also political and public life is something scholars formerly found perplexing and anomalous. But as we come upon new data on the lives that women lead, it becomes clear that one must learn to understand the systematic impact of the strategies women use and to comprehend the forces that constrain the kinds of opportunities women are able to pursue and the symbols and beliefs that are used to define our actions. The desire of feminists to recover hidden facts about our past has led not merely to new information but to new questions about how one ought to understand human societies.

Or has it? Early feminist questions, born in a political context that made clear the injustices and silences that deserved to be addressed, had little need of either paradigm or doubt. Instead, a practical sense that all the data urgently needed to be revealed inspired a drive to hear our sisters speak, without reflection on the categories that would inform our understandings. Thus, feminist scholars over the past ten years provided challenges to certain biases in traditional accounts without supplying the conceptual frameworks necessary to undermine them. While recognizing enemies and blind men among teachers and peers, we failed to recognize *ourselves* as heirs to their traditions of political and social argument.[3] Simultaneously, we embraced and were at pains to redefine some of the gendered dualisms of past work. We found a source for questions in the most egregious errors of the past. But at the same time we stayed prisoners to a set of categories and preconceptions deeply rooted in traditional sociology.

My concern is essentially one of teasing out some of these categories and constraints. I want to "deconstruct"[4] conceptual frameworks that we use as though they were concrete reflections of the world "out there" in order both to free our moral thinking from assumptions bound to sex and to free feminism from the moralisms of our predominantly individualistic modes of sociological understanding. It never hurts to look at our assumptions or to probe the sources of our analytical ill-ease. Discomforts in which moral impulse and intellectual concern are joined may serve as both stimuli and resources if, as with the case at hand, we find ourselves at once excited and disturbed by trends within this clearly inspiring and troubling branch of scholarship.

THE SEARCH FOR ORIGINS

The significance of all these general remarks for an anthropologist like myself becomes clear when we consider the following observation.[5] Few historians, sociologists, or social philosophers writing today feel called on—as was common practice in the nineteenth century—to begin their tales "at the beginning" and probe the anthropological for, say, the origins of doctors in shamans or of Catholic ritual in the cannibalism of an imagined past. Whereas turn-of-the-century thinkers as diverse as Spencer, Maine, Durkheim, Engels, and Freud considered it necessary to look at evidence from "simple" cultures as a means of understanding both the origins and the significance of contemporary social forms, most modern social scientists have rejected both their methods and their biases. Rather than probe origins, contemporary theorists will use anthropology, if at all, for the comparative insight that it offers. Having decided, with good cause, to question evolutionary approaches, most would, unfortunately, go on to claim that data on premodern and traditional forms of social life have virtually no relevance to the understanding of contemporary society.

Yet quite the opposite is true of the vast majority of recent feminist writing. If anthropology has been too much ignored by most contemporary social thinkers, it has achieved a marked though problematic pride of place in classics like *Sexual Politics* and *The Second Sex*. Simone de Beauvoir, Kate Millett, Susan Brownmiller, Adrienne Rich, all introduce their texts with what appears to anthropologists an old-fashioned evocation of the human record. On the assumption that preparing meals, enjoying talk with women friends, making demands of sons, or celebrating their fertility and sexual vitality will mean the same thing to women independent of their time and place, these writers catalogue the customs of the past in order to decide if womankind can claim through time to have acquired or lost such rightful "goods" as power, self-esteem, autonomy, and status. Though these writers differ in conclusions, methods, and particulars of theoretical approach, all move from some version of de Beauvoir's question "What is woman?" to a diagnosis of contemporary subordination and to the queries "Were things always as they are today?" and "When did it start?"

Much like the nineteenth-century writers who first argued about whether or not mother-right preceded patriarchal social forms or about whether or not women's difficult primeval lot as been significantly improved in civilized society, feminists differ in their diagnoses of our prehistoric lives, in their sense of suffering, conflict, and change. Some, like Rich, romanticize what they imagine was a better past, whereas others find in history an endless tale of female subjugation and male triumph. Most, however, find no cause to question a desire to ferret out our origins and roots. Nor would they challenge Shulamith Firestone, who, in her important book *The Dialectic of Sex,* quotes Engels to assert our need first to "examine the historic succession of events from which the antagonism has sprung in order to discover in the conditions thus created the means of ending the conflict."[6] Firestone suggests, in fact, that we seek out the roots of present suffering in a past which moves from history back to "primitive man" and thence to animal biology.

And most recently, Linda Gordon, in her splendid account of the relationship between birth control and developments in American political life, attempts in less than thirty pages to summarize the history of birth control throughout the premodern world, providing her readers with a catalogue of practices and beliefs that is unsatisfying both as history and as anthropology.[7] In a study demonstrating the place of birth control agitation in the history of leftist politics in the United States, changing as it did according to the nature and organization of our families and our economy, anthropology is, unfortunately, evoked primarily to universalize contemporary political demands and thus to undermine our present sense of singularity. Gordon turns to "primitives" to demonstrate the depth of what we think we need and to confirm her sense that even though Eve suffered as much as we do today, we can henceforth be optimistic in expecting female protests to be heard and social expectations, correspondingly, to be altered. To me, there is something wrong, indeed morally disturbing, in an argument that claims that the practitioners of infanticide in the past are ultimately our predecessors in an endless, although perhaps ascendant, fight to keep men from making claims to female bodies.

By using anthropology as precedent for modern arguments and claims, the "primitive" emerges in accounts like these as the bearer of primordial human need. Women elsewhere are, it seems, the image of ourselves undressed, and the historical specificity of their lives and of our own becomes obscured. *Their* strengths prove that we can be strong. But, ironically, at the same time that we fight to see ourselves as cultural beings who lead socially determined lives, the movement back in evolutionary time brings an inevitable appeal to biological givens and the determining impact of such "crude" facts as demography and technology. We infer that birth control is now available to human *choice*. But in the past—the story goes—women's abilities to shape their reproductive fates were either nonexistent or constrained by such logistical facts as a nomadic lifestyle, a need for helpers on the farm, or an imbalance between food supply and demography. We want to claim our sisters' triumphs as proof of our worth, but at the same time their oppression is artfully dissociated from our own because we live with choice, whereas they are seen as victims of biology.

My point is not to criticize these texts. Feminists (and I include myself) have with good reason probed the anthropological record for evidence that appears to tell us whether or not "human nature" is the sexist and constraining force that many of us were taught. Anthropology is, for most of us, a monument to human possibilities and constraints; it is a hall of mirrors wherein what Anthony Wallace called the "anecdotal exception" seems to challenge every would-be law; but at the same time, lurking in the oddest shapes and forms it promises familiar pictures of ourselves, so that by meditating on New Guinea menstrual huts and West African female traders, ritualists, or queens, we can begin to grasp just what, in universal terms, we "really" are.

But I would like to think that anthropology—and feminism—can offer more than that. I would rather claim that when anthropology is asked (by feminists or their enemies alike) to answer troubling ideologies and to give voice to universal human truths, anthropology becomes a discipline limited by the assumptions with which it first began and therefore unable to transcend the biases its questions presuppose. To look for origins is, in the end, to think that what we are today is something other than the product of our history and our present social world, and, more particularly, that our gender systems are primordial, transhistorical, and essentially unchanging in their roots. Quests for origins sustain, since they are predicated upon it, a discourse case in universal terms; and universalism permits us all too quickly to assume—for everyone but ourselves perhaps—the *sociological* significance of what *individual* people do or, even worse, of what, in biological terms, they are.

Stated otherwise, our search for origins reveals a faith in ultimate and essential truths, a faith sustained in part by cross-cultural evidence of widespread sexual inequality. But any analysis that assumes that sexual asymmetry is the first subject we should attempt to question or explain fails in political terms to help us understand the choices we in fact pursue, just as it fails in analytical terms to undermine the sexist biases of much theorizing in contemporary social science.

These biases have their bases in two larger trends within traditional social science thought. First is the overwhelming and pervasive individualism that holds that social forms proceed from what particular persons need or do, activities (where gender is concerned) which seem to follow from presumed "givens" of our reproductive physiology. Second, more as complement than as concomitant of the first trend, is our tendency to think in dualistic terms, opposing individual to social, unconscious psyche to more conscious strategies and rules, biological to cultural law, domestic to political jural bonds, and woman to man. Taken together, these polarities lead both feminists and traditionalists alike to think of gender as, above all else, the creation of biologically based *differences* which oppose women and men instead of as the product of social *relationships* in distinct (and changeable) societies. Individualism, dualism, and biological determinism are thus linked in modern thought because they lead us to seek essential and presumably universal qualities in each sex instead of asking what in the relations of the sexes makes them *appear* the way they do and how the asymmetries that such relations typically entail are causally bound to socially specific forms of inequality and hierarchy.

QUESTIONING QUESTIONS

What are our options? For anthropologists in general, such difficulties begin with the embarrassment accompanying "cultural relativism" in our thought. Inevitably, we face the question of why and how distinctive cultures make a claim on our lives.[8] Can anthropologists describe the "other" without in some way commenting on the generalizations which emerge from observations of its similarities and differences from ourselves? Can students be taught the organization of power in some distant forest world without permitting them as well a glimpse of what they share with the inhabitants of that forest space, of perhaps an essential "human nature" lurking everywhere beneath diversity in cultural norms and rules? More specifically, can feminists be asked to dwell on anthropological details without inquiring if the "other" is, perhaps, an ancestress whose rise and fall describes our present state? Can we not see in women elsewhere our true "sisters," whose distinctive lots, for better or worse, reveal determinants that can tell us what we need and where we ought to go? Most anthropologists I respect remain uneasy with the search for origins and/or pan-human laws, but none has clarified how a discipline born of the contrast between "us" and "them" can claim to learn from others in anything other than our culture's terms. None tells us how to reconcile a distrust of essences and a taste for local and historical detail with the suspicion/fear that women's lot is everywhere, in important ways, the same. How can one write a feminist ethnography without assuming, for example, that learning about women elsewhere must, in fact, provide a set of images that reflect immediately on ourselves?

These difficulties have sources more complex than can be addressed here. What is significant to my immediate concerns, however, is the relationship between dilemmas faced by feminists and those confronted by anthropologists. Wanting to speak and think of change, the feminist must distrust perspectives that stress "deep," essential commonalities in women's styles, relationships, and strengths. At the same time, a desire to discover previously hidden women's lives is rooted in a conviction about the "sisterhood" we share. Thus, on one level it appears that the anthropologists who talk of foreign peoples—so much like (the selfish, rational, existential, or just biologically viable "man") and yet so different from ourselves—are paralleled by those feminists who try to "rank" or otherwise describe our foreign sisters' goals and needs in terms at once related to and distant from our own. The interest in the "other" is, in every case, presented as a telling variant on our historically and politically shaped concerns.

Much more narrowly (although perhaps of more immediate relevance here), the anthropological arguments about whether or not "family" and "kinship" (both, of course, eminently "social" institutions built on what appears to be a biologically given base) are universal facts bear a close resemblance to contemporary arguments concerning both the pattern in and the determinants of such variable though universal terms as "woman" and "man."[9] In both instances, there is the sense that variation is limited, that commonality is necessary and deep. Just as one would not fail, in the name of cultural relativism, to comment on the universal fact that heterosexuality and reproduction figure centrally in the organization of social bonds, so it seems necessary to acknowledge general patterns in our gendered hierarchies and roles, independent of particulars in cultural detail. Gender, much like kinship, seems to have an obvious transcultural core; but in both cases there is also cause to fear that such appearances are "ideological" and misleading. Precisely because our faith in "nature" is so readily evoked in these domains, we may well argue that our common sense must be surrendered lest a prior faith lead us to see what we expect to find and so obscure our grasp of what is really there.

For anthropology, of course, conundrums like these are the stuff of daily talk. When is difference really difference? What phenomena is it legitimate to compare? The rub—where feminists are concerned— is that something much more immediate than liberalism or relativism appears at issue when such questions as these are raised. If I decline to argue (when, let us assume, the natives disagree) that women elsewhere enjoy privileges more constrained than those of men, how can I claim that the American housewife who takes real pleasure in her role is—or at least ought to be—my ally in opposing women's secondary place today? If, instead, I find that certain African women, U.S. housewives, and professional women like myself can all agree on many of the pleasures and disabilities of women's lot, does the community so formed reflect "real" commonalities of concern or rather a political rhetoric that "just happens" to be available?

We may well want to claim that our community is "real," that it is probably true that women everywhere (and for similar reasons) have social roles subordinate to men's, and that given birth and caring for infants are core experiences that women everywhere share. But at the same time, and principally because the organization of gender *does* appear so universally bound up with biological capacities and constraints, we have developed a distrust of observations such as these. A facile "sisterhood" appears too readily to cast biology as the imme- diate cause of women's lot, as though the now-discovered community were the product not of our political life but of our "deeper" and es- sentially presocial bodies. On the one hand, then, we are aware that our attention to commonalities appears not only reasonable but fun- damental to both feminist scholarship and feminist political demands. On the other, it appears that feminists have a particular interest in challenging those unities most apparent to our sight and in question- ing all claims that link the stereotypes and symbols that define a so- cial group to a set of attributes bound up primarily with individual biology.

The argument over nature/nurture thus defines recurrent poles for feminist (as for much anthropological) thought. We seek and resist essences and yet, in doing so, appear recurrently to reproduce a set of arguments that remove us from the concrete forms that gender takes—and from its status, *both* as cause and as consequence, of the social bonds and needs produced in our historically quite various so- cieties.

CATEGORIES AND FALSE CLARITY

My claim thus far has been that certain tensions within feminism, between essentialist universalism and a more relativist concern to understand what sorts of variants exist, have political consequences and roots, which are in some ways paralleled by dilemmas concerning universalism and relativism in anthropology. Universalists stress commonalities in human bodies and in human lives but in so doing tend to focus on "inherent" properties of individuals independent of the social systems wherein individuals are formed, and then fail to probe the systematic ways that "personal" facts, like gender, are in all societies bound up with other forms of social inequality. The feminist use of anthropology—in particular, the search for an original state or cause—has thus tended to exacerbate some of the contradictions that emerge in any search for unity and/or difference across space and time.

But these difficulties are not feminism's or anthropology's alone. Because feminist conundrums may well pave the way to positive critiques of modern social thought, I want now to dwell upon some ramifications of the tensions explicated above, suggesting how three common themes in the interpretation/explanation of gender roles are ultimately related to some of the morally and intellectually most troubling areas in contemporary social science. Overall, my claim is that recent feminist trends continue to reproduce a deep but analytically unexplicated faith that the idea of "women" (and/or gender) is related to all other statuses and roles in a way that parallels the opposition between our "natural" and our "cultural" selves, or, perhaps, between "the individual" and "society." On the one hand, I acknowledge that this belief in many ways makes sense; certainly it corresponds to a persuasive and transcultural form of gender ideology.[10] At the same time, an overemphasis on commonalities and attendant biological forms of cause tends to inhibit systematic thought about those things that feminists can best help their fellow social scientists to learn: the very real cross-cultural variety in views of gender and, more broadly, in conceptions of the self; their roots in different forms of social life; and their implications for human action and relationship in diverse societies. Thus, at the same time that a sense of unity may help to ground our questions and our political demands, feminists who would avoid reproducing the past must first question that unity and, with it, some of the categories most current in contemporary social science.

THE NATURE/NURTURE ARGUMENT

First and foremost, then, is an emergent sense that feminists must criticize the nature/nurture argument in social thought. Without embracing relativisms that deny us a legitimate political voice, we must begin to clarify what has been called the "use and abuse of biology."[11] The reasonable claim that gender must "have something to do" with the biological characteristics associated with sex—and with this, the argument that we must or that we dare not tamper with our "natural" physiology—has, of course, recurred in feminist debates, the proponents ranging from technologists who think that test-tube fertilization and/or birth control will make us free to those who argue for new cults of motherhood, more midwives, or "essentially feminine" forms of relationship and sexuality.[12] The status of "nature" as an inevitable first cause is explicitly entertained by students of sex differences in the young; it is implicit in, for example, de Beauvoir's analysis of the experiences that constitute a "second sex;" and, of course, it figures heavily in the recent claims of sociobiologists. Clearly, arguments that link gender to "some sort" of "natural" source have been put to a variety of uses, each positing somewhat different links between apparently natural causes and their consequences in human society.

At the same time, however, all appeals to nature share certain assumptions. Biologically oriented explanations assume that differences are "really real." Not surprisingly, they tend to emphasize those presumably inborn traits (for example, lactation, ovulation, physical weakness, or propensities for nurturant care) that *differentiate* women from men, casting the average characteristics of two biologically opposed groups as cause for the things we presently believe that men and women "are." Thus, if, overall, women "mother," this social fact reflects endowments in the average woman's genes; and if, overall, men engage in physical aggression more than women, this too reflects important facts about what all men, ultimately, are like.[13] Moreover, if male activities are celebrated more than female activities, such arguments suggest that this fact too reflects either the depth of individual male need or else the sheer superiority of men's biological endowments. Relationships, in such accounts, are contracts forged by individuals who are already fully formed. Natural differences are what make us unite, and from such instrumental unions grows society. The notion that most differences, where gender is concerned, are no more natural than the claim by Bushmen that women need male partners to light fires and shoot game[14] is something the biological determinists seem consistently to disregard.

What is it, then, that fuels this kind of argument? Although most of us would suspect appeals to biological "fact" in an attempt to understand phenomena like racism, elitism, or the privileges of social class, we readily forget the emperor's social clothes in talk of gender. We claim to know that social forms are not transparent products of individual desires, needs, or skills and argue at least minimally that social forms themselves determine much of our capacities and wants. But where gender is concerned, we find ourselves afraid to be skeptical of what appears brute natural "truth." We rarely recognize that our need to give to "nature" its apparent due leads to a form of mechanistic, individualizing thought that stands immediately at odds with the most powerful approaches to inequality now available in social science. Of course, part of the problem is that the pervasive inclination to individualism and empiricism in our work means that all naturalizing claims will tend to have rhetorical appeal, a fact clearly illustrated by the contemporary success of sociobiology. What the feminist experience makes particularly clear, however, is that this rhetoric (like any other) promises much more than it can give. We fear complexity and diversity in our world, craving a "natural" moral law. Yet nature cannot bear the moral burden imposed on it: thus we think poorly and inconsistently about biology. Appeals to nature cannot justify, because they presuppose it, a moral stance, uniting "is" and "ought" or else confusing "being" of a physical sort with the identities and relationships forged within particular societies.

The point is not that our biology does not figure in the construction of our gendered lives but rather that descriptions of the physical self can never help us understand the things we want or the origins of desire in our relationships of conflict, trust, cooperation, and inequality. In other words, what the arguments surrounding gender reveal is that, for reasons we have yet to understand, there is a tendency in our social thought to feel distrustful of society and of sociological accounts and therefore to search for natural essences as often as we can in hopes of finding out the necessary and moral terms on which to base our social lives.

BIASED DICHOTOMIES

A second set of issues follows immediately from those discussed above. These issues emerge in the work of theorists who decline to think of gender in explicitly biological terms but try instead to argue that a grasp of men's and women's social place must be anchored in analyses of the functionally opposed domains in which they act. Thus, it is claimed (with more or less cogency, to be sure) that "woman" everywhere relates to "man" as reproduction to production, expressive to instrumental, domestic to jural-political, natural (maternal) to contingent (paternal) bonds, and family to society.[15] One characteristic of these pairs, of course, is that the first and, it usually emerges, implicitly feminine term appears more closely linked to nature than its mate, suggesting, for example, that "mothering" is apt to be more biologically constrained and less cross-culturally varying a role than "fathering" or "judging." Furthermore, it would appear at once across cultures and within any particular social group that the initial term will be less differentiated and far less institutionally complex than the more "social" term that follows. Not surprisingly, then, one finds a view of history embodied in these pairs wherein reading from left to right often supplies the guiding imagery of accounts of individual growth and of evolutionary progress. Nor, given my remarks above, is it surprising, since the nineteenth century, at least, that the second (instrumental, social, male) emerges either as the progressive or the competitive, morally suspect term, whereas the first tends to be linked to images of an altruism lacking interest or distrust, corresponding to notions that stress either unhealthy stasis or life-giving continuity and morality.[16]

Much as with the biological arguments discussed above, feminists have found a good deal that is attractive in these polarities. Because they speak at once about apparently biological (lactation, childbirth) and more clearly social (the seeming universality of, for example, the family and marriage) sorts of facts, such oppositions as, for instance, that between "domestic" and more "public" realms appear to offer a description that makes sense of social facts apparent in our world while giving equal weight to the activities and determinants of both men's and women's lives. Feminists concerned by the lack of female presence in conventional accounts have thus seen promise in the notion that one needs to explore how "family" and/or "reproductive" roles may interact with the activities described by persons interested in less gendered versions of "political economy." In addition, all reminders of the place that biological reproduction must assume in any human social form have been particularly important for those analysts concerned with the discovery of first causes (we are constrained by child care or else oppressed by men who envy the capacities of our wombs) or mythic origins.

Unfortunately, however, domestic/public and similar analytic frames appear to replicate the difficulties they had sought to overcome.[17] Thinking of the home as women's and assuming women's place is naturally in the home, we fail to probe the possibility that our families are no more natural or universal than our religions or economies. We write of mothering and socialization in a single breath but rarely link these to the economics of the home or the pervasive familism of politics. Thus, an analysis in terms of opposed spheres—whatever its heuristic value or explanatory appeal—is suspect, first because it lets us think of women in terms less fully social than those we use to think of men and second because the opposites themselves derive from preconceptions that assume the nature and social implications of sex-linked endowments. We speak of spheres of women and of spheres of men as though such a separation were the product not of human action in a contradictory world but instead of (virtually) inevitable forms of natural logic.

The point is, ultimately, that a tendency to emphasize roles and contexts that oppose women and men leans heavily on the assumptions of a straightforward biological account. For dualists and biological determinists alike, significant social forms derive directly from a class of differentiating natural "facts," with "nature" bound closely to the "feminine" pole, embracing family, trust, and mothers. Thus, dichotomous thinking tends to dull the analyst's eye to how our loves and interests interact. More disturbing still, it typically sustains a set of pieties about what our families—and our feminism—should be like, permitting use of questionable biofunctional accounts by persons who would universalize what is, in fact, a historically specific faith that families are the natural moral basis of human societies.

PSYCHOLOGY AND SOCIETY

The third area in which feminist arguments at once reflect and lead toward critiques of recent social thought again relates to the above, though here the issues have much less to do with recognition of the institutions in which women make important claims than do the conceptual categories appropriately evoked when we attempt to understand our sisters' lives. Is gender, in the broadest sense, a psychological fact? an ideological disguise? a name for roles, or statuses, or positions and relationships in production? More narrowly, feminists are concerned that neither Marxist nor conventional sociological accounts have properly addressed sex inequalities as social facts. Nor have these accounts theorized about the ways "identities" associated with such things as status, sex, and age must figure equally in subjective life and in the public ordering of society. Thus, feminists have suggested that we recognize "sex-gender systems" as complex psychocultural domains somewhat autonomous from such things as "social organization" and/or "political economy."[18] And even though we learned from Weber about "subjective" features entering into economic realms, a theme emerging in much recent feminist work has been that understanding gender (more than, for example, understanding ethnicity or social class) requires a coupling of "sociological" accounts with depth psychology.

Unlike those theorists who claim a biological base for gendered roles or those who argue that female and male are necessarily defined by the opposition between "domestic" units and "political" society, the argument here has been that gender represents an aspect of identity in all social life. However, unlike the identities linked to the experience of ethnicity or class, gender figures early as an aspect of the developing infant self and so has deeper psychological roots than other categories of human action in adult society. Thus, it is claimed that attention to gender requires a renewed concern not for forgotten families or as yet uncovered facts about our genes but rather for subjective, often inarticulate aspects of identification, opposition, love, and fear, as these are shaped in early life and enter into an adult's experiences of the tension between "unconscious" impulse and "conscious" rule, between individual selfishness and social bond, and between "desire" and "right."

Perhaps the most sophisticated transformation of the nature/nurture opposition that pervades all feminist thought, recent appeals for psychological accounts still retain much of the rhetorical force and limitation of simpler theories that are based on biologically derived dichotomies. As noted earlier, questions of gender require attention to considerations many theorists have ignored—in this case, not the "hidden" facts of reproduction or the organization of the home but equally "hidden" issues linked to individual psychology. While rejecting sheer biology as the basis for a sociological account, theorists who emphasize subjective roots of gender roles tend toward a layered view wherein the inconscious psyche stands closer to the biological self than does the consciousness associated with society. In short, the psychological approach only partially transforms more mechanistic biological accounts because, while recognizing that gender is a feature of all social life, it argues for an explanation anchored largely in the *individual's* mind and body. Furthermore, a tendency to emphasize that gender (but not the motivations and styles associated, for example, with economic life and social class) is organized relatively early in the individual's life leads analysts to ignore the equally subjective bases of other social facts. Similarly, it makes it all too easy to forget that the determinants of gender roles go far beyond the infant's home, including contexts where adults make claims, explain their privileges to their peers, or argue about what is wrong and right.

Stated otherwise, much as with more biologically oriented accounts, talk of the psychological foundations of gendered roles attempts to link unconscious (and relatively presocial) drives to social rule while slighting questions of the public, relatively conscious, cultural forms in terms of which all human actors both interpret and attempt to shape the "outer" worlds and "inner" needs that they confront. No fact of nature in and of itself decides for human actors where that bit of nature leads; similarly, no aspect of unconscious life determines how in any given social form one's dispositions shape and are shaped by their social context. Society does not make our minds, nor does the unconscious make society. Rather, human beings, shaped by histories and relationships they only partly understand, interpret what they desire and see in terms provided by their social world and negotiated with the associates, friends, enemies, and kin with whom they share their lives.

The "individual" and "society" are thus joined in human consciousness throughout every human life, and gender probably figures constantly in the process. It is this fact that makes me wary of psychological accounts that see the gendered self take shape within familial cells that stand outside social wholes, without conceptualizing as well the ways that human beings, through their interactions, must forever reproduce and change the expectations that confer significance and direction to their projects. Thus, while it is obvious that gender is a central issue for developing infant selves and that it is bound up as well with the requirements of our reproductive physiology, we will never understand how gender operates in both our private lives and in society as a whole without examining the collectively forged symbolic terms that make gender both a resource and a constraint in conscious and political interactions among adults. That is, an understanding of the place of gender in unconscious realms will be inadequate until we come to understand how "male" and "female" work as cultural and social facts, whose significance for individuals cannot be analyzed apart from their significance in public life.

Feminists, of course, are not only social thinkers presently attributing more centrality to conscious actors and their specific cultural milieu than they have previously enjoyed in social thought.[19] But by challenging the view that we are either victims of cruel social rule or the unconscious bearers of a set of natural traits that (most unfortunately) demeans us, feminists have highlighted our need for theories that attend to ways in which actors shape their worlds, to interactions in which significance is conferred, and to the cultural and symbolic forms in terms of which expectations are organized, desires articulated, prizes conferred, and outcomes given meaning.

CONCLUSION

Analytical questions often have a practical source. Feminist scholarship—and more generally, the study of the sexes—has been motivated in large part by a desire to confront, refute, or otherwise rework the claim that gender is an individually anchored fact, the product not of social systems but of biology.[20] And yet our very interest in a "first," enduring, and essential cause reveals a lasting faith in biological accounts. Attempts to anchor gender in dynamics that are relatively independent of variety in social life all testify to the power of an assumption that takes gender as a natural fact shaped somehow "outside of" or "prior to" the historical ordering of particular societies.

Such contradictions are, of course, far from surprising. Were biologisms less compelling, they could not so have influenced our debates. Were our arguments more consistent and less ideologically constrained, we would not often find the claims of common sense, political impulse, and analytical regard so diversely ramified and so characteristically out of line. But "nature" does have a particular, morally potent sort of claim within our modern social world; it has the "scientific" status of permitting a reduction to the physically individuated self; and finally, it has the reasonableness of an insistence that however alienated our experience of social role, gender is one social fact associated not with an ideal self but with a concrete body. Surely, no one can easily reject the hold of nature's claims. Yet there are particular and quite predictable ways in which they blind us.

The problem, in its most general form, is that the several oppositions here discussed—nature/nurture, stasis/change, domestic/public, morality/competition, psychology/society—have a variety of long-standing ideological bonds, so that it is difficult to incorporate the insights they include without embracing as well some of the analytical difficulties they embody. All depend on more or less specified assumptions about sex. Therefore, although they may refer to different and nonisomorphic sets of facts, their gendered qualities tend to reproduce a relatively individualized and sexist picture of the working of our gender systems in human societies. None helps us think of power at the same time that we think of sex; none schools us in the contexts and relationships that connect women and men; none helps us understand the place of gender in the ways we think not just of sex but of such diverse things as youth and aging, competition, love and hate—in short, of almost every aspect of our social lives.

In other words, a set of prior understandings gave feminists a strategy and an object to attack. Yet these understandings have inhibited our grasp of just how tenuous our terms and oppositions are and of how adherence to the idioms of the past inhibits the development of a morally and intellectually satisfying feminist sociology. What gendered oppositions hide from view is the quite overwhelming fact that human beings live together in the world and that the seeming ease with which our roles and activities are differentiated and opposed reflects not natural law but human histories wherein our fellows have had cause at once to share and struggle, celebrate and cry.

Feminists are well aware, of course, that women are no more "natural" than men and, furthermore, that gender is no more natural than white racial dominance. We know that it is ludicrous to assume that women everywhere find their place within the home. We try, instead, to ask what forces limit female participation in political or economic realms and make it *seem* as though our separation from the world of men in this regard is born of natural logic. Finally, we know quite well that women's goals and needs are no more hidden and "psychological" than those of men who rule our governments and markets. In short, we recognize that gender is both a personal *and* a political fact, a feature not of individuals apart but of all interactions in human societies. But at the same time that our scholarly writings have revealed the limitations of a set of categories that political concerns have taught us to distrust, they have not yet created discourses that show consistently how we can begin to do without those categories or even radically to revise them. As critics, we feminists have remained, not surprisingly, the partial victims of the categories provided by our society.

My hope here has been less to challenge former work than to reflect on tensions within feminist thought that highlight the connections among ideology, moral impulse, intellectual difficulty, and intellectual promise. There is no question that we have both moral and analytical cause to undermine the individualism so prevalent in contemporary social thought. In doing so, we will in fact begin to think in less dichotomous terms, stressing ongoing action and interaction instead of static "natural" and "cultural" or "individual" and "collective" poles—and understanding meaning as something that happens in, as it yet underlies it, all interactive process. Furthermore, because issues of gender are so deeply intertwined with these enduring categories and dichotomies in our thought, I hope for new insight into our need both to exploit and to criticize the moral bases of our work within the ongoing quest for questions among feminist scholars.

NOTES

1. This paper is at once a commentary on contemporary feminist scholarship and a reflection on my own development as a feminist scholar. It develops certain aspects of the argument in Michelle Rosaldo, "The Use and Abuse of Anthropology: Reflections on Feminism and Cross-Cultural Understanding," *Signs* (1980), 5(3):389–417.

2. See, for example, Carol Gilligan's acticle in this anthology.

3. The use of nineteenth-century accounts of "primitive matriarchy," discussed below, is perhaps the clearest case of feminists' following decidedly nonfeminist forms of social and historical reflection. I hope in subsequent work to show that our "return" is, as they say, no accident; nineteenth-century assumptions about men and women are, I believe, deeply embedded in the categories of contemporary social science, a fact which lends a certain circularity to recent attempts to use these categories to explain why we are as we are.

4. My allusion to Jacques Derrida, *Of Grammatology* (Baltimore: Johns Hopkins University Press, 1976), is intentional. I am concerned to "denaturalize" a set of categories; he is concerned to "denaturalize" The Sign.

5. The discussion in this section draws extensively on Rosaldo, "Use and Abuse of Anthropology."

6. Shulamith Firestone, *The Dialectic of Sex: The Case for Feminist Revolution* (New York: Bantam Books, 1970), p. 2.

7. Linda Gordon, *Women's Body, Women's Right* (New York: Penguin Books, 1975).

8. See Paul Rabinow's article in this anthology, which explores this point in somewhat different form.

9. The particular conundrums anthropologists confront when trying to think about apparently universal "facts" like kinship without prejudging the "essence" of particular cases or embedding causal (and naturalizing) presuppositions in descriptive terms are discussed from different points of view by David M. Schneider, "What Is Kinship All About?" in Priscilla Reining, ed., *Kinship Studies in the Morgen Centennial Year* (Washington, D.C.: Anthropological Society, 1972); Andrew Strathern, "Kinship, Descent, and Locality: Some New Guinea Examples," in J. Goody, ed., *The Character of Kinship* (London: Cambridge University Press, 1973); Steve Barnett and Martin Silverman, *Ideology and Everyday Life* (Ann Arbor: University of Michigan Press, 1979); and Sylvia Sunko Yanagisako, "Family and Household: The Analysis of Domestic Groups, *Annual Review of Anthropology* (1979), 8:161–205. My point here is that discussions of gender—like those of kinship—are torn between appearances of naturalness and universality, on the one hand, and a fear that such appearances are blinding, on the other.

10. For the generality of nature/culture formulations in gender ideologies, see, for example, Sherry Ortner, "Is Female to Male as Nature Is to Culture?" in M. Rosaldo and C. Lamphere, eds., *Woman, Culture, and Society* (Stanford: Stanford University Press, 1974); J. A. Barnes, "Genetrix:Gentor-Nature:Culture?" in Goody, *Character of Kinship*) and Edwin Ardener, "Belief and the Problem of Women," in J. LaFontaine, ed., *The Interpretation of Ritual* (London: Tavistock, 1972).

11. The reference goes ultimately to Friedrich Nietzsche, *The Use and Abuse of History* (New York: Liberal Arts Press, 1949), and, more immediately, to the recent polemic against sociobiology by Marshall Sahlins, *The Use and Abuse of Biology*: An Anthropological Critique of Sociobiology (Ann Arbor: University of Michigan Press, 1976). Both, of course, are relevant—although in different ways—to my discussion.

12. I am thinking here of a range of writers who have wanted to claim an immediate relationship between something like "control of reproduction" and "women's status." Such a correlation is implicit in Firestone, *Dialectic of Sex*, as it is in Adrienne Rich, *Of Woman Born: Motherhood as Experience and Institution* (New York: W. W. Norton, 1976); it is also central to Carl Degler's recent reinterpretation of the meanings of nineteenth-century American demography, *At Odds: Women and the Family in America from the Revolution to the Present* (Oxford: Oxford University Press, 1980).

13. Alice Rossi, "A Biosocial Perspective on Parenting," *Daedalus* (1977), 106(2):1–

31, has made one of the strongest statements of this point, although I think it is a feature generally associated with so-called "sex difference" research.

14. See Lorna Marshall, *The !Kung of Nyae Nyae* (Cambridge: Harvard University Press, 1976) for the Bushman reference. The point could be made equally well, however, for such bits of American folk ideology as the notion that women are good teachers because of "natural" nurturance or that men are good businessmen because of "natural" aggression.

15. The gendered biases of jural-political/domestic are explicated in Yanagisako, "Family and Household," and Rosaldo, "Use and Abuse of Anthropology." For relatively ideological uses of related dichotomies, see Annette Kuhn and Ann Marie Wolpe, eds., *Feminism and Materialism* (London: Routledge & Kegan Paul, 1978), on production/reproduction; Talcott Parsons, expressive *Social Structure and Personality* (New York: Free Press of Glencoe, 1964), on instrumental/expressive; Maurice Bloch, "The Long Term and the Short Term: The Economic and Political Significance of the Morality of Kinship," in Goody, *The Character of Kinship*, on interest/morality; Beverly L. Chinas, *The Isthmus Zapotecs: Women's Roles in Cultural Context* (New York: Holt, Rinehart & Winston, 1973), on formal/informal; and Barnes, "Genetrix:Gentor," on culture/nature.

16. My claim is that in nineteenth-century thought (and, less explicitly, in much social thought today) male and female were opposed in very similar terms, although with different valuations. Herbert Spencer, who was relatively optimistic about progress, feared female entry into the public world as something that would undermine progressive competition and the survival of the fittest, whereas John Ruskin hoped that women would be able to correct some of the excesses of modern capitalism by spreading their maternal influence, for example, through charity.

17. I have developed and criticized an essentially dichotomous account in a recent paper; see Michelle Rosaldo, "Woman, Culture and Society: A Theoretical Overview," in Rosaldo and Lamphere, *Women, Culture and Society;* and Rosaldo, "Use and Abuse of Anthropology."

18. See Gayle Rubin, "The Traffic in Women," in R. Reiter, ed., *Towards An Anthropology of Women* (New York: Monthly Review Press, 1975), for a classic statement of this position, and Nancy Chodorow, *The Reproduction of Mothering* (Berkeley: University of California Press, 1978), and J. Mitchell, *Psychoanalysis and Feminism* (New York: Random House, 1974), for related arguments. Chodorow argues that the version of psychoanalytic theory that she uses is, explicitly and intentionally, sociological and sensitive to variants in configurations of social relations (in a way that might answer some of the reservations expressed here); but this "promise" is not developed in her text.

19. See, for example, Anthony Giddens, *New Rules of Sociological Method* (London: Hutchinson, 1976), and Anthony Giddens, *Central Problems in Social Theory* (Berkeley: University of California Press, 1979).

20. Lest there be some confusion, my emphasis on the relatively asociological cast of much recent feminist thought—and its tendency to focus explanatory attention on the requirements and development of *individual* minds and bodies—is not intended as a rejection of all generalization in feminist social science. Generalities, like particulars, have their moral and analytical place; the issues ultimately concern the links between our general terms and the particulars illuminated by our categories. Given the present state of the art, I want to argue that what we need are general constructs that will help us grasp the particulars of gender systems as public, cultural, and political facts—of vital consequence for, but not determined by, individual biology or psychology.

Five

WANT FORMATION, MORALITY, AND SOME "INTERPRETIVE" ASPECTS OF ECONOMIC INQUIRY

Michael S. McPherson

"We propose to suggest that these wants which are the common starting-point of economic reasoning are from a more critical point of view the most obstinately unknown of all the unknowns in the whole system of variables with which economic science deals."—Frank H. Knight

For the last half century or more, mainstream economics has been shaped—and indeed defined—by the principle that the nature and origins of consumers' tastes and preferences lie outside the proper domain of economic inquiry. This doctrine, aptly characterized by Kenneth Boulding as "the immaculate conception of the indifference curve,"[1] may be losing its hold on the profession. While complacency about want formation has always been a sore point with critics of the mainstream tradition, the last decade has seen an increasing number of attempts from in or near the mainstream to enlarge the conceptual vocabulary and analytical apparatus of economics in ways that permit the "black box" of consumer tastes to be opened to investigation.

How far this trend will go is anybody's guess. But if, in fact, the trend does take hold—if questions about why we want the things we do assume an important place on the economist's agenda—then the implications for the theory and practice of economics are likely to be significant. My theme is that economists are likely to be led by such explorations toward a richer conception of the person than traditional "economic man," and hence toward awareness of some "interpretive"

I wish to thank Lee Alston, Albert Hirschman, Richard Krouse, Donald McCloskey, Andrew Ruttan, Thomas Scanlon, John Sheahan, William Sullivan, Dennis Thompson, and Gordon Winston for helpful comments. Work on the revision of this paper was supported in part by a grant from the Ford Foundation.

aspects of economics: its concern with "meaningful understanding" as well as "causal explanation" of human conduct. Stress on this more complex view of the person and on the interpretive dimension that accompanies it has implications for both the "positive" and the "normative" aspects of economics,[2] as well as for the relation between them, which I try to make clear.

I. THE "GIVEN" NATURE OF WANTS AS A TROUBLED DOGMA

Self-conscious renunciation of any interest in problems of want formation is a surprisingly recent phenomenon among economists. While the greats of classical economics never devoted much systematic analytical effort to these questions, there was no lack of awareness among them that people's wants were in some important measure social artifacts. John Stuart Mill in particular was deeply aware of the problems raised by the social dependency of wants, and both his reformulation of utilitarianism and his sympathetic stance toward socialism resulted largely from this awareness.[3] Alfred Marshall, the great British architect of the "marginal utility" theory in economics, the foundation stone of modern preference theory, regarded his own formulation as quite primitive precisely because it abstracted from social influences on people's tastes. Marshall, indeed, found the primary justification of competitive capitalism not in the efficiency of its use of resources but in its tendency to promote what he saw, in his Victorian way, as a robust and enterprising personal character.[4]

Elevation of the "givenness" of wants and character to a dogma accompanied the formalization and heightened methodological self-consciousness of the 1930s. Theorists like Paul Samuelson and Lionel Robbins, heavily influenced by the philosophical doctrines of logical positivism, wrote books with portentous titles like *The Foundations of Economic Analysis* and *The Nature and Significance of Economic Science,* which strove to put the subject on a rigorously objective foundation. Treating wants as data had, from this viewpoint, several advantages. First, there was the belief that wants could be defined behavioristically—that a complete picture of a consumer's preferences could in principle be built up purely from repeated observations of the choices actually made by consumers—Samuelson's reknowned theory of "revealed preference." Any attempt to inquire into what lay *behind* those choices, on the other hand, invited introspection, mentalistic concepts, and other "unverifiable" constructs to enter economics.

Second, given wants fit nicely with the positivist commitment to a sharp distinction between fact and value. To determine what people want seems uncontroversially a matter of fact, but the question *why* they want it—even if the question is asked in a "positive" rather than a "normative" spirit—bristles with evaluative import. It is a question hard to pursue very far without beginning to wonder whether some wants are better than others. And since the positivist *knows* that question is meaningless—a matter of emotion, not science—perhaps it's best not to begin the journey.

The third point sharpens the second. The work of the thirties brought the first real mathematical proofs of the optimality properties of a competitive economy: competitive allocation maximizes want satisfaction for a given income distribution. The proofs, however, made crystal clear the obvious point that allocation was optimal only relative to existing wants. If the system helped produce the wants it satisfied, it might be the case not so much that the market economy gave people what they liked as that it brought them to like what they got. It plainly enhanced the economists' self-esteem and increased their political usefulness to relegate this embarrassing possibility to the footnotes. The political doctrine of "consumer sovereignty" both supports and is supported by a lack of interest in the origin of wants.

Behind and beyond these methodological and political considerations there undoubtedly lay for many economists an important moral reason for refusing to examine the origin of wants: namely, that to do so would be to undermine a commitment to view the economic agent as an autonomous, free chooser. The simplest, if not ultimately the most convincing, way to express our respect for the autonomy of individuals is to ignore or deny the social determination of wants. Near the end of this essay I shall return to this key problem of personal autonomy, seeking to give an account that can survive the obvious fact that wants *are* influenced by society. But that problem is best approached after a careful look at the role of theories of want formation in economic explanation.

II. THE PROBLEM OF ECONOMIC RATIONALITY

Economists are somewhat schizophrenic in explaining just why want formation can safely be ignored. On one hand is the suggestion, stemming from a positivist understanding of economic method, that the stance is merely a matter of convenience in the scientific division of labor, a handy strategic device. Thus Milton Friedman: "The economist's task is to trace the consequences of any given set of wants. The legitimacy of and justification for this abstraction must rest ultimately . . . on the light that is shed and the power to predict that is yielded by the abstraction."[5] The picture is this: something-or-other causes individual wants, wants cause individual behavior, and these in turn cause aggregate social results. The economist simply cuts into the causal chain at a convenient point.

Now, pragmatically, there is plainly something to this view. If one wishes to explain why bad weather causes the price of wheat to rise, there is no need to probe the deeper intentions of farmers and bread-eaters. But this division of labor is going to work as a general principle only if there are no important feedbacks from the want-satisfying process to the want-forming process (as there might be, say, in long-run economic growth)[6]—else adequate causal stories will have to account for the interactions—and if explanatory approaches useful in explaining the "causes" of wants are sharply different from those useful in explaining the consequences of wants—else there will be little reason for economists to specialize in one and not the other. The "positivist" approach really offers no *reason* to believe that either of these claims holds across the whole range of economic phenomena and explanations. The real reasons for the strong reluctance to engage in the study of want formation lie, I think, elsewhere, in certain philosophic commitments that often go unacknowledged.

There is, I want to suggest, a very strong commitment in economics to view people as *rational,* and to explain social outcomes as the (generally unintended) consequences of individually rational conduct. The stress on rationality is present not only because the "hypothesis" of rationality serves well for predictive purposes—although I am sure that is often the case—but also (and more fundamentally) because of other purposes that economic explanations serve. A central purpose of such explanations is to shed light on the consequences for economic welfare of alternative social arrangements and policies. And this means showing how well these arrangements allow people to realize their intentions—that is, to get what they want. Only models which have some conception of rational actors at their base— actors with ends they are trying to achieve—can perform this function. The classic paradigms of economic explanation—from Adam

Smith's Invisible Hand to Keynes's diagnosis of the systematic failure of a market economy to reach full employment—have had this quality of illuminating the relation between individual and (as we might call it) social rationality. The perhaps surprising result of this reflection— surprising to economists as well as to others—is that economists have all along been aiming to produce explanations which satisfy one of the prime requirements of "interpretive" social science: namely, that such explanations should give "understanding" as well as being "causally adequate."[7]

In my view, it is this wholly defensible commitment to rational explanation, coupled, however, with an unacceptably narrow conception of rationality, which principally accounts for the economist's lack of interest in questions of want formation and preference structure. For rationality is understood in the Humean way, as the strictly instrumental choice of means to *given* ends. And the given ends are the preferences people manifest in their everyday behavior. So these become the starting points of rational conduct—and the stopping points of rational explanations. To *explain* those nonrational or irrational preferences then seems a very mysterious enterprise (I suspect some economists secretly belive that it cannot be done at all, and that the "sciences" that pretend to do so are just a sham) and at any rate radically different from the sort of rational explanation economists produce.[8]

But surely this is a severely impoverished account of human rationality. Even granting what may not be true—that there is some deep level of basic impulse and emotion which is in a Humean way a nonrational starting point for human conduct, it is surely bizarre to view our day-to-day choices among alternative goods, services, and activities as being due to that. To be sure, some of our preferences (as between chocolate and vanilla ice cream) may be just unanalyzable facts (or at least not worth analyzing), but it seems undeniable that in a variety of cases there are *reasons* supporting our preferences, and an analyzable structure to be looked into. The most obvious instance, and one which is quickly coming to be incorporated in economic theory, is that in which particular preferences can themselves be seen as means to the end of deeper preferences—as when ingredients are purchased with an eye toward baking a cake.[9] But people may also have preferences over their own preferences for noninstrumental reasons—wanting, say, to cultivate "good taste" in art—so that the preferences they exhibit are in part the product of rational choice.[10] The overt preferences that a person reveals in action will depend in complicated ways on beliefs and expectations, on deeper ends, on strategic choices made earlier in life, and so on. It is hard to see why a person's attempts to satisfy the preferences he happens to have at some moment can be called "rational," while the critical deliberation that sometimes links these immediate preferences with more basic features of the person's structure of belief and motivation should be denied that description.

When we characterize behavior and the preferences that underlie it as "rational" in this extended sense, we must of course mean "rational" from the actor's point of view. It is desirable to be able to say that a person can act rationally from false beliefs (at least if there is some reason to hold the beliefs) or that it may be quite "rational" for a person to be confused, uncertain, or inconsistent when forced to act (or to develop preferences among alternative courses of action) on limited information and with a limited capacity to analyze it. Thus, actions which plainly "make sense" to the actor may be "irrational" from a broader or fuller perspective. These possibilities are often obscured for economists by the tendency to assume that people have full information and an unlimited capacity to reason.

Broader notions of rationality, then, open up some space between the given wants that are supposed to define "the utility function" and the straightforward maximization of that function. Herbert Simon has for some time argued that it is useful to describe conduct and strategies of action which "make sense" in light of informational and reasoning constraints as "procedurally rational" and to mark this notion off from the "substantive rationality" of choosing the action that would be best with full information and ideal reasoning.[11] Economists typically have analyzed conduct on the hypothesis of "substantively rational" action from given preferences—replacing the actual decision maker with an idealized one and bracketing any interest in the processes by which decisions actually get made. It seems likely that some important features of preferences and patterns of preference formation can themselves be explained as "procedurally rational" responses to the social environment. In a somewhat related vein, Jon Elster has argued the need to recognize a sphere of "imperfectly rational" conduct we display as we try to harmonize conflicting wants and to bring unwelcome desires under control.[12]

These and related developments in theorizing about rationality (like the important work of Amartya Sen[13]) represent extensions and modifications of the economist's choice theory framework, rather than wholesale rejection of it. This suggests that the analytical tools of economics can make a real contribution to understanding want formation and change. This will especially be the case when patterns of preference can usefully be viewed as rational responses to internal and environmental limitations. Thus, to cite a suggestive example, the tenacity with which people sometimes commit themselves to "ideological" views, and their consequent refusal to absorb or confront evidence at odds with their position, may be not simply irrational obtuseness, but a "procedurally rational" response to the need to adopt some conceptual framework to prefilter the riot of information that would otherwise overwhelm their capacity to attend.[14] To change this response, it is not enough to demand that people be more "open-minded"; it is necessary to change the circumstances that make it rational for them to "close up."

But while noting the contributions that an extended choice theory approach can bring to explaining wants and preferences, it is also important to say that there is no reason to think that recognizably economic approaches to understanding want formation can fill all the space. As I explain at more length in section IV, there are some significant limitations to what economists can expect to do in this arena, and attempts to be too universalist or imperialist are likely to end in triviality. The evidence to date, as suggested by the examples I will shortly turn to in section III, is that economists who take an interest in these problems have at least as much to learn from other social sciences as they have to teach.

These admonitions of modesty do not, however, lead to the drawing of a clear line that marks out the areas concerning which economists do and do not have something to say. This, I suspect, is all to the good, since such lines tend to be more misleading than helpful. In the reigning economic view, the rational side of man is fully captured by economics, and everything else is deeply irrational. According to that view, extending the scope of rational explanations of conduct beyond the sphere of markets, as in the "rational choice" theories of politics, has really meant pushing aside other modes of explanation in these areas and substituting economic methods. But notions of rationality that can allow for limitations on knowledge and reasoning capacity and for conflict in preferences suggest that the line between the "rational" and the "irrational" cannot be so easily drawn. When (as in the received view of economics) sociology or psychology are seen as sciences of the irrational and economics as the science of the rational, prospects for meaningful communication between them seem pretty bleak. But when all these subjects are viewed as grappling with actors whose conduct is too complex to be described as simply rational or irrational, prospects for communication, and perhaps even collaboration, seem more hopeful.

III. BROADENING THE NOTION OF RATIONALITY

It would doubtless be valuable to say more at a general level to ground and clarify these broader notions of rationality and to show how they can help in the task of explaining the formation and structure of preferences. But it may be more to the point to support the relevance of this perspective through a brief review of several recent examples of work reflecting these developments.

Tibor Scitovsky in *The Joyless Economy* has attempted to use modern physiological psychology as an explanatory framework for economic behavior.[15] Scitovsky focuses on the notion of physiological "arousal," an index of the state of the nervous system which can be correlated with states of perceived tension (high arousal) or boredom (low arousal). Pleasures are typically felt during transitions out of these uncomfortable states toward a level of "optimal" arousal. Scitovsky at times treads close to the unacceptable reductionist thesis that these levels and rates of change of arousal are somehow the "final cause" or "ultimate determinant" of all our behavior, but he need not (and ought not) be read that way. If pleasure and comfort are seen as two *among* our concerns, and arousal measures as correlates rather than causes of our experience of them, then it turns out that Scitovsky presents an illuminating picture of "procedurally rational" people trying, in the face of some ignorance and uncertainty, to achieve a desirable mix of comfort and pleasure. For comfort is the enemy of pleasure, in the sense that simply maintaining oneself in a state of uneventful homeostasis blocks opportunities for pleasurable relief of boredom and tension. Scitovsky offers not only an interesting account of the "microdynamics" of consumption from this perspective but also an imaginative social criticism (oversimplified here): "mass consumption societies" tend in various ways to make the achievement of monotonous comfort easier than the pursuit of sustainable pleasures (through novelty and creativity), with the result that people acting rationally from their own individual points of view, in light of the environments they face, wind up missing out on some of life's more important pleasures.

Albert Hirschman has employed some of Scitovsky's categories in his analysis of swings in political enthusiasm and activity in Western societies. Hirschman argues that there is a built-in cycle in the preference for "public" and "private" happiness: deep involvement either in the demands of personal life or in politics carries within it "the seeds of its own destruction" as people enter in with too high expectations and find the results eventually giving way to disappointment. Hirschman draws in part on Scitovsky's notion of the pleasure of stimulation giving way to mere comfort, but the psychology he describes is richer. For Hirschman argues that the commitment to private life is more than a concern for personal well-being: it is often supported by an ideology which sees the building of prosperity as the greatest contribution to society—but with results that never quite live up to the promise. In politics too people enter with ideals whose realization is never as complete or satisfying as they hope, so (for this among other reasons) disappointment is built in. Hirschman's aim is in good part to make these shifts in preference—and the large and apparently irrational mistakes that underlie them—"understandable" from the actor's point of view, and his approach therefore fits well that described here. Indeed, as Hirschman says, the "human types" he portrays are far from irrational: "They are *superior* to the 'rational actor' inasmuch as they can conceive of *various* states of happiness, are able to transcend one in order to achieve the other, and thus escape from the boredom of permanently operating on the basis of a single, stable set of preferences."[16]

My last example concerns a whole set of writings, mostly appearing in the last five years, on the problem of "self-command" or "self-control." Here is a point where the simple model of rational action from given preferences breaks down: how can such people ever have trouble doing what they want? And yet we all have trouble getting up in the morning, setting down to work, stopping smoking, keeping up an exercise program, and on and on. These examples all suggest conflicts among preferences, and they lead to all sorts of behavior that is very puzzling from the viewpoint of received economic theory: the emergence of "anti-markets," in which the service is sold of persuading you not to do what you want (SmokEnders, Weight Watchers); the use of strategies of "binding" or "precommitment," which limit your range of choice (setting yourself deadlines, putting the alarm clock across the room); and others. Various attempts are being made to explain the sources and implications of these phenomena. What they have in common is the employment of richer and less rigid conceptions of individual rationality: recognizing, for example, that a person may have not just a single set of preferences, but competing, contradictory ones, and metapreferences over those preferences which rank the sets; that a person's preferences, rather than being stable, may in fact oscillate between alternative states; and that "consistency" of behavior over time is not only hard to achieve but hard to define.[17]

IV. MATTERS FOR REVISION

These examples bring home the point that to the degree economists come to take seriously these lines of analysis, more complex models of the *person* will necessarily play a more central role in economic analysis. Clearly, people as rational actors already populate economic theory, but, for the most part, they have been dealt with summarily: drastically simplified assumptions about their motives have been made to allow attention to turn elsewhere. These simplifications are no doubt useful in some explanatory contexts. But when the roots and structure of preference are at issue, it becomes much more important to look closely at the chooser as an active, deciding, deliberating creature and to attempt to see how the world looks from this creature's point of view. The attempt to reconstruct the world from the actor's perspective has a good deal in common with the exercises in "interpretation" that mark certain approaches in sociology and anthropology.[18] The stress on the actor's perspective; the relativity of conduct to his beliefs and values; the embeddedness of those beliefs and values in a social and historical context—all these interpretive features necessarily come to the fore when want formation is at issue.

This interpretive dimension is, of course, never really absent from social science, since the basic objects of any such science are in a fundamental way defined by a society's beliefs and orientations toward them—"money" is an obvious example. But in much of economics these interpretations are in the background—they are treated as "brute facts" in the sense in which Charles Taylor has employed that term.[19] To render these interpretations problematic—to try to see where they come from and how they are composed—brings the interpretive dimension to center stage. This necessarily implies a relaxation of some of the more dogmatic methodological commitments of mainstream economics, in both its "normative" and "positive" aspects. Some of the implications are prefigured in the examples mentioned above, but others will perhaps be more reluctantly accepted.

The Limits of Behaviorism

Economists have been strongly committed to the view that the only objective evidence of people's goals and preferences lies in their overt actions in the marketplace: people's verbal reports, their responses to questionnaires, the results of introspection, are viewed as hopelessly contaminated sources of evidence on what people "really" want.[20] This behavioristic commitment both stems from and reinforces the radically flattened view of preferences economists employ: taking preferences as brute facts about the person that are revealed in actions. The most obvious way to find out *why* someone wants something or acts in a certain way is to ask him. His response is surely not the last word about his "real motives," but it would seem to be at least the first word, and a necessary item for the analyst to account for. Thus, the fact that people's characterizations of their actions seem often to be at odds with the way they really act—as with cognitive dissonance—can be viewed not as a "brick wall" blocking the use of such evidence but rather as a puzzle to explain (and a revealing one in terms of how people form their wants and intentions).

When we recognize that preferences have analyzable structures—as means to deeper ends, in the conflict between an ideal that is striven for and actual conduct that falls short, or in other ways—it becomes especially important to move beyond observations of overt behavior to understand these phenomena. For precisely the *meanings* that activities and choices have for people, the underlying reasons for their actions, are embedded in these structures. It is just perverse to try to tease these meanings out under the self-imposed discipline of refusing to look at any evidence but "revealed preferences"—a bit like playing charades. The range of materials that might usefully be employed in such investigations includes not only interviews and questionnaires, but historical data and controlled experiments of the sort psychologists do.

Amartya Sen, who has written thoughtfully about the need for richer models of preference structure, has speculated that the ultimate basis for economists' reluctance to examine discursive evidence is a view that the use of language is purely instrumental to economic ends: people say whatever advances their interests with no concern for truth. There is little to recommend this outrageously pessimistic view of human beings, and, as Sen notes, one sad result of the insistence on behaviorism has been "to undermine thinking as a method of self-knowledge and talking as a method of knowing about others."[21]

The Centrality of Culture

The methodological roots of economics are highly individualistic, and indeed the tendency in economics is to explain society as the product of individual choice. But in accounting for wants, the fact that they are in major part a reflection of cultural and social phenomena that precede the individual cannot be overlooked. It is the cultural and social milieu that in large measure endows goods and activities with meaning and presents people with the matrix of constraints and opportunities within which they develop themselves.

This point would be too banal to make were its implications not so frequently overlooked. Some of the examples discussed above, in fact, tend to view preference formation and structure as largely an internal, psychological phenomenon. There is this tendency in Scitovsky's reliance on physiological psychology and in some of the literature on self-control. This is perfectly all right as long as this is understood as a *partial* explanation, but it raises problems if viewed as a general theoretical approach.

For explanations of want formation can never be reduced simply to individual psychology or to biological need. The argument has been rehashed most recently in the controversy over sociobiology:[22] human beings are born with an extraordinarily undifferentiated and flexible biological equipment, a wide range of potentialities, and a highly manipulable set of response mechanisms. They are endowed at birth with a "capacity for culture" and little more. People become human as these primitive capacities are formed and differentiated through becoming embedded in a particular cultural framework. While the possible range of cultures must surely be shaped in some broad ways by the "innate" potentialities of the human organism, there is no plausibility to the notion that the interesting features of a particular culture (such as the wants and preferences its members display) could be derived from or accounted for by the properties of this biological equipment, an equipment which itself evolved in interaction with culture.

The best "bad example" of such reductionist ambitions is provided by the methodological pronouncements that surround attempts by Gary Becker and his associates to elaborate formally the idea that particular wants are means to the ends of deeper wants. As already noted, that notion points to an important aspect of the meaningful structure of preferences and has begun to find a place not only in narrow technical economic analyses but in broader reflections on wants and their formation. The reductionist impulse emerges, however, in the notion that behind every set of particular wants is a certain set of basic wants, everywhere and always the same, with the particular wants serving simply as the adequate means, given available technology and resources, to these simple, universal ends.[23]

This program, however, either dissolves in tautology—as it does if we say everyone's ultimate end is happiness and define "happiness" as "what everyone wants"—or founders on the rock of cultural diversity. It is impossible to believe that the whole of cultural learning is no more than the teaching of means to given ends. People form their ends as well as their beliefs about effective means to ends in cultural contexts. And while it would be true to say that the forming of these ends—religious commitments are a good example—depends on connecting them somehow with basic emotional states like ecstasy or fear, it would be quite wrong to say that the end, once formed, is simply a means to achieving (or avoiding) these emotional states. If that were so, one could get a devout Catholic, apparently devoted to serving God, happily to leave the faith just by showing him that he could achieve the relevant emotional states more easily with drugs. But a devout Catholic couldn't possibly conceive of himself and his faith in that way.[24] In fact, as this example suggests, it may in some cases make more sense to conceive of cultural learning as supplying "ends to given means," rather than the other way around: people (individually) need reasons for doing what (socially) needs getting done. The result may be a rational structure of ends and means for each individual, but the ends have no particular status as pregiven.

History and Specificity

It is revealing to note that Becker's program of viewing preferences as means to ends loses persuasiveness only as it aspires to universality—and the same could be said of some other work in this field. Economists remain powerfully drawn to simple, universal laws and theories, but these are probably not to be found in understanding want formation (or, very likely, in many other arenas of economics). The embeddedness of wants in cultural contexts, their relativity to particular structures of belief and meaning, the inherent complexity of human motivation—all suggest that economists exploring these problems will need to be content with partial explanations, with the elucidation of complexities, and with the understanding of historical particulars, rather than hoping for simple and sweeping truths. General understandings may often have to come, as in Geertz's view of cultural anthropology, from the deeper understanding of particulars.[25] Since this reality cuts against the economist's "compulsion to theorize,"[26] it may pose a large obstacle to pursuit of these lines of inquiry. Nonetheless, some of the more revealing among recent attempts to analyze wants have had something of the quality of "case studies"—as in Hirschman's work, described above—and this is likely to continue.

Although the three foregoing considerations all point out differences between the explanation of want formation and more usual modes of economic explanation, none of them, I think, excuses the analyst from the requirements of theoretical discipline and empirical accountability that I take to be the real marks of the scientific enterprise. Perhaps the greatest and most justifiable fear economists have about relaxing the assumption of given preferences is that without it, "anything goes." Becker, for example, has worried that without the assumption of stable preferences the analyst "might succumb to the temptation of simply postulating the required shift in preferences to 'explain' all apparent contradictions to his predictions."[27]

The point, however, is not to assume unexplained changes in preferences but precisely to explain preferences and how they change. Becker apparently assumes such explanations can't be had, perhaps because, harking back to an argument considered above, they are themselves purely irrational affects. But the analyst who wishes to explain preferences can get the requisite theoretical discipline by proceeding from the hypothesis that wants are a *procedurally* rational response to the limitations and opportunities with which the person is faced, and empirical corrigibility by requiring any explanation to account not only for people's observed behavior (as in any economic explanation) but also for what they say about their wants.

V. WANTS AND CULTURE

It is hard to believe that economics could digest the whole range of problems and approaches I have been reviewing without any impact on its normative standpoint. There is, of course, the possibility that the "normative" and the "positive" are such radically different realms that no real cognitive connections can be drawn between them: any set of positive views can be conjoined with any normative view. But it seems much more plausible and helpful, as Robert Bellah's paper in this volume well illustrates, to recognize that theories in the social sciences have a holistic quality: an underlying vision and conceptual orientation that shape both their explanatory and their moral dimensions.

This kind of view is supported in the present context by the obvious affinity between a propensity to take wants as given in explanatory contexts and a tendency to adopt a narrowly want-regarding utilitarianism in moral contexts. I noted earlier that wants tend to be viewed as "hard facts" by the economist, as the dividing line between rational conduct in the service of given ends and prerational or nonrational "value commitments," and that hence wants are seen as the starting points for the kind of rational explanation economists do. This same view makes it natural to see existing wants as starting points when the aim is to try to promote desirable states of affairs, and to define desirable states of affairs solely in terms of the degree to which for these preexisting wants are satisfied.

Analysis from this starting point marked the great debate surrounding neoclassical welfare economics from the 1930s through the 1960s, with endless discussion about whether and how individual preferences could be aggregated into a social total but with a real lack of serious reflection on the possibility that normative judgments could

be grounded in anything other than or in addition to existing preferences. Neoclassical welfare economics is now often regarded by
economists as a dead end, but its underlying presuppositions continue to shape professional judgments in basic ways. An illustration
is that when economists do examine normative theories which depart
from a want-regarding framework, they often squash the theory down
to fit their want-regarding presuppositions—Rawls's theory of justice,
for example, sometimes gets translated into the wildly implausible
form of a want-regarding theory in which only the wants of the worst-
off individual count, and this caricature is then rejected for its im-
plausibility.[28]

Just as the "wants-are-given" perspective is useful and adequate in
some explanatory contexts, there may well be normative contexts
where all that is in point are questions about how well existing wants
are being satisfied. Surely when we recognize that wants are in part
a social artifact, we can also recognize the damage that results when
a society systematically generates aspirations which it is systematically unable to fulfill. The "fit" between wants and their satisfaction
is always *a* relevant normative question. But it is unlikely that a strictly
want-regarding utilitarianism can survive very well as the basic normative standpoint for an economics which takes seriously the questions about want formation raised earlier in this paper. The view of
the person as a clear-headed maximizer over clearly defined preferences must give way to the image of a more complicated and less
certain actor, attempting to sort out what is worth doing and what
sort of person to be. In this context, giving people what they want
becomes itself an ambiguous enterprise. In Frank Knight's words,
"The chief thing which the common-sense individual actually wants
is not satisfactions for the wants which he has, but more, and *better,*
wants."[29]

Moreover, the particular wants people display will reflect in important ways the cultural milieu in which they are embedded, and economic arrangements are themselves an important part of this milieu.
Thus, the economic system must be thought of not only as a means
of satisfying wants but as a way of creating them. There is, as Bernard Williams has argued, no such thing in economic planning and
policy making as "just following" existing preferences, for preferences are formed partly in anticipation and in response to economic
policies and plans.[30] When we deliberate about alternative social ar-

rangements, we cannot escape the fact that we are deciding in some measure what kinds of people we shall become. A view of economics which pretends to be neutral on these questions will either be driven into silence on all practical issues or, more likely, lend tacit support to the status quo of preferences and of the society that fosters them.

Such reflections might, we can hope, temper the enthusiasm of economists for elaborate schemes of social cost-benefit analysis based on existing wants as *the* adequate framework for all purposes of social evaluation. What is needed but sadly lacking is not wholesale rejection of such analytical techniques but reflection on where they might fit into the deliberative apparatus of a more desirable kind of society.[31]

More generally, we might hope for greater receptivity among economists to the broad ranges of moral reflection which presuppose conceptions of the person richer and subtler than the single-minded maximizer of standard welfare economics. Economics as a moral science is located in the tradition of Western political philosophy, and that tradition is in one important dimension a sustained reflection on the complex interplay between conceptions of human well-being and social arrangements adequate to sustain and satisfy those conceptions. If the education and practice of economists showed more awareness of that tradition, the result might be to help overcome what Bernard Williams has rightly called the "great simple-mindedness" of neoclassical welfare economics.[32]

VI. A NEW PERSPECTIVE ON REASON, AUTONOMY, AND SOCIETY

There are, as Hirschman notes in his contribution to this volume, hopeful signs that economists are in fact coming to take the moral dimensions of social life more seriously. Perhaps this is in some measure a response to philosophical reflections like those considered in section V, but I suspect that a growing awareness that effective economic functioning is highly (and perhaps increasingly) dependent on certain kinds of moral restraints has played a larger role. The work being done along these lines is valuable but, I think, one-sided in its concern for the role morality can play in promoting economic efficiency. After briefly describing these recent developments, I will suggest a further dimension of moral inquiry, one compatible with the new developments in the analysis of want formation sketched earlier, which it is within the power of economists to pursue.

The recent upsurge of economists' interest in morality has stemmed from renewed awareness of the obvious fact (which was well known to Adam Smith) that even a market economy cannot function purely on self-interest or on just any wants: without moral dispositions on the part of most to play by the rules of the game voluntarily, the costs imposed by cheating and by efforts to police the rules would bring the system down overnight. Attention to this insight has given rise to a small but rapidly growing literature in economics examining the function of morality as a means to the end of ensuring economic efficiency.

This attractively down-to-earth approach to moral thought is leading in some interesting directions. Thus, some economists have begun to identify the particular features of markets and commodities which make them especially vulnerable to cheating—features like nonrepetitiveness of transactions and high costs of measuring product or service quality—and hence to determine where the performance of the economy is most dependent on moral restraints.[33] Others have stressed the way in which social institutions like schooling and the family may promote economic well-being by encouraging "tastes" for honest dealing and have employed this fact as both genetic explanation and moral justification for such institutions.[34] The question whether modern "mixed-economy" capitalism can generate the "moral support" needed for efficiency can also be raised in this framework.[35]

Neither is this mode of analysis necessarily confined to market economies. Sen has offered an interpretation of the Chinese cultural revolution as a strategy for modifying attitudes toward work in ways that enhance economic productivity without requiring large inequalities in income to provide incentives.[36]

These developments promise to shed considerable light on the social interest in the wants individuals develop, and in this way to help us get beyond the "wants are given" perspective of neoclassical welfare economics. But, as writers in this vein plainly recognize, these approaches are quite incomplete as a general framework for examining the moral problems raised by the social relativity of wants. For they really take as given the interest we have in promoting efficient exchange and production, and their predominant emphasis is on moral concerns as simply instrumental to promoting that interest. And while we can grant that morality must be "functional" in the broad sense of protecting and promoting central human concerns, it is necessary in a fuller view to recognize the existence of important interests and values beyond the interest in the greater economic output which morality can promote.

In particular, once we recognize that preferences are not given, it surely makes sense to acknowledge that we each have an interest not only in satisfying the preferences we have—which is where the contributions of morality to productive efficiency come in—but also in developing "desirable" preferences in the first place. The latter is obviously a deeply problematic interest to grapple with, since it is unclear from whose standpoint or by what standard our preferences themselves should be judged as more or less desirable. It is understandable that economists, fearful especially of imposing on others their own prejudices about how to live, have drawn back from this level of analysis. But unless economists are willing to explore this question—to push beyond the analysis of morality as a means to greater economic efficiency—they will fail to come to grips with some of the most serious problems raised in the previous section. For the mere fact that existing preferences are being effectively met, even (perhaps especially) if people's moral dispositions are effectively enlisted in that cause, is no proof that people might not do better by having other preferences.

I cannot claim to have any definitive answer to the very deep questions these considerations raise, but I can point to what I believe is a potentially fruitful line of inquiry suggested by the conception of the person and the mode of analysis of want formation developed earlier. Much stress has been laid on the idea that a person's preferences depend very much on his personal history and on the social and cultural background against which they develop. It is perfectly natural, with this view of the person, to go on to wonder whether some environments are more thwarting or encouraging of prospects for favorable development than others. Inquiry can turn from the intrusive and perhaps unavoidably elitist program of deciding which preferences would be "best" for a particular person or for people in general to the more impartial procedural question of guaranteeing a desirable social background for preference development.

The obvious objection is that this move simply slips our prejudices about desirable ways of living in through the back door: the secret criterion for deciding what is a "good" environment for choice is our preexisting commitment to certain kinds of preferences we want to promote. It must be granted that our ideas of more and less favorable conditions for preference development could never be completely independent of our view of the kinds of creatures humans are and the sorts of things they incline to seek; in that sense they can never be totally neutral among possible preferences.[37] But our judgments about good and bad conditions for choice need not reduce to hidden advocacy of a preferred way of living. They have an important *cognitive* component, connected to conditions like awareness of alternatives, scope for reflection, opportunities for free discussion and questioning, and so on. Such conditions suggest criteria for judging the worth of a social environment for preference formation that could be agreed on by people with a broad range of views about what particular ends are most worth seeking. We can safeguard our interest in developing "desirable" preferences without warranting anyone to decide which preferences are desirable for us by ensuring that social institutions and policies encourage environments which meet such broadly acceptable cognitive standards.

This line of thought suggests a relatively straightforward way of giving sense to a principle of respect for "personal autonomy" in political and moral theory. Under favorable conditions for choice we might be said to have more "control" over how we develop, to be less subject to "interfering" forces (whether consciously manipulative or not) that impair our capacity to choose. "Personal autonomy," in this sense of having our preferences develop under favorable conditions, has both instrumental and intrinsic value. Instrumentally, we want to guard ourselves against processes of want formation that may harm us—as, for example, if we are manipulated surreptitiously into developing desires (say for cigarettes) that harm our long-run interest. But autonomy is also important to us intrinsically. Preferences developed under favorable conditions are more truly "our own" and better reflect our choices as autonomous beings. This conception gives expression to a moral commitment to make it possible for people to be in some sense "self-determining" while taking account of the inevitable role of social influences in shaping the person.[38]

I noted earlier that the neoclassical commitment to "consumer sovereignty" stems in part from a moral commitment to the value of personal autonomy: one respects a person by respecting that person's preferences, with no questions asked about how they were formed. The conception of autonomy proposed here can be seen as extending this commitment by defending a person's concern not only to act on the preferences he has but to be afforded protection from constricted or distorting environments for developing wants.

This formulation of the concept of autonomy, while promising, is, plainly, highly abstract. To get anywhere in the criticism of social institutions and policies it will be necessary to describe with some concreteness the social prerequisites for autonomous choice—or, less ambitiously, to identify specific kinds of defects and impairments in the social environment for preference development. This will require better empirical knowledge of what processes of preference development are like: what factors are strategic in shaping the developmental process, what kinds of limitations and opportunities are especially important in shaping outcomes, and so on. Also needed is more investigation of the kinds of environments which make for good choices by actors who are bounded by imperfect information and a limited capacity to process the information they have.

Some of the possibilities can be suggested by looking at illustrations at the levels both of grand theory and of more specific analyses.

In the last decade, two "grand theories" of major importance have emerged which purport to characterize the ideal social conditions for autonomous choice: Habermas' theory of communicative competence and Rawls's theory of justice.[39] The theories are at base quite similar, although they emerge from different traditions and are expressed and defended in different terms. For both, the root condition for ideal autonomy is the presence of a set of social arrangements which can be discursively justified from everyone's point of view and rest on principles publicly acknowledged by all, without any hidden conditions or ideological distortions needed to secure the allegiance of any group. When these conditions are met, the wants of any person or group can be said to correspond to their "real interests," and what Rawls calls the "choice criterion of value," the premise that the worth of a pursuit to a person derives simply from his having chosen it, assumes full force.

Now, an important point to stress is that these clearly moral theories make—and must make—claims about preference development of an explanatory kind. For embedded in such conceptions of autonomy is the notion that defects in the social conditions confronting people will lead to distortions in the wants and personalities they will display, and hence that one can explain the distortions in terms of the defects. Rawls, for example, contends that "excessive" social inequalities tend to promote personality structures prone to envy and (in the poor) the loss of self-esteem.[40] Habermas' program requires him to show that dysfunctional phenomena like the "legitimation crisis" in Western democracies and the "false consciousness" they reflect can be traced in reasonably specific ways to distortions in structures of communication. These analyses are *at once* moral criticisms of existing societies (from the theories' point of view) *and* explanatory hypotheses about preference development.

It follows that in testing these empirical claims we are in some sense assessing the moral theories from which they derive. Any moral view, and in particular any conception of autonomy and its social prerequisites, will provide us with a certain way of "reading" human conduct, and those "readings" can be placed against the facts of how people actually behave and interact. We may, it is true, never be *forced* by the facts to reject any particular moral commitment. But then, as Willard Quine has argued, the same is true in science: there are always a number of places to modify a theory to fit a recalcitrant fact, and we can always hang onto our most cherished commitments if we are willing to pay a high enough price. The idea that moral views are somehow thoroughly independent of the facts stems from the positivist view that such views are ultimately just nonrational facts. But the kind of reconstruction Rawls has offered of moral thought, as a kind of back-and-forth movement between particular beliefs and intuitions and more general principles, clearly provides room for the notion of corrigibility by facts.

Our interest in securing favorable conditions for preference development does not, however, surface only in the context of elaborating such large-scale theories of ideal autonomy and its social prerequisites. Arguments about autonomy bear as well on some quite immediate controversies in political economy, and here too explanatory and moral questions are intertwined. Some examples may suggest the fruitfulness of an autonomy-based perspective in approaching them.

There is, to begin with, the controversy surrounding the role of advertising in "creating wants." Those who disparage the role of advertising often seem to presume that the wants advertising "creates" are bad by some absolute standard, which standard (unless it can be clearly defended) is likely to seem elitist and arbitrary. On the other hand, defenders of advertising often allege that it does not "create" wants at all, but simply dispenses useful information. An autonomy-based view would recognize that advertising helps to create the social environment in which preference development takes place and would ask whether this contribution to the social environment is a help or a hindrance in creating favorable conditions for choice. This view makes clear, against the defenders of advertising, that it is more than *just* information: it is highly selective information at best, packaged in particular ways, and affecting not just particular choices but the entire deliberative process by which people decide how to live. But against the attackers of advertising, this view asserts that the case against advertising must rest not on a priori judgment about the goodness or badness of particular wants but on attention to the *way* wants are formed. The challenge is to articulate clearly the senses in which advertising impairs the environment for choice relative to some reasonably clear-cut notions of what is required to choose well (not only abundant information but encouragement of reflection, questioning, exposure to a full range of alternatives), and then—something not often attempted—to show empirically that the asserted impairments really do wind up affecting people's wants in the way the theory would suggest.

A second example is the relation between political-economic institutions and people's preferences for participation in them. There is a familiar view that limited opportunities for participation by citizens in politics (and by workers in decision making in the firm) are a reflection of a weak preference by citizens (and workers) for such involvement—a "weakness," if you will, in human nature. This view of man may be said to be confirmed by surveys and by a lack of overt discontent with existing arrangements. But maybe people choose not to develop their "taste" for participation because they know it has little chance of being satisfied. A richer participatory environment might call forth more active involvement or, to adapt the example to Hirschman's formulation, discussed above, a more sustained, less spasmodic inclination to involvement. Here again there is a causal hypothesis generated by a moral view, and the empirical challenge is to determine whether an "unfavorable" environment—one that lacks opportunities for participation—is indeed a key determinant of "tastes" for participation.

Finally, there is the interesting fact that some defenders of the market argue not only its want-satisfying properties but also its advantages as an environment for preference development. This argument has been made glancingly by Friedman[41] and at more length by members of the so-called neo-Austrian school.[42] The argument cites the richness of information, the wide opportunity for experiment, and the lack of overt social coercion in market economies. These arguments are, I think, one-sided, overlooking elements of implicit coercion, of bias in the kinds of opportunities and developmental paths opened up and closed off, and other defects in existing market-oriented economies. Nonetheless, this is the *kind* of argument defenders of the market need to make from the standpoint of a concern with autonomy. To explore their claims empirically would plainly be worthwhile, and, interestingly, it would require employing the sort of developmental view of the person argued for here, in contrast to the view employed in more familiar defenses of the market. Moreover, market economies undoubtedly do have important features which protect certain aspects of personal autonomy, and it is necessary to preserve these in advancing alternative conceptions of a desirable political economy.

I have tried with these illustrations to show that drawing out the implications of a concern for autonomy as a moral notion results in the identification of hypotheses and lines of empirical inquiry that social scientists might do well to explore. I have no desire to claim that the territory thus staked out should be explored exclusively by economists, since many of the questions ought naturally to interest sociologists, psychologists, and political scientists as well. But there is good reason to think that economists do have something to contribute. Substantively, all my examples focus on political economic institutions and raise questions about which economists are ordinarily expected to have views—like the social value of advertising or the social worth of the market. Formally, questions about favorable conditions for preference development are closely allied with questions about effective decision making from uncertainty, and this is a subject to which economists have made many of the most important contributions. This is not at all to say that the task of clarifying our moral notions about autonomy can be reduced to a formal optimization exercise, but only that economic analyses of information-handling problems may shed some light in this area, where we know all too little. Such analyses, to cite a simple example, subvert the commonsense notion that more information is always better than less, since a glut of information can readily impair the "information-processing" capacities of the subject.[43] Maximizing available alternatives is not equivalent to creating the best environment for choice, as "liberals" are perhaps sometimes too quick to suppose.

VII. CONCLUSION: REVISION AND RENEWAL IN ECONOMICS

My aim has been to suggest that the issues of want formation to which economists are beginning to attend open up a path which may enrich economists' conception of the person and thereby modify their stance toward problems of both explanation and moral evaluation. The notion that the achievement of "interpretive understanding" of social action and the promotion of social conditions for autonomous choice are central aims in social inquiry have become fashionable in some areas of social science, but it must still seem quite foreign to the positivist self-understandings of most economists. I have tried to show, however, that these commitments can be seen as extensions and deepenings and modifications of the actual practice of economics, which in this and other ways is better than its methodological preachments, rather than as a radical challenge to the foundations of the subject as actually practiced.

I would not argue this way if I did not believe it, but I welcome the diplomatic overtones of this argument as well. I am sure that many of those who, like me, sympathize with the aims of interpretive and critical social science wish that contemporary economics would simply go away. But I see this as neither very likely nor particularly desirable. Rather, what is to be wished for is that contemporary economics, with its substantial intellectual merits and considerable social prestige, discover ways to broaden its intellectual base beyond the overly narrow moral and philosophical commitments that now inform it. Perhaps the strongest reason to hope for this outcome is that most economists want very much to understand the human world. And the creature I have tried to describe—tentative, conflict-ridden, mistake-prone, seeking to do his best in the light of internal and external limitations—is eminently more understandable, in several senses, than the single-minded maximizer of textbook tradition.

NOTES

Epigraph: Frank H. Knight, *The Ethics of Competition and Other Essays* (Chicago: University of Chicago Press) p. 20.

1. Kenneth E. Boulding, *Economics as a Science* (New York: McGraw-Hill, 1970), pp. 118–19.

2. The terms "normative" and "positive" are the ones favored by economists to mark off the distinction between the evaluative and the explanatory dimensions of economics.

3. See Michael S. McPherson, "Mill's Moral Theory and the Problem of Preference Change," *Ethics* January 1982, 92:252–73.

4. See John K. Whitaker, "Some Neglected Aspects of Alfred Marshall's Economic and Social Thought," *History of Political Economy* (Summer 1977), 9(2):161–97.

5. Milton Friedman, *Price Theory* (Chicago: Aldine Press, 1962), p. 6.

6. A valuable argument on these lines is in David Felix, "De Gustibus Disputandum Est: Changing Consumer Preferences in Economic Growth," *Explorations in Economic History* (1979), 16:260–96.

7. I presuppose here that rational explanation is a species of causal explanation. In this and other ways, my account differs from that in Martin Hollis and Edward Nell, *Rational Economic Man* (Cambridge: Cambridge University Press, 1975), from which I have nevertheless learned much.

8. This whole account is much too philosophical for most economists to embrace explicitly, though I think something like it fits their real views pretty well. The author who comes closest to articulating this perspective is Gordon Tullock, "Economic Imperialism," in James Buchanan and Robert D. Tollison, eds., *Theory of Public Choice* (Ann Arbor: University of Michigan Press, 1972), pp. 317–29. The following quotation from Paul Samuelson's influential *Foundations of Economic Analysis* (New York: Atheneum, 1965), suggests the same viewpoint: "In fact, many economists, well within the academic fold, would separate economics from sociology upon the basis of rational or irrational behavior, where these terms are defined in the penumbra of utility theory" (p. 90). Gary Becker, in the introduction to his *Economic Approach to Human Behavior* (Chicago: University of Chicago Press, 1976), states very strongly the view that economics is defined by rational action from given preferences, although for him the preferences that are "given" lie deeper than surface preferences for goods and services.

9. Becker and his students and colleagues at the University of Chicago have been prominent in developing this approach. A useful survey is in Robert T. Michael and Gary S. Becker, "On the New Theory of Consumer Behavior," *Swedish Journal of Economics* (1973), 75:378–95. A related approach is described in Kevin L. Lancaster, "A New Approach to Consumer Theory," *Journal of Political Economy* (April 1966), 74:132–57.

10. The formal idea of a "meta-preference" as a preference among preferences is defined and explored by Amartya Sen in several essays. See especially his "Rational Fools: A Critique of the Behavioral Foundations of Economic Theory," *Philosophy and Public Affairs* (Summer 1977), 6(4):317–44.

11. Herbert A. Simon, "From Substantive to Procedural Rationality," in Frank Hahn and Martin Hollis, eds., *Philosophy and Economic Theory* (Oxford: Oxford University Press, 1979), pp. 65–86. Many of these insights have been developed by Simon and his colleagues over the last several decades in the context of the "behavioral" theory of the firm. For a survey with reference to the implications for the general theory of rational conduct, see James A. March, "Bounded Rationality, Ambiguity, and the Engineering of Choice," *Bell Journal of Economics and Management Science* (Autumn 1978), 9(2):587–608. See also Janos Kornai, *Anti-Equilibrium* (Amsterdam: North-Holland, 1971), ch. 11.

12. Jon Elster, *Ulysses and the Sirens: Studies in Rationality and Irrationality* (Cambridge: Cambridge University Press, 1979).

13. Sen, "Rational Fools," and other work.

14. See Kenneth J. Arrow, *The Limits of Organization* (New York: W. W. Norton, 1974). Of course, one must also note—with Jon Elster in *Ulysses and the Sirens*—that sometimes people *are* irrationally obtuse. The idea of "procedural rationality" should not be used so flexibly as to foreclose the possibility of irrational behavior.

15. Tibor Scitovsky, *The Joyless Economy: An Inquiry into Human Satisfaction and Consumer Dissatisfaction* (New York: Oxford University Press, 1976).

16. Albert O. Hirschman, *Shifting Involvements: Private Interest and Public Action* (Princeton: Princeton University Press, 1982), p. 134.

17. Important examples from a rapidly growing literature include Gordon C. Winston, "Addiction and Backsliding: A Theory of Compulsive Consumption," *Journal of Economic Behavior and Organization*, 1(4) (forthcoming); H. Shefrin and R. Thaler, "An Economic Theory of Self-Control," NBER Working Paper No. 208, revised (Stanford, Calif.: National Bureau of Economic Research, Inc., July, 1978); and Thomas C. Schelling, "The Intimate Contest for Self-Command," *The Public Interest* (Summer 1980), 60:94–118.

18. For a representative sample of writings, see Paul Rabinow and William Sullivan, eds., *Interpretive Social Science: A Reader* (Berkeley: University of California Press, 1979). There is no canonical definition of what interpretive social science is. My own view incorporates the features described in the text but stops short of strong hermeneutical claims that deny the possibility of causal analysis or theoretical generalization in social science. I thus dissent, for example, from many of the claims in Peter Winch's well-known book, *The Idea of a Social Science and its Relation to Philosophy* (London: Routledge and Kegan Paul, 1958).

19. Charles Taylor, "Interpretation and the Sciences of Man," in Rabinow and Sullivan, eds., *Interpretive Social Science,* pp. 25–72.

20. This orientation has been changing, not only because of the considerations advanced in this paper, but because of the growing impact of "attitudinal" surveys and the obvious importance of expectations in understanding inflation.

21. Amartya Sen, "Behavior and the Concept of Preference," *Economica* (August 1973), n.s. 40:258.

22. See, for example, Marshall Sahlins, *The Use and Abuse of Biology: An Anthropological Critique of Sociobiology* (Ann Arbor: University of Michigan Press, 1976); and Michael S. McPherson, "Sociobiological Imperialism and the Sciences of Man," *Berkshire Review* (1978), special issue, pp. 52–64.

23. "One does not argue over tastes for the same reason that one does not argue over the Rocky Mountains—both are there, will be there next year, too, and are the same for all men." George J. Stigler and Gary S. Becker, "De Gustibus Non Est Disputandum," *American Economic Review* (March 1977), 67(2):76.

24. Becker would probably say that the Catholic's *real* end is these emotional states, and he just does not know or will not admit it—and that the proof is that if the drugs become available, there will be fewer Catholics and more druggies. But this short circuit has lots of problems. If the Catholic himself is "tempted" by the drugs, he is likely to do all sorts of things that make no sense according to the assumption that his real aim is just a certain emotional state—things like removing himself from temptation, moving to have drugs outlawed, etc.—all moves to protect his real end, from his point of view: to do honor to God. As for later generations, it may well be that fewer will ever *form* the end of serving God, but that is a different matter.

25. Clifford Geertz, *The Interpretation of Cultures* (New York: Basic Books, 1973).

26. Albert O. Hirschman, "The Search for Paradigms as a Hindrance to Understanding," in Rabinow and Sullivan, eds., *Interpretive Social Science*, pp. 163–80.

27. Becker, *Economic Approach*, p. 6. It is important to remember that the "preferences" Becker wants to treat as stable are the "basic," "universal" preferences discussed earlier.

28. This criticism applies to some of the criticism of Rawls in (among other places) Lester Thurow, *Generating Inequality* (New York: Basic Books, 1975); and section V of the (in many ways excellent) article by Sidney Alexander, "Social Evaluation Through Notional Choice," *Quarterly Journal of Economics* (November 1974), 88:597–624. The mathematically formalized versions of Rawls's theory produced by economicsts almost always misrepresent Rawls in the way the text suggests.

29. Knight, *Ethics of Competition*, p. 22.

30. Bernard Williams, "A Critique of Utilitarianism," in J. J. C. Smart and Bernard Williams, *Utilitarianism: For and Against* (Cambridge, England: Cambridge University Press, 1973), p. 147.

31. An illuminating interchange is that between Stuart Hampshire, "Morality and Pessimism," in Stuart Hampshire, ed., *Public and Private Morality* (Cambridge, England: Cambridge University Press, 1978), pp. 1–22; and James Griffin, "Are There Incommensurable Values?" *Philosophy and Public Affairs* (Fall 1977), 7:39–59.

32. Williams, "Critique," p. 149.

33. Kenneth Arrow, "Gifts and Exchanges," *Philosophy and Public Affairs* (Summer 1974), 1(4):343–62; and Melvin Reder, "The Place of Ethics in the Theory of Production," in Michael Boskin, ed., *Economics and Human Welfare: Essays in Honor of Tibor Scitovsky* (New York: Academic Press, 1979), pp. 133–46.

34. Arrow, *The Limits of Organization*; and Douglass C. North, *Structure and Change in Economic History* (New York: W. W. Norton, forthcoming).

35. Fred Hirsch, *Social Limits to Growth* (Cambridge: Harvard University Press, 1976).

36. Amartya Sen, *On Economic Inequality* (Oxford: Clarendon Press, 1973), ch. 4.

37. Equally, our ideas about what is good for a person can never be completely separated from our notions about what he would tend to choose under favorable conditions. The circle here is not, I think, a vicious one.

38. It should be noted that autonomy as I am using it here is a different notion from that of "personal autonomy" as a developed character trait. The latter (like Mill's "individuality") describes, roughly, a determination to "make up one's own mind" on questions of social importance, to resist conformity. Autonomy as a character trait is discussed in Robert Young, "The Value of Autonomy," *Philosophical Quarterly* (January 1982), 32:35–44. The distinction between these two notions of autonomy is drawn in McPherson, "Mill's Moral Theory." It is perhaps worth stressing that there is nothing especially individualistic about autonomy in the sense used in this paper: there is

no claim that wants are best formed in isolation or that well-formed wants will be wholly or mainly self-regarding.

39. See especially the essays in Jürgen Habermas, *Communication and the Evolution of Society*, Thomas McCarthy, trans. (Boston: Beacon Press, 1979); and John Rawls, *A Theory of Justice* (Cambridge, Mass.: Belknap Press, 1971).

40. These personality structures can themselves be shown in the context of Rawls's theory to be incompatible with his conception of personal autonomy.

41. Milton Friedman, "Value Judgments in Economics," in Sidney Hook, ed., *Human Values and Economic Policy* (New York: New York University Press, 1967), pp. 85–92, esp. p. 91.

42. The most interesting treatments appear in various works of Frank Knight and Friedrich Hayek. See also James Buchanan, "Natural and Artifactual Man," Virginia Polytechnic Institute and State University, 1978.

43. See Arrow, *The Limits of Organization*; and various works of Herbert A. Simon, including "Rationality as Process and as Porduct of Thought," *American Economic Review* (May 1978), 68:1–16.

Six

HISTORY: ETHICS, SCIENCE, AND FICTION

Michel de Certeau

My analysis of historiography must be situated in the context of a question too broad to be treated fully here, namely the antinomy between ethics and what, for lack of a better word, I will call dogmatism. Ethics is articulated through effective operations, and it defines a distance between what is and what ought to be. This distance designates a space where we have something to do. On the other hand, dogmatism is authorized by a reality that it claims to represent, and in the name of this reality it imposes laws. Historiography functions midway between these two poles; but whenever it attempts to break away from ethics, it returns toward dogmatism.

This antinomy between ethics and dogmatism plays an essential role in the history of sciences, especially in the concerns of the social sciences. The organization of a scientific knowledge that took shape during the seventeenth and eighteenth centuries supposed a change in the fundamental postulate of medieval societies: the religious or metaphysical aim of stating the truth of being according to God's will was replaced by the ethical task of creating or making history (faire l'histoire). However, both ambitions were concerned ultimately with establishing a certain order.

Today, this search for a prevailing order has been superseded by the social imperative to produce a more humane world. Now, value is assigned to human beings according to their actions, their functions within a historical economy that is directed by the law of progress, rather than according to their positions within a system of absolutes.

Differentiated and limited disciplines, which organize operations within coherent frameworks, define theoretical hypotheses, specific objects of knowledge, and scopes of investigations. The social sciences, born in modern times, form a set of institutions that express ethical postulates through technical operations. For a long period, these special institutions organized "new crusades" of a technical nature to perform ethical tasks; they are in contrast to other institutions which speak in the name of "reality" and use a dogmatic way of making believe.

However, a new "dogmatism" has appeared, one that has replaced the historical linkage of ethical obligation and technical ability. The scientific establishment has been gradually separating itself from its ethical goals, which for such a long time had motivated and directed its technical operations. It has slowly been losing its foundation in social operativity and transforming its products into representations of a reality in which everyone must believe. I call this dogmatizing tendency "the institution of the real." It consists of the building up of representations into laws imposed by the state of things. Through this process, ethical tasks are replaced by what is supposed to be the expression of reality. A touchstone is the concept of "fiction."

FICTION

"Fiction is a perilous word, much like its correlative, science."[1] Having discussed the fictive aspects of historical discourse elsewhere, I should like here only to specify, in the form of a preliminary note, four possible ways in which fiction operates in the historian's discourse.

Fiction and History

Western historiography struggles against fiction. This internecine strife between history and storytelling is very old. Like an old family quarrel, positions and opinions are often fixed. In its struggle against genealogical storytelling, the myths and legends of the collective memory, and the meanderings of the oral tradition, historiography establishes a certain distance between itself and common assertion and belief; it locates itself in this difference, which gives it the accreditation of erudition because it is separated from ordinary discourse.

Not that it speaks the truth; never have historians pretended to do that! Rather, equipped with apparatus for the critical reading of documents, the scholars efface error from the "fables" of the past. The territory that they occupy is acquired through a diagnosis of the false. They hollow out a place for their discipline in the terrain of received tradition. In this way, installed in the midst of a given society's stratified and interconnected modes of narrative (that is to say, all that this society tells or is told of itself), they spend their time in pursuit of the false rather than in the construction of the true, as though truth could be produced only by means of determining error. Their work is oriented toward the negative, or, to borrow a more appropriate term from Popper, toward "falsification."[2] From this viewpoint, "fiction" is that which the historiographers constitute as erroneous; thereby, they delimit their proper territory.

Fiction and Reality

At the level of analytic procedures (the examination and comparison of documents), as at the level of interpretations (the products of the historiographical operation), the technical discourse capable of determining the errors characteristic of fiction has come to be authorized to speak in the name of the "real." By distinguishing between the two discourses—the one scientific, the other fictive—according to its own criteria, historiography credits itself with having a special relationship to the "real" because its contrary is posited as "false."

This reciprocal determination operates elsewhere as well, although by other means and with other aims. It involves a double displacement, which renders a concept plausible or true by pointing to an error and, at the same time, enforcing belief in something real through a denunciation of the false. The assumption is made that what is not held to be false must be real. Thus, for example, in the past, arguments against "false" gods were used to induce belief in a true God. The process repeats itself today in contemporary historiography: by demonstrating the presence of errors, discourse must pass off as "real" whatever is placed in opposition to the errors. Even though this is logically questionable, it works, and it fools people. Consequently, fiction is deported to the land of the unreal, but the discourse that is armed with the technical know-how to discern errors is given the supplementary privilege of representing something "real." Debates about the reliability of literature as opposed to history illustrate this division.

Fiction and Science

Through a rather logical reversal, fiction may have the same position in the realm of science. In place of the metaphysician's and theologian's discourse, which once deciphered the order of all things and the will of their Author, a slow revolution constitutive of our "modernity" has substituted writings ("écritures" or scientific languages) capable of establishing coherences that could produce an order, a progress, a history. Detached from their epiphanic function of representing things, these "formal" languages in their various applications give rise to scenarios whose relevance no longer depends on what they express but on what they render possible. These scenarios constitute a new species of fiction, scientific artifacts, which are judged not in terms of reality—which they are said to lack—but in terms of the possibilities they generate for producing or transforming reality. The "fiction" is not the photographing of the lunar space mission; it is what anticipated and organized it.

Historiography also utilizes fictions of this type when it constructs systems of correlation among unities defined as distinct and stable—for example, when it investigates the past, but applies hypotheses and scientific rules of the present, or in the case of historical econometrics, when it analyzes the probable consequences of counterfactual hypotheses (for example, the fate of slavery if the Civil War had not taken place).[3] However, historians are no less suspicious of this particular fiction cum scientific artifact. They accuse it of "destroying" historiography, as the debates over econometrics have demonstrated. Their resistance appeals once again to the method that, while supporting itself by "facts," reveals errors. But, again, the method is founded on the relationship that historians' discourse is presumed to have with the "real." In fiction, even of this kind, historians struggle against a lack of referentiality, an injury to "realist" discourse, a break in the marriage they suppose exists between words and things.

Fiction and "Univocity"

Fiction is accused, finally, of not being a "univocal" discourse, or to put it another way, of lacking scientific "univocity." In effect, fiction plays on the stratification of meaning: it narrates one thing in order to tell something else; it delineates itself in a language from which it continuously draws effects of meaning that cannot be circumscribed or checked. In contrast to an artificial language, which is "univocal" in principle, fiction has no proper place of its own. It is "metaphoric"; it moves elusively in the domain of the other. Knowledge is insecure when dealing with the problem of fiction; consequently, its effort consists of analysis (of a sort) to reduce or translate the elusive language of fiction into stable and easily combined elements. From this point of view, fiction violates one of the rules of scientificity. It is a witch whom knowledge must labor to hold and to identify through its exorcism. It no longer bears the mark of the false, of the unreal, or of the artificial. It is only a drifting meaning. It is the siren from whom the historian must defend himself, like Ulysses tied to the mast.

In fact, however, despite the quid pro quo of its different statutes, fiction, in any of its modalities—mythic, literary, scientific, or metaphorical—is a discourse that "informs" the "real" without pretending either to represent it or to credit itself with the capacity for such a representation. In this way, it is fundamentally opposed to a historiography that is always attached to an ambition to speak the "real." This ambition contains the trace of a primitive global representation of the world. It is a mythic structure whose opaque presence haunts our scientific, historical discipline. In any case, it remains essential.

This, then, is the obscure center around which revolve a number of considerations which I should like to introduce concerning the interplay of science and fiction. I shall break these down into three propositions as follows: (1) the "real" produced by historiography is also the orthodox legend of the institution of history; (2) scientific apparatus—for example, computer technology—also has a certain fictive quality in the work of historians; and (3) considering the relationship of discourse to that which produces it, that is, its relationship to a professional institution and with a scientific methodology, one can regard historiography as something of a mix of science and fiction or as a field of knowledge where questions of time and tense regain a central importance.

THE EPIC OF THE INSTITUTION

In general, every story that relates what is happening or what has happened constitutes something real to the extent that it pretends to be the representation of a past reality. It takes on authority by passing itself off as the witness of what is or of what has been. It seduces, and it imposes itself, under a title, which it pretends to interpret (for example, Nixon's last hours in the White House or the capitalist economy of the Mexican *haciendas*). In effect, every authority bases itself on the notion of the "real," which it is supposed to recount. It is always in the name of the "real" that one produces and moves the faithful. Historiography acquires this power insofar as it presents and interprets the "facts." How can readers resist discourse that tells them what is or what has been? They must agree to the law, which expresses itself in terms of events.

However, the "real" as represented by historiography does not correspond to the "real" that determines its production. It hides, behind the picture of a past, the present that produces and organizes it. Expressed bluntly, the problem is as follows: a mise en scène of a (past) actuality, that is, the historiographical discourse itself, occults the social and technical apparatus of the professional institution that produces it. The operation in question is rather sly: the discourse gives itself credibility in the name of the reality which it is supposed to represent, but this authorized appearance of the "real" serves precisely to camouflage the practice which in fact determines that appearance. Representation thus disguises the praxis that organizes it.

The Discourse and/or the Institution

The historian's discourse does not escape the constraint of those socioeconomic structures that determine the representations of a society. Indeed, by isolating itself, a specialized social group has attempted to shield this discourse from the politicization and the commercialization of those daily news stories which recount our contemporary actuality to us. This separation, which sometimes takes on an official form (a corps d'état) and sometimes a corporate form (a profession), makes possible the circumscribing of more ancient objects (a past), the setting aside of especially rare materials (that is, archives) and the codifying of procedures by the profession (that is, techniques). But all this happens not as though the general procedures for making our common "histories" or our everyday news stories (television, newspapers) had been eliminated from their laboratories but, rather, as though they were put to the test there, criticized, and verified by the historians in their experimental setting. It becomes necessary, therefore, prior to analyzing the specific techniques proper to scholarly historical research, to recall what these procedures have in common with the daily production of news stories by the media. The institutional apparatus of history itself, in supporting the researches of its members, blinds them to the ordinary practices from which they pretend to be detached.

Except in marginal cases, erudition is no longer an individual phenomenon. It is a collective enterprise. For Popper, the scientific community corrects any effects of the researcher's subjectivity. But this community is also a factory, its members distributed along assembly lines, subject to budgetary pressures (hence dependent on political decisions) and bound by the growing constraints of a sophisticated machinery (archival infrastructures, computers, publishers' demands, etc.). Its operations are determined by a rather narrow and homogeneous segment of society from which its members are recruited. Its general orientation is governed by sociocultural assumptions and postulates imposed through recruitment, through the existing and established fields of research, through the demands stemming from the personal interests of a boss, through the modes and fashions of the moment, etc. Moreover, its interior organization follows a division of labor: it has its bosses, its aristocracy, its "head research technicians" (often the foremen managing the boss's research), its technicians, its piece workers, and its clerks of all kinds for performing routine mental and physical labors. I leave aside, for the time being, the psychosociological aspects of this enterprise, for example, that recently analyzed as "the rhetoric of university respectability" by Jeanine Czubaroff.[4]

The books that are the products of this factory say nothing about how they are made, or so little as to amount to nothing. They conceal their relationship to this hierarchical, socioeconomic apparatus. For example, does the doctoral dissertation (la thèse) specify its relation to the boss (le patron) upon whom the promotion depends, or to the financial imperatives which the boss himself must obey, or to the pressures exerted by the profession on the choice of subjects for investigation and the methods to be employed? It is useless to insist. Yet one must insist that these determinants do not concern properly scientific imperatives; nor do they result from personal ideologies. But they do concern the weight of a present historical reality on discourses which speak little of this presence while blithely pretending to represent the "real."

To be sure, this historian's representation has its necessary role in a society or a group. It constantly mends the rents in the fabric that joins past and present. It ensures a "meaning," which surmounts the violence and the divisions of time. It creates a theater of references and of common values, which guarantee a sense of unity and a "symbolic" communicability to the group. Finally, as Michelet once said, it is the work of the living in order to "quiet the dead"[5] and to reunite all sorts of separated things and people into the semblance of a unity and a presence that constitutes representation itself. It is a discourse based on conjunction, which fights against all the disjunctions produced by competition, labor, time, and death. But this social task calls precisely for the occultation of everything that would particularize the representation. It leads to an avoidance in the unifying representation of all traces of the division which organizes its production. Thus, the text substitutes a representation of a past for elucidation of the present institutional operation that manufactures the historian's text. It puts an appearance of the real (past) in place of the praxis (present) that produces it, thus developing an actual case of quid pro quo.

From Scholarly Product to the Media: General Historiography
From this viewpoint, scholarly discourse is no longer distinguishable from that prolix and fundamental narrativity that is our everyday historiography. Scholarship is an integral part of the system that organizes by means of "histories" all social communication and everything that makes the present habitable. On the one hand, the book or the professional article and on on the other, the magazine or the television news are distinguishable from one another only within the same historiographical field which is constituted by the innumerable narratives that recount and interpret events. Of course, the "specialist" in history will persist in denying this compromising solidarity. But the disavowal is in vain. The scholarly side of this historiography forms only a particular species of it, a species that merely employs different techniques but is no more "technical" than other closely related species. It too belongs to the widely diffused genus of stories that explain what is happening.

Without ceasing, morning, noon, and night, history in effect "tells" its story. It gives privileged position to whatever goes badly (the event is first and foremost an accident, a misfortune, a crisis) because of an urgent need to mend these holes immediately with the thread of a language that makes sense. In a reciprocal fashion, such misfortunes generate stories; they authorize the historian's or newsmaker's tireless production of them. Not very long ago, the "real" bore the figure of a divine secret that justified the endless narrativity of its revelation. Today the "real" continues to allow an indefinite unfolding of the narrative; only now it takes the form of the event, remote or peculiar, which serves as the necessary postulate for the production of our revelatory discourse. This fragmented god never ceases to give rise to a lot of talk. He chatters incessantly—everywhere, in the news, in statistics, in polls, in documents, all of which compensate by means of a conjunctive narrative for the growing disjunction created by the division of labor, by social atomization, and by professional specialization. These informational discourses furnish a common referent to all those who are otherwise separated. In the name of the "real," they institute a symbol-creating language that generates belief in the process of communication and in what is communicated, thereby forming the tangled web of "our" history.

With regard to this general historiography, I would note three traits common to the entire genus, even though these are likely to be more visible in the species of the "media" and better controlled (or ordered in different modalities) in the "scientific" species.

First, the representation of historical realities is itself the means by which the real conditions of its own production are camouflaged. The "documentary" fails to show that it is the result, in the first place, of a selective socioeconomic institution and of a technical encoding apparatus—newspapers or television. In it everything happens as though the situation in Afghanistan merely displayed itself through the medium of Dan Rather. In fact, the situation is told to us in a story which is the product of a certain milieu, of a power structure, of contracts between a corporation and its clients, and of the logic of a certain technology. The clarity and simplicity of the information conceal the complex laws of production that govern its fabrication. It is a sort of trompe l'oeil, but different from the trompe l'oeil of old in that it no longer furnishes any visible sign of its theatrical nature or of the code whereby it is fabricated. Professional "elucidation" of the past acts in a similar way.

Second, the story which speaks in the name of the real is injunctive. It "signifies" in the same way a command is issued. In this context, the event or the problem of the day (this everyday "real") plays the same role as the divinity of old: the priests, the witnesses, or the ministers of current events make them speak in order to command in their name. To be sure, giving voice to the "real" no longer serves to reveal the secret purposes willed by a god. Henceforth, numbers and data take the place of such secrets. Yet the structure remains the same: it consists of endless dictation, in the name of the "real," of what must be said, what must be believed, and what must be done. And what can possibly be opposed to the "facts"? The law, which is given in numbers and in data (that is, in terms fabricated by technicians but presented as the manifestation of the ultimate authority, the "real") constitutes our new orthodoxy, an immense discourse of the order of things. We know that the same holds true for historiographical literature; many recent analyses show that it has always been a pedagogical discourse, and a normative and militantly nationalist one at that. But in setting forth what must be thought and what must be done, this dogmatic discourse does not have to justify itself because it speaks in the same of the "real."

Third, this storytelling has a pragmatic efficacy. In pretending to recount the real, it manufactures it. It is performative. It renders believable what it says, and it generates appropriate action. In making believers, it produces an active body of practitioners. The news of the day declares: "Anarchists are in your streets; crime is at your door!" The public responds immediately by arming and barricading itself. The news adds: "Reliable indicators show that the criminals are illegal aliens." The public searches out the guilty ones, denounces certain people, and calls for their execution or exile. The media historian's narration devaluates certain practices and assigns privilege to others; it blows conflicts out of proportion; it inflames nationalism and racism; it organizes or disengages certain forms of behavior; and it manages to produce what it says is happening. Jean-Pierre Faye has analyzed this process apropos of Nazism.[6] We know many other instances where such stories, fabricated in series, made history happen. The bewitching voices of the narration transform, reorient, and regulate the space of social relations. They exercise an immense power, but a power that eludes control because it presents itself as the only representation of what is happening or of what happened in the past. Professional history operates in an analogous way through the subjects it selects, through the problematics to which it accords privilege, through the documents and the models it employs. Under the name of science, it too arms and mobilizes a clientele of the faithful. Consequently, the political and economic powers, who often have more foresight than the historians themselves, are always striving to keep historians on their side by flattering them, paying them, directing them, controlling them, or, if need be, subduing them.

SCIENTIFICITY AND HISTORY: THE COMPUTER

In order to establish its own setting and base of power, discourse binds itself to the institutional structure that legitimates it in the eyes of the public and, at the same time, makes it dependent on the play of social forces. Corporate bodies underwrite the text or the image, providing a guarantee to readers or spectators that it is a discourse of the "real" while simultaneously, by its internal functioning, the institution articulates the mode of production on the ensemble of social practices. But there is a reciprocal exchange in the parts played by these two aspects. Representations are authorized to speak in the name of the "real" only if they are successful in obliterating any memory of the conditions under which they were produced. Now it is again the institution that manages to achieve an amalgam of these contraries. Drawing on common social conflicts, rules, and procedures, the institution constrains the activity of production, and it authorizes the occultation of this process by the very discourse that is produced. Carried out by the professional milieu, these practices can then be hidden by the representation. But is this situation really so paradoxical? After all, the exclusion from the discourse of any reference to the conditions that produced it is precisely what actually binds the group (of scholars).

Of course, this practice cannot simply be reduced to everything that makes it part of the category of general historiography. As a "scientific" practice, it has certain specific characteristics. I shall take as an example the functioning of the computer in the field of professional historiography. The computer opens up the possibility of quantitative, serial analysis of variable relationships among stable units over an extended period of time. For historians, it is tantamount to discovering the Islands of the Blessed. At last they will be able to sever historiography from its compromising relations with rhetoric, with all its metonymic and metaphorical uses of details that are supposed to be the signifying elements of the ensemble, and with all its cunning devices of oratory and persuasion. At last they are going to be able to disengage historiography from its dependence on the surrounding culture, out of which prejudgments and expectancies determine in advance certain postulates, units of study, and interpretations. Thanks to the computer, they become capable of mastering numbers, of constructing regularities, and of determining periodicities according to correlation curves—three frequent distress points in the strategy of their work. Thus, historiography becomes intoxicated with statistics. Books are now filled with numerical figures, the guarantors of certain objectivity.

But, alas, it is necessary to disenchant them, though we need not go as far as Jack Douglas or Herbert Simon, who speak of a "rhetoric of numerical figures."[7] A counterpart to the ambition of mathematizing historiography is the historicizing of that particular kind of mathematics known as statistics. We need to identify the following elements of this mathematical analysis of society: its relation to the historical conditions that made it possible; the technical reductions that it imposes methodologically and, thus, the relation between what it treats and what it is unable to take into account; and its effective functioning in the field of historiography, that is, the mode in which it is picked up and assimilated by the very discipline it is supposed to transform. This identification will involve one more way of noting the return of the fictive within a practice that is scientific.

The Necessary Conditions

Nothing seems more extraneous to the avatars through which the historian's discipline has passed than this mathematician's scientificity. In its theorizing practice, mathematics is defined by the capacity of its discourse to determine the rules of its production and to be "consistent" (without contradiction among any of its propositions), "univocal" (without ambiguity), and "constraining" (precluding by its form any denial of its content). Therefore, its writing has at its disposal a certain autonomy that makes "elegance" the internal principle of its development. Actually, its application to the analysis of society is dependent on circumstances of time and place. Despite the fact that the seventeenth-century *Theologiae . . . mathematica* by John Craig, with its "rules of evidence,"[8] already put forth the idea of calculating the probabilities of testimony, it was not until the eighteenth century that Condorcet established the foundations of a "social mathematics" and produced a calculus of "probabilities," which he thought could account for the "motives of belief" and, thus, for the practical choices made by individuals who are joined together in society.[9] Only then did the idea of mathematizable society take shape, the principle and the postulate of all subsequent analyses that take a mathematical approach to social reality.

This "idea" did not just emerge as a matter of course, although the project for a society ruled by reason goes back to Plato's *Republic*. In order for the "langue des calculs," as Condillac called it,[10] to define the discourse of a social science, it was first necessary that a society be understood as a totality composed of individual units and as an aggregate of their respective wills. Thus, "individualism" was born with modernity itself.[11] It is presupposed by any mathematical treatment of the possible relations among individual units, just as it was the necessary presupposition for the conception of a democratic society. Furthermore, three circumstantial conditions connect this idea with a particular historical conjuncture. First is progress in the techniques of mathematics (the calculus of probabilities, etc.), which cannot be dissociated from the quantitative approach to nature and to the deduction of universal laws that is characteristic of eighteenth-century science;[12] then the sociopolitical organization of an administration for rationalizing territory, centralizing information, and furnishing the model for the general management of citizens; and finally, the establishment of a bourgeois elite ideologically persuaded that its own power and the wealth of the nation would be ensured by the rationalization of society.

This triple historical determination, one technical, another sociopolitical, and a third ideological and social, was—and remains—the necessary condition for all statistical operations. In addition is the fact that today scientific progress, a national or international institutional apparatus, and a technocratic milieu combine to support the computer industry.[13] In other words, the mathematization of society does not escape history. On the contrary, it depends on new knowledge and on institutional structures and social formations, the historical implications of which are developed across the entire field of this "ahistorical" methodology.

The Reduction of History

A further point is that mathematical rigor pays the price of restricting the domain in which it can be employed. Already in Condorcet we find a threefold reduction. In his "social mathematics" Condorcet assumes that one acts according to what one believes, that belief can be reduced to a number of "motives of belief," and that these "motives" are reducible to probabilities. He wants, indeed, to carve out of the real a mathematizable object. Therefore, he leaves out of his calculation an enormous mass of material, that is, the tremendous social and psychological complexities surrounding the choices people make. His "science of strategies" assembles simulacra. What, finally, did this mathematical genius calculate about the society he pretended to analyze? The price of the rigorous novelty in his method is the transformation of its object of study into a fiction. From the end of the eighteenth century, as Peter Hanns Reill has shown in connection with the emergence of German historicism,[14] the mathematical model was rejected for the sake of evolutionism (which is concurrent with the historicization of linguistics);[15] it was restored, in history as well as elsewhere, by the macroeconomic structuralism of the twentieth century.

Today only drastic restrictions permit the use of statistics, which is still an elementary form of mathematics, in historical studies. So from the very outset of the statistical operation, one can retain only as much of the material being studied as is susceptible to arrangement in a linear series; and this kind of data favors, for example, electoral history or the history of urban planning, to the detriment of other histories, which are left to lie fallow or are relegated to amateurs. One must define the units to be treated in such a way that the statistical sign (the numbered object) is never identified with things or with words, in which case historical or semantic variations would compromise the stability of the sign and, thereby, the validity of calculations. In addition to these restrictions necessitated by the "cleaning" of the data are those imposed by the limits of the theoretical instruments themselves. For example, it would be necessary to have access to a "fuzzy logic" capable of treating categories like "a little," "rather," "perhaps," etc., categories that are characteristic of the field of history. However, despite recent research which sets out from notions of "proximity" or "distance" between objects and introduces "fuzzy" relationships into computational analysis,[16] the computer algorithms continue to be reducible to three or four formulas.

We have all witnessed the elimination of certain material from a historical study because it could not be treated in accordance with the rules imposed by this computational methodology. I could recount the transformations in historical research concerning, for example, the *Etats-Généraux* of 1614 or the *Cahiers de doléance* of 1789, objects finally rejected and placed outside the narrow field of inquiry accessible to the computer. At the elementary level of the analysis and breakdown of material into units, the mathematical operation excluded entire areas of historicity, and for its own good reasons. it creates an immense amount of refuse, rejected by the computer and piled up all around it.

Functions of the Computer

To the degree that they are honored in the actual practice of the historian, these constraints produce a technical and methodological auditing of sorts. They generate some effects of scientificity. To characterize these effects, one might say, in general, that wherever it is introduced into the computation, calculation multiplies hypotheses and enables the falsification of some among them. On the one hand, combinations among the elements that have been isolated will suggest previously unthought-of relationships. On the other, the computation of large numbers will prohibit interpretations founded on particular cases or on received ideas. There is, thus, an expansion of what is possible and a determination of what is impossible. Computation proves nothing. It increases the number of legitimate formal relations among abstractly defined elements, and it designates the hypotheses to be rejected on the grounds that they are poorly formulated, unexaminable, or contrary to the results of the analysis.[17]

But this being so, computation ceases to be fundamentally concerned with the "real." It amounts to no more than a managing of formal units. Actual history is, in fact, thrown out of its laboratories. Consequently, the reaction that the computer produces in historians is extremely ambiguous. Simultaneously, they want it and they don't want it. They at once are seduced by it and rebel against it. I do not speak here of theoretical compatibility but of a factual situation. It must have some significance. In examining how it works, we can mark out at least three aspects of the way the computer actually functions in historiographical work.

Data Storage and Analysis. In distinguishing, as one must, among the computer sciences (where statistics plays a lesser role), probability theory, statistics itself (and applied statistics), and the analysis of data, it could be said that, in general, historians confined themselves to the last sector, the quantitative treatment of data. In the field of history, the computer is used essentially to build new archives. These archives, public or private, duplicate and then eventually replace the older archives. There exist remarkable data banks, such as the Inter-University Consortium for Political and Social Research (ICPSR) of the University of Michigan at Ann Arbor; or the archival banks created in France at the *Archives Nationales* by Remi Matthieu and Ivan Cloulas (which are concerned with the administration of townships in the nineteenth century) and at the *Minutier central* of the Parisian notaries.

This extensive development of computer-assisted historical research is still restricted largely to the archivistic, which is a discipline traditionally taken to be "auxiliary" and distinguished from the interpretive work that historians reserve as their proper concern. Although in transforming documentation it also transforms the possibilities of interpretation,[18] the computer is nonetheless lodged within a particular sphere of the historiographical enterprise, at the interior of the preestablished framework that used to protect the autonomy of the historians' hermeneutics. It is permitted only an "auxiliary" place, determined once again by the old model, which would distinguish the assembling of data from the elucidation of meaning and order the techniques in a hierarchy. In principle, this pattern of work permits the historian to utilize computation without having to bow to its rules. No doubt it explains why, as Charles Tilly asserts, at the level of intellectual proceedings there have been few epistemological confrontations between mathematical and interpretive operations in the field of historiography, so that, despite tensions, porosities, and reciprocal displacements, the field maintains a sort of epistemological bilingualism.[19]

Acknowledgment of Power. Rather than employing the computer for the sake of the formal operations that it sets in motion, historians use it as a source of more solid and extensive data. The computer appears in their work in its current image of technocratic power. It is introduced into historiography by virtue of a socioeconomic reality rather than by virtue of a system of rules and hypotheses such as is proper to a scientific field. (This is the reaction of a historian, not of a mathematician.) The computer is inscribed in the historian's discourse as a massive and determinant contemporary fact.

Consequently, each book of history must include a minimal base of statistics, which both guarantees the seriousness of the study and renders homage to the power that reorganizes our productive apparatus. The two gestures, one of conformity with a contemporary technical method and the other of dedication to the reigning authority, are inseparable from each other. They are one and the same. From this point of view, the tribute that contemporary erudition pays to the computer will be the equivalent of the "Dedication to the Prince" in books of the seventeenth century: a recognition of obligation to the power that determines the overall rationality of an epoch. Today, the institution of computerized information processing, like the princely and genealogical institution of old, appears in the text under the aegis of a force that is right and takes the lead over the discourse of representation.

In relation to these two successive seats of power, historians are in the position of being equally near them and yet foreigners. They are in attendance on the computer just as in the past they were in attendance on the king (auprès du roi). They analyze and mimic operations that can be carried out only at a distance. They utilize them, but they are not in command of them. In sum, they do work in history, but they do not make history. They represent it.

Authentication. On the other hand, the historians' dedication to this scientificity accredits their texts. It plays the role of the authoritative citation. Among all the authorities to which the historiographical discourse may refer, it is this one that lends it the most legitimacy. In the final analysis, what always accredits the discourse is power, because power functions as a guarantee of the "real," in the manner in which gold bullion validates banknotes and paper money. This motive, which draws the representational discourse toward the center of power, is more fundamental than psychological or political motivations. Power today takes on the technocratic form of the computer. Therefore, to cite its operations is, thanks to this "authority," to bestow credibility on the representation. By the tribute it pays the computer, historiography produces the belief that it is not fiction. Its scientific proceedings express once again something unscientific: the homage rendered to the computer sustains an old hope of making historical discourse pass for discourse on the "real."

A corollary to this problematic of making others believe (something) by citing a source of power is the more general problematic of the "belief" that is bound to a citation of the other. The two are connected, power being the "other" of the discourse. I shall take as an example the relationship that one particular discipline maintains with another. In my own experience of collaborations between historians and computer scientists, a reciprocal illusion makes each group assume that the other discipline will guarantee what it otherwise lacks— a reference to the "real." Of the computer sciences, the historians ask to be accredited by a scientific power capable of providing a certain "serious" quality to their discourse. Of historiography, the computer scientists, disquieted by the very ease with which they are able to manipulate formal units, require some ballasting for their computations, something of the "concrete" derived from the particulars of the historian's erudition. Each plays the role in the other's field by compensating for the two conditions of all modern scientific research: its limitation, which is the renunciation of totalization, and its nature as an artificial language, which is the renunciation of the possibility of being a discourse of the "real," or of representation.

In order to come into being, a science must resign itself to a loss of both totality and reality. But whatever it has to give up in order to establish itself returns in the guise of the other, from which it continually awaits a guarantee against the lack that is at the origin of all our knowledge. The specter of a totalizing and ontological science reappears in the form of a belief in the other. The reintroduction, which is more or less marginal, of this model of science expresses the refusal of the loss and bereavement that accompanied the break between discourse (writing) and the "real" (presence). It is not surprising that historiography—which is undoubtedly the most ancient of all disciplines and the most haunted by the past—should become a privileged field for the return of this phantom. The use of the computer in the field of historiography cannot be dissociated from what it enables historians to make others believe, nor from what it presupposes they believe themselves. This superabundance (this superstition) of the past plays a part in the way historians employ modern techniques of investigation. So it is that in this very relation to scientificity, to mathematics, to the computer, historiography is "historical"—no longer in the sense that it produces an interpretation of previous epochs but in the sense that it is reproducing and recounting what modern sciences have rejected or lost and constituted as "past"—a finite, separate entity.

SCIENCE FICTION, OR THE PLACE OF TIME

This combination may be what constitutes the essence of the historical: a return of the past in the present discourse. In broader terms, this mixture (science and fiction) obscures the neat dichotomy that established modern historiography as a relation between a "present" and a "past" distinct from each other, one being the producer of the discourse and the other being what is represented by it—one the "subject," the other the "object" of a certain knowledge. This object, presumed to be exterior to the work of the laboratory, in fact determines its operations from within.

The presence of this combination is frequently treated as the effect of an archaeology that must be gradually eliminated from any true science or as a "necessary evil" to be tolerated like an incurable malady. But I believe it can also be understood as the index of a peculiar epistemological status and, therefore, of a function and scientificity to be reckoned with in its own right. If this is the case, then we must bring to light those "shameful" aspects that historiography believes it must keep hidden. The discursive formation which will then appear is an interspace (between science and fiction). It has its own norms, and these do not correspond to the usual model, which it is always transgressing but which one might like to believe, or to make others believe, it obeys. This science fiction, science and fiction, like other "heterologies," operates at the juncture of scientific discourse and ordinary language, in the same place where the past is conjugated in the present, and where questions that are not amenable to a technical approach reappear in the form of narrative metaphors. To conclude, I would like to specify a number of questions which an elucidation of this mixture of science and fiction must consider.

A Repoliticization

Our sciences were born with that "modern historical act that depoliticized research by establishing "disinterested" and "neutral" fields of study supported by scientific institutions. This act of neutralization continues in many instances to be organizing the ideology proclaimed in certain scientific communities. But the further development of what this act made possible has tended to invert its neutralizing effects. Having become actual seats of logistic power, scientific institutions have fitted themselves into the system they serve to rationalize, a system that links them to each other, fixes the direction of their research, and ensures their integration into the existing socioeconomic framework. These effects of assimilation naturally weigh most heavily on those disciplines which are the least technologically developed. And this is the case with historiography.

It is therefore necessary today to "repoliticize" the sciences, that is, to focus their technical apparatus on the fields of force within which they operate and produce their discourse. This task is preeminently that of the historian. Historiography has always been lodged at the frontier between discourse and power. It is a battlefield for a war between sense and violence. But after having believed for three or four centuries that it was possible to dominate and to observe this relation—to situate it outside of knowledge in order to make it an "object" for knowledge and to analyze it under the category of a "past"—we must recognize today that the conflict between discourse and power hangs over historiography itself and at the same time remains an integral part of it. Historical elucidation unfolds under the domination of what it treats. It must make explicit its internal and prevailing relation to power (as was the case in the past for the relation to the prince). This explication is the only means available to prevent historiography from creating simulacra. Assuming the guise of a scientific autonomy, those simulacra would have the effect of eliminating any serious treatment of the relationship that a language of sense or of communication maintains with a network of forces.

Technically, this "repoliticization" will consist in "historicizing" historiography itself. By a professional reflex, historians refer any discourse to the socioeconomic or mental conditions that produced it. They need to apply this kind of analysis to their own discourse in a manner that will make it pertinent to the elucidation of the forces that presently organize representations of the past. Their very work will then become a laboratory in which to test how a symbolic system articulates itself in a political one.

The Coming Back of Time

In this way the epistemology that would differentiate an object from the subject and, consequently, reduce time to the function of classifying objects will be modified. In historiography, the two causalities, that of the object and that of time, are connected. For three centuries, maybe the objectification of the past has made of time the unreflected-on category of a discipline that never ceases to use it as an instrument of classification. In the epistemology that was born with the Enlightenment, the difference between the subject of knowledge and its object is the foundation of what separates the past from the present. Within a socially stratified reality, historiography defined as "past" (that is, as an ensemble of alterities and of "resistances" to be comprehended or rejected) whatever did not belong to the power of producing a present, whether the power is political, social, or scientific. In other words, the "past" is the object from which a mode of production distinguishes itself in order to transform it. Historical acts transform contemporary documents into archives, or make the countryside into a museum of memorable and/or superstitious traditions. Such acts determine an opposition which circumscribes a "past" within a given society: in this way, a drive to produce establishes a relationship with what is not part—with a milieu, from which it cuts itself off; with an environment, which it must conquer; with resistances, which it encounters; etc. Its model is the relationship that a business undertakes with its raw material or with its clients, inside the same economic area. Documents of the "past" are thus connected to a productive apparatus and are treated according to its rules.

In this typical conception of the expansionist "bourgeois" economy, it is striking that time is exterior, is considered "other." Moreover, as in a monetary system, it appears only as a principle of classification in relation to those data which are situated in that exterior, objectified space. Recast in the mold of a taxonomic ordering of things, chronology becomes the alibi of time, a way of making use of time without reflecting on it, a way of banishing from the realm of knowledge the principle of death or of passing (or of metaphor). Time continues to be experienced within the productive process; but, now, transformed from within into a rational series of operations and objectified from without into a metric system of chronological units, this experience has only one language: an ethical language which expresses the imperative to produce.

Perhaps in restoring the ambiguity that characterizes relationships between object and subject or past and present, historiography could return to its traditional task—which is both a philosophical and a technical one—of articulating time as the ambivalence that affects the place from which it speaks, and thus, of reflecting on the ambiguity of place as the work of time within the space of knowledge itself. For example, the "archaic" structure that transforms the use of the computer into a metaphor, while still maintaining its technical function, makes evident an essential, temporal experience, that is, the impossibility of identifying with a given place. A "past" reappears through the very activity of historiographical production. That the "other" is already there, in place, is the very mode through which time insinuates itself.[20] Time can also return within historiographical thinking by means of a corollary modification concerning the practice and understanding of the object instead of that of place. Thus, "immediate history" can no longer distance itself from its "object," which, in fact, envelops it, controls it, and resituates it in the network of all other "histories." So, too, with "oral history" when it is not content to transcribe and exorcise those voices whose disappearance was formerly the condition of historiography. If professionals apply themselves to the task of listening to what they can see or read, they discover before them interlocutors, who, even if they are not specialists, are themselves subject/producers of histories and partners in a shared discourse. From the subject-object relationship, we pass to a plurality of authors and contracting parties. A hierarchy of knowledges is replaced by a mutual differentiation of subjects. From that moment, the particular place of the relationship that the technicians maintain with others introduces a dialectic of all these places, that is, an experience of time.

Subjects and Affects

That the particularity of the place where discourse is produced is relevant will be naturally more apparent where historiographical discourse treats matters that put the subject/producer of history into question: the history of women, of blacks, of Jews, of cultural minorities, etc. In these fields one can, of course, either maintain that the personal status of the author is a matter of indifference (in relation to the objectivity of the work) or that the author alone authorizes or invalidates the discourse (according to whether he or she is part of it or not). But this debate requires what has been concealed by an epistemology—namely, the impact of subject-to-subject relationships (women and men, blacks and whites, etc.) on the use of "neutral" techniques and in the organization of discourses that are, perhaps, equally scientific. For example, from the fact of the differentiation of the sexes, must one conclude that a woman produces a different historiography from that of a man? Of course, I do not answer this question, but I do assert that this interrogative puts the place of the subject in question and requires a treatment of it unlike the epistemology that constructed the "truth" of the work on the foundation of the speaker's irrelevance. Questioning the subject of knowledge demands that one rethink the concept of time, if it is true that the subject is constructed as a stratification of heterogeneous moments and that, whether scholars are women, blacks, or Basques, they structure the subject by their relations to the "other."[21] Time is precisely the impossibility of an identity fixed by a place. Thus begins a reflection on time. The problem of history is inscribed in the place of this subject, which is in itself a play of difference, the historicity of a nonidentity with itself.

This double movement, which, in introducing time, disturbs the security of place and of the object of historiography, also recalls the discourse of affect or of passions. After having been central in analyses of society until the end of the eighteenth century (through Spinoza, Hume, Locke, and Rousseau), the theory of passions and of interests was slowly eliminated by an objectivist economics, which, in the nineteenth century, replaced it with a rational interpretation of the relations of production, retaining only a residue of the old formulation and, thereby, anchoring the new system in the notion of "needs." After a century of being rejected, the economics of affects came back in the Freudian mode as an economics of the unconscious. With *Totem and Taboo, Civilization and Its Discontents,* and *Moses and Monotheism,* an analysis is presented, necessarily connected with an unconscious, which articulates anew the subject's investments in collective structures. Like ghosts, these affects constitute in themselves a return of the repressed in the order of a socioeconomic reasoning. They make it possible to formulate, in theory or in historiographical practice, questions which have already found expression in the work of Paul Veyne on the historian's desire,[22] of Albert Hirschman on disappointment in economics,[23] of Martin Duberman on the inscribing of the sexual subject in its historical object,[24] and of Regine Robin on the structuration of the historiographical process by the mythic scenes of childhood.[25] Studies of this kind inaugurate a different epistemology from that which defined the place of knowledge in terms of a position "proper" to itself and measured the authority of the "subject of knowledge" by the elimination of everything concerning the speaker. In making this elimination explicit, historiography returns once again to the particularities of the commonplace, to the reciprocal affects which structure representations, and to the multiple pasts which determine the use of its techniques from within.

A Scientific Myth as Ethical Discourse

The fact that identities of time, place, subject, and object assumed by classical historiography do not hold, that they have been stirred by forces that trouble them, has been for a long time underscored by the proliferation of fiction. But this is a part of historiography which is held to be shameful and illegitimate—a disreputable family member that the discipline disavows. This is all the more curious when one considers that in the seventeenth century historiography was placed at the opposite extreme: at that time, the generalist historian gloried in practicing the rhetorical genre par excellence.[26] During the space of three centuries, the discipline has passed from one pole to the other. This oscillation is already the symptom of a status. It will be necessary to specify its transformation and, in particular, to analyze the progressive differentiation which, by the eighteenth century, separated the "sciences" from the domain of "letters"; historiography was found stretched between these two domains to which it was attached by its traditional roles of "global" science and of "symbolic" social conjunction. It has remained so, albeit under different guises. But improvements in its technique and the general evolution of knowledge have increasingly led it to camouflage its links, inadmissible to scientific thought, with what had been identified during the same period of time as "literature." This camouflage is precisely what introduces into contemporary historiography the simulacra that it refuses to be.

In order to grant legitimacy to the fiction that haunts the field of historiography, we must first "recognize" the repressed, which takes the form of "literature," within the discourse that is legitimated as scientific. The ruses that the discourse must employ in its relationship to power in the hope of using that power without serving it, the manifestations of the object as a "fantastic" actor in the very place of the "subject of knowledge," the repetitions and returns of times that are supposed to be irrevocably past, the disguises of passion under the mask of reason, etc.—all concern fiction in the "literary" sense of the term. And fiction is hardly a stranger to the "real." On the contrary, as Jeremy Bentham already noted in the eighteenth century, "fictitious" discourse may be closer to the real than objective discourse.[27] But another logic comes into play here, which is not that of the positive sciences. It began to reemerge with Freud. Its elucidation will be one of the tasks of historiography. From this perspective, fiction is recognizable where there is no fixed, "univocal" position proper to itself, that is, where the "other" insinuates itself in the place of the "subject of knowledge." The central role of rhetoric in the field of historiography is precisely an important symptom of this different logic.

Envisaged then as a "discipline," historiography is a science which lacks the means of being one. Its discourse undertakes to deal with what is most resistant to scientificity (the relation of the social to the event, to violence, to the past, to death), that is, those matters each scientific discipline must eliminate in order to be constituted as a science. But in this tenuous position, historiography seeks to maintain the possibility of a scientific explanation through the textual globalization produced by a narrative synthesis. The "verisimilitude" that characterizes this discourse is its defense of a principle of explanation and of the right to a meaning. The "as if" of its reasoning (the enthymematic style of historiographical demonstration) has the value of a scientific project. It maintains a belief in the intelligibility of things that resist it the most. Thus, historiography juxtaposes elements that are inconsistent and even contradictory and often appears to "explain" them; it is through historiography that scientific models are reconnected with what is missing from them. This relating of systems to what displaces them or metaphorically transforms them corresponds as well to the way time appears to us and is experienced by us. From this perspective, historiographical discourse is, in itself, the struggle of reason with time, but of reason which does not renounce what it is as yet incapable of comprehending, a reason which is, in its fundamental workings, *ethical*. Thus it will be in the vanguard of the sciences as the present fiction of what they are only partially able to achieve. An affirmation of scientificity rules this discourse, which conjoins the explicable with the not yet explicable. What is recounted there is a fiction of science itself.

Continuing to maintain its traditional function of "conjunction," historiography links the cultural, legendary manifestations of a time to what, in these legends, is already controllable, correctable, or prohibited by technical practices. It cannot be identified with its practices, but it is produced by what those practices trace, erase, or confirm in the received language of a given milieu. The traditional model of a global, symbolizing, and legitimating discourse is thus still in evidence here, but worked by instruments and controls that belong specifically to the productive apparatus of our society. Furthermore, neither the totalizing narrativity of our culture's legends nor its technical and critical operations can be assumed to be absent or eliminated, except arbitrarily, from what finally results in a representation—the historical book or article. From this point of view, each of these representations, or the mass they form taken together, could be compared to myth if we define myth as a story permeated by social practices—that is, a global discourse articulating practices which it does not talk about but which it must respect, practices that are at once absent from its narrative and yet oversee it. Our technical practices are often as silent, as circumscribed, and as essential as were the initiation rites of the past, but henceforth they are of a scientific nature. It is in relation to these technical practices that historical discourse is elaborated, assuring them a symbolic legitimacy and, at the same time, "respecting" them. They depend on historical discourse for their social articulation, and yet they retain control over it. Thus, historical discourse becomes the one possible myth of a scientific society that rejects myths—the fiction of a social relationship between specified practices and general legends, between techniques that produce and demarcate places in society and legends that propose a symbolical ambiguity as an effect of time. I shall conclude with a formula. The very place established by procedures of control is in itself historicized by time, past or future; time is inscribed there as the return of the "other" (a relationship to power, to precedents, or to ambitions), and while "metaphorizing" the discourse of a science it turns it into the discoure of a social reciprocity and of an ethical project. While place is dogmatic, the coming back of time restores an ethics.

NOTES

1. Michel de Certeau, "La fiction de l'histoire," *L'écriture de l'histoire,* 2nd ed. (Paris: Gallimard, 1978), pp. 312–58.

2. Karl Popper, *The Logic of Scientific Discovery,* (London, Hutchinson, 1959).

3. See Ralph Andreano, ed., *La nouvelle histoire économique* (Paris: Gallimard, 1977), p. 258.

4. Jeanine Czubaroff, "Intellectual Respectability: A Rhetorical Problem," *Quarterly Journal of Speech* (1973), 59:155–64.

5. Jules Michelet, "L'héroisme de l'esprit," *L'Arc* (1869), 52:7–13.

6. Jean-Pierre Faye, *Les langages totalitaires* (Paris: Hermann, 1973).

7. Jack D. Douglas, "The Rhetoric of Science and the Origins of Statistical Social Thought," in *The Phenomenon of Sociology,* Edward A. Tiryakian, ed. (New York: Appleton-Century-Crofts, 1969), pp. 44–57; Herbert W. Simon, "Are Scientists Rhetors in Disguise? An Analysis of Discursive Processes Within Scientific Communities," in *Rhetoric in Transition,* Eugene E. White, ed. (University Park: Pennsylvania State University Press, 1980), pp. 115–30.

8. John Craig, *Theologiae christianae principia mathematica* (London, 1699); cf. the Latin text and a translation of his "rules of historical evidence" in *History and Theory,* Supplement 4, 1964.

9. Marquis de Condorcet, *Mathématique et société* (Paris: Hermann, 1974).

10. Etienne de Condillac, *Oeuvres,* vol. 23, *La langue des calculs* (Paris: C. Hovel, 1798).

11. See C. B. Macpherson, *The Political Theory of Possessive Individualism* (Oxford: Clarendon Press, 1962); and Alan Macfarlane, *The Origins of English Individualism* (Cambridge: Cambridge University Press, 1978).

12. See Morris Kline, *Mathematics in Western Culture* (New York: Oxford University Press, 1972), pp. 190–286.

13. See, for example, "IBM ou l'émergence d'une nouvelle dictature," *Les temps modernes* (October 1975), no. 351.

14. See Peter Hanns Reill, *The German Enlightenment and the Rise of Historicism* (Berkeley: University of California Press, 1975), p. 231.

15. See Michel de Certeau, Dominique Julia, and Jacques Revel, "Théorie et fiction (1760–1780): De Brosses et Court de Gébelin," *Une politique de la langue* (Paris: Gallimard, 1975), ch. 4.

16. See, for example, Charles Corge, *Informatique et démarche de l'esprit* (Paris: Larousse, 1975).

17. On the subject of computer-assisted historical analysis, see Charles Tilly, "Computers in Historical Analysis," *Computers and the Humanities* (1973), 7:323–35.

18. See François Furet, "Le quantitatif en histoire," in Jacques Le Goff and Pierre Nord, eds., *Faire de l'histoire,* vol. 1 (Paris: Gallimard, 1974), pp. 42–61.

19. Tilly, "Computers," pp. 333–34.

20. For a fuller analysis of this problem about the "return" of the past in the present, see Michel de Certeau, "Histoire et psychanalyse," in Jacques Le Goff et al., eds., *La nouvelle histoire* (Paris: CEPL, Retz, 1978), pp. 477–87.

21. The same problem poses itself at the collective level, as is shown, for example, by the difficult relationship that the new black African historiography, of a nationalist type, maintains with the ethnic plurality of its object-subject. See Bogumil Jewsiewicki, "L'histoire en Afrique et le commerce des idées usagées," *Canadian Journal of African Studies* (1979), 13:69–87.

22. Paul Veyne, *Comment on écrit l'histoire* (Paris: Seuil, 1971).

23. Albert O. Hirschman, *The Passions and the Interests: Political Arguments for Capitalism Before Its Triumph* (Princeton, N.J.: Princeton University Press, 1977).

24. Martin Duberman, *Black Mountain: An Exploration in Community* (New York: Dutton, 1973).

25. Regine Robin, *Le cheval blanc de Lénine ou l'histoire autre* (Bruxelles: Complexe, 1979).

26. See Marc Fumaroli, "Les mémoires du XVIIe siècle au carrefour des genres en prose," *XVIIe Siecle, 1971,* nos. 94–95, pp. 7–37; F. Smith Fussner, *The Historical Revolution: English Historical Writing and Thought, 1580–1740* (Westport, Conn.: Greenwood Press, 1962), pp. 299–321.

27. Jeremy Bentham's theory of linguistic fictions and of "incomplete symbols" enables him to analyze the effective operations connected with a logic of "as if"; cf. C. K. Ogden, *Bentham's Theory of Fictions* (London: Kegan Paul, 1932).

PART II

ISSUES OF FOUNDATION

Seven

METHOD AND MORALITY

Richard Rorty

What, then, is moral theory? It is all one with moral *insight,* and moral insight is the recognition of the relationships at hand. This is a very tame and prosaic conception.—John Dewey

SCIENCE WITHOUT METHOD

Galileo and his followers discovered, and subsequent centuries have amply confirmed, that you get much better predictions by thinking of things as masses of particles blindly bumping each other than by thinking of them as Aristotle thought of them—animistically, teleologically, anthropomorphically. They also discovered that you can get a better handle on the universe by thinking of it as infinite and cold and comfortless than by thinking of it as finite, homey, planned, and relevant to human concerns. Finally, they discovered that if you view planets or missiles or corpuscles as point masses, you can get nice, simple predictive laws by looking for nice, simple mathematical ratios. These discoveries are the basis of modern technological civilization. We can hardly be too grateful for them. But they do not, *pace* Descartes and Locke and Kant, point any epistemological moral. They do not tell us anything about the nature of science or rationality. In particular, they were not due to the use of, nor do they exemplify, something called "the scientific method."

The tradition we call "modern philosophy" asked itself, "How is it that science has had so much success? What is the secret of this success?" The various bad answers to these bad questions have been

A revised version of this paper appeared as "Method, Social Science, and Hope" in the *Canadian Journal of Philosophy* (December 1981), 11:569–588.

variations on a single bad metaphor; namely, that the "new science" discovered the language which nature itself uses. When Galileo said that the book of nature was written in the language of mathematics, he didn't mean that his new reductionistic, mathematical vocabulary *happened* to work; he meant that it worked *because* that was the way things *really were*. He meant that that vocabulary worked because it fit the universe as a key fits a lock. Ever since, philosophers have been trying, and failing, to give sense to these notions of "working *because*" and "things as they *really are*."

Descartes explicated these notions in terms of the natural clarity and distinctness of Galilean ideas—ideas which, for some reason, had been foolishly overlooked by Aristotle. Locke, struck by the unclarity of the notion of "clarity," thought he might have better luck with a program of reducing complex ideas to simple ideas. To make this program relevant to current science, he used an ad hoc distinction between ideas which resembled their objects and those which did not. This distinction was so dubious as to lead us, via Berkeley and Hume, to Kant's rather desperate suggestion that the key only worked because we had, behind our own backs, constructed the lock it was to fit. In retrospect, we have come to see Kant's suggestion as giving the game away. For transcendental idealism opened the back door to all the teleological, animistic, Aristotelian notions which the intellectuals had repressed for fear of being old-fashioned. The speculative idealists who succeeded Kant dropped the notion of finding nature's secrets. They substituted the notion of making worlds by creating vocabularies, a notion echoed in our century by maverick philosophers of science like Cassirer and Goodman.[1]

In an effort to avoid the so-called "excesses of German idealism," many philosophers in the last hundred years have tried to use notions like "objectivity," "rigor," and "method" to isolate science from nonscience. They have done this because they thought that the idea that we can explain scientific success in terms of discovering "nature's own language" must, somehow, be right—even if the metaphor could not be cashed, even if neither realism nor idealism could explain the imagined "correspondence" between nature's language and current scientific jargon. Very few thinkers have suggested that maybe science doesn't have a secret of success—that there is no metaphysical or epistemological or transcendental explanation of why Galileo's vocabulary has worked so well so far, any more than there is an explanation of why the vocabulary of liberal democracy has worked so well so far. Very few have been willing to abjure the notions that "the mind" or "reason" has a nature of its own, that discovery of this nature will give us a "method," and that following that method will enable us to penetrate beneath the appearances and see nature "in its own terms."

Kuhn and Dewey are among the few who have suggested that we give up the notion of science traveling toward an end called "correspondence with reality" and instead say merely that a given vocabulary works better than another for a given purpose.[2] If we accept their suggestion, we shall not be inclined to ask "What method do scientists use?" Or, more precisely, we shall say that within what Kuhn calls "normal science"—puzzle-solving—they use the same banal and obvious methods all of us use. They check off examples against criteria; they fudge the data enough to avoid the need for new models; they try out various guesses, formulated within the current jargon, in the hope of coming up with something which covers the unfudgeable cases. We shall not think there is or could be an epistemologically pregnant answer to the question, "What did Galileo do right that Aristotle did wrong?" any more than we should expect such an answer to the questions, "What did Plato do right that Xenophon did wrong?" or "What did Mirabeau do right that Louis XVI did wrong?" We shall just say that Galileo had good ideas and Aristotle less good ideas; Galileo was using some terminology that worked, and Aristotle wasn't. Galileo's terminology was the *only* "secret" he had—he didn't pick that terminology because it was "clear" or "natural" or "simple" or in line with the categories of the pure understanding, or anything else. He just lucked out.

The moral that seventeenth-century philosophers *should* have drawn from Galileo's success was a Whewellian and Kuhnian one; namely, that scientific breakthroughs are not so much a matter of deciding which of various alternative hypotheses are true but of finding the right jargon in which to frame hypotheses in the first place.[3] But, instead, as I have said, they drew the moral that the new vocabulary was the one nature had always *wanted* to be described in. I think they drew this moral for two reasons. First, they confused the fact that Galileo's vocabulary was devoid of metaphysical comfort, moral significance, and human interest with the fact that it worked. They vaguely thought that it was *because* the Galilean scientists were able to face up to the frightening abysses of infinite space that they were so successful, and identified their distance from common sense and from religious feeling—their distance from decisions about how people should live—as part of the secret of their success. So, they said, the more metaphysically comfortless and morally insignificant our vocabulary, the more likely we are to be "in touch with reality" or to be "scientific" or to describe reality as it wants to be described and thereby get it under control. Second, they thought the only way to eliminate "subjective" elements—those which might be merely part of *our* vocabulary but not of nature's—was to eschew terms which could not be definitionally linked to those in Galileo's and Newton's vocabularies, terms denoting "primary qualities."

These intertwined mistakes—the notion that a term is more likely to "refer to the real" if it is morally insignificant and if it occurs in true, predictively useful generalizations—gave substance to the idea of "method" while presupposing "an absolute conception of reality."[4] This is reality conceived not simply as "whatever it is that our representations represent" but as somehow represented apart from our representations, as it looks to itself, as it would describe itself if it could. Bernard Williams and others who take Cartesianism seriously think not only that this notion is unconfused but that it is one of our intuitions about the nature of knowledge. By contrast, I believe that it is merely one of our intuitions about what counts as being philosophical. It is the Cartesian form of the archetypal philosophical fantasy—first spun by Plato—of cutting through all description and all representation to a state of consciousness which, *per impossibile,* combines the best features of inarticulate confrontation with the best features of linguistic formulation. This fantasy of discovering, and somehow *knowing* that one has discovered, "nature's own vocabulary" seemed to become more concrete when Galileo and Newton formulated a comprehensive set of predictively useful universal generalizations, written in the language of mathematics, From their time to the present, the notions of "rationality," "method," and "science" were inextricably bound up with the search for such generalizations.

Without this model to go on, the notion of "a scientific method," in its modern sense, could not have been taken seriously. The term would have retained the sense it had in the period prior to the new science, for people like Bacon. In that sense, to have a method was simply to have a good comprehensive list of topics or headings—to have, so to speak, an efficient filing system. In its post-Cartesian philosophical sense, however, it does not mean simply ordering one's thoughts but filtering them in order to eliminate "subjective" or "noncognitive" or "confused" elements, leaving only the thoughts which are "nature's own." This distinction between the parts of one's mind which do and don't correspond to reality is, in the epistemological tradition, confused with the distinction between rational and irrational ways of doing science. If "scientific method" means merely being rational in some given area of inquiry, then it has a perfectly reasonable "Kuhnian" sense—it means obeying the normal conventions of your discipline, not fudging the data *too* much, not letting your hopes and fears influence your conclusions unless those hopes and fears are shared by all those who are in the same line of work. In this sense, "method" and "rationality" simply name a decent respect for the opinions of one's fellows. But epistemologically centered philosophy has wanted notions of "method" and "rationality" which are *not* relativized to a community at a time, notions which describe the way in which the mind is naturally fitted to learn "nature's own language."

If one believes, as I do, that the ideas of an "absolute conception of reality" and of "scientific method" are neither clear nor useful, then one will see the interlocked questions, "What should be the method of the social sciences?" and "What are the criteria of an objective moral theory?" as badly posed. In the remainder of this paper, I want to say in detail why I think these are bad questions and to recommend a Deweyan approach to both social science and morality, one which emphasizes the utility of narratives and vocabularies rather than the objectivity of laws and theories.

"VALUE-FREE" SOCIAL SCIENCE AND "HERMENEUTIC" SOCIAL SCIENCE

There has recently been a reaction against the idea that students of man and society would be "scientific" only if they remained faithful to the Galilean model—if they found "value-neutral," purely descriptive, terms in which to state their predictive generalizations and left evaluation to "policy makers." This has led to a revival of Dilthey's notion that for human beings to understand human beings "scientifically," we must apply non-Galilean methods.[5] From the point of view I wish to suggest, the whole idea of "being scientific" or of choosing between "methods" is confused. Consequently, the question about whether social scientists should seek value neutrality along Galilean lines or, rather, should try for something more cozy, Aristotelian, and "softer"—a distinctive "method of the human sciences"—seems to me misguided.

I have said that the Galilean model suggested that scientists should produce predictively useful generalizations and that they should use a descriptive terminology which lacks moral significance, preferably one "reducible to physics." But philosophers of science excuse such disciplines as paleontology and geology for offering narratives rather than laws. Nor are such disciplines asked to supply "reductions" of their vocabulary to that of chemistry or physics. This is because fossils and rocks are as good as atoms as far as "objectivity" goes. Once religious fundamentalism was set aside, nobody suspected that geologists might be substituting their own suspiciously "subjective" vocabulary for nature's. So no philosopher feels impelled to give a "rational reconstruction" of geological inquiry. Further, the fact that geology and meteorology are not much better at prediction than is psychoanalysis does not lead anybody to call them pseudo-sciences. The assurance that it is only complexity and not "subjectivity" that hampers our predictions is enough to keep them respectable. Again, in biology, where we do have both laws and accurate predictions, nobody is worried about actually giving "reductions" of the biological predicates. Occasionally we get bland assurances that the reduction could be performed if necessary, but there are no suspicions to be assuaged by actually doing so.

In fact, we could not press the notion of "reducibility" if we wanted to. There is no conceivable way in which one could give necessary and sufficient conditions for the application of a descriptive term in a "higher-level" science in the terms of a "lover-level" one (and, a fortiori, for the terms of any social science in behaviorese). Language simply does not work that way. Talk about "reducibility" survives largely because there is thought to be at least one clear case of reducibility—that of values to fact, of "ought" to "is," of evaluation to description. The post-Galilean concern for "being rigorously scientific" boils down, in practice, to concern about keeping this distinction sharp. Consequently, it has seemed natural to those who wanted a "science of man" to picture layers of "descriptive" sciences, with sociology at the top and physics at the bottom, connected by vertical relations of reducibility—with an entirely unconnected, "unscientific" level of activity ("policy making," "evaluating," etc.) separated by an ontological and methodological divide. Philosophers worry about whether sociology and political science and psychoanalysis are "scientific" while leaving paleontology and botany to do as they please because it is only at the upper levels of the "descriptive" pyramid that there is any danger of contamination from the evaluations going on nearby.

I suggest, therefore, that "physicalism," "behaviorism," and "reductionism" be set aside as outdated shibboleths and that we should focus on "descriptivism"—on the thesis that we should segregate the "evaluative" terms in a language and use their absence as one criterion for the "scientific" character of a discipline or a theory. In fact, however, this thesis is hard to make intelligible. There is, after all, no way to prevent anybody's using any term "evaluatively." Words do not intrinsically have or lack "normative" meaning. If we concentrate on use rather than meaning, we are no better off. If you ask somebody whether he is using "repression" or "primitive" or "working class" normatively or descriptively, he might be able to answer in the case of a given statement made on a given occasion. But if you ask him whether he uses the term only when he is describing, only when he is engaging in moral reflection, or both, the answer is almost always going to be "both." Further—and this is the crucial point—unless the answer *is* "both," it is just not the sort of term which will do us much good in social science. Predictions will do policy making no good if they are not phrased in the terms in which policy can be formulated.

Suppose we picture the "value-free" social scientist walking up to the divide between "fact" and "value" and handing predictions to the policy makers who live on the other side. They will not be of much use unless they contain some of the terms which the policy makers use among themselves. What the policy makers would like, presumably, are rich juicy predictions, like "If basic industry is socialized, the standard of living will (or won't) decline," "If literacy is made more widespread, more honest people will be elected to office," and so on. They would like hypothetical sentences whose consequents are phrased in the terms which might occur in morally urgent recommendations. When they get predictions phrased in the sterile jargon of "quantified" social sciences ("maximizes satisfaction," "increases conflict"), they are quite right to tune out. The only sort of policy makers who would be receptive to most of what presently passes for "behavioral science" would be the rulers of the Gulag, or of Huxley's *Brave New World,* or a conspiracy of those who personify Foucault's "forces of domination." One can excuse Foucault for reasoning that if *this* is what social science is like, then it *must* be merely an instrument of domination.[6] For only those who make policy in terms so thin as hardly to count as "moral" at all—terms which never stray far from definitional links with "pleasure," "pain," and "power"— would find such social science of use.

The issue between those who hanker after "objective," "value-free," "truly scientific" social science and those who think it should be replaced with something more hermeneutical is thus not really a quarrel about "method." It is a quarrel about the sort of terminology to be used in moral and political reflection. There is no disagreement about how to get the best predictions of what people will do under various conditions, nor about the fact that it would be very handy to know what the consequences of any given action would be. To phrase the issue as being between alternative conceptions of what it is to "understand" people or societies is, I think, an unfortunate attempt to straddle the gap between an unclear "methodological" issue and a clear moral issue. To say that something is better understood in one vocabulary than another is always an ellipsis for the claim that a description in the preferred vocabulary is most useful for a certain purpose. If the purpose is prediction, then one will want one sort of vocabulary. If it is evaluation, one may or may not want a different sort of vocabulary. (In the case of evaluating artillery fire, for example, the predictive vocabulary of mechanics will do nicely. In the case of evaluating human character, the vocabulary of stimulus and response is beside the point.)

To sum up this point, we need to disjoin two requirements on a vocabulary: (1) it contains descriptions which permit predictively useful, univeral generalizations, and (2) it contains descriptions which help one decide what to do. Value-free social science assumed that a thin "behavioristic" vocabulary would be useful for predicting human behavior. This suggestion has not panned out very well; the last fifty years of social science research has not notably increased our predictive abilities. But even if it *had* succeeded in offering predictions, this would not *necessarily* have told us whether it could be useful in deciding what to do. The debate between friends of value freedom and friends of hermeneutics has often been conducted as though to show that if a given vocabulary satisfies either requirement then it will satisfy the other. Friends of hermeneutics have protested that behaviorese was not a good vocabulary for moral reflection because it was inappropriate for "understanding" people; they argued that this inappropriateness is shown by its inability to suggest predictive laws. But it is not a good vocabulary for moral reflection anyway—for *moral* reasons. We just don't want to be the sort of policy makers who use those terms for deciding what to do to our fellow humans. Conversely, friends of value freedom, insisting that as soon as social science finds its Galileo (who is somehow known in advance to be a behaviorist) the first requirement will be satisfied, have argued that it is our duty to start making policy decisions in suitably thin terms so that our "ethics" may be "objective" and "scientifically based." For only in that way will we be able to make maximal use of all those splendid predictions which will shortly be coming our way. Both sides make the same mistake in thinking that there is some intrinsic connection between the two requirements. It is a mistake to think that when we know how to deal justly and honorably with a person or a society we have any idea of how to predict and control it, and a mistake to think the converse.

The idea that only a certain vocabulary is suited to human beings or human societies, that only that vocabulary permits them to be "understood," is the seventeenth-century myth of "nature's own vocabulary" all over again. If one sees vocabularies as instruments for coping with things rather than as representations of their intrinsic natures, then one will not think that there is an intrinsic connection or an intrinsic lack of connection between "explanation" and "understanding"—between being able to predict and control people of a certain sort and being able to sympathize and associate with them, to view them as fellow citizens. One will not think that there are two "methods"—one for explaining somebody's behavior and another for understanding his nature. One will not confuse the regulative ideal that it would be nice to have a single vocabulary which is useful for every possible purpose with the confused idea that the vocabulary of prediction or of moral deliberation (or, for that matter, of aesthetic appreciation or religious fellowship) is the one which gets people "right."

Both sides in the quarrel between "objectivity" and "hermeneutics" should realize that the natural process of give and take between the vocabulary we use for prediction and control and the one we use for moral deliberation changes both vocabularies. It changes them in unpredictable and uncontrollable, and sometimes in immoral, ways. Foucault is doubtless right that the social sciences have coarsened the moral fiber of our rulers. Something happens to politicians who are exposed to endless tabulations of income levels, rates of recidivism, cost-effectiveness of artillery fire, and the like—something like what happens to concentration camp guards. The guards in the Gulag see that nothing matters to the prisoners save bread and pain, so they cease to think of the prisoners in the terms they use for their fellow guards. The rulers of the liberal democracies come to think that nothing matters but what shows up in the expert's predictions. They cease to think of their fellow citizens *as* fellow citizens. Conversely, the friends of value freedom are doubtless right when they say that any departure from liberal *Zweckrationalität,* any attempt to avoid such hard problems of social engineering as raising income levels and lowering recidivism by thinking in "hermeneutical," "textualist" terms, is a temptation to avoid the responsibility to take hold of social forces and use them to alleviate human suffering. They are also right when they say that Nazi and Communist rhetoric depends heavily on replacing liberal jargon with Hegelian jargon. But all this simply shows that any vocabulary—liberal or Marxist, behaviorist or "critical," Greek or Christian—can be an instrument of immoral behavior. The mistake of both sides is to think that if we get—from the psychological laboratory, from the texts of Marx, from the Christian Gospels, from Heidegger—the "right" vocabulary, we shall automatically be rendered morally good.

I am not saying that we are doomed to predict in one vocabulary and deliberate in another but only that it is no disaster if we do so. For all we now know, someday we may achieve the sort of synthesis of which Dewey dreamed—a single vocabulary for all our activities, a vocabulary that contains no hint of a descriptive-normative distinction. But, in the meantime, we should not take this distinction with any great seriousness. We should look at any new development within the human sciences with two questions in mind: Does it increase our capacity to predict and control? Does it increase our sense of what it is important to consider in moral deliberation? We should avoid asking several other questions, for example, "Is it really scientific?" "Is it an instrument of domination?" or "Is it liberating?" "Is it really scientific?" is an oblique and confusing way of asking, "Does it help predict and control, and can it therefore be accepted even by those with different goals?" "Is it an instrument of domination?" is an oblique and confusing way of raising the question, "Do we need to guard against its misuse?"—a question which is as relevant to physics as to sociology. "Is it liberating?" is an oblique and confusing way of raising the question, "Does it give us a sense of what we have overlooked in our previous moral deliberations?" "Domination-vs.-liberation" is a useful moral distinction, but it only causes confusion when used within the pseudo-subject of "methodology." In particular, it causes us to think that there is something impossible or something intrinsically nasty and inhuman about trying to predict people by Galilean-style laws. But it is no easier or harder to be nasty in that style than in the style of Marx or of Freud.

EPISTEMIC AND MORAL PRIVILEGE

The current movement to make the social sciences "hermeneutical" rather than Galilean is a good thing if it is taken as meaning that narratives as well as laws, redescriptions as well as predictions, serve a useful purpose in helping us deal with the problems of society. In this sense, the movement is a useful protest against the fetishism of social scientists who worry about whether they are being "scientific." But this protest goes too far when it waxes philosophical and begins to draw a principled distinction between man and nature, announcing that the ontological difference dictates a methodological difference. When it is said, for example, that "interpretation begins from the postulate that the web of meaning constitutes human existence,"[7] this suggests that fossils, for example, might get constituted *without* a web of meaning. But once this sense of "constitution" is distinguished from the causal sense (in which houses are "constituted of" bricks), to say that "X is constituted by Y" can be reduced to the claim that you can't know anything about X without knowing a lot about Y. To say that human beings wouldn't be human, would be merely animal, unless they talked a lot is true enough. If we can't figure out the relation between a person, the noises that person makes, and other people, then we won't know much about them. But one could equally well say that fossils wouldn't be fossils, would just be rocks, if we couldn't grasp their relations to lots of other fossils. Fossils are constituted *as* fossils by a web of relationships to other fossils, and if we can't grasp some of these relationships the fossil will remain, to us, a mere rock. *Anything* is, for purposes of being inquired into, "constituted" by a web of meaning.

To put this another way, if we think of the distribution of fossils or the migratory behavior of butterflies as texts, then we can say that paleontology or zoology, at some stages, follow "interpretive" methods. That is, they cast around for some way of making sense of what is happening by looking for a vocabulary in which the puzzling object is related to other objects so as to become intelligible. Before either discipline becomes "normalized," nobody has any clear idea of what sort of thing might be relevant to predicting where similar fossils might be found or what the butterflies might do next. To say that "paleontology is now a science" means something like, "Nobody has any doubts what sorts of questions you are supposed to ask, and what sort of hypotheses you can advance, when confronted with a puzzling fossil." Similarly, to say that hermeneutical methods are not required to read the daily newspaper is to say that nobody has much doubt about what counts as a misprint, what as an expression of prejudice, and what as a pointless cliché. I believe that being "interpretive" or "hermeneutical" is not having a special method but simply casting about for a vocabulary that might help. When Galileo came up with his reductionistic and mathematized vocabulary, he was successfully concluding an inquiry which was, in the only sense I can give the term, hermeneutical. The same goes for Darwin. I do not see any interesting differences between what they were doing and what biblical exegetes, literary critics, or historians of culture do. So I think that it would do no harm to adopt the term "hermeneutics" for the sort of by-guess-and-by-God hunt for new terminology which characterizes the initial stages of any new line of inquiry.

But although this would do no harm, it also would do no particular good. It is no more useful to think of people or fossils on the model of texts than to think of texts on the model of people or of fossils. It only appears more useful if we think that there is something special about texts—for example, that they are "cultural" or "intentional" or "intelligible only holistically." But I do not think that there is a sense of "cultural" in which language users count as having a culture and butterflies do not and which is relevant to the success of inquiry into behavior. Nor do I think that "possessing intentionality" means more than "suitable to be described anthropomorphically, as if it were a language user." The relation between actions and movements, between noises and assertions, is that each is the other described in an alternative jargon. Nor do I see that explanations of fossils are less holistic than explanations of texts; in both cases, one needs to bring the object into relation with many other different sorts of objects in order to tell a coherent narrative which will incorporate the initial object.

Given this attitude, it behooves me to offer an explanation of why some people do think that texts are very different from fossils. I have suggested elsewhere in arguing against Charles Taylor,[8] that they make the mistaken assumption that somebody's *own* vocabulary is always the best vocabulary for understanding what he is doing, that his own explanation of what is going on is the one we want. This mistake seems to me part of the confused notion that natural science has, or should get hold of, the vocabulary which the universe uses to explain itself to itself. In both cases, we are thinking of our explanandum as if it were our epistemic equal or superior. But this is not always correct in the case of our fellow humans and is merely a relic of pre-Galilean anthropomorphism in the case of nature. There are, after all, cases in which the other person's, or culture's, explanation of what it is up to is so primitive or so nutty that we brush it aside. The only general hermeneutical rule is that it is always wise to ask what the subject *thinks* it is up to before formulating our own hypotheses. But this is an effort at saving time, not a search for the "true meaning" of the behavior. If the explanandum can come up with a good vocabulary for explaining its own behavior, this saves us the trouble of casting about for one ourselves. From this point of view, the only difference between an inscription and a fossil is that we can imagine coming across another inscription which is a gloss on the first, whereas the relation between the first fossil and the one next door, though perhaps equally illuminating, will be described in a nonintentional vocabulary.

In addition to the mistake of thinking that a subject's own vocabulary is always relevant to explaining it, philosophers who make a sharp distinction between man and nature are, like the positivists, bewitched by the notion that irreducibility of one vocabulary to another implies something ontological. Yet the discovery that we can or cannot reduce a language containing terms like "is about," "is true of," "refers to," etc., or one which contains "believes" or "intends" to a language which is extensional and "empiricist" would show us nothing at all about how to explain language users or intenders. Defenders of Dilthey make a simple inversion of the mistake made, for example, by Quine when he says that there can be no "fact of the matter" about intentional states of affairs because different such states can be attributed without making a difference to the behavior of the elementary particles.[9] Quine thinks that if a sentence cannot be paraphrased in the sort of vocabulary which Locke and Boyle would have liked, it does not stand for anything real. Diltheyans who exaggerate the difference between the *Geistes-* and the *Naturwissenschaften* think that the fact that it cannot be paraphrased is a hint that it represents a distinctive metaphysical or epistemic status or a need for a distinctive methodological strategy. But surely all that such irreducibility shows is that one particular vocabulary (Locke's and Boyle's) is not going to be helpful for describing certain explananda (people and cultures). This is no more metaphysically significant than, to use Putnam's analogy, the fact that if you want to know why a square peg does not fit into a round hole, you had better not describe the peg in terms of the positions of its constituent elementary particles.[10]

The reason definitional irreducibility is made such a big deal, it seems to me, is that it *is* important to make a *moral* distinction between the brutes and ourselves. Therefore, looking about for relevantly distinct behavior, we have traditionally picked our ability to know. In previous centuries, we made the mistake of hypostatizing cognitive behavior as the possession of "mind" or "consciousness" or "ideas" and then insisting on the irreducibility of mental representations to their physiological correlates. When this became *vieux jeu*, we switched from mental representations to linguistic representations. We switched from mind to language as the name of a quasi substance or quasi force which made us morally different. Thus, recent defenders of human dignity have been busy proving the irreducibility of the semantic instead of the irreducibility of the psychical. But all the Ryle-Wittgenstein sorts of arguments against the ghost in the machine work equally well against the ghost between the lines—the notion that having been penned by a human hand imparts a special something, textuality, to inscriptions, something which fossils can never have.[11]

As long as we think of knowledge as representing reality rather than as coping with reality, mind or language will continue to seem numinous, and "materialism" or "behaviorism" and the Galilean style will seem morally dubious. We shall be stuck with this notion of "representing" or "corresponding to" reality as long as we think that there is some analogy between calling things by their "right"—that is, their conventional—names and finding the "right"—that is, "nature's own"—way of describing them. But if we could abandon this metaphor and the vocabulary of representation which goes with it, as Kuhn and Dewey suggest we might, then we would not find language or mind mysterious, nor "materialism" or "behaviorism" particularly dangerous. If the line I am taking is right, we should not think of our distinctive moral status as "grounded" in our possession of mind, language, culture, feeling, intentionality, textuality, or anything else. All these numinous notions are just expressions of our awareness that we are members of a moral community, phrased in one or another pseudo-explanatory jargon. This awareness is something which cannot be further "grounded"—it is simply taking a certain point of view on our fellow humans. The question of whether it is an "objective" point of view is not to any point.

This idea can be made a bit more concrete as follows. I said that, *pace* Taylor, it was a mistake to think of somebody's own account of his behavior or culture as epistemically privileged. He might have a good account of what he is doing or he might not. But it is not a mistake to think of it as morally privileged. We have a duty to listen to his account not because he has privileged access to his own motives but because he is a human being like ourselves. Taylor's claim that we need to look for *internal* explanations of people or cultures or texts takes civility as a methodological strategy. But civility is not a method, it is simply a virtue. The reason we invite the moronic psychopath to address the court before being sentenced is not that we hope for better explanations than expert psychiatric testimony has offered. We do so because he is, after all, one of us. By asking for his own account in his own words, we hope to decrease our chances of acting badly. What we hope from the social sciences is that they will act as interpreters for those with whom we have difficulty talking. This is the same thing we hope for from our poets and dramatists and novelists. Thus, for example, the contrast which Hirschman draws between good and bad political science,[12] like Rabinow's contrast between anthropology in the manner of Geertz and in the manner of Boas,[13] seems to me a contrast between fellow feeling and moralizing condescension—between treating men as moral equals and as moral inferiors.

Just as I argued above that it is a mistake to think that there is a principled distinction between explanation and understanding or between two methods, one appropriate for nature and the other for man, I have been arguing here that the notion that we know a priori that nature and man are distinct sorts of objects is a mistake. It is a confusion between ontology and morals. There are lots of useful vocabularies with which the nonhuman-human or thing-person distinction simply does not mesh. There is at least one vocabulary—the moral—and possibly many more, for which the distinction is basic. Human beings are no more "really" described in the latter sort of vocabulary than in the former. Objects are not "more objectively" described in any vocabulary than in any other. Vocabularies are useful or useless, good or bad, helpful or misleading, sensitive or coarse, and so on; but they are not "more objective" or "less objective" nor more or less "scientific." The whole idea of an "ontological distinction" is, like that of a "methodological distinction," an attempt to do the impossible: forecast which vocabularies will be most useful in the future. Any such attempt by philosophy to tell the rest of culture the limits within which it can work is doomed. The best that can be said for such attempts is that they are confused efforts to do the morally right thing: to insist on the Christian idea that man is a "natural kind" and thus that human beings have dignity rather than mere utility.

MORALS WITHOUT PRINCIPLES

Here I want to argue that the notion of "moral theory" or "moral principle" is almost always misleading and that it has caused unnecessary confusion in our thinking about the cultural role of the social scientist and of the philosopher. Since Kant and Bentham, a genre of moral philosophy has grown up which identifies moral perfection with doing justice to others and takes for granted that we already possess the vocabulary necessary to determine whether we are doing justice to others. In this tradition, the only remaining problem for moral thought is to split the difference between Kant and Bentham—between the categorical imperative and the utilitarian principle as formulations of "the moral law."

This reduction of morality to formulating "the moral law" has two roots: the Christian and the Galilean. On the one side, it is an attempt to update and make respectable the Judeo-Christian notion that all the laws and the prophets can be summed up in respect for one's fellow humans. On the other, it is an attempt to secularize ethics by imitating Galileo's secularization of cosmology—finding nice, elegant little formulae from which one can deduce what to choose, just as Galileo gave us nice, elegant little formulae with which to predict what will happen. This Kantian symmetry between "laws of nature" and "laws of freedom" is adopted even by those who find Bentham and utilitarianism more to their taste than Kant and universalizability, just insofar as they make a distinction between "moral theory" and "empirical social science." Moral philosophy—considered as the discipline, invented by Sidgwick, which has as its task to reconcile Kant and Bentham—takes for granted that what is wanted is "directive rules of conduct" and that we know the words in which to state such rules.[14] When Aristotelians, or Kierkegaardian Christians, or Marxists, or Nietzscheans argue that there is more to moral philosophy than that—that we may not yet know the words which would permit us to deal justly with our fellows—they are said to confuse morality with something else, something "religious" or "aesthetic" or "ideological." When philosophers like Iris Murdoch protest that what is needed is not rules that synthesize the utilitarian principle and the categorical imperative but rather a morally sensitive vocabulary, they are seen as doing something rather odd and "literary," not to be confused with "moral theory."[15]

The social sciences have usually taken this Christian-Galilean notion of "moral theory" for granted. Social scientists inclined toward utilitarianism, for example, Skinner, have thought that "the theory of behavior" could just replace moral theory, since the only morally relevant factors are observable satisfaction and dissatisfaction. Those inclined toward Kant have used the jurisprudential model: the moral philosopher explains points of the moral law as the judge explains points of the civil law, whereas the social scientist, playing the role of juror, makes determinations about matters of fact, "prudential" matters. But the differences between these two conceptions are less important than their common agreement on what it would be like to have a "moral theory."

This Christian-Galilean way of looking at morality should never be mentioned without respect. It has been responsible for the triumphs of liberal democracy. It is taken for granted by such champions of human decency as John Stuart Mill, George Orwell, Andrei Sakharov, and John Rawls. These are the people who tell us that what really matters is not Kierkegaardian or Murdochian subtlety but eliminating suffering, giving human beings a chance to live in the light. But our respect for this tradition and our hope that it will endure should not blind us to the fact that moral deliberation is rarely a matter of invoking principles. It rarely conforms to the juridical model. The puzzle cases—the ones where we hope that perhaps the social sciences might finally be of some use—are ones where we grope for the correct vocabulary to describe the situation, not the ones where we are torn between the demands of two principles. The moral philosopher's fiction of live moral and political questions being resolved by finding the "morally relevant features of the situation"—that is, those that can be described in the thinnest possible vocabulary, the vocabulary in which classical moral principles are stated—should not be taken seriously.[16] It is a handy regulative idealization, like the division of function between judge and jury, but no more than that, and not a very useful one. Sidgwickian moral philosophy, like Weberian social science, has made remarkably little contribution to the solutions we have found for our moral and political problems.

If we can think of consulting this sort of "moral theory" as merely one moment in the course of deliberation and of reading through the reports of behavioral scientists as another moment, then we shall have a more realistic sense of the role which social science and philosophy play than is given by the usual judge-and-jury model (or by the notion that the social scientists can now do better through observation and experimentation what the moral philosophers once hoped to do in their studies). In particular, we shall not worry too much about just how "empirical theories of behavior" and "moral theory" are supposed to fit together, because the whole idea of "theory" will not seem as compelling as it did when theories were seen as guesses at "nature's own vocabulary," the vocabulary in which the object itself (human behavior or the moral law) has always wanted to hear itself described. To be useful for the deliberative process, both the moral principles and the predictions may have to be paraphrased in still a third vocabulary, one which we may have to whip up especially for the occasion. If we think of deliberation in this way, then we shall be able to think of Marx as well as Mill, Nabokov as well as Orwell, Solzhenitsyn as well as Sakharov, Murdoch as well as Rawls, as aiding our attempts to figure out the right thing to do.

As I am using the term "deliberation," it is simply what we do when our habits or principles leave us undecided. Then we have no clear sense of how to proceed—no "method"—and we look around. Deliberation is being "hermeneutic" about the moral situation we find ourselves in—casting about for a vocabulary which may help us decide what to do. To think of this as the *typical* moral and political situation is to give up notions of "a scientific approach to political choice" or "an objective grasp of human relationships" or "a clear distinction between description and evaluation." It does seem, to me, typical, and, consequently, I think that we need to get rid of the jargon which the Christian-Galilean tradition has constructed. We need to see moral theory as Dewey saw it, as "all one with moral *insight* . . . the recognition of the relationships at hand." Dewey spent his life campaigning against the notion that moral thought consists in looking for classical moral principles of the Bentham-Kant-Sidgwick type. He asked us to see the ability to cope with nature and the ability to do the right thing as achieved by much the same processes. He made fun of questions about "the ontological status of values" or the "epistemological status of policy judgments."

Dewey's way of looking at morals and politics chime with those of Hegel and Marx. All three insist on the need to supplement principles with vocabularies which mark out the morally relevant features of a situation. Their point is that unless we can wield terms like "citizen," "family," "state," "irresponsible," "social class," "alienated," "fanatic," "ownership," "legal," "intemperate," "neurotic," and the like, we are not going to be able to apply any moral principles. We are not going to make reasonable judgments about how to maximize pleasure, nor about which beings are to be assigned dignity rather than mere utility. They also suggest that if we have the vocabulary, we can skip the principles, since our mastery of the vocabulary shows a mastery of the ways in which our culture thinks about pleasure or about human dignity. The social philosophies of Hegel and of Dewey—

and even, I think, of Marx—are a search for human perfection, as something distinct from justice. They regard justice and the elimination of suffering as goals to be taken for granted, but they see such goals as resembling "holiness" in being too abstract to do the moral agent or the policy maker much good. Their real concern is with the possible forms of human relationships that might come to exist if we changed ourselves and our societies in various ways. They see accounts of the ways in which people are presently conducting themselves as useful chiefly in providing hints about ways in which they might conduct themselves differently. They think of moral insight as what you achieve when you grow up and stop thinking in terms of right and wrong, permitted and forbidden, legal and illegal. For them, the search for principle is a primitive stage of moral development. What counts as moral sophistication is the ability to wield complex and sensitive moral vocabularies, and thereby to create moral relevance. In their eyes, what makes the modern West morally advanced is not its clear vision of objective moral truths but its sense of new cultural and moral possibilities. Rather than borrowing from the philosophy of science the notion that we are finally discovering "nature's own moral vocabulary," Hegel and Marx and Dewey see us as making rather than finding, creating morality rather than discovering it.

If we adopt this point of view, we shall see moral philosophy as continuous with the social sciences and both as continuous with literature. We shall see all three as attempts to find ways of describing our relationships to our fellows which help us figure out what to do. We shall think that the failure of the social sciences to find Galilean-style predictive generalizations does not greatly matter and that the failure of Sidgwick-style moral philosophy to provide algorithms for resolving moral dilemmas does not greatly matter either. We shall see *Black Boy* and *An American Dilemma*, *Babbitt* and *Middletown*, as doing pretty much the same thing. We shall not see "methodological" chasms between Murdoch's essays and her novels, nor between Macauley and Tolstoy, nor between Rousseau and Schiller, nor even between Plato and Sophocles. We shall not think that by being "scientific" or "philosophical" one genre of writing can attain an "objectivity" which another, "literary," kind cannot. We shall not agree with Habermas that to avoid "relativism" we must insist on "universal truth claims."[17] We shall think of universal truths as nice to have, if we can get them, but something which we know how to get along without. We shall see the aim of all these various contributions to the deliberative process—those which aim at universal truths and succeed, those which aim at such truths and fail, and those which do not even attempt such claims—as grist for the same mill. We shall see the achievements of both the social sciences and the moral philosophy of the last hundred years as consisting not of carrying out their self-proclaimed aims but of having made us educated, liberal policy makers of the West able to talk in less reductive and less condescending terms about people very different from ourselves—people who are stupid, or crazy, or poor, or foreign, or primitive. We shall see them as, incidentally, having told us some new truths and, much more important, as having made us morally better.

NOTES

Epigraph: John Dewey, "Moral Theory and Practice," *Early Works of John Dewey*, vol. 3 (Carbondale: Southern Illinois University Press, 1972), p. 94.

1. See Ernst Cassirer, *Substance and Function* (New York: Dover Publications, 1953); and Nelson Goodman, *Ways of Worldmaking* (Indianapolis: Hackett, 1978).

2. See Thomas S. Kuhn, *The Structure of Scientific Revolutions,* 2nd ed. (Chicago: University of Chicago Press, 1970); and John Dewey, *Reconstruction in Philosophy* (New York: Mentor Books, 1950).

3. See William Whewell's criticism of John Stuart Mill's inductivism in, for example, his *Novum Organum Renovatum* (London, 1858).

4. I borrow this phrase from Bernard Williams' *Descartes: The Project of Pure Enquiry* (Harmondsworth: Penguin, 1978), p. 65.

5. For recent discussion and development of Dilthey's ideas, see Georg Henrik von Wright, *Explanation and Understanding* (London: Routledge & Kegan Paul, 1971); and Charles Taylor, "Interpretation and the Sciences of Man," *Review of Metaphysics* (1971), 25.

6. Foucault's best discussion of the role of social science as an instrument of domination is, perhaps, his *Discipline and Punish* (New York, Vintage Books, 1979).

7. Paul Rabinow and William M. Sullivan, "The Interpretive Turn: Emergence of an Approach," in Paul Rabinow and William M. Sullivan, eds., *Interpretive Social Science: A Reader* (Berkeley: University of California Press, 1979), p. 5.

8. See the symposium "What Is Hermeneutics?" with contributions by Charles Taylor, Herbert Dreyfus, and Richard Rorty, in *Review of Metaphysics* (September 1980), vol. 34.

9. See the exchange between Noam Chomsky and Willard V. O. Quine in Donald Davidson and Jaako Hintikka, eds. *Words and Objections,* (Dordrecht: Reidl, 1969); and my discussion of Quine's thesis of the "indeterminacy of the *Geisteswissenschaften*" in Richard Rorty, *Philosophy and the Mirror of Nature* (Princeton: Princeton University Press, 1979), pp. 192–209.

10. As far as I know, Putnam has used this analogy only orally and not in print. For similar antireductionist remarks, however, see Hilary Putnam, *Meaning and the Moral Sciences* (London: Routledge & Kegan Paul, 1978), pp. 55–77.

11. See Gilbert Ryle, *The Concept of Mind* (London: Hutchison, 1949), ch. 1; and Ludwig Wittgenstein, *Philosophical Investigations* (Oxford: Blackwells, 1953), secs. 412ff.

12. Cf. Albert O. Hirschman, "The Search for Paradigms as a Hindrance to Understanding," in Rabinow and Sullivan, *Interpretive Social Science*, pp. 163–79.

13. Paul Rabinow, "Humanism as Nihilism," in this volume. Unlike Rabinow, however, I see no need to go beyond Geertz, since (for reasons offered below) I see no need to avoid what Rabinow calls "a complete aesthetization of anthropology."

14. See Henry Sidgwick, *The Methods of Ethics,* 7th ed. (London: Macmillan, 1907), p. 3. Compare p. 5: "We are generally agreed that reasonable conduct in any case has to be determined on principles."

15. See Iris Murdoch, *The Sovereignty of Good* (New York: Schocken Books, 1971). Murdoch sums up the cluster of ideas which characterize Christian-Galilean moral thought as it has developed within recent analytic philosophy: "The very powerful image with which we are here presented is behaviouristic, existentialist, and utilitarian in the sense which unites these three conceptions. It is behaviorist in its connection of the meaning and being of action with the publicly observable, it is existentialist in its elimination of the substantial self and its emphasis on the solitary omnipotent will, and it is utilitarian in its assumption that morality is and can only be concerned with public acts. It is also incidentally what may be called a democratic view, in that it suggests that morality is not an esoteric achievement but a natural function of any normal man. This position represents, to put it another way, a happy and fruitful marriage of Kantian liberalism with Wittgensteinian logic solemnized by Freud" (pp. 8–9). Note, in this connection, Carol Gilligan's use of Murdoch's point of view in her essay in this volume. Much of what Gilligan criticizes in Kohlberg seems to me to stem from Kohlberg's restriction of the term "morality" to its Christian-Galilean sense.

16. For a definition and explanation of this notion of "classical moral principle," see J. B. Schneewind, "Moral Knowledge and Moral Principles," in G. A. Vesey, ed., *Knowledge and Necessity* (London: Macmillan, 1970). See also Schneewind's "Moral Problems and Moral Philosophy in the Victorian Period," in S. P. Rosenbaum, ed., *English Literature and British Philosophy* (Chicago: University of Chicago Press, 1971), especially the distinction between private and public moral problems at pp. 192ff.

17. I have tried to deal with the charge of "relativism" brought against Deweyan ways of thinking in Richard Rorty, "Pragmatism, Relativism, and Irrationalism," *Proceedings and Addresses of the American Philosophical Association* (August 1980), 53(6):719–38. I think that the attempt to avoid "relativism" by finding "universals" is, once again, the idea that someday we shall hit upon a vocabulary which bears its "objectivity"—its being "nature's own"—on its face. This vocabulary, or the principles stated in it, are fantasized to be so compelling that to be acquainted with them is sufficient to bring everyone into line, once and for all.

Eight

WITHERING NORMS: DECONSTRUCTING THE FOUNDATION OF THE SOCIAL SCIENCES

Reiner Schürmann

"The division of philosophy into 'physics,' 'ethics,' and 'logic' yields a compartmentalization. With that begins a process that comes to completion in the discipline's prevailing over the subject matter dealt with in that discipline. What belongs to the 'subject matter' is decided by the perspectives and trends of inquiry which, for the sake of its own survival, the discipline prescribes as the only possible ways of objectifying the subject matter" (*Her*, 233f).[1]

One may wonder whether the question of morality in the social sciences is one that could arise at any given moment in the history of Western reflection on human society. It seems to be typical, rather, of our postmodern era. It needs to be situated in terms of its locus in the history of what Heidegger describes as the "compartmentalization" of sciences. In what context does morality in the social sciences at all become an issue? This is a typically contemporary problem not primarily because previous generations lacked our capacity for global destruction or for recombinant DNA technology—military overkill and gene splicing, too, have their moments in history when they can appear. They too are phenomena that reveal and enforce a certain order in history; they too appear when a concrete historical process comes to completion. The very quest for a coherent and, if possible, systematic link between the problems of the human and social sciences—for example, anthropology, economics, law, and psychology (to say nothing of, more generally, technological and, more specifically, military problems)—and morality indicates a desire for a rational organization of these various fields. However, their connection seems more difficult to achieve today than that of an analogous body of disciplines at the time of Aristotle, or of the medieval *Summae,* or of Descartes' "tree of knowledge," or of Hegel's system.

If a certain disintegration has separated moral discourse from the various types of discourse in the social sciences, this loss of a center, of a focal point for knowledge, may help us understand what has happened to us since classical Greece as well as in which direction the order of phenomenal interconnectedness—and therefore of discourse—may develop in the future. The breakup of discursive unity indicated by our no longer juxtaposing "ethics" with other disciplines such as "physics" and "logic" may provide us not with a calamity but with an opportunity to reverse the predominance of discipline over subject matter; it may force us to think of the subject matter of the social sciences in a manner different from that dictated by the tradition that runs rather smoothly from Aristotle to the end of the nineteenth century. This chapter will suggest that there are good reasons—"topological" ones, to speak precisely—why it is difficult today to coordinate a moral discourse with a sociological, psychological, or anthropological one. Our ignorance in this respect may be the symptom of a historical turn as decisive as the Socratic, or at least Aristotelian, turn which inaugurated the process that Heidegger described as "objectifying the subject matter."

EPOCHAL PRINCIPLES AND THE HYPOTHESIS OF CLOSURE

"The *nomos* is not only the law but more originally the injunction contained in the dispensation of being. Only such injunction is capable of inserting man into being. Only such insertion is capable of sustaining and obligating. Otherwise, all law remains merely the artifact of human reason. More essential than establishing rules is that man find his way into the truth of being and that he dwell there. Such dwelling alone provides the experience of something we may hold on to. It is the truth of being that provides guidance for behavior" (*BWr*, pp. 238f).

It used to be the awesome task of philosophers to secure an organizing first principle on which theoreticians of ethics, politics, law, etc., could depend in order to anchor their own discourse rationally. These points of ultimate moorage provided legitimacy to the *principia,* the propositions held to be self-evident in the order of intelligibility. They also provide legitimacy to the *princeps*, the ruler or the institution retaining ultimate power in the order of authority. In a word, they provided norms. They laid out the paths by which analysis and explication were guided and which ultimately characterized a given epoch. When these first principles are questioned, however, the network of exchange that they opened becomes confused, and the order they founded declines. In Heidegger's terminology, the "truth of being" undergoes a reversal.

A principle—the sensible substance for Aristotle, the Christian God for the medievals, the *cogito* for the moderns—has its ascent, its period of reign, and then its decline and end. We can trace this cycle in a mode of phenomenal interconnectedness instituted by a first principle. Thus, we can pinpoint the *archē*, the origin, as the founding act of an era. We can also unearth the theoretical and practical foundations on which that era rested, its origin in the sense of both *principium* and *princeps*. The question is, however, whether or not we can speak of an origin from which has issued that very lineage of representations that have been considered authoritative and measure giving. Can we speak of a beginning and an end to the various guises that the awesome task of constructing a "first philosophy" or "general metaphysics" has assumed? Is the disintegration that is felt in the human and social sciences an indicator that these principles have a pedigree, a genealogy, and a necrology? I believe we have more to gain from hastening the withering away of what I call "epochal principles" than from attempts at their resuscitation.

Securing ultimate points of reference used to an an awesome task because of its practical implications: the epochal principles provided the ground on which we could justify our moral beliefs. Any representation of what is ultimate "in the order of becoming, of being, and of knowing" (Aristotle) naturally translates itself into what is held to be the true moral code. In his "Letter on Humanism," Heidegger enunciated a radical shift in analysis which allows one to speak of withering norms: before designating a "law," *nomos* designates the modality of phenomenal interconnectedness, that is, the way things, *for some time*, stand in relation to one another, the structure within which they can be experienced. This fabric of interaction is describable. For example, a university can be situated by its links (as is the case today in Europe) to state bureaucracy, political parties, ideological warfare, public funds, national prestige, etc. A few centuries ago universities were situated within a phenomenal network composed rather of rising urban centers, rural overpopulation and misery, a cosmopolitan clergy, the authority of one text and of a dead language, the promotion of a single doctrine, etc. By contrast, in the United States, to discover by what ties universities are linked to phenomena such as higher culture, industry, adolescence, and the military, one merely has to look at a campus composed, for instance, of a Rockwell Hall, Carnegie Building, Mellon Hall, Westinghouse Hall, etc.

What is scientifically possible at a given age as well as what is morally necessary depends on the general phenomenal interconnectedness and its modality as stamped by an epochal principle. The scientific "you can," no less than the moral "you ought," results from a form of domination: not of man over man, nor of class over class, but of some ultimate representation over all and any kind of discourse and action.

The first to draw a genealogy of those figures esteemed highest for an age was Nietzsche. In a single page he spelled out what has become the model for today's deconstructionists and archeologists of knowledge. Under the title "How the 'True World' Finally Became a Fable," [2] Nietzsche enumerated six states of the metaphysical first principle. At each stage it served to regulate and sanction all things knowable and doable for a time, and through these stages it progressively exhausted itself in that function. These stages were Plato's "virtuous man," Christian salvation, Kantian duty, positivism, the "free spirit" of skepticism, and finally Nietzsche's own joyful nihilism, at which stage the "true world" has become a fable. What Nietzsche saw fading away was not just any one representation of an ideal but the sequence itself of ultimate standards for thinking and acting. His "gay science" consisted in saluting the "high point of humanity" when the old quest for an unshakable and indubitable ground has come to an end and when "innocence is restored to becoming."

Nietzsche's genealogy of metaphysics allows us to further specify the concept of epochal principles. They rest entirely on the representation of a relationship which Aristotle called the *pros hen*, relation to the one. They are an entity to which knowing and doing—theory and practice—are referred as to a yardstick. Whether such a point of reference is substantive or merely formal makes no difference for the discovery of structures in phenomenal interconnectedness. In Aristotle the *pros hen* relation properly obtained only in the context of fabrication, in which all steps of manufacturing are oriented toward the object to be produced and in which the "idea" to be realized in wood or marble serves as the working measure. From the *Physics* to the *Metaphysics* occurs that *metabasis eis allo genos* (transition into another kind), that undue transposition by which the *pros hen* relationship became the heart of any first philosophy and this first philosophy a doctrine of an ultimate ground.

Nietzsche's genealogy also allows us to introduce another technical term which will serve to designate the locus to which our ignorance concerning morality in the social sciences points—"hypothesis of closure." Nietzsche's genealogy of the "ideal world" operated on the hypothesis that the centuries in which theory and practice could be measured by some one ideal yardstick had come to an end. Hence the subtitle given by him to that outline, "History of an Error."

Epochal principles and the hypothesis of closure constitute the two coordinates of Heidegger's "deconstruction [*Abbau*] of metaphysics." His indebtedness to Nietzsche is patent when Heidegger enumerates the epochal principles that in his view have ruled over Western history: "ideas, God, moral law, the authority of reason, progress, the happiness of the greatest number, culture and civilization." But his indebtedness is patent also when he places this sequence under the hypothesis of closure. Metaphysics is that historical space, he writes, wherein it becomes our destiny that these figures "lose their constructive force and become nothing" (*QCT,* p. 65). Thus, deconstruction is the method of laying bare the sequence of epochal principles under the presupposition of the hypothesis of closure. Heidegger is very cautious about this hypothesis, preferring to move "about" the line that encircles the closed field of metaphysics rather than "across" that line (*über die Linie* in the sense of *de linea* rather than of *trans lineam*) (*QB,* pp. 35f). Elsewhere, however, he clearly states that to raise the question "What is metaphysics?" already amounts, "in a certain way, to having left metaphysics behind" (*WM,* p. 9). What counts is that the method of deconstruction is a topological one: it assigns us our place, namely, on the borderline where "special metaphysics" is uprooted from "general metaphysics," the body of human and social sciences from "first philosophy," or still more generally, cultural discourse from philosophical discourse. Thus, the point of departure of this entire enterprise is not really innovative. It is the traditional wonderment before the epochs and their slippages. How is it possible to account for the fact that in the heart of an epochal enclosure (those enclosures called "polis," "Roman Empire," "Middle Ages," etc., or, according to a scarcely more discriminating division, "seventeenth," "eighteenth," or "nineteenth" centuries) certain practices are possible and even necessary, while others are not? How does it happen that a revolution was impossible in the Middle Ages? Just as an International was impossible during the French Revolution and a Cultural Revolution was impossible at the moment of the First International? Or, according to a perspective that is less alien to the question of the "principles" than it may seem, how does it happen that a Duns Scotus, although surnamed *Doctor Subtilis,* could no more write a critique of pure reason than Kant a genealogy of morals? How does it happen, in other words, that a domain of the possible and necessary is instituted, endures for a time, and then cedes under the effect of a mutation? "How does it happen?" This is a descriptive question asking for the conditions that make norms possible and that should not be confused with the etiological question, "Why is it that . . . ?" The causal solutions brought to bear on these phenomena of mutation, whether they are "speculative," "economic," or whatever, leave us unsatisfied because of the causal presupposition they cannot question—which they cannot *situate,* for this presupposition is only an epochal incidence of the *pros hen* schema.

Within the closed field of metaphysics, the constellations of phenomenal interconnectedness are governed by the representation of a most real ground. "The *principia* are such as stand in the first place, in the most advanced rank. The *principia* refer to rank and order. . . . We follow them without meditation" (*SvG,* pp. 40, 42). This is not to say that they have any efficacy of their own—an idealist construction for which Marx had already derided Proudhon: "Each principle has had its own century in which to manifest itself. The principle of authority, for example, had the eleventh century, just as the principle of individualism had the eighteenth century. Consequently, it was the century that belonged to the principle, and not the principle that belonged to the century. In other words, it was the principle that made the history."[3] No hypostatization of this kind can occur in the deconstruction, since it remains confined to describing modalities of presence. These modalities have nothing noumenal, nor are they empirical facts; the deconstruction is not a historicist enterprise. Between the Scylla of noumenal history and the Charybdis of mere historicism, it follows the middle road of the categorial.

The hypothesis of closure rests entirely on a phenomenology of technology, which, for Heidegger, is essentially ambiguous. In the global reach of technology, principial thinking comes to its fullest deployment. At the same time, this climax may signify its consummation. To Heidegger, the ambiguity of technology is suggested by the lines of the German poet Friedrich Hölderlin, "But where danger is, grows / The saving power also."[4] Technology is essentially Janus-like, looking backward with the most rigidly principial gaze ever and forward with what can be described as anarchy; backward with the gaze of reason turned into rationality and forward with the "enlightened" gaze of reason ("enlightened" in the Kantian sense of "thinking for oneself").

THE "PRINCIPLE OF ANARCHY"

"The greater the work of a thinker—which is in no way measured by the extent and number of his writings—all the richer is what remains unthought in that work, that is, what emerges for the first time thanks to it, as having not yet been thought" (*SvG*, pp. 123f).

We now are in a position to look anew at the question—better, the confessed ignorance—What is the moral significance of contemporary developments in the social sciences? Perhaps this ignorance is not accidental or due to lack of some specific power of insight. In any case, it can be paralleled with a few "confessions" of ignorance in Heidegger's writings, of which the above quotation is only one example. Other such confessions of his ignorance have to do, for instance, with the political system best suited for a technological era (*GFPJ*, 16); with the works of Plato (*QCT*, p. 18), Descartes (*EP*, p. 25), and Kant (*KPM*, p. 206); and with Heidegger's *Being and Time* (*KPM*, p. 253).

A very distinct ignorance seems to prevail at the moments of transition between epochs, at the "decisive" moments (*decidere*, Latin, "to cut off" or "to set apart"). What if the avowal of ignorance were integral to the constellation of presence in postmodernity? What if this ignorance were so necessary to the contemporary order of discourse that without such a confession, the social sciences would no longer constitute a text or a fabric governed by internal laws? The deconstruction cannot dispense with the assumption that an epochal discourse constitutes an "autonomous entity of internal dependencies."[5] Can it be said, then, that beyond the compartmentalizations which primarily serve the disciplines' own survival, the "archive" of all that is said about human society today is structured according to rules that are few in number, one of which directly concerns this ignorance? That this ignorance is closely woven into the texture of theorizing because on the level of discourse it echoes a break, a rupture, a *Kehre* ("turning") in the ways things, words, and actions enter into mutual exchange today? In Heidegger's own itinerary, the "turning" in his thinking is merely experienced as the reverberation of a turning in the order of things. He describes technology as the *Gestell,* "enframing." Referring to Hölderlin, he can say, "The essence of 'enframing' is the danger. . . . In the essence of this danger there conceals itself the possibility of a turning such that . . . with *this* turning, the truth of the coming to presence of being may expressly enter into whatever is" (*QCT,* p. 41). As we shall see, "the truth of the coming to presence of being" designates nothing more and nothing less than the withering away of the epochal principles, a modality of presence such that the "fable" of the ideal world—Heidegger's notion of *epochē*—is no longer necessary to give it coherence and cohesion. The "truth" (*alētheia*) of being designates the utterly contingent flux of interchange among things without the governance of a metaphysical first principle.

A society gets the philosophy and the social sciences it deserves. Under the sway of the *Gestell,* no one should be surprised that the analytical model has come to dominate in philosophy and the purely explanatory model in the social sciences. It is, therefore, rather superficial to lament a split between philosophy and the social sciences. In either field the calculative pull would be reversed by the "turning." Even more, the political reality in which we live, no less than analytical and behaviorist thinking, is rooted in metaphysics. It too, then, is directly challenged by the epochal reversal. So is morality. The question of morality is the question, "What ought I to do?" As the ground on which to rest a theory of action recedes, the postmodern "turning" in the way things are present to one another must appear as the moment of the greatest danger. Ever since Socrates, philosophers have consistently repeated that "virtue is knowledge," that practical reason receives its architecture from pure reason, and that *theōria,* since it is what is most noble within our reach, prescribes the routes to *praxis.* But the method of deconstruction no longer allows one to claim that *agere sequitur esse,* that action follows from being. Even worse, it not only disrupts the unity between the moral or "practical" and the scientific or "theoretical" discourse, but by depriving thinking and acting of their model or canon, it renders them both literally *an*-archic.

The method of deconstruction thus not only deprives norms of their metaphysical guarantees; it leads to the pulverization of a speculative base upon which life finds its steadiness, its legitimation, and its peace. Deconstructing metaphysics amounts to dismantling what Kant called the "doctrines" of first philosophy. The deconstruction interrupts and throws out of gear the derivations between first philosophy and practical philosophy. It does more than disjoin the ancient unity between theory and practice. It is the method of raising the question of phenomenal interconnectedness, the "question of being," in such a way that questions of action and morality already find their solution—their dissolution, rather, since the ground on which they can become a question at all is lost.

To ask, "What ought I to do?" is to speak in the vacuum of the place deserted by the successive representations of an unshakable ground. The epochal constellations of presence have always already prescribed not only the terms in which the question of morality can and must be raised (in ousiological, theological, transcendental, and linguistic terms) but also the grounds from which it can and must be answered (substance, God, *cogito,* and discursive community), as well as the types of answers that can and must be adduced (hierarchy of virtues, hierarchy of laws—divine, natural, and human—hierarchy of imperatives, and hierarchy of discursive interests: cognitive or emancipatory). The deconstruction of the historical constellations of presence thus shows that one can speak of the closed unity of the metaphysical epoch at least in one respect: the concern with *deriving* a practical or moral philosophy from a first philosophy. "Metaphysics" is then the title for that ensemble of speculative efforts with a view to an *archē* for both the theoretical and the practical discourse. In the light of the deconstruction, that ensemble appears as a closed field. The hypothesis of closure or, as we can now say, of transition toward anarchic presence, toward a mode of interconnectedness deprived of any ultimate principle, functions doubly (even though the opposition between system and history needs to be revised). It is a *systematic* closure inasmuch as the norms of action formally "proceed from" the corresponding first philosophies. And it is a *historical* closure because the deconstructionist discourse can arise only from the boundary of the era over which it is exercised. The hypothesis of closure confers its ambiguity on much of contemporary philosophizing, which is still enclosed in the problematic of ultimate roots (hence such late forms of feuds about the *archē* as the debate over value commitment and value neutrality or the debate about "is" and "ought," etc.) but already outside the fief where philosophy can secure any unshakable ground.

The hypothesis of closure also confers its radicality on the deconstructionist move: action bereft of *archē* is thinkable only at the moment when the problematic of "being"—inherited from the closed field of metaphysics but subject on its threshold to a transmutation—emerges from ontologies and dismisses them. If in the epoch of postmodernity (in short, since Nietzsche) the question of presence no longer seems capable of articulating itself as a first philosophy, and if the withering away of epochal principles makes it impossible to separate what is cognitive from what is normative or what is scientific from what is ethical, then in the epochal constellation of the twentieth century the possible discourse about society as well as the possible action in society prove to be essentially *an*-archic.

"Anarchy" is only the complement of the two premises I have advanced, namely, that (1) traditional doctrines of *praxis* refer this concept to an insurpassable first science from which proceed the schemata that are applicable to a rigorous reasoning about action, that is, to moral doctrine, and (2) in the age of the closure of metaphysics, this procession from or legitimation by a first science proves to be *epochal*—regional, dated, finite, and "finished" (in both senses of the word, complete as well as terminated). Correlatively, here anarchy refers to both the tradition and its closure. Indeed, the prime schema which practical or moral philosophy has traditionally borrowed from first philosophy is the reference to an *archē,* the *pros hen* relationship. This attributive-participative schema, when translated into the doctrines of *praxis,* results in the ordering of acts to one measure-giving focal point. Throughout history, none of the continual displacements or transferences of this focal point has destroyed the attributive, participative, and therefore normative pattern itself. The *arche* always functions in relation to action just as substance functions in relation to its accidents, imparting them sense and *telos*.

In the epoch of closure, on the other hand, the regularity of the principles that have reigned over action can be laid down. The schema of reference to an *arche* then reveals itself to be the product of a certain type of thinking, of an ensemble of philosophic rules that have their genesis, their period of glory, and their decline. Anarchy in this sense does not become operative as a concept until the moment when the great sheet of constellations that fix presence in constant presence folds up, closes in on itself. The body of social and human sciences appears without a common discourse—and action, without principle—in the age of the turning, when phenomenal interconnectedness becomes irreducible to a norm-providing paradigm. If these are the contours of the program of deconstruction, the necessity of an avowal of ignorance begins to be glimpsed: the very question of a moral criterion for the social sciences pertains to principial constructions.

The most adequate expression to cover the whole of these premises would be the "principle of anarchy." The word "anarchy," though, clearly lends itself to misunderstanding. The paradox of this expression is nonetheless instructive as well as dazzling. Is not the backbone of metaphysics—whatever the ulterior determinations by which this concept would have to be specified—the rule always to seek a first principle from which the world becomes intelligible and masterable, the rule of *scire per causas*, of establishing "principles" for thinking and doing? "Anarchy," on the other hand, now designates the withering away of such a rule, the relaxing of its hold. It designates the retrieval of the premetaphysical happening of *phyein* or *physis*. This paradox is dazzling because in two words it points within and beyond the closure of metaphysics, thus exhibiting the boundary of that closure itself. The paradox that the expression "principle of anarchy" articulates locates the deconstructionist enterprise and indicates the place where it is situated: still implanted in the problematic of *ti to on* ("What is being?") but already uprooting it from the schema of the *pros hen*, which was connate to that problematic. It is still a principle but a principle of anarchy. It is necessary to think through this contradiction. The principial reference then appears to be counteracted, both in its history and in its essence, by a force of dislocation, of plurification. The referential logos becomes "archipelagic speech" and a "pulverized poem" (*parole en archipel* and *poème pulvérisé*).[6] The deconstruction is a discourse of transition. By putting the two words "principle" and "anarchy" side by side, what is intended is to prepare oneself for this epochal transition.

The anarchy that is at issue here is the name of a history affecting the foundation of action, a history where the bedrock yields and where it becomes obvious that the principle of cohesion, be it authoritarian or rational, is no longer anything more than a blank space deprived of legislative, normative power. Anarchy expresses a destiny of decline, the decay of the principles to which Westerners since Plato have related their acts and deeds in order to anchor them and to protect them from change and doubt. Indeed, "in principle," all people do the same thing.

The avowal of ignorance concerning the moral criterion for research in the social sciences now appears more coherent, or at least better inscribed in the general unity of the epochal texture exhibited by the deconstructionist method. If, on the one hand, the question of moral criteria can become an issue only within principial modes of phenomenal interconnectedness, and if, on the other, the lineage of epochal principles comes to an end in the age of closure, then weighing the advantages and inconveniences of the different moral theories is a rather untimely way of approaching discourse in the social sciences today.

From Heidegger's writings, the inevitability of ignorance can be shown in several ways. First is the best-known factor, the opposition between thinking and knowing. In Heidegger, no dialectic links thought and knowledge; no synthesis makes it possible to pass from one to the other. "Science does not think." This opposition, inherited from Kant, establishes two territories or continents between which there is neither analogy nor even resemblance. "There is no bridge that leads from science to thought" (*BWr*, p. 349). We "think being" and its epochs, but we "know beings" and their aspects. There is a generalized ignorance, then, that strikes thought in all its advances. Heidegger invokes this necessary poverty of philosophy so conspicuously only because it is the lieutenant of a necessity within the "history of presence" (*Seinsgeschichte*).

Furthermore, for Heidegger the matter of thinking is, on the boundary line that encircles a long history, to "repeat" or retrieve presence itself, to "win back the originative experiences of metaphysics through a deconstruction of representations that have become current and empty" (*QB*, p. 93). If this long history actually reaches its end, then, in a crisis, the structure of this field gets out of order; its principles of cohesion lose their efficacy; the *nomos* of our *oikos,* the "economy" that encloses us, produces fewer and fewer certainties. The moment when an epochal threshold is crossed is inescapably one of ignorance.

Finally, the necessary ignorance concerning moral criteria and their respective merits results from the constellation of presence whose dawn is described to us as a cessation of principles, a dethroning of the very principle of epochal principles, and the beginning of an economy of passage, that is, of anarchy. In the epoch of transition, then, words, things, and actions together would constitute the public realm in such a way that their interaction is irreducible to any systematization.

Nonetheless, it must be added that the avowal of ignorance on the part of the deconstructionist is of course a feint, one that is more than strategic—unless the word "strategy" is understood not in relation to human actions and the art of coordinating them but in relation to the economies of presence. Then we see that there are strong reasons for feigning. Indeed, after having outlined the withering away of principles, it is difficult to avoid questions of the following type: How, then, is one to evaluate action at all? What is your theory of the state? of property? of law in general? What will become of defense? of our highways? . . .

Heidegger, to stay with him, makes himself scarce. After one of the most direct developments of what could be called ontological anarchy—expressed at this juncture by the concept of "life without why," borrowed from Meister Eckhart (via Angelus Silesius)—Heidegger concludes, "In the most hidden ground of his being, man truly is only if in his way he is like the rose—without why." The "without why" points beyond the closure; therefore it cannot be pursued. The brusque halt of the development—"We cannot pursue this thought any further here" (*SvG*, pp. 72f)—as well as the feigned ignorance are inevitable when "another thought" is attempted. To strengthen this point a little further, a life "without why" certainly means a life without a goal, without *telos;* also, it is said that "in the most hidden ground of his being"—hence, totally—man must be deprived of *telos.* For man to be "in his way like the rose" would be to abolish practical teleology. It is clear that the objections rebound: But without *telos* action would no longer be action. Indeed. Hence the necessity of the feint.

ANARCHIC PRESENCE AS MEASURE FOR THINKING AND ACTING

"*Poiein* takes *physis* as its measure, it is *kata physin*" (*Her*, p. 367).

The phenomenology of the technological "turning," as it reveals the cessation of modalities of presence governed by epochal principles, entails a few consequences concerning morality and the social sciences.[7] The first consequence is easiest to see and perhaps easiest to tolerate. It is a certain breakdown in the "compartmentalization" of the social and human sciences. The reason for this breakdown is, however, not the one that is frequently invoked when scientists complain about the impermeability of partitions between disciplines, namely, that man or human nature is one and that therefore the inherited division into fields of research is artificial. On the contrary, there is no unitary dream that moves the phenomenological deconstruction the way I have tried to outline it. The figure of "man" as *one* is precisely the chief epochal principle instituted with the Socratic turn, the turn due to which "the specific feature of all metaphysics consists in its being 'humanistic'" (*BWr*, p. 202). The properly principial role of man dates back merely to the beginning of modernity: "modern man is barely three hundred years old" (*Her*, p. 132). With the turn out of the epochal, principial, and metaphysical—that is to say, humanistic—history, man as one can no longer serve as the measure for discourse in the sciences called "social" and "human." What is measure-giving is rather the event of *phyein*, or, as Heidegger calls it, the *Ereignis*, the "event of appropriation." It is therefore not the unitary figure of man that leads to the observation that with the technological age, "the discipline prevails over the subject matter dealt with in that discipline." The partitions are artificial not because this subject matter is ultimately simple but because once the *epochē* is overcome, it appears, on the contrary, as irreducibly multiple.

A second consequence is the discovery that a subject matter so irreducibly multiple requires multiple modes of discourse. "Only a manifold thinking will succeed in entering the discourse that corresponds to the 'matter' of that subject matter."[8] A "plurivocity in discourse" is required to respond to "the all-playing structure of never resting transmutation" (*QB*, p. 105) in a modality of presencing no longer obfuscated by the "fiction" of an "ideal world," that is, a presencing no longer "withholding" (*epechein*) itself. The ceaseless transmutation in the constellation of presence and therefore in discourse beyond the technological closure is what Heidegger opposes to the "reification" that he deplores in the social and human sciences. There exist too few rather than too many types of discourse about "man and his society."

The third consequence is the fact that the plurification in thinking and speaking as it results from the hypothesis of closure involves a subversion—an overturn (*vertere*) from the foundations (*sub*)—that does not stop with the mere wish for discursive proliferation. The domain most thoroughly and decisively structured by the *pros hen* relation is grammar. Metaphysical thinking has to be seen as the universalization of the relation by which a predicate is attributed to a subject. This primary attributive relation is what would have to be unlearned if the borderline of the metaphysical field were at all to be transgressed (that is, if metaphysics were to be "worked through" as one surmounts, *verwindet*, grief or pain). At the end of his last public lecture, Heidegger complained about the chief obstacle. "This lecture has spoken merely in propositional statements" (*OTB*, p. 24). He suggests that all we can do is "to prepare somewhat the transmutation in our relation to language" (*OWL*, pp. 135f). "The difficulty lies in language. Our Western languages are, each in its own way, languages of metaphysical thinking. It must remain an open question whether the essence of Western languages is in itself marked with the exclusive stamp of metaphysics . . . or whether these languages offer other possibilities of utterance" (*ID*, p. 73).

A fourth consequence concerns ethics—the one domain besides grammar in which the *pros hen* relation has held sway without challenge. Aristotle enunciated the methodological teleocracy in the very first lines of the *Nicomachean Ethics*: "Every art and every inquiry, and similarly every action and pursuit, is thought to aim at some good." In all our undertakings, we aim at some *telos*. This reign of the end, couched in the question "What is the good for man?" constitutes the guiding thread of all moral research and doctrine. Without the representation of a measure-giving end, no such doctrine can be conceived.

But teleocracy cannot survive the transition toward an order of presence where "innocence is restored to becoming," to the flux, to perpetual transformation. Heidegger proposes ever new concepts and metaphors to suggest this abolition of teleocracy in action. One of these is the metaphor "woodpaths," the tracks used for the felling and cartage of timber. What is peculiar about such tracks is that they lead nowhere. "In the wood are paths which mostly wind along until they end quite suddenly in an impenetrable thicket. They are called 'woodpaths' " (*EGT*, p. 3). Like these cart tracks, doing—as opposed to making—when freed from the representations of *archē* and *telos*, would follow an itinerary that ends in the impenetrable. In Heraclitus' terms, human action would be *kata physin*, following the way things enter into mutual relations. As such, it would be irreducible to the representation of an "end for man" which sanctions the morality of his ventures.

In yet another attempt at conceptualizing the overcoming of teleocracy, Heidegger quotes Nietzsche's declaration of faith that directly contradicts the Aristotelian declaration of faith in teleology: " 'The absence of an end in itself' is our principle of faith."[9] In all of these attempts at subverting teleocracy, what is at stake is the confinement of the rule of end to the domain where it initially and genuinely obtains, namely, to fabrication. Aristotle's *Physics,* Heidegger charges, is the "foundational book of Western philosophy" (*MW*, p. 224) precisely because of the rule of end established in it—the rule of end which Aristotle translates into his key concepts of *entelecheia* and *energeia*.

The fifth and final consequence is that in attempting to answer the question, "What ought I to do?", thinking has nowhere else to turn than to itself. (Thinking is understood as pure response to *phyein*, to "coming-to-presence," "presencing," "appearing.") Indeed, after Parmenides and to a certain extent against the modern opposition between subject and object, Heidegger holds that the basic traits of thinking and those of presencing are the same. As Hannah Arendt puts it, "If there is anything in thinking that can prevent men from doing evil, it must be some property inherent in the activity itself." Moral evil does not stem from the election of some wrong end or maxim or principle. Arendt speaks of the "interconnectedness of non-thought and evil."[10] The measure for good and evil that thinking finds in itself is *physis,* the emergence out of concealedness, a measure, to be sure, that has nothing permanent. But it is a demanding measure nevertheless. "Thoughtlessness is an uncanny visitor who comes and goes everywhere in today's world" (*DTh*, p. 45). The contrary of "thinking," then, is not feeling or willing. Nor is it the body or the animal. The contrary of thinking is *hybris* or *adikia*, "extracting oneself from the transitory while" and "striking the insurrectionary pose of persistence" (*EGT*, p. 42), which is precisely the chief characteristic of all epochal principles.

The plurification of discourse and the "anarchic presence" which is its condition locate or situate the question of moral guidelines for the social sciences within the closed field of principial and "archic" thinking. From the point of view of moral theory—more precisely of the genesis of the moral law—the closure of this field can be seen as implicit already in Kant and as becoming more and more explicit with Nietzsche and Heidegger. Indeed, since the Kantian moral law is constituted or "declared" by the transcendental subject, its transgression lies ready as a possibility in its very legislation; even more, inasmuch as the subject is the "master" of what it enacts, the act of transgression is identical with the act of legislation. In Nietzsche, the moral law appears as one of the obstacles that the will to power sets up for its own preservation and enhancement. The establishment of the law is thus quite expressly already its transgression. In Heidegger, finally, the moral law has as its condition of domination the rise of principial thinking in classical Greece. As an immobilization of the flux of *phyein*, the formation of the moral law constitutes, here most evidently, its own transgression—a transgression toward that full sense of *physis* which Aristotle discarded for the sake of a "first philosophy" guided entirely by the representation of ends; a transgression, in other words, toward a mode of acting purely "according to [anarchic] presencing" (*kata physin*).

The French poet René Char may have sensed this same withering away of any measure-giving first principle at the end of the epochal economies structured by *pros hen* relations when he wrote, "Amont éclate" ("Upstream bursts").[11] And he may have felt the same urgency of hastening the fall of what remains of them so as to set free a more original multiplicity. "Cette part jamais fixée, en nous sommeillante, d'où jaillira DEMAIN LE MULTIPLE" ("That part never fixed, asleep in us, from which will surge TOMORROW THE MANIFOLD").[12]

NOTES

1. The abbreviations below, which appear in parentheses in the text, refer to Martin Heidegger's works that are available in English; all translations quoted are, however, mine.

BWr Basic Writings, David F. Krell, ed. (New York: Harper & Row, 1977).

DTh Discourse on Thinking, John M. Anderson and E. Hans Freund, trans. (New York: Harper, Torch Books, 1966).

EGT Early Greek Thinking, David F. Krell and Frank A. Capuzzi, trans. (New York: Harper & Row, 1975).

EP The End of Philosophy, Joan Stambaugh, trans. (New York: Harper & Row, 1973).

GFPJ "Only a God Can Save Us Now," David Schendler, trans., in *Graduate Faculty Philosophy Journal* (1977), 6(1):5–27.

Her Gesamtausgabe, vol. 55, *Heraklit* (Frankfurt: Vittorio Klostermann, 1979).

ID Identity and Difference, Joan Stambaugh, trans. (New York: Harper & Row, 1969).

KPM Kant and the Problem of Metaphysics, James Churchill, trans. (Bloomington: Indiana University Press, 1962).

MW "On the Being and Conception of *Physics* in Aristotle's *Physics* B, 1," Thomas Sheehan, trans., *Man and World* (1974, 7: 219–270.

OTB On Time and Being, Joan Stambaugh, trans. (New York: Harper & Row, 1972).

OWL On the Way to Language, Peter Hertz, trans. (New York: Harper & Row, 1971).

QB The Question of Being, Jean Wilde and William Kluback, trans. (New Haven: College and University Press, 1958).

QCT The Question Concerning Technology, William Lovitt, trans. (New York: Harper & Row, 1977).

SvG Der Satz vom Grund (Pfullingen: Neske, 1957).

WM "Einleitung," in *Was ist Metaphysik?* 8th ed. (Frankfurt: Vittorio Klostermann, 1960).

2. Friedrich Wilhelm Nietzsche, *The Portable Nietzsche,* Walter Kaufmann, ed. and trans. (New York: Viking, 1968), pp. 485f.

3. Karl Marx, *The Poverty of Philosophy* (New York: International Publishers, 1963), p. 115.

4. Quoted *QCT* 42.

5. See Louis Hjelmslev, *Concerning the Foundations of Linguistic Theory* (in Danish) (Copenhagen, 1943); and *Language* (in Danish) (Copenhagen, 1963).

6. René Char, *La parole en archipel* (Paris: Gallimard, 1962), the title and p. 73.

7. The five consequences mentioned here are worked out from what I find suggested in some texts by Heidegger.

8. Martin Heidegger, preface to William Richardson, *Heidegger: Through Phenomenology to Thought* (The Hague: Martinus Nijhoff, 1963), p. xxii.

9. Friedrich Nietzsche, *The Will to Power,* quoted in Martin Heidegger, *Nietzsche* (Pfullingen: Neske, 1961), 2:283.

10. Hannah Arendt, *The Life of the Mind* (New York: Harcourt Brace Jovanovich, 1977), 1:179f, cf. 4.

11. René Char, *Le nu perdu* (Paris: Gallimard, 1962), p. 48.

12. René Char, *Commune présence* (Paris: Gallimard, 1964), p. 255.

Nine

BEYOND INTERPRETATION: HUMAN AGENCY AND THE SLOVENLY WILDERNESS

Stephen G. Salkever

CONTEXTUALISM AND EMPIRICISM

Social science, like any other sort of inquiry, has always begun with a conception of its object or subject matter. In the case of social science, that object is human action, and so it seems safe to say that every social scientist presupposes a definition of what is human, an idea that serves to focus and distinguish the concerns of the social scientist from those of the logician, the physicist, or the biologist. These ideas or models of man have the character of perceptions rather than of inferences: they express insights into those aspects of our prescientific experiences of human action which should be seen as organizing and giving significance to the rest. At this very abstract level, the social scientist (like every other human inquirer) appears to face a paralyzing quandary of the kind that since Plato and Aristotle has been called an *aporia,* a logical knot or perplexity. We need a definition of the human to study humans, but we have no grounds for distinguishing an acceptable definition from an unacceptable one, since the definition is itself the only common ground we have.

But the perplexity is not as puzzling as it seems, nor should it be taken to imply that the healthiest social science is the least reflective social science. The fact that the fundamental conceptions of the human are perceptions or express perceptions does not mean that they may not be subject to justification and criticism. The following are four substantial reasons for accepting a proposed definition: (1) it relies on an essentially nonprivate experience; (2) it does not commit those who accept it to a self-contradiction; (3) it is neither trivial nor insufficiently fruitful; and (4) it does not derive its plausibility from a false or misleading analogy. These criteria are not meant to be final, and questions can be raised about each of them, both as to their epistemological basis and as to their practical value. At best, they provide a language for talking about what definitions are acceptable and why some definitions are better than others, thus serving to overcome the apparent arbitrariness of those definitions which are inevitably presupposed by any social science.

My goal here is to show that considerations stemming from the third and especially the fourth criteria suggest that the definitions of the human which underlie both the empiricist and the interpretive or contextualist[1] approaches to social science are inadequate. My contention is that a better definition is possible, one which supports the idea of a social science which is both objective and critical (or evaluative), a social science which might be called functionalist in an Aristotelian sense. Initially, I aver that the best social science must ask three questions concerning any human action or institution: how could I have predicted it? (the question of empiricists and physicists); what does it mean to the actor? (the question of contextualists and textual critics); and, most important, what is it for? (the question of functionalists and ethologists). Functionalist social science is not an entirely separate alternative to empiricism and contextualism but rather a way of preserving and encompassing both of these apparently mutually exclusive approaches to the study of humanity.

The first two criteria, nonprivacy, or commonness, and noncontradiction, or logical coherence, are fairly uncontroversial requirements for all rational discourse, although more will be said in the second part of this paper about the first criterion when I defend the theoretical foundations of a functionalist social science. But the third criterion, that the perception expressed in the basic definition be neither trivial nor insufficiently fruitful, leads directly to the heart of the empiricist-contextualist controversy that dominates current thought about the social sciences. Both sides agree that some definitions clearly fail this test like, for example, the claim that humans are featherless bipeds; however true the definition may be, it sheds absolutely no light on the questions which motivated us to take up our inquiries concerning human actions in the first place. Still, the controversy between the empiricist and contextualist conceptions is by no means easy to resolve. Since laws predicting the behavior of uniquely free or creative agents cannot be developed, the contextualist image of man is scientifically barren for empiricists. Conversely, the empiricist assumption that there is no essential difference between human and nonhuman things prevents, according to contextualists, the development of any distinctly *social* science. Each side claims that its opponent's definition blocks the way to interesting investigation: empiricists charge that the contextualists impede the formulation of universal predictive laws of human behavior, whereas contextualists charge that empiricists eliminate the possibility of understanding the full meaning of an action.[2] The controversy seems insoluble in terms of the fruitfulness criterion as such, since each side is in fact deeply suspicious of the other's notion of just what we expect from social science in the first place.

A more promising situation involving the fruitfulness condition is presented by the claim that both the empiricist and the contextualist positions are inadequate because neither sheds any light on the obviously interesting question of how to distinguish a good from a bad action. Empiricists hold that social science must be as free from moral predicates as physics, and contextualists say that moral issues are resolvable only by reference to the cultural context or system of meanings within which the action occurs. This charge, that contextualist no less than empiricist social science necessarily leads to an unilluminating value neutrality, has come largely, though not exclusively,[3] from the critical theorists of the Frankfurt school. In Habermas' terms, social science must begin with a conception of the human which will illuminate the problem of distinguishing a systematically restricted context of communication from one which is not [4] or of distinguishing a legitimate from an illegitimate system of domination.[5] A similar objection is made in Leo Strauss's complaint that the purely contextualist or interpretive social scientist "would have to bow without a murmur to the self-interpretation of his subjects," no matter how irrational or vicious these subjects may appear to be.[6] In sum, the images of man which inform both empiricist and contextualist social science bar us from making, as social scientists, any judgments concerning the relative rationality or virtue of the societies or people we seek to understand.

It might be argued that this apparent weakness of empiricism and contextualism is in fact a strength. Although these approaches provide no transcontextual basis for evaluation, they may be fruitful in bringing to our attention the fact that such evaluation is so difficult as to be practically impossible, thus leading us in the end to a criticism of the evaluative questions themselves because they are unreasonable.

Aristotle suggests this idea in the first book of the *Nicomachean Ethics,* in a passage much cited by those who would like to appropriate him, as it were, for the contextualist position: "Problems of what is noble and just, which social science [*politikē*] examines, present so much variety and irregularity that some people believe that they exist only by convention [*nomos*] and not by nature [*physis*]."[7] This is not Aristotle's last word on the subject of the possibility of evaluative objectivity; but there is no doubt that both empiricist and contextualist social science can and do provide a salutary preventive against imprudent or ethnocentric moralizing. One might even be tempted to conclude that even if these approaches are not entirely accurate, they are, from a practical standpoint, effective *pseudē kala* (noble lies). However, the moral question raised by critical theorists and others is not an illegitimate one, and its reasonableness can be defended by a consideration of the fourth criterion. Much of the persuasive force of both the empiricist and the contextualist positions derives from an acceptance of a misleading analogy, which they (as well as the proponents of critical theory) share.

The fourth criterion is directed at the metaphysical framework within which the perceptions expressed by the central definition occur. However, these perceptions are not inferences drawn from metaphysical premises but rather the perceptions of human beings who as profit maximizers or self-interpreters are viewed on the basis of the conception that human beings are interrelated with the rest of the world. The definitions express the perceptions of lines or limits between the human and the nonhuman. To use Aristotelian language, they are rational rather than sense perceptions, and their adequacy depends in part on the adequacy of the metaphysical presuppositions which provide their setting. The usefulness of this condition depends on the premise that these settings or foundations are not themselves arbitrary; they are, of course, very abstract, but since they do involve claims about the real character of the world, there is no good reason to assume at the outset that they are beyond criticism.

Since they are so abstract and general and since they concern matters which are utterly beyond sense experience, these claims are usually presented in the form of analogies: the world is like a mind, or a machine, or a body, or chaos. Both empiricists and contextualists share a common metaphysical framework, a framework that involves a mistake which infects both their conceptions of the human, to which it gives rise. Their common background turns on and derives its rhetorical power from a false analogy between animals and machines, an analogy that was fixed in the philosophical literature by Descartes, who used it as a way of illustrating the fundamental metaphysical duality of mind and body.[8] Animals, according to Descartes, cannot properly be said to *act* at all; rather, "it is Nature which acts in them, according to the arrangement of their organs; just as we see how a clock, composed only of wheels and springs, can reckon the hours and measure time more accurately than we can with all our prudence."[9] From this common and, I think, distorted beginning, the empiricist-contextualist controversy takes its bearings: empiricists claim that humans are just like animals and so can be understood by the same methods employed in measuring the performance of machines, whereas contextualists urge that humans, unlike machines, have an inward dimension of consciousness and so cannot be understood in terms suitable for understanding the behavior of animals.

The use of imagery expressing the insight in early empiricist thought that humans are animals and hence machines is well known. Two instances will illustrate this point. In Hobbes' *De Cive* we find the following: "For every man is desirous of what is good for him, and shuns what is evil, but chiefly the chiefest of natural evils which is death; and this he doth, by a certain impulsion of nature, no less than that whereby a stone moves downward."[10] Similarly, a century later, in the second book of the *Treatise*, Hume raises this question: "For is it more certain, that two flat pieces of marble will unite together, than that two young savages of different sexes will copulate?"[11] In each instance, Hobbes and Hume are attempting to specify the *way* in which nature acts on and in us for the sake of placing the science of man on the same secure footing as the natural sciences, a foundation made possible by the identification of the animal and the mechanical, the living and the nonliving. Although the monism of Hobbes and Hume appears un-Cartesian, it can be argued that the main intention (and surely the main consequence) of Cartesian dualism was to open the way for the application of the science of mechanics to the study of all of nature.[12]

A contextualist alternative to empiricist social science was developed (as a reaction to empiricism) in social and political thought at least as early as the eighteenth century. This view stressed the ways in which human beings are *agents,* self-determining actors, rather than mere animals trapped in the world of nature understood as passive *res extensa.* Such a position is clearly expressed by Rousseau in the *Second Discourse:* "Nature commands every animal, and the beast obeys. Man feels the same impetus, but he realizes that he is free to acquiesce or resist; and it is above all in the consciousness of this freedom that the spirituality of the soul is shown."[13] The moral consequences of this contextualist reaction can be seen very clearly in the work of Edmund Burke. Burke's famous contention that there are no natural rights of man, only common law rights of Englishmen, depends upon the assumption that nature is not in any way a source of value or of standards of evaluation but that ideas of good and evil are created by and derived from the rules which human beings create in the formation and maintenance of cultures (Aristotle's *nomoi*).

This idea, that moral rules are a derivative or distillate of prior cultural activity, forms the cornerstone of the (conventionalist) moral vision of contextualism and has been well expressed in this century by Michael Oakeshoot: "Moral ideals are a sediment; they have significance only so long as they are suspended in a religious or a social tradition, so long as they belong to a religious or a social life."[14] Mention of Burke and Oakeshott here should not be taken to imply that contextualism is always on the "conservative" side of every political issue. It is well to remember that Burke was not only opposed to the French Revolution but was for the same contextualist reasons opposed (unlike Marx) to British imperialism in India, to the oppression of the Irish, and to the attempt to prevent American independence. What is central to contextualist social science is not its conservatism but rather its conception of human beings as agents entirely distinct in the inwardness of their conduct from the passive and uninteresting realm of nature, the meaningless world of mere *res extensa.* My intention is not to criticize the moral or political consequences of either empiricism or contextualism but rather to suggest that a plausible alternative to both is available, an alternative whose superiority lies in depicting and promoting a social science which is both objective (because founded on determinations of a common nature) and evaluative. Such an understanding of social science can be reached only after loosening the powerful grip that the analogy between the animal and the mechanical has on our imaginations.

Before considering the character and plausibility of such a change, I would like to bring the contextualist definition of the human as active and unnatural into clearer relief by considering a poem of Wallace Stevens, "Anecdote of the Jar."[15]

I placed a jar in Tennessee,
And round it was, upon a hill.
It made the slovenly wilderness
Surround that hill.

The wilderness rose up to it,
And sprawled around, no longer wild.
The jar was round upon the ground
And tall and of a port in air.

It took dominion everywhere.
The jar was gray and bare.
It did not give of bird or bush,
Like nothing else in Tennessee.

Prior to the interposition of the jar, that archetypal human artifact, nature is simply a slovenly wilderness, busily consumed by the formless and meaningless process of reproducing birds and bushes and whatever else goes on in uncivilized places like Tennessee. Not only are the works of man utterly distinct from the works of nature, but nature itself is really nothing at all until meaning and focus is imposed on it by human intention. Humans make meanings, animals make animals. The force of the poem is to draw attention to the unbridgeable gap between the human world, the world of meaning and culture, and the natural world, the world of mechanistic process.

This is the contextualists' picture of the limit and definition of the human world, vividly portrayed in Hannah Arendt's distinction between the common human "world" built up by the words and deeds of men and the animalic life to which we are linked only by our "labor," but not at all by the thoughts and actions which are the constituents of genuinely human culture, the true subject matter of social science. Arendt writes, "And it is true that the use of the word 'animal' in the concept of *animal laborans,* as distinguished from the very questionable use of the same word in the term *animal rationale,* is fully justified. The *animal laborans* is indeed only one, at best the highest, of the animal species which populate the earth."[16] The world or, better, worlds (as opposed to mere earth) within which human beings constitute, describe, or interpret themselves through words and deeds cannot be seen from the outside, since no objective perspective or Archimedean point is available to the social scientist, who can only attempt to understand other persons as they understand themselves. Only the jar can reveal the meaning of the jar; there is no place to stand in the slovenly wilderness of birds, bushes, and other laboring animals.

For some contextualists, like Hannah Arendt and Charles Taylor, such an objective perspective is possible for the natural scientist, the measurer of *res extensa;* for others, like Richard Rorty, nature itself is only a product of human intention, and natural science simply one jar among many. For both moderate and strong contextualism, however, human agency is self-constituting and thus beyond justification and critique. For empiricism, on the other hand, "human agency" is a fiction, and human action can be conceived of and explained as just one more type of reactive behavior without reference to any supposed moral qualities. Whatever their differences, the proponents of self-definition and internality find common ground with the adherents of necessary external causality in the denial of the possibility of objective evaluation or criticism of human conduct and in the denial of the purposes of particular actions and institutions. This common ground is no accident, revealing as it does a common commitment to a metaphysical framework which defines the human relative to an unexamined acceptance of the identity of animal and machine.

But there are good reasons for questioning this acceptance. The first of these is indirect. Although all of the classic social scientists and philosophers mentioned above are committed in principle to the impossibility of transcontextual judgments of value, very few have refrained from practicing the rational justification and critique which their conception of their science would seem to forbid. Empiricists like Hobbes and Hume as well as contextualists like Nietzsche and Heidegger make practical criticisms and recommendations which depend for their meaning on the possibility of some transcontextual propositions concerning the human good or the difference between better and worse human lives. In other words, all presuppose and indeed display some conception of objective human needs, of what human life requires if it is to be fully human.[17] This tension between the self-understanding and the practice of the classic social scientists or practical philosophers (I think it is now clear that there is no good reason to distinguish between these two kinds of inquiry) suggests the reasonableness of trying to see whether some reconciliation is possible.

BEING A KIND OF ANIMAL

An evaluative social science cannot do without a conception of human needs or interests which are independent of human invention.[18] Human needs may be understood by human agents, but they cannot be created or constituted by such agents if social science is to have access to a point of view which criticizes and recommends according to its understanding of the situation. Can anything of evaluative import be said about human needs that is not simply arbitrary or a reflection of the rules and goals of particular cultures? Recently, there have been two major kinds of attempts at such a theory of needs or interests which offer some hope of a solution: structuralist and critical theories of human development, such as those of Lawrence Kohlberg and Habermas;[19] and something which might be called a naturalist approach, one which adopts some of the insights of evolutionary biology and ethology. Although the former effort is less disputed and more familiar to social scientists, the second offers a more defensible account of the human good (and so of human needs relative to that good), largely because it avoids the abstraction of man from nature.

These alternatives to contextualism and empiricism are functionalist, that is, they hold the subject matter of social science to be an organized system (whether an individual, a group, or a species) that is defined or bounded by a condition or state of that system which describes its proper or characteristic functioning or working.[20] By contrast, both contextualism and empiricism deny that there is any objective way of determining goals or proper functions. Kohlberg and Habermas, on the other hand, present positions which are functionalist (or even teleological) in the sense that they hold that human actions can be fully understood only in the light of a conception of a goal or way of life which can be called a successful realization of a

potential for humanness. For Kohlberg, this way of life is characterized by a tendency to act according to ethical rules which satisfy
certain formal requirements of a Kantian sort, such as universality
and consistency. Habermas' counterpart is the life lived by members
of an ideal community of speakers, agents who are motivated solely
by the persuasive force of their speech and whose conduct thus exemplifies the specifically human interest in autonomy and responsibility. According to Habermas, this conception of the ideally human
is not an arbitrary creation but is instead a result obtainable by a
more or less Husserlian reflection on the structure of the distinctive
human faculty, that is, language. He writes, "The human interest in
autonomy and responsibility is not mere fancy, for it can be comprehended a priori. What raises us out of nature is the only thing whose
nature we can know: *language*. Through its structure, autonomy and
responsibility are posited for us."[21]

For both Kohlberg and Habermas, the best human life (or proper
human functioning—Aristotle's *ergon*) involves a decisive transcendence of or turning away from the world of nature, the realm of external compulsion and the slovenly wilderness, to the realm of inner
direction and the Kantian community of ends in themselves.[22] This
is a noble view and one which draws much rhetorical force from the
traditions of Christian transcendence and Cartesian dualism. But
without some grounding in either an a priori reflection on the implicit
interests of rational beings (through which goals are *posited for us*)
or an empirically based universal theory of human development, both
of which grounds are subject to serious debate, the structuralist and
critical positions are in danger of reduction to the contextualist position, whose moral neutrality they hope to overcome but whose conception of man as the sole locus of meaning and intention they share.
Before we accept the necessity of conceiving the human as diamet-
rically opposed to the merely animal (because of the shared Cartesian
assumption that transcendence is the only alternative to mechanistic
materialism), we should be clearer about just what the merely animal
is.

The problem, then, is to find a non-Cartesian basis for a social science which can avoid both the reduction of human activity to reaction to nonhuman pressures which characterizes empiricism *and* the
arbitrary abstraction of man from nature characteristic of contextualism, structuralism, and critical theory. In what follows I will argue

that a more plausible theory of human nature is currently available, a theory which provides the biological foundation for a social science which is both naturalist and nonreductionist.

Modern biology is an elaboration of the Darwinian theory of evolution, a theory whose central hypothesis is that the physiological and behavioral traits of organisms develop in response to a set of adaptive pressures collectively known as natural selection. That is, within a population of living things, these traits (called phenotypes) will tend to persist over time, and on the average, these traits contribute best to the survival and reproduction within a given environment of the organisms which display them. The mechanism for the transmission of phenotypic traits from generation to generation was not known by Darwin, but since the development of Mendelian genetics and the discovery of DNA, biologists know that these traits are the visible signs of information stored in the genetic code (or genotype) of the organism. The gene itself is not a structural unit like a molecule but rather a functional unit which corresponds to a certain section of the DNA material present in the chromosomes in every cell of the organism and which in effect provides a program for the development and behavior of its bearer. Genotypic change is the result of an apparently random or blind process called mutation; the vast majority of mutations are pathological and cause the death or disability of those afflicted by them. But some mutations contribute to adaptive success and so are likely to spread throughout the population. The process of evolution is thus generally described as one of blind variation and selective retention, although "selective" here in no way implies the presence of any intending or choosing agent supervising the process.

In animals, the relationship of genotype to behavioral phenotype, of the biological starting point to the way of life of the individual animal, is not from mechanical cause to necessary effect. Evolutionary biology in effect liberates us from the Cartesian analogy by showing that many animals are not slaves to biological compulsion. By establishing a way of understanding human beings as animals without seeing animals as (or as if they were) cleverly constructed survival (or aggression or whatever) machines, contemporary biology in effect provides the theoretical basis for an evaluative social science by restoring the Aristotelian concepts of potentiality and actuality to natural science. This central thesis about the potentiating rather than determining relationship of genotype to phenotype is explained by

David Barash in the following way: "Behavior is not contained some-how within a gene, waiting to leap out like Athena, fully armored, from the head of Zeus. Rather, genes are blueprints, codes for a range of potential phenotypes. In some cases the specification may be very precise. . . . In others, the blueprint may be so general as to be al-most entirely at the disposal of experience."[23] Similarly, Edward Wilson characterizes the development of every organism as a process of "prepared learning" rather than as a set of genetically determined or controlled automatic responses to external stimuli.[24]

The tightness of the genotypic blueprint, or the narrowness of the limits within which individuals develop, varies considerably across species; in some species, such as social insects, Cartesian mecha-nism seems almost entirely appropriate. Furthermore, within species, certain phenotypic traits—such as eye color and schizophrenia in hu-mans—seem to be more firmly subject to genetic control than others. But for most mammalian species, at any rate, the behavior or way of life pursued by an individual animal is not reducible to a predictable response to forces beyond its control. Rather, the character (Aris-totle's *hexis*) or disposition of the animal to pursue certain goals in certain ways is the result of a process of development for which the genetic code provides only a potentiating beginning or a limit, a range of possibilities within which the identity of the individual is further specified by cultural or personal factors.

This indeterminacy (within limits) of individual development is es-pecially true of humans, but it is true of us because of the kind of animal we are and not because we somehow transcend animality. To say that we are animals is not at all to say that we are machines but rather to say that we are beings for whom certain fundamental and shared problems (which should be called needs rather than drives) are established by our genotype. The range of possible ways of being a particular kind or species of animal is limited by nature, but the way of life lived by an individual (the priorities, habits, and prefer-ences the individual develops) is not determined for it in advance. The extent of this indeterminacy, which provides the space within which agency comes into play, is variable across species but does not require any transcendence of the natural order; it only describes the way some animals live, humans more than any others. To understand a species is not to grasp hidden forces or drives which push its mem-bers about from place to place. Rather, it is to grasp the limits, needs, or problems that supply the setting within which members of the species lead problematic lives and the ways in which those limits are different from those pertaining to members of other species.

In the concluding section, I argue that a consideration of the nature of the human species (which can be expressed in Aristotelian terms as an understanding of the formal and final causes of human action) and of typically human problems and the materials at hand for solving these problems serves as the objective cornerstone of an evaluative social science. Before developing this point, however, let us consider whether such a social science can satisfy the first of the adequacy criteria described earlier, the requirement that the central definition of the human must not reflect some uncommon or essentially private insight. Such consideration is necessary because the idea of species or natural groupings may surely appear to be an insight of just this kind, the product of an outmoded and indefensible essentialist ontology. This problem is absolutely crucial; as Habermas says, the possibility of a social science which is Aristotelian in form, if not in content and detail, is "unthinkable without the connection to physics and metaphysics in which the basic concepts of form, substance, act, potency, final cause, and so forth are developed." The difficulty, according to Habermas, is that "today it is no longer easy to render the approach of this metaphysical mode of thought plausible."[25] Habermas' challenge is an important but not a fatal one. In the present context, the difficulty is to defend the idea that species are real or natural rather than arbitrary or wholly conventional designations. A small step in this direction may be made by a brief reflection on the curious history of the concept of "species" in modern biological thought.

Aristotle argued not only that species of living things are real rather than mere names but that such groupings are fixed and eternal.[26] The discovery in the nineteenth century that the characteristics of organisms have an evolutionary history led Darwin and most of his followers to urge that species designations were merely names imposed upon groups of individuals: individuals are real and natural; groups are conventional and arbitrary. The assumption during this period was that biologists had to choose between believing in evolution and therefore rejecting the notion of species as anything more than a mental construct, on the one hand, and believing in the natural differentiation of species and therefore rejecting evolution, on the other.[27] Given the power of the evolutionary hypothesis, it is not surprising that the triumph of evolution signaled the temporary death of species, an event which cheered individualists and caused despair among those moral philosophers who saw the rejection of the reality of species differentiation as a justification for a pathological individual egotism. But as the evolutionary framework became widely accepted, biologists began more and more to accept the notion, made plausible by the experience of studying animal life, that organisms are related to one another as groups of naturally distinct kinds or populations, which are once again called species. The only quarrel among contemporary biologists focuses on whether the boundaries which delimit species are genetic or morphological or something else.[28] The consensus of present-day biologists does not provide anything like conclusive proof of the objective status of species or natural kinds. However, it does render this premise more plausible by showing that a commitment to the view that speciation is a common feature of the natural world does not require or imply, in scientific practice at any rate, a commitment to any pre-Darwinian theory of fixity. Aristotle, for instance, may have been very wrong on the issue of historical evolution but quite right about natural kinds.

NATURE AND CULTURE: OVERCOMING THE REDUCTION/TRANSCENDENCE DILEMMA

From a biological point of view, the naturalist contention that human action is continuous with animal life (via the concepts of genotype-phenotype and species nature) provides a clear picture of the ways in which humans are different from machines and thus indicates a way of asserting that we are in important respects self-determining agents without resorting to romantic and implausible notions of human transcendence or quasidivinity. The next step is to examine some of the consequences of the naturalist understanding of human life for moral philosophy and social science. My argument is that although defining human beings as a natural kind does not provide precise answers or rules that can then be applied by social scientists, some kinds of questions or lines of inquiry are, however, better than others. I also suggest that social science must pose precisely the same questions that arise in situations of practical choice and is in that sense utterly continuous with common life while at the same time potentially critical of that life.

Before centering on the content of human nature, let us focus on what is meant by characterizing an animal in terms of its nature. Mary Midgley describes these terms as follows: "The nature of a species, then, consists in a certain range of powers and tendencies, a repertoire, inherited and forming a fairly firm characteristic pattern, though conditions after birth may vary the details quite a lot."[29] The crucial distinction here is that what we inherit, as members of a species, is a set of problems and a set of capacities (or potentials for solving these problems) and not simply one or more powerful and controlling hidden drives or motives, like aggressiveness or territoriality or libido. The characteristic problems of a species, which establish the limits within which a certain kind of life can be lived in a certain environment, are not immediately or directly perceivable at the level either of phenotype or of genotype. Instead, those problems, which partially constitute the species and are inherited rather than created by individuals, can be seen only by observing behavioral traits and attempting to say what those characteristics are for by interpreting institutions and actions as if they were proposals about how to solve those fundamental problems we want to identify.

This kind of indirect perception of basic questions by careful examination of characteristic answers can never achieve perfect precision, but the kind of understanding achieved is neither trivial nor without evaluative import. Possible answers to the question "What is it for?" can include "nothing" (as with the human appendix) or the suggestion that some common practices are inadequate solutions to the definitive problems (maladaptions). For simpler species, those for which there is very little variance among the ways of life lived by species members, fairly precise answers can be given to this functionalist question, though even with insects surprises are still possible. As the way of life of the species members becomes less regular and predictable, the constitutive problems become more difficult to specify; but in every case the life of the animal is grasped as reflecting a sort of practical inference, an attempt to develop a set of inherited potentialities in such a way as to solve a set of inherited problems. Given the genotype-phenotype model of biological potentiality, this language of intentions is not misleadingly anthropomorphic; intentionality and self-directedness are common features of animal life and are not dependent on any exclusively human or transcendent will.

Understanding behavior in this way may be called functionalist or teleological in the sense that behavior is to be understood and evaluated relative to a set of problems and potentialities posited for each animal by its nature. This functionalism is Aristotelian and does not involve the supposition of any overall natural plan or directive intelligence; nor does it require any doctrine of orthogenesis.[30] A functionalism of this kind is critical relative to a broad conception of the proper activity of the organism and thus differs decisively from what might be called the *tout comprendre, tout pardonner* functionalism of cultural relativist anthropology. It is also different from Parsonian functionalism, which has dominated much of contemporary sociology and political science, since it begins with a set of provisional and corrigible claims about objective human needs and problems rather than with a list of the characteristic or necessary functions of social or political systems. Parsonian functionalism is potentially critical, but since it generally avoids considering questions of basic human needs, its normative or critical judgments often appear to be arbitrary or merely ethnocentric, reflecting an uncritical acceptance of the ways in which human needs are met by modern Western technological societies.

Perhaps the best developed model or analogue for an adequate functionalist social science is that provided by medicine. For the physician, physical features of an individual organism become intelligible in the light of a basic conception of the problems confronting this self-directing physical system and in the light of a general sense of a healthy or well-functioning state of the organism relative to those problems.[31] To understand a patient is to understand him or her as being more or less healthy relative to some stable and objective standard of physical well-being, the kind of standard the Greeks called *aretē*. This word is now ordinarily translated "virtue," but in the political philosophy of Plato and Aristotle it refers simply to the characteristic or definitive excellence of the subject of any functional analysis. Functionalist analysis of this sort is in fact common in social science (Robert Merton's account of the way in which urban political machines serve the "latent" function of socializing new immigrants into the culture of large American cities is a good example) but is almost never recognized as such,[32] because of the supposed impossibility of speaking objectively or impartially about fundamental human needs. But the claim of the unique indefinability of the human loses much of its force once we separate the question of whether there are constitutive human needs from the question of whether humans are merely *res extensa*.

Although not impossible, the problem of understanding human nature is difficult. This difficulty stems from the point stressed by all contextualist social science, the fact that we are cultural animals, beings who are in at least some respects self-defining. This is the characteristic human trait known as pseudospeciation,[33] the universal human tendency to erect cultural and linguistic barriers between groups of conspecifics in a way which parallels the way biological evolution separates species. But from a functionalist point of view, the fact that we inherit a cultural as well as a biological tradition is the beginning of inquiry rather than the conclusion. If cultural life, or even culturally derived identity, is a universal phenotypic trait of human beings, then what is culture for? What purpose does cultural life serve relative to fundamental human needs and problems, and how well are these functions performed by different cultures or different forms of life? These needs, which we assume exist by virtue of our common humanity, can be seen only indirectly, and so we will never be in a position to achieve precise knowledge concerning them. However, some answers to the question of the human purpose or function of culture are more plausible than others.

The least plausible solution would claim that culture is simply the most efficient means of mazimizing fitness or human survival. Culture may, of course, have provided some adaptive advantage for early man over alternative ways of living, but it is also possible that culture was an adaptive disadvantage which was offset by other concomitant advantages. At any rate, is is apparent that the significance of culture for human life goes beyond survival. As Arendt says, from the point of view of individual survival "action seems a not very efficient substitute for violence, just as speech, from the viewpoint of sheer utility, seems an awkward substitute for sign language."[34] Cultural life reflects the plasticity or openness which is part of the human problem, the fact that our biologically inherited genotypic limits or range of possibilities are extremely broad, more so than those of any other animal. This essentially human need for self-definition beyond that which is provided by nature (or genotypic inheritance) is a difficulty as well as an advantage in two senses: first, because it means that we cannot do without cultural as well as natural limits in order to lead healthy lives; second, because it suggests the possibility of error in the fundamental practical inferences which these cultures exhibit. The practical inferences contained in the rules and concepts of a human cultural group differ from those made by members of other species not because they are uniquely free but rather because they are uniquely (in degree if not in kind) prone to error. There is, moreover, no remedy for this problematic quality of specifically human life: culture is something which we cannot neglect or transcend as long as we are naturally or genotypically humans; as long, in other words, as we are what Aristotle called the political animal—a being that, as Marx says in his accurate paraphrase of the Aristotelian formulation of man as *zoon politikon,* is "not merely a gregarious animal, but an animal which can individuate itself only in the midst of society."[35]

The need for culture thus reflects not only the need for survival but a need for (or a natural lack of) identity and personal coherence which is unique or uniquely sharp in humans. However, cultures are not all equally successful in solving the problem of identity; the choices and limits implicit in our cultural inheritance may be more or less correct in their assessment of what, under the circumstances, constitutes the best human way of life. That is, the plasticity of our nature means that we must set priorities for ourselves concerning which of many possible goals should be pursued, in which order, and in what way. The answer to this problem of priorities is a claim (made by our culture) about how our lives should be organized; each culture, therefore, can be read as making a claim (sometimes clear and univocal, sometimes ambiguous) about what the best human life is or about human virtue. The problem of virtue (or how we should live) exists for all animals but is especially problematic in humans, given the lack of specific instructions in our genotype, and it is this problem that cultures in effect (or function) attempt to solve. But these solutions are neither arbitrary nor always correct; the fact that human nature is plastic must not be taken to imply its nonexistence. As Midgley says, "All moral doctrines, all practical suggestions about how we ought to live, depend on some belief about what human nature is like. . . . Very often these beliefs are wrong. When they are so, they are often evolutionarily implausible. Some understanding of ourselves as an animal species can therefore help us to avoid subscribing to them."[36] The point to be made here is that cultural life serves a necessary function in the development of a specifically human form of life and that the work of inherited or traditional cultures in the development of human individuals is therefore both indispensable *and* corrigible or criticizable.

Cultural rules need not, then, be seen as constituting our world from scratch. Rather, they reflect judgments about what, given natural and environmental limits, human flourishing or virtue is like and about how to develop and support it in a particular place and time—judgments, in other words, about both the ends and the means of human life. Since they are judgments of this sort rather than free creations, they are subject to criticism and justification by us as social scientists and as citizens insofar as we are capable of making similar judgments based on similar considerations. This capacity for making sound judgments about goals or ends can be called rationality (as distinct from the strictly instrumental intelligence by which we select the best means to already posited ends) and is a capability which is uniquely powerful, though perhaps not utterly unique,[37] in humans. Both individual rationality and culture (or the process which Aristotle calls habituation or character formation) are ways of completing the development of a healthy or virtuous human being (or the reverse), a development which is begun by the genotypic instructions which we all share by virtue of biological evolution. Neither culture nor critical rationality is by itself sufficient for the development of virtuous human beings; without culture, reason would simply have too much work to do, whereas without rationality, the goals we pursue are neither fully nor securely our own. To say that habitual or traditional culture is simply a stage on the way to an utterly independent rationality, as Marx thought, has the character of a prayer rather than a sound assessment of human possibility.

Perhaps the best cultures are those which demand neither too much nor too little exercise of human rationality. In Aristotelian terms, every culture (or *polis*) must provide a way of solving the problems of survival and reproduction (of living, *zēn*), of friendship and harmony (of living together, *suzēn*), and of individual rationality (living well, *eu zēn*). There is no one ideal or simply best culture or way of life, since environmental and social circumstances will partially determine the alternatives possible for any given culture. Sometimes the problems of survival or those of internal harmony or trust (problems of cultural integration) will be so great as to leave little room for the development of rational individuals. The irreducible variety of settings within which the problem of establishing a coherent order of priorities must be solved means that the objective basis which an understanding of the constitutive problems and possibilities of human nature provides takes the form of a hierarchy of ends or goals (such as *zēn, suzēn* and *eu zēn*) but not that of a set of universally valid or applicable rules of action.[38] Both good political judgment and good social science must combine a sense of natural developmental goals with a sense of the options available in the cultural context which is the focus of either our action or our analysis.

Insofar as this understanding of human nature is correct, it allows us to see that any social science (or any culture) which neglects one aspect of the human problem (survival, community, or rationality) for the sake of addressing another will be inadequate. In this sense, contextualist social science is inadequate because it stresses the problems of community at the expense of those concerning individual rationality. Kohlberg's stage six (his highest stage of development, in which orientation to choice and action is in terms of abstract universal ethical principles) and Habermas' ideal speech community, on the other hand, are misleading because they pay insufficient attention to the human need for habituation and community. In general, acceptance of a functionalist conception of human nature will mean denial of the adequacy of any universal rules of conduct, whether of a Kantian or of a utilitarian kind.[39] Instead, any satisfactory moral philosophy will have to take the form of an agent (virtues and vices) morality rather than of an act (rule) morality.[40] This is true not on logical grounds but because only an agent morality can adequately express the developmental goals and problems of the particularly complex kind of animal that humans happen to be.

My analysis is not intended to provide the basis of a wholly new kind of systematic social science, since a thoroughly new beginning is neither desirable nor necessary. Instead, it has been meant to show that the sorts of questions that thoughtful social scientists and historians have always asked, questions about the value of various cultures, institutions, and ways of life, are in fact perfectly reasonable ones and that they should not be discarded in favor of inquiries which presume that human actions are either externally determined or transcendentally self-creating and which hence conclude that such actions are either beneath or beyond justification and critique. These questions are also those which are always posed by competent political actors. The only significant difference between practical philosophy (taken to include social science and moral philosophy) and practice itself is that the former pursues at leisure those issues which must be resolved by acting human beings under pressure.

NOTES

1. The interpretive approach is presented and defended by Charles Taylor, "Interpretation and the Sciences of Man," in Paul Rabinow and William M. Sullivan, eds., *Interpretive Social Science: A Reader* (Berkeley: University of California Press, 1979), pp. 25–72. "Contextualist" is a word frequently used to describe this position and is the one I think best captures its spirit. See Davis Hoy, *The Critical Circle: Literature, History, and Philosophical Hermeneutics* (Berkeley: University of California Press, 1978), pp. 68–72. The definition of the contextualist position which I adopt throughout is very close to Leo Strauss's characterization of "fully developed historicism" in *What Is Political Philosophy? and Other Studies* (Glencoe, Ill.: Free Press, 1959), p. 26.

2. For a review of the controversy, see J. Donald Moon, "The Logic of Political Inquiry: A Synthesis of Opposed Perspectives," in Fred Greenstein and Nelson W. Polsby, eds., *Political Science: Scope and Theory* (Reading, Mass.: Addison-Wesley, 1975), pp. 131–228.

3. A very balanced criticism of both sides is Brian Fay and J. Donald Moon, "What Would an Adequate Philosophy of Social Science Look Like?," *Philosophy of Social Science* (1977), 7:209–27.

4. Jürgen Habermas, "Hannah Arendt's Communications Concept of Power," *Social Research*, (1977), 44:3–24.

5. Jürgen Habermas, "Legitimation Problems in the Modern State," *Communication and the Evolution of Society*, Thomas McCarthy, trans. (Boston: Beacon Press, 1979), pp. 178–206.

6. Leo Strauss, *Natural Right and History* (Chicago: University of Chicago Press, 1953), p. 55.

7. Aristotle, *Nicomachean Ethics*, J. Bywater, ed. (London: Oxford University Press, 1894), 1094b14–16, my translation.

8. My discussion of this analogy between animals and machines owes a great deal to that of Hans Jonas in his chapter "The Philosophical Aspects of Darwinism," *The Phenomenon of Life: Toward a Philosophical Biology* (New York: Dell, 1966), pp. 38–63.

9. René Descartes, *Discours de la Méthode*, Geneviève Rodis-Lewis, ed. (Paris: Garnier-Flammarion, 1966), part 3, pp. 80–81, my translation.

10. Thomas Hobbes, *De Cive*, Sterling P. Lamprecht, ed. (New York: Appleton-Century-Crofts, 1949), pt. 1, ch. 1, p. 26.

11. David Hume, *A Treatise of Human Nature*, L. A. Selby-Bigge, ed. (Oxford: Clarendon Press, 1888), bk. 2, pt. 3, sec. 1, p. 402.

12. This point is made by Jonas, "Philosophical Aspects," pp. 54–55, nn. 7–8.

13. Jean-Jacques Rousseau, *Discourse on the Origin of Inequality*, Roger D. Masters and Judith R. Masters, trans. (New York: St. Martin's Press, 1964), p. 114.

14. Michael Oakeshott, *Rationalism in Politics* (New York: Basic Books, 1962), p. 36. The relationship of Oakeshott to the contextualist position is noted by Habermas, "Legitimation Problems," p. 204: "It is only a small step from this conservative appropriation of the great traditions in terms of language games to the traditionalism of a Michael Oakeshott."

15. *Poems by Wallace Stevens*, selected by Samuel French Morse (New York: Random House, 1959), p. 21.

16. Hannah Arendt, *The Human Condition* (Chicago: University of Chicago Press, 1958), p. 84.

17. I defend this claim in Stephen G. Salkever, "Freedom, Participation, and Happiness," *Political Theory* (1977), 5:391–413.

18. That is, it cannot be both evaluative and impartial or scientific.

19. Lawrence Kohlberg, "Moral Stages and Moralization: The Cognitive-Developmental Approach," in Thomas Lickona, ed., *Moral Development and Behavior* (New York: Holt, Rinehart, & Winston, 1976), 31–53.

20. This kind of functionalism is discussed, characterized as Aristotelian, and defended by K. V. Wilkes, *Physicalism* (Atlantic Highlands, N.J.: Humanities Press, 1978), pp. 55–64.

21. Jürgen Habermas, *Knowledge and Human Interests,* Jeremy J. Shapiro, trans. (Boston: Beacon Press, 1971), p. 314.

22. The Kantian character of Habermas' goal is noted by Richard Bernstein, *The Restructuring of Social and Political Theory* (Philadelphia: University of Pennsylania Press, 1978), pp. 205–13.

23. David Barash, *Sociobiology and Behavior* (New York: Elsevier North-Holland, 1977), p. 41.

24. Edward O. Wilson, *On Human Nature* (Cambridge, Mass.: Harvard University Press, 1978), ch. 3.

25. Habermas, "Legitimation Problems," p. 201.

26. This is the position generally attributed to Aristotle, although his explicit remarks on this issue are few and far between. See Marjorie Grene, *A Portrait of Aristotle* (Chicago: University of Chicago Press, 1963), pp. 229–32. For a discussion of the complexities of the Aristotelian positon concerning the fixity of species, see Stephen R. L. Clark, *Aristotle's Man* (Oxford: Clarendon Press, 1975), pp. 28–47.

27. See Ernst Mayr, "Species Concepts and Definitions," in Ernst Mayr, ed., *The Species Problem,* American Association for the Advancement of Science, Publication Number 50 (Washington, 1957), pp. 1–19.

28. The status of the species problem in current biological thought is discussed by Michael Ruse, *The Philosophy of Biology* (London: Hutchinson University Library, 1973), pp. 126–39.

29. Mary Midgley, *Beast and Man: The Roots of Human Nature* (Ithaca: Cornell University Press, 1978), p. 58.

30. A strong case that Aristotle's teleology is of this sort is made by Allan Gotthelf, "Aristotle's Conception of Final Causality," *Review of Metaphysics* (1976), 30:226–54; and by Martha Craven Nussbaum, *Aristotle's "De Motu Animalium"* (Princeton: Princeton University Press, 1978), pp. 59–99.

31. My understanding of function and functionalism is substantially the same as that defended by Christopher Boorse in "Wright on Functions," *Philosophical Review* (1976), 85:77: "In every context where functional talk is appropriate, one has to do

with the goals of some goal-directed system. . . . Functions are, purely and simply, contributions to goals."

32. See Robert K. Merton, "Manifest and Latent Functions," *Social Theory and Social Structure* (New York: The Free Press, 1957), pp. 19–84. One notable exception is a paper to which my analysis here owes a great deal: Roger D. Masters, "Politics as a Biological Phenomenon," *Social Science Information* (1975), 14:7–63. See also Fred H. Willhoite, "Primates and Political Authority: A Biobehavioral Perspective," *American Political Science Review,* (1976), 70:1110–26; and the analysis of the function of religious institutions in Donald T. Campbell, "On the Conflicts Between Biological and Social Evolution and Between Psychology and Moral Tradition," *American Psychologist* (1975), 30:1103–26.

33. Midgley, *Beast and Man,* pp. 307–8.

34. Arendt, *The Human Condition,* p. 179.

35. Karl Marx, *Grundrisse,* Martin Nicolaus, trans., in Robert C. Tucker, ed., *The Marx-Engels Reader,* 2nd ed. (New York: W. W. Norton, 1978), p. 233.

36. Midgley, *Beast and Man,* p. 166.

37. For a discussion of rationality in the decision making of hamadryas baboons, see Christopher Boehm, "Rational Pre-Selection from Hamadryas to *Homo Sapiens:* The Place of Decisions in the Adaptive Process," *American Anthropologist* (1978):, 80:265–96.

38. This is Leo Strauss's characterization of the classical "natural right" position in Plato and Aristotle in *Natural Right and History,* pp. 162–63.

39. See Robert McShea, "Human Nature Ethical Theory, *Philosophy and Phenomenological Research* (1979): 39:386–401.

40. Arguments for agent morality are presented in Stephen G. Salkever, "Virtue, Obligation, and Politics," *American Political Science Review* (1974), 68:78–92; in Lawrence Becker, "The Neglect of Virtue," *Ethics* (1975), 85:110–22; and in James D. Wallace, *Virtues and Vices* (Ithaca: Cornell University Press, 1978).

Ten

AN INTERACTIONAL MORALITY OF EVERYDAY LIFE

Norma Haan

Because social scientists' claims of value neutrality are no longer tenable—for reasons made clear in several chapters in this volume—and because many moral ideas that social scientists inadvertently use can withstand neither public scrutiny nor professional debate, social science faces a crisis of legitimation. This difficulty might be alleviated if social scientists were to examine their moral bases, work to construct a theory based on wide consensus, and then come to use moral theory reflectively and openly.

My observations and analyses over some years of actual moral actions, coupled with certain new recognitions and rediscoveries in psychology, suggest to me that the construction of an empirically based, consensual theory of everyday morality may be possible. I describe such a formulation here as a working model.

OUR EVERYDAY INTEREST IN MORALITY

People have intense interest in morality. In a way, morality is a vast and inescapable conspiracy in which we all participate. Clearly the morality of everyday life is not a capacity that resides exclusively in individuals; it is social interchange in itself. Lay morality seems to consist of shared understandings about the character that exchanges must have in order to sustain and enrich individual and collective lives. So critical is morality for our well-being that invariably we all

I wish to thank the many people who made comments on earlier drafts of this paper, but especially Eliane Aerts, Tom Andrae, Lynne English, Frederick Gordon, Richard Holway, Vicky Johnson, Andrew Phelps, Neil Thomasen, and Jerome Wakefield.

join in this compelling compact. As parents, we go to the greatest lengths to ensure our offspring's morality because we are certain that their commitment to morality will be elemental to their future welfare. Probably as a result of the great energy we all exert to induce the young to share our moral commitments and to retain our own, all people, even the most heinous criminals, work to maintain a sense of themselves as moral by whatever justification—accurate or distorted. Only for brief moments and in very limited ways do we admit our inevitable falls from grace. Interestingly, according to Plato's report, the Sophist Protagoras held the same view that "all men properly say they are righteous whether or not they really are. Or else if they do not lay claim to righteousness they must be insane."[1] (Our Freudian-informed insights tell us that those who wear guilt on their sleeves are engaged in some venture other than self-criticism.)

The view of the self as a moral entity starts early. The parents of a four-year-old boy, regarded by his teachers as a child of moral sensitivity, described how he defends his moral position when he hits his younger brother. He shouts *before* he is reprimanded, "It was an accident; it was an accident." When his brother was a baby, the father heard the then three-year-old boy chant sing-song fashion, "Crush the baby, kill the baby, crush the baby's head." When the father asked about the song, the boy removed himself from responsibility. He said it was "just a song" (the time-honored distinction we make between thought and action) and that "Indians sing it" (displacing responsibility onto those peoples who seem forever to exemplify savagery in the fantasies of American whites).

In addition, we have only to recall Adolph Eichmann's contention that he was a moral being—he merely performed his job when he gave orders to murder thousands of Jews. Thus, we all work to preserve our belief in ourselves as moral beings—ordinary criminals, the boy, and Eichmann, as well as social scientists.

I want to understand this powerful and compelling morality of practical life. Consequently, in recent years my associates and I have been observing and listening to adolescents and young adults practice morality, recently extending our observations to preschoolers at play. Two examples of moral discourse among eighteen-year-olds will illustrate the interactive, dialogical aspects of the morality that I think must be reflected in the theory.

With the often direct wisdom of the untutored, a friendship group of eighteen-year-old university students confronted the question of governing themselves within an experience where they fully simulated being the sole survivors of a world disaster. First, they wished to avoid selecting a leader because, they said, everyone should be equal; they wanted leadership to be decided by simple rotation, and they would vote on particular decisions. When the specter of tie votes and, later, the rights of the minority came to their minds, concern and debate ensued. The following dialogue is only lightly edited for the sake of brevity, and I have added comments in brackets to draw attention to the implications of these young people's key considerations.

Phil: Then we'll just talk and talk and vote and vote. [Persistent attempts to understand each other might lead to consensus.]

Hilda: We'll need a coin, too. [Random draws are sometimes the only solution.]

Cissy: Everyone would have to listen and respect each other. [Without these properties of dialogue, moral solution is impossible.]

Betty: What if that doesn't happen?

Ray: The best we can hope for is mutual cooperation, but beyond that, we're just going to have to try. [No assurance of perfect compliance can be given beforehand.]

Charles: If we have *any* rule that we'll all accept—without having to evoke it—it is everyone has to accept the right of argument. Every person must be able to talk without their talk being oppressed or interrupted. [The core moral right lies in the procedure of making one's case known; for a right to be a moral right it must be accepted, not legislated.]

Ed: We'll have to have every individual evaluate everyone else's ideas.

Ray: But you can't force that on other people! When someone has an opinion just allow him to express it totally. [Again, a moral right must be accepted for itself; it cannot be enforced.]

Hilda: Is your rule that everyone has to cooperate?

Phil: It's not a rule, it's expected. It is an agreement—that's what we're doing—we're doing a mutual agreement. [A vision of how to achieve moral balances guides the group.]

Ray: It's a mutual agreement to listen to other people. We've all agreed on a mutual agreement.

Betty: There is still a problem: what if someone doesn't want to follow the other seven people? Are you going to force him? [How binding is the moral balance on all concerned?]

Charles: I thing we all would realize we can't be loners. It's like a dance; I want to count the steps in fourths and the rest of you count in eighths, then I should realize that the dance won't work. [The social interdigitation of people cannot be questioned; acceptance of this fact makes human affairs work.]

Phil: We are supposed to have basic life supports in here [part of the simulation], so I don't think that a situation where we are *so* desperate that we can't get agreement is going to arise—or should arise. We're just going to have to work things out as they come up. [Considerations of survival do make procedures of achieving moral balances more delicate; however, the participants are not that desperate yet.]

Charles: But you can't ask someone to go against their principles. [The majority has responsibility to the dissident.]

Cissy: But maybe we'll change our minds if we listen, respect, and vote, or maybe he'd change his mind; we can listen and vote again. [Continual dialogue and exchanges of facts and opinions and expressions of need are the way to moral balances.]

Betty: I would still want to act on my principles.

Eve: But, Betty, just try to convince us of them! If you believe something so *strongly,* you could change our minds. [Matters don't have to be left at A vs. B; recognition of our social interdigitation leads to A = B.]

Charles: Betty, you're twisting situations. We would probably find out we had the *same* morals if we really talk. [Dialogue uncovers our shared morality.]

Cissy: It's really hard; there are no clear answers for that, Betty. You just have to see what's going to happen. [There are no ultimate, perfect moral protections. We have to take risks.]

Betty: Would you take action against me if I opened the door [to the outer contamination] and the group didn't want me to?

Charles: You'd be acting violently by doing that. You'd not be respecting everybody else. If we forced you to stop, we'd just be saying there has to be fair representation. [Action must be based on the same standards as talk.]

Thus, this group of eighteen-year-olds regards its morality as a process which they themselves keep in motion through the mutuality of their acceptances and fates and the commonality of their morals; their morality is not a given; instead, it is continually sought but not always securely or perfectly achieved.

An audio-recorded voice informs the group that a survivor of unknown condition is outside the group's cell; the group decides that everyone should voice an opinion, one at a time, about whether to let him in. The following statements are exemplary of the positions taken.

"That could be one of us. We may have the disease a little bit now for all we know. He is alive and we are alive, let him in." [The bonds of intersubjectivity hold.]

"If we leave the guy out there and then one of us gets sick, are we going to kick one of us out? We could set a precedent." [Our self-interest is synonymous with his.]

"To be human we have to sacrifice some things, and if we're selfish then we lose our values." [Our interest in being human is synonymous with his welfare.]

"We could help him get better. Also, he may not have a disease, so we have to take a chance." [Facts are important, but we don't know all the relevant ones, so to be human, risks have to be taken.]

"We already agreed to support everybody else, right? Just because he wasn't originally a part of our group doesn't mean we should reject him." [We made a universal agreement.]

"If more people join, we can come up with more ideas and better decisions." [Dialogue and balance are *the* forms of our morality.]

The group gives another argument for their socially bonded view of life when an audio voice "patches" them through to other cells and finally to a cell where a man wishes to commit suicide because of the desperate conditions.

Phil: I think his obligations come through the fact he's alive even if he doesn't know the people he's stuck with; he's obligated because he's in circumstances that overpower his right to kill himself.
Betty: What do you mean?
Phil: If he says he can kill himself, there's no reason why everybody else can't do the same and he wouldn't agree to that, so there's his obligation! He wouldn't want to start anything like death by chain reaction. [One's social bondedness holds even when facing death.]

Thus, they identify the value of life itself in interactional, secular terms, however some of them might consecrate life in their religious, spiritual beliefs.

Another such friendship group hotly argued with one another following a morally intense "game" experience that established an oppressive three-class society where socioeconomic mobility was not possible and where two members, Mike and Bob, had wielded total power. All other members had belonged to the lower or the middle class.

Bob: I have a question, Mike. What if you honestly thought you were the best leader—say you had a Ph. D. and your people were all illiterate. You knew you could satisfy their needs. Wouldn't you think you *should* take over? [Those with "superior" moral knowledge, he suggests, should lead.]

Mike: No. I'd explain to them, but if they didn't like my ideas that would be that. Maybe they'd ask me back later when things didn't work out for them. [His understanding of the social hazards of benevolent paternalism is not complete.]

Jane: But that isn't the real problem here. You leaders could have been open-minded and all that, but that still wouldn't necessarily mean we'd have an opportunity. We just couldn't get anywhere. [Kindness without participation is insufficient.]

Bob: Jane, you seemed to be thriving on being equal. What about when Mike and I said let's get back to the first, fair rules, but you guys wouldn't go for it. You're contradicting yourself. We gave you the opportunity for everything to be equal and fair, but you didn't go for it. [A logical contradiction, he thinks.]

Jane: But you were *giving* it to us! Besides, we weren't really going to be equal. You were still going to be in power, and what we wanted was a real voice. [Gifts without voice do not make a moral balance.]

Nancy: We wanted a chance to exercise our little power; we were getting organized to revolt against you, and then you said you wanted us to *forget* what you had done! That would mean we'd give up our organizing. [Their interests as active agents are at stake.]

Bob: Look, I was just asking to be treated normally. I had tried to be fair and think of good rules, so I was hurt when you wouldn't do it. [His intentions were good, so he should be forgiven, he thinks.]

Mike: Yeah, it was a matter of trust. I was really surprised that you didn't trust us. [It was the lower class's fault for not trusting!]

Ted: But you had screwed us already; it takes time to get over that. [Moral exchanges have a history.]

Janice: We *at least* had the right to be mad at you! I don't think you had the right to tell us to forgive you. It didn't mean we were going to do something bad to you. How could we promise *not* to be mad at you? [Morality is not just factual; our feelings are legitimate too. People are accountable over time for what they do.]

Thus, this group draws a precise distinction from its experience: having or being *given* the nominal conditions of justice is not morally sufficient; instead, people want a voice and opportunities to participate in the process of determining their own living conditions. Altruism from those who have power is inferior to the legitimate right of people to work for their own good. Thus, the society of prescribed just conditions is second best to the society of participation.

HISTORICALLY INGRAINED ASSUMPTIONS ABOUT THE SOURCES AND NATURE OF MORALITY

Because the morality I am trying to describe arises out of the practicalities of human experiences, it is at odds with Platonic-Judeo-Christian formal, idealistic morality that has traditionally been the "official," or received, moral wisdom. Interestingly, everyday morality does seem more consonant with the fifth-century naturalistic, empirical moral theories of the Greek Sophists which Platonism replaced.[2] Habitually but subtly our thinking about morality seems directed by several Platonistic assumptions; thus, some of these implicit assumptions must be explicated so the very different nature of everyday morality can become clear. In fact, these assumptions seem to obscure the simpler features of everyday morality, at least as I now formulate it.

First is our assumption that if a moral theory is adequate, it should provide clear and absolute guidance for all important problems of living. Formulations of everyday morality have usually been depreciated, charged with being relativistic, as were the Sophists' theories by the Platonists; but this indictment, which implies that everyday morality is uncertain and therefore inferior, needs examination. A moral theory can contain both relativist and absolutist categories and still be logically consistent. Relativism and absolutism are not necessarily mutually exclusive. Moral theories have different aspects, some of which may be wisely absolute and others wisely relativistic. Nonetheless, absolute claims attract human beings because they seem to deliver the especially important social security of moral clarity. Socrates, Plato, and Aristotle, each in a different way, argued against the Sophists' naturalistic uncertainties to construct their ideal, formal theories of absolute standards, some say as anodynes for the political disorders of their time.[3] Thereafter, in the opinion of many, from Bacon to Popper, the Platonic view of fixed, ideal moral ideas merged with Judeo-Christian thought and influenced the course of history. This confluence seems responsible for our assumption that the most convincing and awesome moral theories are Platonistic.

For example, the popular contemporary theory of the psychologist Lawrence Kohlberg is based on Platonic assumptions, a stance he explicates in his paper "Education for Justice: A Modern Statement of the Platonic View." Kohlberg writes, "Virtue is . . . always the same ideal form regardless of climate or culture. . . . virtue is knowledge of the good. He who knows the good chooses the good. . . . virtue is philosophical knowledge or intuition of the ideal form of the good. . . . Its teachers must in a certain sense be philosopher-kings."[4]

In opposition to our expectancies that morality should provide not only certain guidance but also perfect solutions, I suggest that a successfully universalistic theory of morality cannot actually prescribe beforehand what particular moral conclusions should be reached; instead, only the procedures that people use to relate to one another's minds about a multitude of moral circumstances can logically be prescribed. Thus, everyday morality is absolute, but in a different way from Platonic theories. Certain ambiguities must be tolerated and certain risks must be taken in everyday moral discourse, as the eighteen-year-olds argued. However, scholars and citizens generally believe that probabilistic, not fully prescriptive moral theories are inferior because they seem to retreat from the certainty promised by the strong claim of all-embracing moral standards.

Second, instead of attempting to understand everyday morality, scholars and citizens have seemed to make the assumption and accept the idea that moral theories can only be "best" theories (knowledgeably proposed by the wise elite) and that "true" theories are impossible to construct. Still faced with variety in humans' cherished values, we have settled for the idea that "best" is different for different people; therefore, many different moral schemas can and must exist. So far Kohlberg's work stands as the only comprehensive attempt to build an empirical basis for a universal moral theory. For a time Kohlberg seemed to have hold of this problem, for he claimed his theory was not merely a best theory. Instead, he claimed, the universal stages of moral development he posited were empirically found and verified;[5] however, critics have not agreed that his evidence is persuasive.[6]

As social scientists increasingly investigate morality, constant attention needs to be given to the likelihood that a purportedly empirical theory is merely the morality of the theorist, my own present formulation not excepted. My defense is that I make my definition of morality explicit as to its grounds and possible empirical support;[7] my colleagues and I are checking "reality," and the formulation we propose takes everyday practice as the starting point. Whatever the success of our venture, the possibility that an empirically based moral theory can be constructed, using an epistemological definition of truth as consensus, has not yet been fully explored. This was not Kohlberg's strategy. He has imposed his theory on reality as has been done for centuries.

A third assumption is that moralities must be in the form of complete, formalized systems rather than being described in the more proximate forms that emerge from the details of human interchange. Surely, this way of constructing a complete morality must spring from an ingrained supposition that morality can only be known to us when it is presented by a higher authority or by morally elite figures—God in the Judeo-Christian tradition, philosopher-kings for Plato, the cognitively elite in philosophic traditions, or people of higher moral stage in the Kohlberg theory. Only these superior figures are thought to "know" morality; thus, they and their emissaries are able to assume the responsibility of teaching morality to ordinary people. In contrast, I argue that everyday morality has no other source than the experiences and agreements of people themselves.

To the extent that a morality is assumed to be worthy only when it provides certain, perfect, complete solutions and is proposed by an elite, differences in people's moral character are accepted. Leaders can then employ morality and manipulate guilt as an instrument of political control. People's deep commitments to their collectivities make them highly vulnerable and responsive to arguments that this or that course of action is morally good or bad for the group. Leaders' public judgments of moral merit quell the efforts of the disadvantaged to promote their own good: those of lower status are guilty—intrinsically unworthy—and have not earned the right to expect more. In an example of such leaders' manipulations of morality to place blame elsewhere, Jean Bethke Elshtain analyzed Jimmy Carter's 1980 State of the Union message and found that he used the word "discipline" nine times.[8] Inflation, Carter implied, is due to moral laxness; therefore, we should pay by sacrifice. The people caused inflation because they did not live within their means; unscrupulously they went into debt, were not work productive, and neither saved not conserved. To the temporary relief of the citizenry, Ronald Reagan does not speak of morality but rather acts on the conclusions of Carter's premise. The financially elite have already demonstrated they are morally more worthy; consequently they surely will in their benevolence allow their rightfully won advantages to "trickle down." In the morality of everyday life, however, specialists are not needed to explicate morality. Instead, all are expected to know and speak their minds so that responsive, accurate moral balances can emerge.

In the fullness and certainty of its prescriptions, the dominant morality has been based on a fourth assumption: morality is regarded as the instrument for controlling "innate" human selfishness and brutishness. However, to assume an inborn brutishness is naive and unwarranted empiricism that confuses human solutions that were historically necessary in deleterious social and personal conditions with those that can occur in different or better environments and times. Furthermore, this is already a moral judgment of humanity, one that empiricists are not allowed to make as a starting premise. If selfishness and brutishness were actually innate, morality could logically be only prohibitive in nature. However, if our commitments to intersubjectivity and the individual's will to appear moral (if not to be moral) are as strong as we contend, morality cannot be prohibition; it is, rather, mutual regulation, an interwoven attempt not merely to survive but also creatively to enhance and make sense of our lives.

RECENT RECOGNITIONS AND DISCOVERIES IN PSYCHOLOGY THAT PERMIT NEW VIEWS OF MORALITY

Perhaps the task of constructing an empirical formulation can now be more fruitful, because psychology is moving on several fronts toward fuller and more accurate views of humans and their interactions. Under the impact of Piaget's thoughts and work, we relearned that the mind is active, rational, and constructivist, thereby restoring the more commonsensical view that the behaviorists banished in the 1920s. If the mind is actively constructivist, morality must then be inductive and creative rather than compliant and rule deductive.

Earlier mechanistic psychologies were ones of fixed entities—for instance, of traits, faculties, id, ego, and the IQ. These entities came alive only when stimuli were applied, in the manner of a motor, but now the psychologies of entities are being replaced by psychologies of processes. "Permanent" features of humans are now constructed to be more "intelligent" and malleable, and their definitions almost always retain some idea of meaningful organization, like structures, schemas, patterns, and expectancies. Thus, "moral character" as a fixed faculty now seems less likely than moral responsiveness as sensitivity and skill in social interaction.

Recognition grows that the human condition is invariably conflictual or problematic in some degree; we actually seem to enjoy problems and conflicts, at least of a mild sort. Accordingly, the earlier psychological ideas that assumed human behavior operates to reduce tension or achieve durable homeostasis or peace can be seen as machine analogies rather than truths. Thus, we see that moral decisions are not likely to be occasional dramatic incidents; instead, moral dialogues and negotiations must be continual occurrences.

We psychologists increasingly admit that psychologies oriented toward describing the individual, self-contained human psyche can only produce partial truths, because reciprocity among people constructs the person; therefore, social meanings and motives are becoming prime psychological variables. The inadvertent endorsement of excessive individualism by past psychologies and moral theories is revealed as the politically biased product of a particular historical time.

Also, psychology is moving toward the explicit recognition that humans are thoroughgoing social beings from birth and that babies are far less egocentric than we had thought; child development research increasingly focuses on the social cognition of babies and parents and their attachments to each other. In this milieu social allegiances become the backbone of empirical moral theory.

Some psychologies now make distinctions between facilitative and deleterious human situations and the human choices these allow or prevent. Thus, our empiricism becomes less raw but more differentiated and intelligent, and some psychologists dare to take the critical-evaluative position openly to inquire about conditions that support the achievement of truth and morality among peoples.

Finally a cautious definition of human nature is being advanced by the consensus of neobehaviorists and constructivists alike: a human being is one who cannot tolerate powerlessness (or, as it is variously put, helplessness or noncontingency), and as a consequence the human behaves badly under oppressive conditions. Thus, a desideratum of everyday morality may be its facilitation of people's free participation in moral evaluations and decisions.

GUIDELINES FOR INVESTIGATING A MORALITY OF EVERYDAY LIFE

Social scientists' attempts to construct an empirical formulation of morality are not necessarily guaranteed success. Moral philosophers' disputations over the centuries warn us that the task is not an easy one. As matters now stand, psychologists with no theory investigate moral questions "eclectically," and others investigate moral matters without seeming to realize that their research concerns morality. Clearly, the enterprise I advocate is difficult and hazardous and perhaps one only the foolhardy would undertake. Certain guidelines define the limits of social science's responsibilities and capabilities.

In this and subsequent sections, I often write as if social scientists are the ones who should propose and investigate moral theory, but I do not exclude philosophers. Their analyses are critical and necessary in the construction of research-based formulations. Still, empirical theorizing is what social science does; so I write here as though the problem were exclusively one of social science.

The Limitations of Social Science

Rudner suggests that social scientists are in the grip of the "reproductive fallacy," according to which all there is to humans and their affairs is thought to be within science's purview and thus potentially amenable to prediction and control.[9] (Sullivan describes how policy science has the same ambition in his paper in this volume.) Similarly, many scholars (Rawls is an exception) seem to think that a moral theory is deficient, if not wrong, if it does not account for *all* moral phenomena; of course, in practice, theorists often reduce people and their morality to fit theories. As Einstein is reported to have said, we overlook the fact that describing the taste of chicken soup is not the same as tasting chicken soup. The rich inventiveness of a single human being, much less a collectivity of human beings, means social science cannot adequately mirror life; it must intelligently choose to study the forms of morality that are likely to be common to humankind. I suggest, of course, that we would do well to stick to the processes of morality.

Thin Foundational Values as Moral Grounds

Rawls makes an important identification of "thin" values and argues that only thin values can recruit wide agreement.[10] I appreciate this idea. Social scientists' acceptance of the epistemological definition of truth as an examined and tested consensus logically means that the pivotal value chosen as a basis for morality (that is, the naturalistic fallacy committed) must also be thin in order to recruit wide agreement. For an empirical theory, we need a key value that all people, irrespective of personality, religion, sex, historical time, or society would tend to endorse if they had the opportunity freely to consider all possible choices. Assumptions of "strong" or "thick" values properly occur only in parochial contexts, where consensus over a diverse society is not required. The actual value basis of everyday morality, because it must serve the vastly diverse needs of human commerce, is probably also thin; if it were otherwise, men could not relate to women nor whites to blacks nor Eskimos to Indians, and so on.

Moral Action as the Central Feature

The aspect that is taken as the starting point for constructing a moral formulation determines its character. Although moral development, motivation, and cultural-situational variations can be empirically investigated, moral action—its conditions, history, and social contexts—is the logical entry for social science. Now that psychologists admit that the mind is constructivist, they must logically make action the focus of research about morality. Habermas observes that people act when they talk.[11] In moral conflict each person's talk is surely a form of action. Viewing the mind as self-constructing leads to the conclusion that people's moral thinking and decisions are their own (instead of being reproductions of others' or society's teachings) and that their enactments are intelligently and rationally responsive to the peculiar characteristics of each situation. Thus, the parameters of a person's moral actions, constructed in relation to particular kinds of situations and cultures, which also have moral parameters, and the parameters of the person-context interactions all need to be discovered.

Action is regarded, in everyday life, as the only authentic criterion of moral truth. Understanding the conditions for disparities between what people think and what they do could lead to understanding moral default, callousness, and courage. Although many societies have attempted to hold people morally responsible for their thoughts, programs of thought control invariably fail or are imperfectly enforced. Reported thoughts are readily simulated; authentic thoughts become private and the controller finds that evidence is inaccessible. Probably, for all these reasons, people's actions are universally taken as the legal criterion of responsibility.

Much theorizing in psychology has viewed morality as a mirror of society. (Even in Kohlberg's theory, the various moral stages represent compliance with conventions until the person is adult *and* reaches the principled level; very few people—about 5 percent—achieve the latter.) This view is increasingly countered, however, by evidence that not only heroes resist the definitions of bad societies but also ordinary people, who resist impositions of social definitions that are not to their good in more devious and covert ways. Recent accounts of Nazi concentration camps, where social structures were explicitly designed to achieve human degradation, tell a different story from Bettelheim's and Frankl's widely accepted psychoanalytically based descriptions of inmates' moral regression and infantilism, both of which they contrasted with their own performances. Despite massive and torturous oppression, inmates created their own moral systems, acted secretly on their moral understandings, and recreated their networks as key members were killed.[12] Bettelheim's and Frankl's interpretations now appear as classical, conceptual distortions in the service of a believed theory.

Working for One's Own Good in Balance with Others Working for Their Good

Understandably, people generally regard their own good as morally relevant and justifiable. Yet moral theories slight and some even discourage the idea of people as moral objects to themselves, convictions that are probably due to assumptions that curbing human selfishness is the raison d'être of morality. Still, people's interest in their own good and their efforts to achieve that good, *whatever it might be,* can hardly be denied the status of a moral right within the context of others' rights to advocate their own good, of "society's" rights, and of expectancies that parties will jointly discover and promote their mutual good. The unthinking, racist position is sometimes maintained that people in some other cultures do not have the same interest in their own good "as we do." For instance, General Westmoreland commented that the Vietnamese didn't value their lives the way "we" do. To the contrary, people's interest in their lives—with whatever goodness it has or could have—protects society.

Morality as Social Enhancement vs. Warding Off Human Selfishness

Definitions of morality as prohibitive are usually justified as necessary for group survival; however, this reasoning produces a poor and unhappy account of morality. Morality also functions to satisfy and enhance people and groups, as my associates and I have observed in our research. Well-functioning friendship groups of university and high school students "solve" the moral problems we present and then exude confidence and satisfaction with themselves, and members claim their experience has helped them better understand themselves and their fellows. Poorly functioning hierarchically dominated groups are almost rent asunder by the same problems and react by desperately placing great prohibitions on themselves. Nevertheless, the design of most moral systems echoes common assumptions that morality functions solely for the group's survival. For instance, in Rawls's otherwise humane theory, two key concepts are safeguards against human perfidy and self-interest. They come into play as people are imagined to be choosing their principles. The first is the veil of ignorance—none can know his/her present talents or future advantages or else he/she would choose selfishly; the second is the original position—all citizens are required to start this imaginary discussion with the same resources. These stipulations arise from an adversarial view of morality that often further assumes that one party's self-interest is moral while the other's is not, a consequence that can only strain their future relations. Understandings resulting in moral balances between people or societies can enrich and facilitate relations. Interestingly, the pleasures of morality were featured in the Sophists' moral systems: "Harmonization was such as to confer direct pleasure on each and all. This allowed the economic objectives . . . to assume equal importance with the moral ones. . . . The other part was represented by the increased opportunities in society for expressing the equally hedonistic urge to amity and fellowship. For this, too, was part of the urge to live and to live well. In short, the citizen was properly a hedonist, a philanthropist, and an egalitarian all in one."[13]

A MORALITY OF INTERACTION

The following is a brief description of the formulation of the everyday morality that I am testing.

The Moral Dialogue
Interaction is the invariant and distinctive feature of everyday moral consciousness, as it is regarded, experienced, and lived out in the minds of two people, within a single person who is initially of several minds, between people and society, and between societies. (Hereafter, I refer to all these combinations by the term "parties.") Moral claims, ideas, and facts are weighed and priorities set between parties until some balance is found, but the need for resolution never ceases—new considerations always arise. Thus, moral tensions are ubiquitous, and moral resolutions are constantly created, instead of occasionally reproduced.

Despite these obvious features, morality has not often been defined in interactional terms. Instead, it has been regarded as a quiescent capacity, resident in individual people, and activated only by the appearance of a moral problem. Then, it is thought, the person "looks up" a solution by matching the problem to a previously learned rule or principle (in the form of a nominal duty, consequence, or right). A person who has a properly developed moral character will choose the proper rule and behave accordingly to remove the problem. In this view, moral adequacy depends on the extent and accuracy with which the individual has learned the rules (of interest to psychologists, who tend to regard society's rules as immutable) and/or the comprehensive goodness of a particular set of rules (of interest to philosophers, who argue about which set of rules is best). The person who selects and acts on the most abstract and generalized rule, despite the peculiar needs of the parties and irregularities of the situation, is celebrated.

When social interaction is taken as the pivotal feature of morality, a different view of moral processes, decisions, guidelines, and individual capacities emerges. Some moral contretemps occurs between parties; then discussion must take place, whether literally or only in the mind of one person, because people do not tolerate moral disequilibrium for long. Relations must be reequilibrated, whether falsely or authentically. If they are not, the participants' commitments to each other begin to decay. Many inequities are never discussed in real life, but that does not prevent participants from angrily conducting imaginary dialogues within their own minds.

Moral dialogues literally and continuously occur as major or minor events throughout any given day and throughout the given lifetime of any person; these occurrences are not merely expository devices for the exegesis of theory. As minor events, dialogues often go unmarked. Dramatic and all but irresolvable episodes, like the ones philosophers concoct to confound one another or psychologists use to "test" subjects, are rare. People's expectancies of engaging in moral dialogue become so clear and strong as organized patterns of social thought and interchange (as was shown in the earlier examples of the eighteen-year-olds) that the social schema of moral dialogue can be regarded as the prime moral structure.

Dialogue is an exploration of mutual thought—a joint reflective inquiry into the facts and parameters of the moral issue at hand. Initially, parties make fumbling, awkward attempts to defend their views; but faced with antithesis, they back off in order to clarify the problem. Thus, statements of antithetical positions serve to identify the parameters of the issue. As its features are identified, elaborated, and finally simplified, the parties can begin fully to comprehend each other's views. For one person to understand another, attitudes of passivity, receptivity, and amity are required, and people must cast off their self-preoccupation. That people do cognize each other's moral positions is evidence of how important are moral motivations and how comprehensive the social embeddedness of humans. The dialogue persuades and corrects both parties despite their initial intentions. Typically, each party brings out cognitive-affective information. Sometimes people prefer and choose the best rational-cognitive argument (such is our commitment to logic and reality), but the objective circumstances do not always override the emotional importance of less rational views.

More often than not, each party's position is embedded in the other's position, and common grounds or compromises can be discovered. It is unreal to think that A and B are always completely opposed to each other or that a victory for A means a loss for B. The dialogue is as much to discover A's and B's similarities—parties have implicitly agreed to abate their narcissism by participating—as it is for them to press their differences. Only unthinking, overwrought partisanship defeats the dialogue's purpose. "Losing" is not necessarily devastating to participants in these dialogues, because "immorality" is a matter of what a person is doing, which can always be changed. "Immorality" in the dominant Platonic theories is a deficiency in moral capacity or character, a matter pertaining to who the person is, which cannot be readily changed.

The Moral Balance

Dialogical parties intend to strike a moral balance, that is, an agreement which equilibrates this particular contretemps because it wins both parties' endorsement. In the best circumstances, the achieved balance rests on the parties' creation of equity because they discover that they have common interest. But other balances are workable: compromises of advantages, wherein all receive smaller advantage than they initially wanted; compromises of disadvantages, wherein all suffer some disadvantages; or choice of the lesser of two evils. In real life, solutions are often rational, which is not always the same as their being logically impeccable. Given the complexity of human interchange and the unique needs of each person, we all expect to suffer occasional minor injustice, if it is not perpetuated and if it is the only nearly rational solution available. Various phrases express our understanding of moral balance, for example, "making it right with everybody," "evening things up," and "restoring the peace." Again, the highly organized meanings surrounding the idea of moral balance warrant the supposition that it is also a major moral structure.

The Moral Ground

The feature of dialogues that makes them moral is the question of grounding. However, from a psychological frame, motives for acting morally—"Why be moral?"—are not grounds. Instead, they are the empirical reasons why people pragmatically come to want to be moral, given our existence as social creatures who interact in ways that generate moral motivations. Thus, the questions "Why be moral?" can be expected to have empirical answers.

However, "What is moral?"—the key value or the grounds—must have a different kind of answer, a philosophic-logical one. People might universally endorse a definition of morality that guarantees that both one's own good and the good of others *should* be served as equitably as possible. (Such grounds have often been proposed.) Thus, I make a thin, ontological assumption about the desires and rationality of people: that equity-serving dialogues are the vehicle for people's rationally considered and socially experienced desires. Given an informed, unencumbered choice, surely all people would hope to present their morally relevant claims and have them considered than not. This wish is differentiated by practical experiences that inform us when we are very young that our moral claims can be validated only reciprocally, within the context of others' claims.

Various features of moral dialogues that promote accurate and full exchanges of views come to be valued: all should be allowed to speak, none should dominate, and any can veto. These are not, however, grounds in themselves. Instead, they merely provide assurance that parties' interests will be heard and served, most of the time and over time.

Science relates to people's psychology in a fashion similar to the morality described here, and perhaps this explains why some people now turn to scientific techniques with cautious hope that the outlines of a "true" morality of everyday moral exchange may be discerned, one that can take the place of the "best" theories usually proposed. The structure of science and the structure of this morality provide ways for people to diminish their narcissistic interpretations of the world, rise above their self-containment and self-consideration, and meet the minds of others. Both structures attain these goals by following a set of procedural principles that are expected eventually to yield consensual outcomes. Both rest their cases on the procedure that gives all related evidence, whether provided by those high or low in status, even-handed acceptance and evaluation to ensure that the most penetrating, informed, and convincing resolution will have the greatest likelihood of being chosen. Both are expected and known frequently to yield recognizably imperfect solutions or superficially perfect solutions that are, nevertheless, forever liable to revision as new evidence is presented and new circumstances arise. Both are human triumphs—we bootstrap ourselves by assuming a third-person observer's attitude toward ourselves—we rebuild our raft plank by plank while we are at sea, Otto Neurath is supposed to have said. These are attempts to achieve objectivity; both science and morality undertake this task despite the difficulties of knowing more than the self. To get to know more than the self is done only by knowing others and the circumstances of their worlds. To know more than the self is the expected emancipatory outcome of both interactional morality and science.

Moral Motivations

The question of why people are willing to consider others' moral claims has some empirical answers, although clearly much more needs to be known. For instance, investigations of child abuse and juvenile delinquency indicate that children who are treated without consideration of their needs and whose wishes for equity-promoting dialogues are persistently thwarted become adults who treat others or their own children in the same way. The intense concern of juvenile delinquents for their peers is explained by the fact that they are more likely to have equity-promoting dialogue with them than with adults or society in general. However, the strongest empirical support for the force and pervasiveness of moral motivations is the complex justifications people construct to "prove" their moral purity. Freud's theory of the unconscious and the ego defenses is essentially centered on his observation that people cannot bear to think of themselves as immoral.

Although individual moral motivations are often posited, they are more often multiple and related; they can be classified as follows.

Motivation to Conserve One's Identity in Social Exchange. Conservation of one's identity is a strong motivation, quite aside from moral considerations. However, one cannot be a person to oneself unless one is a person to others, and given the social requirements and enhancements of our rearing, an important part of personhood is our belief in the self as moral; thus, we are motivated to conserve our view of ourselves as moral.

Guilt Motivating Morality. From the interactional view, guilt is a mismatch in identity—a matter of inconsistency—between the moral person one thinks one is and the immoral person one is afraid one has been. Guilt is not simply the anxiety of being caught; nor can it simply be the historic voice of the parent, given people's continuous construction of new meanings. Guilt surely must operate to produce moral consideration; however, extreme guilt usually produces excuses and unthinking distortions.

Motives Arising from Rational Considerations. Rational reasons are motives enough in themselves. Various theorists have proposed that motivation arises from enlightened self-interest (Kurt Baier), from recognition that altruism makes sense in view of one's future needs (Thomas Nagel), from self-interest traded off against others' self-interest (Rawls), or from guidance logically derived from one's extant imperative principles (Kohlberg).[14]

Motives as Intersubjective Accountability. Piaget declared that children first avoid contradicting their own logic in the presence of others, an observation he used in support of his view that the social basis and requirements of logic make it a moral imperative in itself.[15] Swanson argues that people require one another to be what in fact they publicly allow themselves to seem to be.[16] I have argued that accuracy in intrasubjectively assessing and expressing one's own needs and accuracy in intersubjectively assessing others' needs and the situation are normatively expected because our social life ultimately depends on such accuracy to sustain, enhance, and make sense of our lives.[17] Thus, intersubjective honesty for Piaget, rectitude for Swanson, and accuracy for Haan all exemplify integrity among people, a matter of good faith.

The development of children's moral intersubjectivity literally depends on their experiencing others as accountable, that is, knowing "good faith" rather than betrayal. Tangible loss is only one reason why people cannot tolerate bad faith. Of equal anguish to people are foiled expectancies. They risk themselves on the possibility that others are credible and feel like fools if they are "taken in" or "set up." Entering a moral dialogue is risky because the self is then exposed, but it is the actualization of people's root knowledge that they have no alternative but isolation and alienation.

The Self and Other in Interactional Morality

Given the social nature of human life, equity-promoting dialogue is what people normatively seek and commonly cherish; however, everyday solutions seldom maximize one person's claim, especially not at any given point in time. Thus, "losses" to the self as the price of commitment to others are inevitable, but they are countered by life-giving and -enhancing compensations that persuade most of us to continue to commit ourselves to others.

A morally adequate "taking all parties' claims into account" requires that all parties be able to speak and desirous of speaking so that the import of their claims can be known and not overlooked or slighted. Thus, people's subjective self-interest and their third-person view of themselves as legitimate moral objects are as necessary to the moral dialogue as are their concerns for others as moral objects. That selves must guiltlessly receive their deserts in order to function givingly is an insight of modern psychology. If the self is not adequately considered by the self and if the self does not require the other to consider the self's claims, the stage is set for a morally corrupt, possibly masochistic relation. At some level of awareness and enactment, the self's anger and the others' guilt are entailed. Therefore, a thin, shaky line divides altruism and masochism. Solid moral balances are struck only when parties' claims are legitimately taken into account and negotiated. Balances cannot be benevolently achieved. Thus, we can see why the magnanimity of the welfare state morally violates rather than pleases its recipients; instead of impersonal gifts, people much prefer what is legitimately theirs.

Equity-promoting dialogue seems to be a variant of the ideal speech situation as it is envisioned by Habermas and by Rawls; however, there are important differences between the two. For Habermas the ideal speech situation is a means of discovering truth as consensus (not morality);[18] for Rawls it is a device to explicate the conditions he thinks are necessary in order for ideal moral contracts to be drawn.[19] However, I mean that equity-promoting dialogues literally occur and that people "believe" in equity (because of all the warrants and on the grounds I have proposed above), to the extent that they will support equity *against* their own desires! Equity is so critical in human interchange that people lie to themselves when they deprive others of it (for instance, by insincere dialogue) or when they themselves are deprived of equity and cannot bear to recognize their own powerlessness. Life without equity or hope of achieving equity is socially unbearable and without meaning.

In ideal circumstances, dialogues are likely to result in both parties taking the agreed-on action because their decisions are public and particular instead of private and general, as are decisions in the Platonic formulations. Because dialogical decisions are already a kind of action, preparation and consummation flow in sequence, and the usual disjunctures between private judgment and public act are less likely to occur. All eyes are on the resolutions. Moreover, the particular considerations of the situation and the parties involved are likely to match resolutions with the circumstances of the situation and the needs of the parties; thus, resolutions are less likely to be vacuous and grandiloquent or awkward to enact.

Development of Interactional Morality

Participation in moral exchanges begins when people are two or three years old. Recent studies of preschoolers' ideas about morality[20] and observations by my colleagues and I indicate that their morality is not physicalistic, as Piaget's early work suggested, and not oriented to propitiating power, as Kohlberg avers.[21] Nonetheless, as people grow older, they become more skilled in moral interchanges gradually, because understanding intersubjectivity is not an easy matter, The various concerns, intransigencies, priorities, and conditions of each party need to be considered, integrated, compromised, or discarded, and the possibilities for resolution are numerous and complex.

Capability of logical, philosophical reasoning is clearly not a precondition of higher development in the interactional system; instead, experiences in intersubjective exchanges, which occur in even the most "primitive" societies, are required. Who can say life among the Hopi Indians or the Sherpa of Nepal is morally inferior to life in New York City? In fact, moral experiences of sufficient social meaning to facilitate development may be few in number the more complex the living situation and society. Complexity tends to diffuse responsibilities and confuses knowledge of contingencies. Research concerning the responses of bystanders who have witnessed accidents and injuries indicates that people reared in cities are less likely to help victims than are those reared in small towns.[22]

Two critical differences between the interactional formulation and Kohlberg's Platonic system are the latter's assertions that morality develops in stages and that the logical stages, described by Piaget, are necessary but insufficient preconditions of moral development. Setting aside the moral-political implications of this elite position that only those of higher logical stages can be morally "adequate," there are further countering empirical reasons for disagreeing. Children's experiences with morality are very different from their experiences with the invariance of the physical world (the experiences Piaget has shown are involved in the evolution of logical stages). A child's experience that gravity pulls is never contradicted, but people often morally contradict each other and themselves. Circumstances A and B, which seemingly differ in the smallest degree, can have vastly different implications. The small boy I described earlier knows that if his brother does not cry after being hit, the social results are different from those when his brother cries even a little bit.

Interactional morality does not evolve from the child's learning fixed moral categories and then progressively integrating and reintegrating these at different stages. Instead, moral development evolves from the considerably more situationally and intersubjectively responsive skill of coming to know how to engage in exchange, to know when, why, and how much to give in terms of the others' claims and needs and one's own, when all involved are deserving and all have a future together, invariably interacting and mutually needful and committed to each other. The invariant authority of the physical world probably has no counterpart in the everyday social world. More inventiveness, fluidity, and flexibility are required in moral dialogues and resolutions that can be embraced within stages, which, if not literally true, can be conceptually useful only if they represent invariant structures. Gradualism is the kind of learning involved in interactional morality.

Dialogues That Do Not Achieve Equilibration Among Parties

Full accounts of exceptional dialogues are not possible here, but three main kinds seem to exist: actual imbalances that are, nevertheless, legitimated—for instance, between parent and child; false balances that have a surface appearance of legitimation; and imbalances arising from exploited differences in social power like status or caste.

Several aspects of parent-child relations prevent full moral exchange and true equilibration. Unique to this dyad is the fact that children do not initially make a free, autonomous commitment to enter into the relationship with parents—they do not ask to be born— nor can they ordinarily terminate the relationship if it lacks moral equity. However, parents do (presumably) make a free, autonomous commitment to bear children. Entailed in that commitment are the parents' intentions "to rear" children—that is, to enhance children's development, power, and integration until they are "grown up" and,

in less obvious ways, when they are adults. Children do not recipro-
cate moral concern equal to their parents', at least not until the parents are aged. In their own turn, the children will take disproportion-
ate moral responsibility for their children. (As Rawls whimsically said,
only the first generation of parents is deprived by this arrangement.[23]) Another reason why these moral exchanges are imbalanced
is that children are morally immature. Parents settle for less sensitive, less adequate resolutions, which attenuate their own good simply because children cannot grasp social nuances and lack power to
enact commitments. In other words, equity is achieved, transcendentally and historically, by parents' awareness that they become morally
indentured as they bear children and that their compensations are
different in kind and come at a different time.

Thus, moral agreements achieved between parents and children
are not literally equilibrated as are normative balances and are only
eventually equilibrated by the transcendental meanings of parents'
commitments in bearing and rearing children. Plainly, the actual imbalance is socially legitimated and socially required.

Legitimated imbalances can also occur between people of unequal
personal resources; in fact, they *should* occur if long-term equity is
to be sustained. Thus, we agree, for example, that special expenditures should be made to fix building entrances so that physically
handicapped people can enter and participate in work and social life.
At the same time, people of lesser power and resources violate the
terms of the moral dialogue if they expect to receive in all ways or in
ways not relevant to their handicaps.

False balances can arise from insincere, conscious freeloading or
from unconscious folie à deux. However, moral theories that contain
extensive provisions for the prevention of freeloading—a phobic response to sin—tend to make adversaries of discussants, no matter
what their commonalities, and thereby close off opportunities for moral
understanding to evolve. However, if a participant proves to be insincere on repeated appraisals, dialogue becomes futile. Sincere participants will protect themselves and their groups first by withdrawal but
perhaps later by force, as they are entitled to do because they must
be moral objects to themselves.

False balances based on the willingness of partners to accept
inequitable relations—for instance, sadomasochistic pairs—seem to
counter the grounds asserted here that all people want equity. The

first easy explanation is to take the ontological stance that because all people basically want equity, parties would not knowingly or freely enter into a sadomasochistic relationship, and any happiness they report is false. In other words, the argument of neurotically diminished capacity could be advanced.

However, I argue that if the partners could be induced to reflect on their sadomasochistic choice, they would agree to the proposition that relations between master and slave are morally corrupt and would not recommend that relationship to their offspring or to future generations, although they might not choose to change their own ways. Their actual choices for themselves are not moral ones; neither party asks, "Should I (in a moral sense) enslave this masochist?" or "Should I enslave myself to this sadist?" Instead, strategic and instrumental considerations of safety, security, and gains dominate their choices. Their moral evaluations, if these could be secured without evoking guilt and arousing distortions, would be revealed by their recommendations for their offspring and future generations. Over the course of history, oppressed people have hoped that their descendants would secure equity even when the cost of their gaining equity in their own lifetimes has been too high. What people actually choose is not synonymous with what they prefer. Sociohistoric necessities distort choice.

When a moral problem arises between two people or two societies of unequal power, no basis exists, within the interactional formulation, for discussants of greater power to dominate the dialogue. Merit, for instance, does not legitimate the use of power in dialogue; to use advantage extraneous to the issue is bad faith that disrupts dialogue or leads to unsatisfactory conclusions, outcomes that are evident when oppressed groups are dominated; they resort to underground strategies of sabotage and nonproductive pseudostupidity. However, if the oppressed's strategies become morally insensitive, they lose appeal to observers who might otherwise be moved to enter the dialogue to ensure society's moral equilibration.

Individual psychological statuses also lead to false moral consciousness. People can crystallize their basic approach to moral dialogue and negate moral information; they do not see the conflict, and, therefore, they are unperturbed. Stressful situations may cause some participants to accept or invent false balances that seem to protect their sense of self-consistency as moral beings. In other words, they

choose compartmentalization instead of disintegration. Finally, deleterious life situations can positively favor participants' personal incli-
nations to accept false balances.

SOCIETY AND INTERACTIONAL MORALITY

The society that rests on dialogue with its citizens is the organizational example par excellence of interactional morality. However, this
simple, not new stipulation for organization is seldom enacted by societies. At its root, it mandates the radical move that those who are
not now heard be heard. The eighteen-year-olds described in our example, who had just experienced a benevolent "monolithic" society,
understood the profound but subtle distinction between creating justice and being given justice. Perhaps the distinction, which means
either power or powerlessness for the self, cannot be entirely grasped
by the powerful unless they have fully experienced the emotion of
powerlessness.

Above all else, collectivities are moral orders; societies are created
and bonded and survive and flourish by reason of their moral agreements, which are forever being invented and reinvented to reflect the
concerns of each generation or the shifting concerns of people over
their lifetimes. From the standpoint of interactional morality, open
moral dialogue generates the social and personal sensibility in citizens that morally legitimates societal relations; thereby structures of
meaningful social order are created; and order need not be pursued
for its own sake. This sequence of events is the reverse of those ty-
pifying the traditional, official Platonic moralities, in which the proper
moral order is the starting point that structures the nature of the
moral operations that are finally expected to provide citizens with
personal sensibility.

Societies' official moralities, received by the populace in treatises
and from wise men, have usually differed from the everyday morality
practiced by citizens or by officials in their private lives. An impediment to the widespread practice of interactional morality is that we
have so far constructed few institutionalizations of it. The telling
question, which when answered reveals the relation of a social-moral
system to citizen participation, is, "By what means does social morality come to be understood by citizens within their lifetimes? Is it revealed to them or achieved by them?" Platonic theories put the citi-

zen in the position of learning or, at best, rediscovering the extant, traditional moral categories; the interactional formulation puts citizens in the more difficult role—and, some would say, society in the more risky position—of constantly working to achieve moral agreements.

Empirical reasons exist for thinking that each generation goes through the processes of creating its morality in its everyday life, whatever its response to the received morality. In other words, to "be moral," people must actually and authentically participate in building the morality they endorse and use; it is *not* morality, in the common-sense meaning and usage of the word and concept, for persons merely to comply with or follow traditions or the latest novelty. Both ideas— that the constructivist mind must produce its own morality and that the person's morality must be self-motivated—are entailed in the ways we think about morality in everyday exchanges. Admission that the minds of people are active and constructing makes it necessary also to concede that human groups do not achieve permanent solutions; nor should they want to, given the complexities, inventiveness, and fortunate obstinacy of members and the complications that nature itself creates.

Although everyday moral ideas may seemingly have less influence than the official morality, it is common morality that judges the social-moral issues of the day to determine a society's legitimacy. Often social dissidents are those whose life positions give them possibilities of recognizing and articulating disparities between the official statements and the actuality: being a woman, black, or poor makes such differentiations clear. Expanding or contracting disparities between everyday and official moralities (as these are discussed in this volume by Flacks) may account for the cycles of privatism and public protests. Given human bondedness, people's withdrawal to privatism may often be an intelligent, self-protective move away from participation in a society that appears immutable, rather than an indication of personal selfishness or passivity, as leaders who seek to legitimate their activities often suggest. Despite the fluidities of people and their affairs, our social history suggests that moralities of ideal, fixed categories which support the status quo have usually been officially favored in the stead of inductive and dialogical methods of testing and redeeming moral claims that are responsive to change and to claims from all views relevant to the issue.

Official moralities of ideal, fixed categories are easily professed, and leaders are like all other people in wanting to think of themselves as morally impeccable; consequently legitimation is a chronic problem of many societies. The U.S. government's need to legitimate itself during the Vietnam War provides an example of distorted justification. Hampshire describes the policy makers' defensive reactions;

"Under the influence of bad social science and bad moral philosophy that usually goes with it, they oversimplified the moral issues and provided an example of false rationality. . . . They thought that their opponents were sentimental and guided only by their unreflective emotions." [24]

The pull of membership in human collectivities complicates society's practice of morality. Happily, the pull ensures our morality, but it leaves us vulnerable to our leaders' moral blandishments and accusations. We can be persuaded that our group is morally superior and that therefore it is imperative that we save the world by shaping it to our image. Or we can be persuaded that our group is guilty, so morally reprehensible that we deserve our poor fate on this earth. When leaders use moral words to manipulate, our commitments to the collectivity make us susceptible to belief. Therefore, the citizenry needs full understanding of the false and authentic moral meanings of group membership. Our membership in collectivities is both our hope and our Achilles' heel. When leaders seek to promote equity-seeking dialogue, their language is different; they neither blandish nor discipline but instead coordinate and participate as members of the dialogue.

In an unjust society, interactional morality can still flourish on some levels or within small intimate groups, but a just society cannot exist without interactional morality. As I see it, justice is merely the more formal, nominal end product of equity in interaction, but equity itself cannot be achieved without equitable participation. However, equitable interaction in face-to-face groups is not sufficient to build a society with institutional forms that support equity. To me, formalized moral ideas are nothing more than reified adulterations of intellectualized restatements of aspects of interactional morality, preferred or more persistently used by problem solvers with special intellectual training. Therefore I am proposing that interactional morality is the more basic description and that the Platonic moralities are the intellectuals' phobic reactions to social uncertainty.

The special moral situation of the disadvantaged provides an example of the disjunctures of the official, received morality when it is applied to real lives. For the disadvantaged to believe in the reality of society's formal moralizations is not sensible; society cannot be legitimate for them. What they want is participation so that they can work for their own good. The contradiction is well illustrated by Kohlberg's attempt to "raise" the morality of women convicts, most of whom were prostitutes and blacks.[25] Had this intervention been successful, and apparently it was not, the women's belief in Kohlberg's conventional stages of formal morality could not have helped them adapt in prison or on the streets. In neither setting could there have been opportunities for them to live according to Kohlberg's categories of justice. Clearly their prostitution reflects a far larger problem of socioeconomic stress than a private one of their personal moral inadequacy. People cannot be asked, except with great clarity, to sacrifice their certain good for an uncertain theoretical good in the future. The more remote justice is from the actual experience of people, the less intelligent it is for them to accept society as morally legitimated.

SUMMARY AND CONCLUSIONS

I have described a working formulation of interactional morality based on the thin assumptive value that people have the right to pursue their own good and to have their good equitably considered. In addition to this assumption of value, I constructed an empirical, naturalistic, and pragmatic formulation of the morality of everyday life. Its main ideas, I argued, are those commonly used by people. Thus, my hope was to construct a theory that is "true" in the sense of recruiting wide consensus, not a theory that would merely be "best" from positions resting on strong assumptions of value. The implicit, central function of most moral theories appears to be the control of "innate" human selfishness. In contradistinction I argued that people's development of powerful moral motivations is all but inevitable and that the critical moral problem for humankind is not the control of selfishness but instead society's facilitation or deterrence of our competence and accuracy in practicing the morality that we invariably endorse.[26]

In any event, moral motivation is a subject for empirical investigation, and the idea of "innate" selfishness is without evidential support; it is an anachronistic, covertly political definition of human nature which has provided the rationalization for the elite's using morality as an instrument of political manipulation—people's commitments to their collectivity make them susceptible to charges of moral unworth.

Formal theories of a priori standards seem to have blanketed the morality of equitable participation ever since Plato and Aristotle discredited the empirical and naturalistic moralities of the Sophists with charges of relativism. Plainly no moral theory is without both its relativism and its absolutism, because life cannot be absolutely ordered but at the same time we cannot reason together and relate to each other without some standardizations. Thus, these arguments for and against relativism are partly spurious. The question for moral theory rather concerns which elements are absolute and which are relative. Platonic moralities propound eternal substantive verities, whereas the moralities of everyday life can do no other than prescribe the processes that people use to solve moral problems. The perfectly just society based on eternal verities is a commonplace promise, but it is the participating society that we probably need and realistically want.

In our theories and investigations, we social scientists seem, quite haphazardly, to use whatever moral assumptions are at hand, whatever moral assumptions were embedded in the theories we embraced as graduate students, or, when we are deeply involved, our personal moral ideas. Our past to the contrary, it is as Quine said: we need not be enslaved to the assumptions we grew up with, because we can "cunningly" readjust our understandings.[27] If we can eventually identify anchor points of the morality of everyday life, which I argue exists, we might forestall an open and discrediting war of social scientific ideologies. As we admit our value base—as most chapters in this volume indicate we must and will—open conflict about the "proper" best morality for social science could ensue. If we had a consensual theory, tied to the realities of everyday life, we might circumvent this wasteful struggle and overcome our chronic haggling about picayune problems of methodology, disagreements that often disguise our moral confusion. But then social science would be reconstructed.

NOTES

1. Eric Havelock, *The Liberal Temper in Greek Politics* (New Haven: Yale University Press, 1957), p. 169.

2. *Ibid.*, pp. 11–21, passim.

3. *Ibid.*, p. 347; also see W. K. C. Guthrie, *The Sophists* (Cambridge: Cambridge University Press, 1971); and Leo Strauss, "The Liberalisms of Political Psychology," *Review of Metaphysics* (1959), 12:390–439.

4. Lawrence Kohlberg, "Education for Justice; A Modern Statement of the Platonic View," in Nancy Sizer and Theodore Sizer, eds., *Moral Education: Five Lectures* (Cambridge: Harvard University Press, 1970), p. 58.

5. Lawrence Kohlberg, "From is to Ought: How to Commit the Naturalistic Fallacy and Get Away with It in the Study of Moral Development," in Theodore Mischel, ed., *Cognitive Development and Epistemology* (New York: Academic Press, 1971).

6. See, for instance, F. E. Trainer, "A Critical Analysis of Kohlberg's Contribution to the Study of Moral Thought," *Journal for the Theory of Social Behavior* (1977), 1:41–63; Norma Haan, "Two Moralities in Action Contexts," *Journal of Personality and Social Psychology* (1978), 36:286–305; Charles Levine, "Role-Taking Standpoint and Adolescent Usage of Kohlberg's Conventional Stages of Moral Reasoning," *Journal of Personality and Social Psychology* (1976), 34:41–46; Elizabeth Simpson, "Moral Development Research," *Human Development* (1974), 17:81–106; and H. Reid and E. Yaronella, "Critical Political Theory and Moral Development," *Theory and Society* (1977), 4:479–504.

7. Haan, "Two Moralities."

8. Jean Bethke Elshtain, "The Love Song of J. Carter," *The Nation,* April 26, 1980, p. 497.

9. R. S. Rudner, *Philosophy of Social Science* (Englewood Cliffs, N.J.: Prentice-Hall, 1966).

10. John Rawls, *A Theory of Justice* (Cambridge: Belknap Press, 1971).

11. Jürgen Habermas, *Communication and the Evolution of Society*, Thomas McCarthy, trans. (Boston: Beacon Press, 1979).

12. Terence Des Pres, *The Survivors* (New York: Oxford University Press, 1976); Bruno Bettelheim and M. B. Janowitz, *Social Change and Prejudice* (New York: Free Press, 1964); Victor Frankl, *From Death Camp to Existentialism* (Boston: Beacon Press, 1962).

13. Havelock, *The Liberal Temper*, p. 393.

14. Kurt Baier, *The Moral Point of View* (Ithaca, N.Y.: Cornell University Press, 1958); Thomas Nagel, *The Possibility of Altruism* (Oxford: Clarendon Press, 1970); Rawls, *The Theory of Justice;* and Kohlberg, "From Is to Ought."

15. Jean Piaget, *The Psychology of Intelligence* (London: Routledge & Kegan Paul, 1950).

16. Guy E. Swanson, "Self Process and Social Organization: An Interpretation of the Mechanisms of Coping and Defense," unpublished ms., 1968.

17. Norma Haan, *Coping and Defending: Processes of Self-Environment Organization* (New York: Academic Press. 1977).

18. Habermas, *Communication.*

19. Rawls, *The Theory of Justice.*

20. For example, see John Darley, Ellen Klosson, and Mark Zanna, "Intentions and Their Contexts in the Moral Judgments of Children and Adults," *Child Development* (1978), 49:66–74; at least twenty other reports suggest that young children's morality is more differentiated.

21. Jean Piaget, *The Moral Judgment of the Child* (1932; rpt., New York: Free Press, 1965); Kohlberg, "From Is to Ought."

22. Bibb Latané and John Darley, *The Unresponsive Bystander* (New York: Appleton-Century-Crofts, 1970).

23. Rawls, *The Theory of Justice*.

24. Stuart Hampshire, ed., *Public and Private Morality* (Cambridge: Cambridge University Press, 1978), p. 51.

25. Lawrence Kohlberg, Peter Scharf, and Joseph Hickey, "The Justice Structure of the Prison—A Theory and an Intervention," *The Prison Journal*, (1973), 51:3–14; also Peter Scharf and Joseph Hickey, "The Prison and the Inmates' Conception of Legal Justice: An Experiment in Democratic Education," *Criminal Justice and Behavior* (June 1976), 3:107–22.

26. Jürgen Habermas, *Legitimation Crisis* (Boston: Beacon Press, 1975).

27. Willard V. O. Quine, *The Ways of Paradox* (New York: Random House, 1966).

Eleven

INTERPRETIVE SOCIAL SCIENCE VS. HERMENEUTICISM

Jürgen Habermas

Let me start with a personal reminiscence. When I first argued in 1967 that the social sciences could not dismiss the hermeneutic dimension of research and that attempts to repress the problem of interpretation would lead to distortions, I had to face two basic types of objections.[1] First was the insistence that hermeneutics was not a matter of methodology at all. The problem of interpretation, as Hans-Georg Gadamer argued, originates in nonscientific contexts, be it in everyday life, in history, art, and literature, or, generally, in coping with the continuation of traditions. Philosophical hermeneutics is designed for elucidating commonsense processes of understanding, not for a systematic attempt at or procedure for collecting and analyzing data. Gadamer conceived of "method" as something opposed to "truth," which can be attained only by skillful and prudent understanding. Hermeneutics, he said, as a practice, is at best an art and never a method—with regard to science, a somewhat subversive force that undermines a systematic approach.[2] The second type of objection came from the advocates of mainstream social science, who offered an almost complementary argument. The problem of interpretation, they said, lies in its mystification. There are no general problems of interpretation, only particular problems that are solvable with standard research techniques. A careful operationalization of theoretical terms, that is, tests of the validity and reliability of instruments, provides safeguards against the experimenter's effects by preventing the difficulties that arise from the otherwise unmanageable and unanalyzed complexity of ordinary language and everyday life.

Thus, in the mid-sixties the lines of controversy viewed hermeneutics in the social sciences either as a blown-up substitute for Heideggerian ontology or as merely a problem of trivial difficulties due to imperfect measurement procedures. Since then, this constellation has changed remarkably. The main arguments of philosophical hermeneutics have become more or less accepted, not in terms of a philosophical doctrine but as a research paradigm *within* the social sciences, within anthropology, sociology, and social psychology. This is what Paul Rabinow and William Sullivan have christened "the interpretive turn."[3] In the course of the seventies, several tendencies inside and outside academia have been advantageous to the breakthrough of the interpretive paradigm. Let me mention only a few of them.

First, there was the Popper-Kuhn debate and the rise of a postempiricist philosophy of science that has demolished the authority of logical positivism and therewith dissolved the vision of a (more or less) unified, nomological science. One offshoot is a shift in the history of science from normative reconstructions to hermeneutically more sensitive approaches.

Then, there was the failure of mainstream social science to keep its theoretical and practical promises. Sociology did not live up to the standards set by Parsonian theory building; Keynesian economics failed on the level of effective policies; and in psychology, learning theory—the one major example of dependable behavioral science—ultimately failed. This opened the door for alternative approaches based on phenomenology, later Wittgenstein, philosophical hermeneutics, critical theory, etc.[4] These could be recommended simply because they offered alternatives to the prevailing objectivism—not so much by reason of any acknowledged superiority.

Next were two moderately successful approaches that provided guidelines for an interpretive type of social science: structuralism in anthropology and linguistics and, less convincingly, in sociology; and genetic structuralism in developmental psychology—a model which holds out promise for the analysis of social evolution, the development of world views, moral belief systems, legal systems, etc.

Another tendency was a neoconservative shift in the philosophical climate, which has also meant a shift in the background assumptions of social scientists. There has been, on the one hand, a certain revival of biologistic approaches, which had been politically discredited for several decades (for example, sociobiology and genetic intelligence research), and on the other hand, a return to relativisms, historicisms, existentialisms, Nietzscheanisms of all kinds, ranging from the harder disciplines, such as the philosophy of science and linguistics, to the softer areas, including cultural studies, literary criticism, and architectural ideologies. Both these tendencies are indicators of the same syndrome, expressed as the widespread belief that whatever is universal in culture, if anything, is due more to the natural state of man than to any rational infrastructure of human language, cognition, and action, that is, of culture itself.

TWO MODES OF LANGUAGE USE

In the interests of connecting the problem of interpretation with the topic of the social sciences and morality, let me first explain what I mean by hermeneutics. Any meaningful expression—be it an utterance, verbal or nonverbal, or an artifact, such as a tool, an institution, or a scripture—can be bifocally identified, both as an observable event and as an understandable objectification of meaning. We well might describe, explain, or predict a noise that is equivalent to the phonetic utterance of a sentence without having any idea of what this utterance means. To grasp (and state) its meaning, one must participate in some (actual or imagined) communicative actions, in the process of which one must use that very phrase in such a way that it is intelligible for speakers, hearers, and bystanding members of the same speech community. Richard Rorty mentions an extreme case: "Even if we could predict the sounds made by the community of scientific inquirers of the year 4000, we should not yet be in a position to join in their conversation."[5] The contrast between "predicting their future speech behavior" and "joining in their conversation" appeals to the important distinction between two different modes of employing language. Either you *say what is or is not the case* or you *say something* to somebody else so that the hearer *understands what is said.* Only the second mode of using language is internally, or conceptually, bound to the conditions of communication. To say how things are does not necessarily depend on some sort of real or fictitious communication; one does not have to make a statement or perform a speech act. One may, instead, say to oneself "p" or just "think that p." To understand what is said does, on the other hand, require participation in communicative action. There must be (or at least be imagined) a speech situation where a speaker in communicating with a hearer about something gives expression to what the former means. However, in the case of the cognitive and uncommunicative use of language, there is only one fundamental relation implied; let us call it the "about" relationship between sentences and something in the world. In contrast, when language is employed for the purpose of coming to terms or reaching a consensus with somebody else (be it only to agree or disagree), there are three such relationships: in giving expression *of* a belief, the speaker communicates *with* another member of the same speech community *about* something in the world. Epistemology deals only with this last relationship between language and reality, but hermeneutics has to cope simultaneously with the tripartite relationship within utterances: expressions of the speaker's meaning, expressions for establishing the speaker's interpersonal relationship with the hearer, and expressions about something in the world. Furthermore, we are forced by a fourth relationship that arises from any attempt to clarify what it means for a speaker to know how to say something and for a hearer to know how to understand what is said; that is, the relationship between a given utterance and sets of all possible utterances made in the same language.

Hermeneutics looks at language while it is at work, as it is employed in reaching a common understanding or shared view among participants. The optical metaphor of the observer taking a "view" should not obscure, however, the fact that language, in its communicative use, is embedded in relationships that are much more complicated and as fundamental as the "about" relationship (and its correlated intentionality). In saying something within an everyday life context, the speaker refers not only to something in the objective world (as the totality of what is the case), but simultaneously to something in the social world (as the totality of legitimate interpersonal relationships) and to something in the speaker's own subjective world (as the totality of manifestable subjective experiences to which the speaker has privileged access).

This is how the tripartite network between utterance and world presents itself *intentione recta,* that is, from the speakers' (and the hearers') perspectives. The same network can be analyzed *intentione obliqua,* from the perspective of the life-world or from the background of shared assumptions and procedures, in which any particular piece of communication is inconspicuously embedded from the very beginning. From this viewpoint, language serves three functions: cultural reproduction, or keeping traditions alive (this is the angle from which Gadamer develops his philosophical hermeneutics); social integration, or coordinating the plans of different actors in social interaction (this is the point from which I would develop a theory of communicative action); and socialization, or the cultural interpretation of needs (this is the perspective from which G. H. Mead projected his social psychology of identity formation).

In short, while the cognitive and noncommunicative use of language demands a clarification of the "about" relationship, whether in terms of intentionality, propositional attitudes, directions of fit, or conditions of satisfaction, the communicative use of language confronts us with the problem of how this "about" relationship is linked with the relationships of "being shared *with*" and "being an expression *of*." And this problem might be analyzed in terms of ontological and deontological worlds of claims to validity, yes/no reactions, and conditions for rational, motivated consensus.

We can see now why saying something and understanding what is said rely on more complicated and much more demanding presuppositions than just saying (or thinking) what is the case. Those who observe or believe or intend to bring about "p" take an *objectivating* attitude toward something in the objective world. Those who participate in processes of communication, saying something and understanding what is said—whether this is a perception, belief, or intention stated; a promise, order, or declaration made; or a wish, feeling, or mood expressed—have to take a *performative* attitude. This attitude allows for changes between the third person, or objectivating, the second person, or conformative, and the first person, or expressive, attitudes. The performative attitude allows for a *mutual* orientation toward validity claims (such as truth, normative rightness, and sincerity), which are raised with the expectation of a "yes" or "no" reaction (or a quest for further reasons) on the part of the hearer. These claims are designed for critical assessment so that an intersubjective recognition of a particular claim can serve as the basis for a rationally motivated consensus. At the same time, by taking a performative attitude, speaker and hearer get involved in those functions that processes of communication fulfill for the reproduction of the life-world both speaker and hearer share.

INTERPRETATION AND THE ISSUE OF OBJECTIVITY

If one compares the third-person attitude of those who just say (or think) how things are (the attitude of scientists, among others) with the performative attitude of those who try to understand what is said (interpreters, among others), the methodological consequences of a hermeneutic dimension in research come to the fore. Let me indicate three of the more important implications of hermeneutic procedures.

First, interpreters sacrifice the superiority of observers' privileged positions, since they are involved in the negotiation about validity claims. By taking part in communicative actions they accept an equal standing with those whose utterances they want to understand. They are no longer immune to the latter's and their own "yes" or "no" reactions but give in to a process of mutual criticism. Within a communicative process, whether actual or not, there is no a priori decision as to who has to learn from whom in order to reach a common understanding.

Second, in adopting a performative attitude, the interpreters not only give up a position of superiority to their subject matter, but they also face the issue of the context-dependency of their interpretation. They cannot be sure, in advance, that they and the hearer start from the same background assumptions and practices. The interpreters' global preunderstanding of the hermeneutic situation can be checked piece by piece, but it cannot be challenged as a whole.

Third, as important as the issues of the interpreters' disengagement in questions of validity and the decontextualization of interpretations is the fact that everyday language ranges over nondescriptive utterances and noncognitive validity claims. In everyday life we more often agree—or disagree—on the rightness of actions and norms, on the adequacy of evaluations and standards, on the authenticity or sincerity of self-expressions, than we do on the truth of propositions or theories. The knowledge employed in saying something is more comprehensive than strictly propositional or truth-related knowledge. To understand what is said, the interpreters have to grasp knowledge that relies on further validity claims. This is why a correct interpretation is not just true, like a true proposition; one should say rather that it matches, suits, or fits the meaning, the *interpretandum,* which the interpreters are supposed to explicate or account for.

These are three consequences of the fact that understanding what is said requires participation and not merely observation. It should be no surprise that any attempt to base science on interpretation, therefore, leads into difficulties. One major obstacle is the problem of how to measure symbolic expressions as reliably as physical phenomena. In the mid-sixties, Aaron Cicourel provided a good analysis of the hermeneutic problems of transforming context-dependent symbolic expressions, the meanings of which are intuitively at hand, into "hard" data.[6] The difficulties are due to the fact that what is understood in a performative attitude has to be translated into what can be perceived from a third-person point of view. The performative attitude, which is necessary for interpretation, admits of regular transitions between first-, second-, and third-person attitudes; for the purpose of measurement, the performative attitude has to be subordinated to just one of them, the objectivating attitude. Another major obstacle is the impact of values on fact-stating discourse. These difficulties spring from the fact that the theoretical frame for an empirical analysis of everyday behavior must be conceptually connected with the frames of the participants' everyday interpretations. *Their* interpretations are linked, however, with both cognitive *and* noncognitive claims to validity, whereas theoretical propositions are related only to truth. Charles Taylor and Alvin Gouldner have convincingly argued against the possibility of value-neutral languages in the social science field.[7] This position is, or can be, supported from different philosophical quarters, Wittgensteinian and Quinean as well as Marxian.

In short, every science that admits meaningful expressions as part of its object domain has to cope with the methodological consequences of the participatory role of an interpreter, who does not "give" meaning to things observed but instead explicates the "given" meaning of expressions that can be understood only from within processes of communication. These consequences threaten the very context-independence and value-neutrality that seem to be necessary conditions for the objectivity of theoretical knowledge.[8]

Must we conclude that Gadamer's position should also be accepted within and for the social sciences? Is the interpretive turn lethal for the strictly scientific standing of all nonobjectivistic approaches? Should we agree with Rorty's recommendation to put the social sciences side by side with the humanities, with literary criticism, poetry, and religion and with educated conversation in general? Should we admit that the social sciences at best contribute to our *Bildungswis-*

sen—supposing they are not going to be replaced by something more serious, in any case, for example, neurophysiology or biochemistry? I observe among social scientists three major reactions to these (or equivalent) questions. If we keep the claims to objectivity and to explanatory power separate, we might distinguish "hermeneutic objectivism" from "radical hermeneuticism" and "hermeneutic reconstructionism."

Some play down the more dramatic consequences of the problem of interpretation by returning to some version of an empathy theory of *Verstehen*. This theory rests on the assumption that we can crawl into another person's mind and meaning and can separate our interpretations from connections with our own hermeneutical situation. This would allow us to retain the claim to objectivity and to ignore theoretical claims. However, I think this way out has been blocked by Gadamer's critique of the early Dilthey's *Einfühlungstheorie*.

Some no longer hesitate to extend radical hermeneuticism, be it for Gadamerian or for Rortian reasons, to that field which unfortunately and mistakenly has been for some time claimed as the proper domain of the social sciences. They give up, be it with unease or with rather hopeful feeling, the claim both to objectivity and to explanatory power. One of the consequences is a kind of moral relativism, which means that different approaches will merely mirror different moral attitudes and convictions.

Some who face the problem of interpretation are prepared to drop the conventional postulate of value neutrality, abstain also from assimilating the social sciences to the model of pure nomological science, and yet advocate the desirability *and* possibility of approaches which promise to generate some sort of objective and theoretical knowledge. This position needs justification.

PRESUPPOSITIONS OF RATIONALITY IN INTERPRETATION

Let me first mention an argument that when fully developed would show that the interpreters' participatory involvement at the same time deprives them of the privileges of an observer's, or third-person, position and yet provides them with the means for maintaining a position of negotiated impartiality from within. The paradigm case for hermeneutics is the interpretation of a traditional text. The interpreters appear at first to understand the sentences of the author; then they have the disturbing experience that they do not adequately understand the text, that is, not to the extent that they can respond to the author. The interpreters take this to be a sign that they are embedding the text in another context than the author did, that they are starting with other questions. This disturbance in communication marks the initial situation. They seek, then, to understand why the author—in the tacit belief that certain states of affairs obtained, that certain values and norms were valid, that certain experiences could be attributed to certain subjects—made certain assertions in the text, observed or violated certain conventions, and described certain intentions, dispositions, feelings, and the like. Only to the extent that the interpreters grasp the reasons that allow the author's utterance to appear rational do they understand what the author could have meant.

Thus, the interpreters understand the meaning of the text only to the extent that they see why the author felt entitled to put forward (as true) certain assertions, to recognize (as right) certain values and norms, and to express (as sincere) certain experiences. The interpreters have to clarify the context, which the author must have presupposed to be common knowledge of the contemporaneous public, if the difficulties which the text now presents did not arise when it was written. This is explained by the immanent rationality which the interpreters must impute to all utterances insofar as they ascribe to them accountability that they have no reason to doubt. The interpreters cannot understand the semantic content of a text if they are not in a position to present to themselves the reasons that the author might have adduced in the initial conditions. And because it is not the same thing for reasons to be sound as for them to be taken to be sound—be they reasons for asserting facts, for recommending norms and values, or for expressing desires and feelings—the interpreters cannot present reasons to themselves without judging them, without taking a positive or negative position on them. It may be that the interpreters leave certain validity claims undecided, that they choose not to regard certain questions as decided, as the author did, but to treat them as problems. But interpreters can elucidate the meaning of an opaque expression only by explaining how this opacity arises, that is, why the reasons the author might have given in the original context are no longer acceptable to us.

In some sense, all interpretations are rational interpretations; interpreters can do no other than appeal to standards of rationality which they themselves have adopted as binding for all parties, including the author and his/her contemporaries (if they only could, and would in fact, enter that communication which the interpreters take up). Such an implicit appeal to presumably universal standards of rationality, even if it should be in a way inescapable for any dedicated interpreters, is, of course, not at all a proof for the soundness of that presupposition. But our intuition—those claims to truth, normative rightness, and sincerity that are meant to be universally acceptable under proper condition—should at least be sufficient reason to look, for a moment, at a type of metahermeneutical analysis which focuses on various conditions for the validity of meaningful expressions and performances.

I am thinking of the rational reconstructions of the know-how of subjects, who are entrusted to produce valid expressions and who trust themselves to distinguish intuitively between valid and invalid expressions. This is the domain of such disciplines as logic and metamathematics, of epistemology and the philosophy of science, of linguistics and the philosophy of language, of ethics and the theory of action, of aesthetics, of the theory of argumentation, etc. These disciplines all have the common intention of giving accounts of the pretheoretic knowledge and intuitive command, let us say, of the rule systems by means of which competent subjects generate and evaluate valid expressions and performance, such as correct inferences; good arguments; true descriptions, explanations, or predictions; grammatical sentences; successful speech acts; effective instrumental actions; adequate evaluations; and authentic self-expressions. To the extent that rational reconstructions explicate the conditions of validity for particular classes of expressions and performances, they can explain deviant cases and, therewith, gain a type of indirect legislative authority or *critical* stance. To the extent that rational reconstructions push differentiations between particular validity claims beyond the limits where they have been traditionally drawn, they can establish new analytical standards and therewith assume a *constructive* role. Finally, to the extent that rational reconstructions succeed in their search for very general conditions of validity, they can claim to identify universals and thus to produce a type of *theoretical* knowledge. It is on this plane that *transcendental* arguments containing the inescapability of presuppositions enter the scene.

Precisely these three characteristics (the critical stance, the constructivist twist, and the transcendental flavor) have often seduced philosophers into mistaking some sort of reconstructions for ultimate foundations, or *Letztbegründen*. It is important to see that rational reconstructions, like all other types of knowledge, have only a hypothetical status. They may very well start from a false sample of intuitions; they may obscure and distort the right intuitions; and they may, even more often, overgeneralize particular cases. They are in need of further corroboration. What I accept as an antifoundationalist criticism of all strong a priori and transcendentalist claims does not, however, block attempts to put rational reconstructions of supposedly basic competences on trial and to test them indirectly by employing them as input in empirical theories.

These are either genetic theories designed for an explanation of the ontogenetic acquisition of cognitive, linguistic, and sociomoral competences (the emergence of innovative structures of consciousness and their institutional embodiments in history); or they are theories designed for the explanation of systematic deviances (for example, speech pathologies, ideologies, and research programs that degenerate). The nonrelativist, Lakatosian type of interaction between the philosophy and the history of science is a case in point; what was learned from contexts of justification and what was first codified in terms of a pseudonormative methodology of nomological sciences were then tested against the background of what historians have had to say about the contexts of discovery and the empirical conditions and mechanisms for the growth of scientific knowledge.

THE EXAMPLE OF KOHLBERG'S THEORY OF MORAL DEVELOPMENT

I would like to take up the example of Lawrence Kohlberg's theory (which has recently, but not always for the right reasons, come under attack) for the sake of backing the second claim, that social sciences can be conscious of their hermeneutic dimension and yet remain faithful to the task of generating theoretical knowledge. I have chosen this example for three reasons.

First, Kohlberg's theory focuses on morality as an object, whereas the objectivity of the theory itself seems to be affected by the in-built preference for one moral theory as against others. Second, Kohlberg's theory represents a quite peculiar division of labor between the rational reconstruction of moral intuitions (philosophy) and the empirical analysis of moral development (psychology). And third, Kohlberg's declared intentions are at the same time risky and relevant—they challenge anybody who does not mutilate either the social scientist or the moral and political philosopher in themselves (that is, I expect, the authors in this volume).

Allow me to present the following responses, highly condensed and obviously in need of elaboration. First, there is an obvious parallel between Piaget's theory of cognitive development (in the narrow sense) and Kohlberg's theory of moral development. Both concentrate on the explanations of *competences*, which are defined as the ability to solve certain sets of empirical-analytical or moral-practical problems. Problem solving is objectively measured by the truth claims of descriptive statements, including explanations and predictions, or by the rightness of normative statements, including justifications of actions and norms of action. Both authors describe the target competence of young adults in terms of (more or less explicit) rational reconstructions of formal-operational thought and of postconventional moral judgment. Kohlberg also shares with Piaget a constructivist *concept of learning.* It is based on the assumptions that knowledge should be analyzed as the product of processes of coming-to-know; that learning is a process of problem solving, in which the learning subject is actively involved; that the learning process is guided by the insights of those involved in the extent that it can be internally reconstructed as leading from some interpretation X_1 of a problem to another interpretation X_2 of the same problem so that the subject can explain in the light of the second interpretation why the former is false, but not vice versa.[9]

Following this same line of reasoning, Piaget and Kohlberg construe a hierarchy of distinct levels of learning, or "stages," each defined in terms of a relative equilibrium of operations, which become increasingly complex, abstract, general, and reversible. Both authors make assumptions concerning the internal logic and the irreversibility of direction of learning processes, concerning learning mechanisms (of interiorization of schemes of action, instrumental, social, or discursive), concerning the initial conditions of the organism (stronger or weaker maturationism), concerning stage-specific stimulus inputs and related phenomena of decalage, retardations, promotions, etc.

Kohlberg adds assumptions on the interaction between sociomoral, and cognitive development.

Second, the danger of a naturalistic fallacy arises in view of the delicate, and in our context more important, complementarity of rational reconstruction and empirical analysis. Piaget in his later writings, and particularly since *Biologie et Connaissance,*[10] tends to assimilate his approach to systems theory. The concept of equilibrium, which imparts relative stability to the processes of problem solving, is measured by the internal criterion of the extent of reversibility, and it is also mixed up with connotations of a self-maintaining system's successful adaptation to changing environments. One can, of course, try to combine the structuralist and the systems models (as is attempted in social theory with the action model or life-world model and the systems model); but combining them is different from assimilating one to the other. The peculiar strength of developmental cognitivism is obscured by any attempt to reinterpret in *functional* terms the superiority of high-level achievements, as they are measured in terms of the *validity* of attempts to solve problems. We would not seriously need rational reconstructions at all if it were the case that what is true or morally right could be sufficiently analyzed in terms of what is effective in maintaining a system's boundaries. Kohlberg avoids this naturalist fallacy, although the following could well be understood as ambiguous:

Our psychological theory of morality derives largely from Piaget, who claims that both logic and morality develop through stages and that each stage is a structure which, formally considered, is in better equilibrium than its predecessor. It assumes, that is, that each new (logical or moral) stage is a new structure which includes elements of earlier structures but transforms them in such a way as to represent a more stable and extensive equilibrium.

Kohlberg then clearly states: "These 'equilibration' assumptions of our psychological theory are naturally allied to the formalistic tradition in philosophic ethics from Kant to Rawls. This isomorphism of psychological and normative theory generates the claim that a psychologically more advanced stage of moral judgment is more morally adequate, by moral philosophic criteria."[11]

Next, there is one strategic difficulty in theory formation that makes Kohlberg's theory different from Piaget's. Both explain the acquisition of universal competences in terms of culturally invariant patterns of development, where the pattern is determined by what is taken to be the internal logic of related learning processes. But cognitive universalism as compared with moral universalism is the easier position to defend—though still controversial—and is supported by a great deal of evidence that the level of formal operations determines the level of hypothetical moral reasoning about observable states and events. Kohlberg has assumed the tasks of (1) defending a universalist and cognitivist position against a moral relativism and a skepticism that are deeply rooted in empiricist traditions (and bourgeois ideologies) and (2) proving the superiority of some sort of formalistic Kantian ethics as compared with rule utilitarianism and (non-Rawlsian) contractarianism. There is an established discourse among contemporary moral philosophers that occurs within the context of defending (1) and (2). Although counterarguments are not readily at hand, my guess is that Kohlberg could win on the first issue (of universalism/cognitivism). On the second issue (of distinguishing his stage 6, formalistic morality, from his stage 5, contractual moral theories), Kohlberg's position is not philosophically very strong. A statement like the following is not acceptable if one wants to establish ethical formalism in terms of the *procedural rationality* of practical discourses: "A morality on which universal agreement could be based would require a different foundation. It would require that moral obligation be directly derived from a substantive moral principle which can define the choices of any man without conflict or inconsistency." When Kohlberg refers, however, to "ideal role-taking" as the "appropriate procedure" of practical decisions, he is well guided by intuitions and ideas expressed in the pragmatic Peircian *and* Meadian reinterpretations of Kantian principles in terms of participation in an idealized "universal discourse." Kohlberg finds this same intuition of *allgemeine-Zustimmungsfähigkeit* also in Rawls' theory: "A just solution to a moral dilemma is a solution acceptable to all parties, considering each as free and equal, and assuming none of them knew which role they would occupy in the situation."[12]

Now, let us assume that we could succeed in the defense of moral universalism. A second difficulty still remains. Kohlberg adopts a deontological position and maintains, for good reasons, I think, that postconventional moral consciousness rests on insight into the autonomy of moral discourse; this autonomy is gained by the separation of the mode of moral reasoning from all other modes of reasoning, whether related to fact stating, art criticism, therapy or something else. What is at stake is not the truth of propositions, the adequacy of evaluations or corresponding standards of appreciation, or the sincerity of self-expressions, but only the rightness of actions and of norms of actions: "The question is, is it morally right?"[13] From this question, the rational reconstruction on which Kohlberg must rely follows a type of normative theory in two distinct senses of the word "normative," as truth and as rightness. This theory is "critical" in the sense of explaining the conditions of certain kinds of validity claims— in this respect moral theories do not differ from reconstructions of what Piaget calls formal operational thought (logics and methodologies also assume legislative and constructive roles). As moral theories they are, however, not only critical but "normative" in the sense that they do not appeal to truth but to normative rightness as the standard for their own validity. In view of this, Kohlberg's starting point is different from Piaget's and also more complicated.

Should we conclude that a theory of moral development is somehow poisoned by the normative status of the particular kind of rational reconstruction which is built into it? Is Kohlberg's theory only pseudoempirical, a hybrid which can neither claim the dignity of a moral theory, plainly with normative standing, nor meet the standards of respectability of an empirical science, the theoretical propositions of which should be capable of being true or false—and exclusively so? I think the answer is no.

Kohlberg's own stand on the issue of how the philosophical reconstruction of moral intuitions relates to the psychological explanation of how people acquire these intuitions is not without ambiguity. First, let us consider the stronger claim that both are part of the same theory. This "identity thesis" claims "that an ultimately adequate *psychological* theory as to why a child does move from stage to stage, and an ultimately adequate *philosophical* explanation as to why a higher stage is more adequate than a lower stage are one and the same theory extended in different directions."[14]

The main support for this contention is derived from the constructivist concept of learning: subjects who move from one stage to the next should be able to explain why their judgments on the higher level are more adequate than those on the lower—and it is this line of the lay person's natural moral reasoning which is reflectively taken up by moral philosophers. This affinity is due to the fact that both the psychologist's subjects and the moral philosopher adopt the same performative attitude of a participant in practical discourse. In both cases, the outcome of moral reasoning, whether it is an expression of the layperson's moral intuition or the expert's reconstruction of it, is evaluated in the light of claims to normative rightness. The psychological theorists' attitude and the type of claim are however, different. Psychologists appropriately conceive of their subjects' learning process in terms of how the subjects would criticize lower-level judgments and justify higher-level judgments; but they, contrary to the subjects (and to their reflecting alter ego, the moral philosopher), describe and explain these judgments in a third-person attitude so that the outcome of *their* own reasoning is exclusively related to claims of propositional truth.

This important distinction is blurred by formulations like the following: "The scientific theory as to why people factually do move upward from stage to stage, and why they factually do prefer a higher stage to a lower, is broadly the same as a moral theory as to why people *should* prefer a higher stage to a lower."[15] Kohlberg rightly insists on the complementarity of the philosophical to the psychological theory:

While moral criteria of adequacy of moral judgment help define a standard of psychological adequacy or advance, the study of psychological advance feeds back and clarifies these criteria. Our psychological theory as to why individuals move from one stage to the next is grounded on a moral-philosophical theory which specifies that the later stage is morally better or more adequate than the earlier stage. Our psychological theory claims that individuals prefer the highest stage of reasoning they comprehend, a claim supported by research. This claim of our psychological theory derives from a philosophical claim that a later stage is "objectively" preferable or more adequate by certain *moral* criteria. This philosophic claim, however, would be thrown into question for us if the facts of moral advance were inconsistent with its psychological implications.[16]

This "complementarity thesis" states the case more adequately than the identity thesis does. The success of an empirical theory which can only be true or false may function as a check on the normative validity of hypothetically reconstructed moral intuitions. "The fact that our conception of the moral 'works' empirically is important for its philosophic adequacy." It is in this way that rational reconstructions can be put on trial or "tested," if "test" means an attempt to check whether pieces complementarily fit into the same pattern. In Kohlberg, the following is the clearest formulation: "Science, then, can test whether a philosopher's conception of morality phenomenologically fits the psychological facts. Science cannot go on to justify that conception of morality as what morality ought to be. . . ."[17]

Finally, the relation of mutually fitting together suggests that the hermeneutic circle comes to its full closure only on the metatheoretical level. The empirical theory presupposes the normative validity of the reconstruction by which it is informed, and yet this validity becomes doubtful as soon as the reconstruction does not "work empirically." This testing has, on the other hand, an impact on the hermeneutic dimension of research. The generation of data is "theory-guided" in a stronger sense than are normal interpretations. Compare the following two statements:

In Europe, a woman was near death from a very bad disease, a special kind of cancer. There was one drug that the doctors thought might save her. It was a form of radium for which the druggist was charging ten times what the drug cost him to make. The sick woman's husband, Heinz, went to everyone he knew to borrow the money, but he could only get together about half of what it cost. He told the druggist that his wife was dying, and asked him to sell it cheaper or let him pay later. But the druggist said, "No, I discovered the drug and I'm going to make money from it." So Heinz got desperate and broke into the man's store to steal the drug for his wife. Should the husband have done that? Why?

A man and wife had just migrated from the high mountain. They started to farm, but there was no rain, and no crops grew. No one had enough food. The wife got sick, and finally she was close to dying from having no food. There was only one grocery store in the village, and the storekeeper charged a very high price for the food. The husband asked the storekeeper for some food for his wife, and said he would pay for it later. The storekeeper said, "No, I won't give you any food unless you pay first." The husband went to all the people in the village to ask for food, but no one had food to spare. So he got desperate, and broke into the store to steal food for his wife. Should the husband have done that? Why?[18]

The first is Kohlberg's famous Heinz dilemma, which illustrates the method for eliciting relevant responses from American children—utterances being scored according to moral stages. The second statement is a translation of the (supposedly) equivalent dilemma which Kohlberg used for testing children in a Taiwanese village. I have no idea how strongly the Chinese version is loaded with Western biases; however weak this translation may be in view of the difficult hermeneutic task, it sheds light on the task itself. Only if the theory is correct should we be able to find context-sensitive equivalents for the Heinz dilemma in all cultures, so that we get Taiwanese answers comparable with the American ones on relevant dimensions of the theory. It is part of the theory that theory-relevant stories can be translated from one context into another—and the theory gives the cues for how it should be done. If it cannot be done without violence and distortion, the very failure of hermeneutic application indicates that the postulated dimensions are imposed from without and are not the result of a reconstruction from within.

Let me conclude by emphasizing that these considerations about the methodological structure of ontogenetic theories with in-built reconstructions of presumably universal moral intuitions have relied on Kohlberg's theory for illustrative purposes. They are not questions that concern the substantive parts of the theory: whether Kohlberg's reconstruction of a formalistic ethical theory needs improvement; whether, in particular, the formalistic approach to ethics unduly ignores contextual and interpersonal aspects of a kind of "situated" moral meaning; whether the Piagetian concept of developmental stages is too strong; and whether Kohlberg is wrong (cognitively biased) in his assumptions about the relation of moral judgment and action. I have different opinions on different issues—but this might be best left for discussions with the experts.

NOTES

1. Jürgen Habermas, "Logik der Sozialwissenschaften," *Philosophische Rundschau* (Tübingen), 1967).

2. Hans-Georg Gadamer, *Hermeneutik und Ideologikritik* (Frankfurt: Suhrkamp, 1970).

3. Paul Rabinow and William M. Sullivan, eds., *Interpretive Social Science: A Reader* (Berkeley: University of California Press, 1979).

4. Richard J. Bernstein, *Restructuring Social and Political Theory* (New York: Harcourt Brace Jovanovich, 1976).

5. Richard Rorty, *Philosophy and the Mirror of Nature* (Princeton, N.J.: Princeton University Press, 1979), p. 355.

6. Aaron Cicourel, *Method and Measurement* (Glencoe, Illinois: Free Press, 1964).

7. Charles Taylor, "Interpretation and the Sciences of Man," *Review of Metaphysics* (1971), 25; Alvin Gouldner, *The Coming Crisis of Western Sociology* (New York: Basic Books, 1970).

8. Let me add that with the distinction between sciences which are based on hermeneutical *procedures* and those which are not, I am not advocating a dualism be-

tween *ontological* features of different domains or regions of reality (culture vs. nature, values vs. facts, or similar neo-Kantian demarcations, most conspicuously produced by Windelband, Rickert, and also Cassirer). What I advocate, instead, is the *methodological* distinction among sciences which either do or do not rely on "understanding what is said" as the conditon for access to their object domain. Although all sciences have to, of course, cope with problems of interpretation on the metatheoretical (which became the focus of the postempiricist philosophy of science; cf. Mary Hesse, "In Defence of Objectivity," *Proceedings of the British Academy,* 58:275–92 (London: British Academy, 1972), only some of those with a hermeneutic dimension of research have to cope with interpretation on the basic level of the *generation of their data.* This is the reason Anthony Giddens speaks of a problem of "double-hermeneutics"; see his *New Rules of Sociological Method* (London: Basic Books, 1976). In this methodological definition of hermeneutically based sciences, I am at odds with Rorty's conception of hermeneutics as an act confined to abnormal discourses. Certainly, it is the breakdown of routinized communication and interpretation that most often provokes hermeneutic efforts in everyday life. But the need for interpretation does not arise only from situations where one is either puzzled or feels the Nietzchean thrill of the exciting, new, and creative. It emerges as well from more trivial encounters with what *happens* to be less familiar. Under the microscope of ethnomethodologists and philosophers, even the most commonsensical features of everyday life are transformed into something stronger. This artificial need for interpretation, for interpretation as a critical enterprise, is the case in the social sciences. Hermeneutics is not reserved for the noble and the unconventional; at least, this gentleman's concept of hermeneutics does not apply to the methodology of the social sciences.

9. Cf. the discussion between Stephen Toulmin and David W. Hamlyn in the latter's "Epistemology and Conceptual Development," in Theodore Mischel, ed., *Cognitive Development and Epistemology* (New York: Academic Press, 1971), pp. 3–24.

10. Jean Piaget, *Biologie et Connaissance* (Paris: Gallimard, 1967).

11. Lawrence Kohlberg, "The Claim to Moral Adequacy of a Highest Stage of Moral Judgment," *Journal of Philosophy* (1973), 70(18):632, 633.

12. Lawrence Kohlberg, "From Is to Ought: How to Commit the Naturalistic Fallacy and Get Away with It in the Study of Moral Development," in Mischel, ed., *Cognitive Development and Epistemology,* p. 213.

13. *Ibid.,* p. 215.

14. *Ibid.,* p. 154.

15. *Ibid.,* p. 223.

16. Kohlberg, "The Claim to Moral Adequacy," p. 633.

17. Kohlberg, "From Is to Ought," p. 223.

18. *Ibid.,* pp. 156.

PART III

SOCIAL APPLICATIONS AND SOCIAL POLICY

Twelve

REFLECTIONS ON THE FORM AND CONTENT OF SOCIAL SCIENCE: TOWARD A CONSCIOUSLY POLITICAL AND MORAL SOCIAL SCIENCE

Wolf-Dieter Narr

The proper study of social science is still man.

There is no lack of problems confronting all of us today. The danger of a worldwide war is increasing, and regional wars and organized murders occur so frequently as to have become commonplaces. The unequal social and material differences among societies on all the continents of the world are still increasing, and famine and malnutrition are an existential condition in many countries. Racial conflict and oppression in various forms continue in both developed and undeveloped countries. And, last but not least, large-scale human suffering is produced by the very institutions of liberal democracies, which tend toward bureaucratic states with some scattered areas of resistance at best.

The urgency of these problems prompts a call for social scientists to respond to them and offer some resolutions, and as quickly as possible. What is social science[1] good for if it fails to confront and tackle these dangers and difficulties? Reflecting on the moral responsibility of social science may seem a remote task, to be discussed during quiet days by the "soul-searching" people among social scientists rather than by the "doers" in their midst. However, as soon as one looks at the actual situation of social science this proves to be untrue. Self-reflection is a vital part of the work of every social scientist.

Speaking with "armed simplicity,"[2] one can state that social science does not fulfill its functions in any satisfying way, especially in regard to problem-solving expectations. Generally speaking, social science *reacts* to social problems; it does not anticipate them. Social science perceives problems in the conventional terms of today's society; it does not take a fresh and radical look at the problems. Social science does not inform us about and analyze problems by reflecting on them in their contextual entirety; it emphasizes the segmentalistic view and approach which are already dominant in modern societies where social science exists as a profession. In other words, social science is a dependent variable of the dominant patterns of present-day, highly developed capitalistic societies; it is more active in support of the strong bureaucratic tendencies of these societies than it is in strengthening the possibilities for the emancipation of people from them.

Especially from a democratic-moral point of view, social science does not fulfill its own or the public's expectations related to its enlightening capacity. In this respect Rousseau's famous answer to the question "Have the sciences and the arts made any contribution to the improvement of moral behavior?"[3] has to be repeated for social science too, although the reason for the negative answer would have to be modified and expanded. Why should social scientists be better people, and why should they not succumb to the dialectic of enlightenment,[4] as society in general does?

From a strictly professional point of view, social science does not keep its promises either. It functions primarily as an agent of socialization which corroborates existing patterns of perception and problem solving. This function is carried out mainly by the social science institutions at universities and research centers. Its second main function is as an agent for legitimation, as a coproducer, and especially as a "diffuser" of the main ideologies of societies. Here, social science plays a minor but important part within the context of "technology and science as ideology."[5] Ideology implies—in a strict sense, going back to Marx's definition of the term—false consciousness, which may serve, intentionally or unintentionally, as a kind of curtain to prevent people from observing, understanding, and acting on their own; or in Festinger's terms, ideology can be called an institutionalized "cognitive dissonance."[6]

The third function of social science is to "reduce complexity"[7] by its capacity to analyze and explain the structure of reality, that is, to show the web of hidden structures behind the seemingly incomprehensible ocean of events. In this capacity as a data-gathering and data-explaining science, social science remains extremely conventional and, at its best, instrumental. That is to say, social science does not add new dimensions and fundamentally new views to the dominant mode of perceiving reality. The social scientist plays the part of a social engineer who takes the structure and the basic functions of the "given machine" for granted. Like the government, the state, the economy, and so on, all in their given structure-oriented frames of reference, social science operates from a basically uncritical point of view and shrinks from radical analyses of anticipated problems which resist treatment according to customary patterns of perception.

This failure to function in a more original and imaginative capacity can be explained if one understands the "costs" which develop because social scientists insist on their discipline being accepted as a *science*. Paradoxically, it is just this insistence on consequences that impedes social science from functioning according to its promises and its abilities. The theoretical and practical longing for this scientific status[8] implies, among other things, a concept of science that is asocial and apolitical. Such a yearning for "purity" denies the dialectical relation of social science to its social and political "objects" and also to its own economy, politics, and society in general. Ignoring the basic premises of the founders of social science—Hobbes, Locke, Rousseau, Kant, Smith, and many others—contemporary social scientists neglect the fundamental fact that every scientific analysis starts from and is based on a historical conception of humankind (an anthropological notion) and is based on a conception of "good" and "bad" societies. All results of an analysis and all conclusions drawn from it are, in fact, valuable and estimable only in regard to the anthropological and social concepts on which the analysis is based. (See the schema at the end of this introduction.)

The problem with mainstream social science is not its failure to take this or that political point of view but its apolitical politics. Claiming to pursue scientific activities and to construct general models of behavior and organization, social scientists are actually hidden persuaders of one political point of view or another, of this or that political model, as, for instance, the American way of life or the German "model." Almost all theories and analyses influenced by Talcott Parsons, for example, can be shown to have this hidden outcome of persuasion.[9] Similar arguments could be made for the political implications of mainstream comparative political studies by Gabriel Almond, Sidney Verba, Walt Rostow, and others.[10] The developmental models of these scholars function as a kind of "scientific" imperialism. Their concepts and vocabulary of systems analysis reveal political biases of a seemingly suprapolitical, theoretical tool, but its political implications and consequences can be shown rather easily.[11] These models and theories function as powerful ideologies because of their scientific pretensions. In addition to their lacking analytical power—in a qualified sense of the term scientific—the toll they take when applied to real issues and real people is almost incalculable, especially when adapted to the problems of underdeveloped countries.

How are we to avoid this situation? Both science and social science make sense only as long as their results lie within explicated, objectified, and generalized limits. When these results contain mere opinions or are true for only one situation, we do not need scientists, let alone social scientists. Are there any criteria and procedural rules that may guarantee such objectifications and generalizations within explicated limits? Certainly, one has to start by acknowledging that there are some basic difficulties that cannot be solved by some masterful method once and for all. Some of the most intriguing difficulties are the following:

1. Since there is no such thing as an absolute ethic that defines what is "good" and what is "evil," there is no possible knowledge that can present us with a clear-cut rank order of basic human needs.[12] Therefore, we do not possess an absolute, suprahistorical yardstick to measure and qualify social events and social institutions.

2. Since there is no absolute moral measure and no absolute knowledge of human needs, the absolute "Gestalt" of the "normal" human society cannot exist. Nor will it ever be possible to detect such a "model" of man and society by means of science.

3. Since there is no method and, of course, no legitimating methodology,[13] social scientists will never be able to discover or construct characteristics of people and typical elements of societies that are universal facts and held beyond specific historical time and space but are at the same time socially relevant. Socially relevant facts are specific mediations (organization, form, modification, and so on) of universal needs and problems—for instance, that human beings cannot survive without food.

Three consequences are implicit in these three difficulties. First, general assumptions about the "nature" of human beings and the "nature/essence" of society have to be made explicit, because they are never natural in a prehuman definition of the term but are historically nurtured to a socially constructed and practical nature.

Second, moral criteria ("good"/"bad," "basic" and "superficial" human needs, and so on) are socially defined. Social science, which is concerned with society as a "moral entity" (the broad variations of norms and sanctions and the organizations that define the various societies) has to recognize the genesis and the functions of organized moral codes and, at the same time, reflect on its own relation to these various moral codes (because it is part of this or that "moral" world).

Third, any results of social science analysis can be proven (and therefore can make sense) only in the context of a socially defined time and a socially defined space, that is, for specifically structured and organized societies at a specific time. Any social science that issues assertions beyond socially conceived and mediated time and space loses its human context, that is, its object. It becomes a pretension, a mere timebound ideology.

Once these difficulties are recognized, the consequences for the criteria and procedures of social science seem almost self-evident. First, the basic anthropological, social, and political assumptions which influence any scientific analysis must be made explicit. These basic assumptions influence the scientific process more than is usually accepted in the neo-Kantian tradition.[14] Second, any social science analysis has to state quite clearly what kind of society and what kind of problems it is attempting to relate to. The interconnected degrees of specificity and generality have to be qualified. Third, the important postulate of thorough explication of assumptions is not sufficient.[15] For social science it is of utmost importance for its validity and reliability that it be aware of the permanent dialectical relationship between itself and the social "object" with which it is dealing. The dichotomy between the "subject" (the social scientist) and the "object" (the social problem) does not exist. There is permanent hidden and open feedback, and sometimes "subject" and "object" even change places. Social science must always be aware of both being affected by the "object" and affecting the "object."

Finally, in regard to criteria and procedures, social science is itself a social phenomenon to be explained and qualified in the context of a specific society. Therefore, the form and content of social science (that is, its organization and its tasks) have an important and decisive impact on its own quality. The social form and the social content of social science are conditioned by a given society; whether the content and form of social science are supporting each other or impeding each other, what kind of tasks are perceived, and what kinds of organizational forms are chosen determine the quality of social science. Scientific pretensions are dependent on them.

Because the social reality of social science, as represented by the perception of its tasks and by the realization of its organization, is so important, I will now focus on the content and the form of social science. My analysis begins with two assumptions. First, as long as social science claims to be more than a derivative branch of dominant tendencies and interests, it has to get its set of problems (tasks and duties) from its own analysis of existing society and its own analysis of its own capacity. The proper functions of social science are not arbitrary ones but can be derived from an analysis of existing society. Second, whatever the perceived tasks of social science may be, the realization of these tasks is defined by the way social science is organized, that is, by the form of social science. Therefore, it is also necessary to analyze the adequacy of the connection between tasks and forms, as well as to change the forms if one comes to the conclusion that social science does not fulfill its purposes. Before launching on this analysis, however, let us review the following schema, which outlines the value-relatedness of the scientific process of social science.

The Permanent Constitution and Regulation of the Analytical Process of Social Science by Values

Note: Not an allegedly value-free or merely value-related social science but only a value-explicit and a value-reflecting social science, as an outspoken moral political science, has the capacity to become a human science in a nonideological way.

1. Prescientific concepts
    a. Image of the human being
        i. Individualistic (Hobbes, Locke)
        ii. Social conception (Aristotle, Marx)
        iii. Optimistic assumption of "human nature" (Erasmus of Rotterdam)
        iv. Pessimistic assumption of "human nature" (Luther, Hobbes)

      v. In between, the human being as a set of ambiguous abilities (Gehlen)

   b. Image of the "good" or "bad" society

2. Specific premises
   a. Accepting the structure and functions of society as basically given, that is, analyzing problems in a society, or starting from a fundamentally critical point of view
   b. Analyzing the problem of a given society as a totality

3. Purposes (frame of reference)
   a. Analyzing "abnormal," anomic behavior from the point of view of the stability of a given group, institution, or society
   b. Hypothesizing the "normality" of a given group or society from the anomic point of view
   c. Qualifying stability or security from the systems point of view or from the perspective of an autonomous citizen, etc.

4. Selection of topic, or qualification of relevance (roll-call analysis of voting behavior of senators, key determinants of world market)

5. Selection of dimension of analysis and of data
   a. Subjective dimension (what people articulate, for instance, in regard to work satisfaction)
   b. Objective dimension (for instance, structure of workplace, workload, etc.)

6. Criteria for the reliability and validity of data
   a. Opinions, behavior patterns, activities, the output of institutions, etc., taken at face value, as "givens," so to speak
   b. Data qualified according to a hierarchy of factors and generation of data then analyzed

7. Kind of theory used and how it is applied
   a. Theory as abstract model and data subsumed
   b. Theory as an explanatory process starting with the phenomena concerned

8. Conception of the social "object" (how much and in what way the subject-object relationship is realized)

9. Perception of the relation between phenomena concerned and society as a totality (what kind of interdependence or indifference is assumed)

10. The relationship between the "facts" and the "theories" being worked with (what is falsifying what; dialectical relationship or not?)

11. Level of generality (assumption about the explanatory and perhaps practical power of an analysis)

12. Endpoint: degree of the "security" of results

a. To gain a reputation
b. To achieve a political program enlightening critical people
c. To function as a tool for praxis

This list of "indicators" of a scientific process is not exhaustive. Most of these indicators are interrelated and influence one another. The individualistic conception of human beings influences the frame of reference, the criteria with which one analyzes and qualifies institutions, and the level of one's analysis. Therefore, the process of social science analysis is governed by a dynamic web of values. The possibility of arriving at results that are objective and that can be generalized is not found outside the web of values and the social object but precisely within them.

THE TASKS OF SOCIAL SCIENCE: CONTENT

My purpose here is a constructive one, not a critical one. I will not analyze why the subjects of social science today are similar to an almost arbitrary scattergram of dots. For when one takes a second look at these apparent scattergrams, one discovers areas of dot congestion. Indeed, when one undertakes a "causal" analysis, one will detect some very important factors that regulate the selection of subjects—the way they are handled in a nonarbitrary way, especially the factor of organization. I will focus on criteria and procedural rules for a nonarbitrary selection and analysis of these selected topics; that is, on the duties of social science. My presentation may be influenced by my own professional competence as a political scientist or political sociologist. I assume that the main direction will be the same if one starts from another perspective of social science as long as one takes the same premises for granted and applies the same criteria.

The Premises of Social Science

The first premise is that social science is, by the very nature of the problems it deals with, a moral science. This is almost self-evident. Social science would not be necessary if we lived in an utopian world of harmony. The interconnected phenomena of scarcity, conflict, inequality, domination, exploitation, and war create permanent problems for a stable and legitimate social order. But these phenomena as such and their historical dynamics—which jointly constitute the phenomenon of social change—did not bring social science into existence for reflection on the social order; they are as old as mankind. Social science was born when the quantity and quality of social relations and social interconnections increased in such a way that large-scale organizations, especially large-scale production, became possible, on the one hand, and the problem of how to steer a given society in all its complexity, how to rationalize social activities, became urgent, on the other. In short, social science is a latecomer among those that first started to instrumentalize nature and now tend to instrumentalize human society itself. Social science as a kind of Epimetheus (an ex post facto thinker) arrived in the laboratory of the industrial society when the dialectic of the Enlightenment could no longer be overlooked. At its earliest stages, a mood of optimism about the possibility of rationalizing society prevailed. Comte, Saint-Simon, Darwin, Marx, and Spencer are in this respect representatives of the same generation.

At the outset, the problem of a good social order is hypothesized, and together with it the problem of the "education of mankind."[16] How are the norms and sanctions of a society, its web of regulations and its basic patterns of behavior, to be organized in such a way that people can live together in peace and yet allow each person to fulfill his or her needs? In other words, to paraphrase Simmel, how is it possible to have at the same time society *and* individual authenticity and integrity of all its members?[17] In this respect Rousseau's famous formulation of the basic problem still holds true: "How can a state be built where there is no single unfree person, where the individual within society does not sacrifice the slightest bit of his natural right of liberty?"[18]

The possibility for a social science originates in exactly the same human and social condition as the possibility for a moral science or ethic. "The possibility of ethics is based upon the fragile relation between human beings and between human beings and things. Ethic and morality are only necessary when discordance begins to question the harmony of social life so radically that the chance of people's actually living together is no longer a sufficient guarantee of security.[19]

In short, the raison d'être of social science as a moral science is directed positively toward a good society and negatively toward a bad society, each the historically specific realization of human existence at a given time. Whatever is done by social scientists touches on moral problems in this sense and serves, in the end, to realize specifically qualified societies, along a spectrum with good and bad at its end points.

The main tasks of social science are therefore consciously or unconsciously grouped around the following questions: What kind of moral relations ("norms" or "sanctions") exist in a given society? How do these specific moral relations come into being? What kind of mechanisms condition individual and collective behavior and make sure that it turns out according to the given moral relations? What are the effects of a socially institutionalized moral on institutions and on individuals? Is there a stratification of norms and sanctions, a class-related hierarchy? In short, what is the status of freedom and equality as strictly correlated phenomena?

The second premise of social science is that it has a basic frame of reference. "Yet I contend," writes Thomas Szasz, "that as psychotherapy, psychoanalysis is meaningless without an articulated ethic."[20] No doubt this assumption holds true for all branches of social science, even if they are normally not applied sciences. Without such an "articulated ethic"—not to be identified as a global or abstract postulate—social science could not avoid functioning as an ideology or serving as an instrument of manipulation. Social science would lose its cognitive-analytical capacity without articulated concepts of "good" and "bad" societies, of "normal" and "abnormal" behavior, of "health" and "illness." At the very least, it must develop criteria and procedures to study why social relations are institutionalized in one way or another and how the specific institutionalizing of norms and sanctions (which, in turn, are linked to the division of labor, that is, to the social arrangement of production and reproduction) affects people collectively, on the one hand, and every individual member of a society, on the other. A formulated moral concept is necessary to discover, to analyze, to judge, and to imagine any alternative modes of production and organization.

Some of the main weaknesses of Marxism—let alone conventional "bourgeois" social science—can be seen in its resistance to articulating an ethical frame of reference. The critique of intellectual criticism of society (the left Hegelians) and the critique of the rationally constructing utopians, who did not grasp the real dynamics of capitalistic society, and, finally, his insistence on "socialism as a science" seduced Marx and quite a few Marxists into becoming true believers in a more or less dialectic development of nature and society as such.

Their emphasis on scientific analysis to analyze and to understand the capitalistic formation of society overshadowed the fact that exactly this kind of legitimate analysis and theoretical generalization has always been influenced by moral attitudes and a moral frame of reference. The lack of an "articulated ethic" is, to some extent, the reason for the following shortcomings of latter-day Marxism: the exaggerated emphasis on objective development, understood as more or less autonomous progress; the corresponding belief in "objective development"; and the underestimation of specific historical circumstances, on the one hand, and of subjective conditions and the present needs of subjects, on the other. Individuals had to obey "history," viewed as an objective force; the "subjective" was transformed into the "objective" conditions of the proletariat. Thus, within Marxism, individual and collective behavior have never been studied sufficiently.[21]

What can be shown in respect to Marx and Marxism holds true even more for conventional social science. At best, so-called norms are really subjective value heavens of each social scientist, who usually plays two separate roles: a "moral" one and a "scientific" one, though these two roles may, occasionally, be conjoined. In contrast to such harmony—by a strange division of labor—is the postulate that social science has to have an "articulated ethic." This postulate assumes two premises: first, that the moral concept influences the scientific process permanently—that is, the scientific process is morally regulated, or even constituted; second, that the moral concept cannot just be constructed arbitrarily by the individual social scientist—the moral concept is part and parcel of the dialectical relationship between the scientific "subject" and the scientific "object." Therefore, the moral concept tells us how the "object" is perceived, how the "object" will be treated, what the "subject" can understand at all in regard to the "object," and how the "object" dominates the "subject" secretly or openly. Therefore, the frame of reference is not an abstract tool that can be taken out of a scientific storage house. The frame of reference must be developed with respect to the "object" studied and the specific interest of the analyst. Thus, the old scholastic saying is still valid: *adaequatio rei atque cognitionis* [22] (the method must be in adequate proportion to the object).

Every frame of reference that guides an analysis is a mediated mixture of general and specific elements. Some of the general ones are a specific conception of the relation of the individual to the society and the mechanisms linking the two;[23] a conception of individual and collective freedom, which are related and constitute each other, though in different ways, depending upon one's theory; a conception of the proper organization of norms and sanctions; and, of course, a clear understanding of the categories "norm" and "sanction."

It goes without saying that the methodology one refers to and the method one uses are dependent on the chosen frame of reference, as they are dependent on the "selected" object and the interest of the analyst with respect to it. Again taking for granted that the abovementioned more general elements of any sufficient frame of reference are correct, any methodology or any applied method has to be dialectical in at least three ways. First, it has to take into consideration the dynamic relationship between an individual phenomenon and the totality of a given society and its history;[24] what and who are influencing what and whom; and what constitutes the feedback mechanisms. Second, it has to be aware of the genetic dimension of social phenomena; they are always products in a general sense, that is, produced by specific conditions and interests, and often are producers themselves. Third, social scientists themselves and their conceptions of social science have to be reflective of the social context of a given society, as both the product and the producers of this social context.

THE FUNCTIONS OF SOCIAL SCIENCE

The functions of social science, as seen against the background of urgent but not permanently soluble problems, make it a consciously moral science, one that cannot avoid being a participant in the social world; for otherwise it becomes strictly ideological and an instrument of manipulation. It must respond to the changing aspects of problems according to a chosen frame of reference, whose general elements can be formally pointed out, as can, therefore, some general functions of social science. Following are four of its basic and interrelated functions.

Information
Fulfilling this function is rather difficult, but not primarily because the amount of information in complex and large societies increases daily. The main difficulties derive from the fact that information itself

is part of the structure of inequality and the struggle for power and that therefore it is difficult to get information at all, to publish it, and to transmit it to the people who need it. The function of information can therefore be implemented only if social science is theoretically and empirically able to isolate gaps in given information and correctly reinterpret that information. In a way, social science has to institutionalize counterinformation to counter the conventional and dominant policies of information. Transmitting information to a public which is able to grasp it is one of the most crucial problems facing social science. At present, it does not perform this function because it is itself an agent of information policy and because it pretends to have "professional" standards by using a hermetic vocabulary.

Social Analysis and Judgment

The quality of information depends very much on the ability of social science to analyze present-day reality and hence reduce the structural complexity of its basic components. Otherwise, the abundant data that emanate from all kinds of official and semiofficial sources every day will never be of a quality that can be understood and used by the public. Analysis requires a radical differentiation and qualification of interests and mechanisms which constitute the phenomena one is concerned with. Analysis is not to be misunderstood as fundamentalism; the latter uses a reductionist approach, that is, it reduces all phenomena to factors "in the last instance." Analysis fulfills its task of making matters comprehensive only if it links phenomena to a set of most important factors. In turn, the abstract factors, for instance, economic, social, and political structures, have to be mediated again with the concrete phenomena. In regard to the process of abstraction from the phenomenon level and in regard to reapplication of these abstract factors in order to explain the phenomena, it is very important to be aware of the structure of mediation and its factors. The factors mediating the "last causes" (i.e., crucial conditioning factors) with the phenomena have to be taken seriously by themselves. Analysis, therefore, implies theory-building, that is, the formulation of a set of interrelated categories that help clarify reality.

Orientation

Weber provides a fine legacy for focusing consciously and scientifically on the "is" and on the "ought." The "ought" adheres to the realm of irrational values; the "is" is part of the rational world, can be touched, seen, and proven. Science does not have any competence outside this factual world. If one takes this external reasoning, which divides reality into nicely separated blocks, for granted, the function of orientation is out of the competence of social science. But besides some misunderstandings of Weber and some quite exaggerated generalizations of his neo-Kantian point of view by some of his followers and by the "professional" pretensions of institutionalized social science, this division of the dimensions of reality is an artificial one itself. Not only is social science, according to Weber, value-related, but one of its foremost tasks is to analyze the relationships (adequate or inadequate) between chosen ends and the chosen means to implement these ends. What Weber fought against was the scientific pretensions of constituting values "scientifically," to articulate—speaking paradoxically—moral decisions from the foundation of amorality, that is, science. When one grasps the meaning of the value-relatedness of social science—necessarily going beyond Weber—one comes to the conclusion that social science cannot be anything other than a moral science. When one combines this value-relatedness with the task of analyzing comprehensively and specifically the means-end relation, it becomes crystal clear that social science has the effect and the function of orientation. "Orientation" means to make people understand what is going on, to make people able to weigh human costs and consequences about measures taken, decisions, institutionalized procedures, and so on.

Imagination

Although the other three functions are not well implemented by social science today, the function which is almost totally missing is that of imagination—indeed, a very disciplined imagination. Social science has the noble and important duty (and in a way its most political one, too) to combine its analytical and critical power to propose, according to its frame of reference, alternative modes of organization. In other words, not just any kind of imagination is asked for, although as a reader of social science literature one would be very glad to catch sometimes some small "bone" of imagination, an imagination against the background of analytical precision, that is to say, the historically specific identification of social problems. What is needed is not more futurologist studies but disciplined imaginations and proposals of alternative modes of social organization and social problem solving, modes which transcend the basic structures and procedures of present-day society but which nevertheless yield "realistic" solutions to present-day problems. How can a "good" society be realized with the resources, and the limits on those resources, of today—materially and immaterially speaking—taken together and synthesized with the knowledge gained by analysis? This kind of disciplined imagination would be drawn from our knowledge primarily of the lost and not of the winning causes in history. It would have to exploit the long, partly hidden, partly suppressed history of suffering, one of the best sources for getting valid criteria for the definition of "human authenticity," "human integrity," "human identity," and the other characteristics of a true democracy. This kind of disciplined imagination would, in turn, function as one of the most sensitive and promising analytical tools. Social science would function as a detective story, to use Ernst Bloch's phrase.[25]

ORGANIZATIONAL ELEMENTS OF SOCIAL SCIENCE: FORM

If one studies the critically articulated purposes, tasks, and implemented analyses of social science today, one is struck by its conventional approach. The image of a biased scattergram comes to mind again. The functions of social science mentioned above are not fulfilled in any satisfying way, although social science is—at least in the developed capitalistic, the so-called Western countries—well institutionalized, organized, and studied by whole "armies" of scholars.

Why is this the case? Why has there been such enormous progress in the institutionalization of social science during the last three decades of growth but no equivalent progress of analytical power, theory building, and disciplined imagination? Sometimes the two progress in an inverse relationship. There are, of course, many reasons for this situation, all of which must be analyzed systematically and historically in the context of the respective societies. One reason can be found in the dominant "paradigm" of social science, a more or less mechanistic conception of the natural sciences and their procedures, that is, the stupefying denial of the very quality of social science, its moral dimension in a "subjective" and an "objective" respect.[26]

Another reason with which I shall deal now is to be found in the surprising fact that social science very rarely reflects on its own materialistic "infrastructure," that is, the way in which it is organized and institutionalized. Social science has been professionalized at some stage in its development without enough thought given to the impact of the process or the form of professionalization on its content and on its purposes and their implementation. In a self-defeating way,[27] social science has neglected to reflect on the means-end relationship with respect to its own professional organizations. May I argue again that the main institutions of social science—the professional organizations, the university departments, and the research institutes— are institutionalized in such a way that they guarantee the dominance of given conventions: they impede imaginative research; they socialize students of social science in an adaptive way; they hinder the fulfillment of the moral political role of social science; and they ensure instead that the mainstream of social science functions primarily as an ideology and a manipulative instrument.

I shall try to qualify these harsh statements to some extent in regard to the institutionalized patterns of teaching and the institutionalized patterns of research by pointing out general organizational elements that can be found in almost every social science department.

FORMS OF TEACHING SOCIAL SCIENCE

I shall focus here primarily on the given organizational elements of social science as far as teaching at universities is concerned. The purposes of social science and their implementation, as well as the organizational forms in which social science is incorporated, are not primarily or even exclusively defined by social scientists themselves. Nevertheless, the latter do, as a social group, take an active part in and are able to change, at least to some degree, the purposes and the organizational patterns that are perceived, pursued, chosen, and finally institutionalized. Therefore, we start with the following assumptions.

First, the socialization of social scientists plays a decisive role in regard to what they do in a later stage professionally, that is, when they become scholars. This assumption is not invalidated by the well-founded observation that a university education functions primarily to form attitudes and not to transmit cognitive skills.[28] Although students are socialized before they come to the university (and nonuniversity factors also play an important role), specific departmental socialization cannot be underestimated. Second, the purpose of the socialization of social science students should be to let students become self-conscious and "sovereign": to give them the freedom to uncover new problems, to tackle these problems without anxiety, and to solve them in a methodical way. Third, it is therefore necessary to care for the student as a whole person. Cognition and self-consciousness, and cognitive abilities and courage, are, as Kant observed, closely related. The teaching institution must be aware of the social conditions of learning behavior.

Looking at the instrumentation with which and in which students of social science are taught and social scientists teach, one discerns the following characteristics, which define the ecology of learning. These characteristics condition the general effect of teaching and learning far beyond the specific abilities and engagements of teachers and students.

First, the methods of teaching today are almost the same as they have been during the last fifty years or more, except for the brief period of the 1960's, when much experimentation took place. The general rule is a mixture of seminars and lectures which are presented discretely. That is, the focus changes from lecture to lecture and from seminar to seminar. Integration of the discrete elements has to be achieved by the student. The presentation of the subject matter of this segmented curriculum is done by specialists. One seminar is about "theory," another about "empirical research," a third about "methods," and so on. Even the different aspects of a specific social science are compartmentalized, let alone the spectrum of social science as a whole, which is lost almost totally.

Second, the presentation of the learning "load" in a discrete form is supplemented and implemented by an almost atomistic body of teachers. There is little if any cooperation. The teachers know very little about the students whom they instruct or about their fellow teachers and what they are teaching. Everybody is his own king or her own queen. This kind of social and scientific atomism among professors is usually considered a sign, if not the very foundation, of academic freedom; but it is a strictly negative freedom.

Third, the curricula of the social sciences are very different, and each one is oriented not to the problems, abilities, and needs of the students but to the reputation of a specific branch of social science—

the reputational paradigm. The curriculum which is implemented conceives of the student, and the teacher too, as a receiver, not as a codeterminer or self-conscious producer.

Fourth, there is a built-in split between theory and practice in regard to the subject matter of each specific social science. The organization of the curriculum makes sure that the split is deepened by the above-mentioned discrete form of teaching.

Fifth, it is almost impossible to overestimate the habitual and the cognitive effects of the system of grading, which along with the final examinations create a competitive atmosphere, isolate the students from one another, and produce a general other-directedness in cognitive perspectives and behavior patterns.

Sixth, the split between theory and practice in the modes of teaching and learning is paralleled by the cleavage between the cognitive and noncognitive aspects of student life. By definition, the departments take care of the cognitive aspects only; either they do not care what else happens to the student, or they accept uncritically the "social" function of sororities, fraternities, and the like.

In sum, the form of teaching is extremely conventional. It is passed on from one generation to the other as though the social situation were the same, as though teachers and students were the same. Progress in teaching and learning is at its best in transmitting sophisticated technical skills, consistent with the goals of the dominant natural science paradigm followed by all social sciences. But the cognitive and habitual costs of this one-sided progress and the encompassing conventionality are enormous: increased isolation, increased segmentalization, and increased inability to integrate the role of professional with the role of human being. It would be unjust, of course, and analytically wrong to blame the organization of the teaching and learning process and of the university as a whole for these insufficiencies. Social science itself is to blame also, for merely mirroring the general tendencies of society instead of using its tools to analyze and then try to modify or change these conventional patterns.

FORMS OF RESEARCH

How issues are perceived and, especially, how they are managed are determined to a great extent by the process of socialization inside social science itself. What has been observed in regard to the process of teaching is corroborated by observing the process of research. Some hints must suffice. It may be noted in passing that the professional newcomer among the social sciences, the so-called research of research, focuses primarily on the various histories of science, on methodological questions, or on the scientific community as a kind of asocial entity of only cognitively interested scholars. Therefore, the intriguing and important social process of reflection on the social, political, economic, and psychological dimensions of the organization of social science itself is not in any way institutionalized.

First, the constitutional principle of atomism in regard to teaching also constitutes the "social" organization of research. The almost unrestricted individualism and the consequent arbitrariness of issue perception and issue analysis are, nevertheless, rather limited. The patterns of recruitment of scientific personnel and the patterns of achievement orientation ensure this kind of "academic individualism," which does not usually cross certain conventional borders. Everything is possible; but some issues and modes of issue analysis are more probable than others. Some modes of research are almost impossible, partly because of the atomistic situation and partly because of the hidden criteria and regulations inside and outside the university.

Second, the other side of this atomistic situation and its concomitant academic individualism is a lack of cooperation among the sciences, both the natural and the social sciences. Cooperation is possible, no doubt—it does happen sometimes—but it is, institutionally speaking, not supported. The effect of this lack is very significant. Social problems are tackled segmentally as given entities and very rarely in their proper context. In the same way, social consequences, the internal sociality of the theory and practice of natural sciences, for instance, are not discussed adequately and sufficiently. The academic perception of reality is thus strangely but not surprisingly analogous to the bureaucratic problem.

Third, I mentioned a double split between theory and practice in regard to the teaching and learning process. This split is deepened as far as research is concerned; it makes social science research apolitical by its very existence. The relation between theory and practice is rather different among the various social sciences. Some social science professions function almost as economic or other interest groups;

others are almost totally restricted to the sphere of the university. But either the theoretical perspective (and the critical distance) is nearly lost (in some of the applied political sciences), or the practical application of scientific models is nothing less than an applied abstraction (as is the case and the problem with economics) or, finally, the theory-building has its own academic momentum. The political practice of using social science as an instrument of ideology and manipulation is not a part of the research process itself, or of the structure of expectations of academic research. People who are not organized or who do not have a significant financial capability are only abstractly considered.

I shall not deal here with patterns of recruitment, although they shape social science research conspicuously, or with the mechanisms that define and diffuse the patterns of reputation, which are based on the totally superficial criterion "publish or perish." Instead, I will conclude these remarks with one of the most difficult problems of social science and of all science—the problem of "issue generation." How can one make sure that academic research is socially relevant? Many options have been discussed: to "open" universities, to "infuse" social interest groups and their representatives into the university, or to connect the university departments in some way with interest groups as a kind of institutionalization of a link between theory and practice. I cannot deal in this context with these proposals and some of their applications. I would like instead to dwell on one deliberation that was lost after the student movement vanished. If one were able to introduce democracy to the academic institutions and at the same time to maintain their high degree of autonomy, two achievements could probably be gained simultaneously. One would be an open discussion of issues by a constituency that is somewhat mobile; the other would be some social distance from dominant interest groups and the bureaucracy that tries to functionalize research according to its own ideas.

CONCLUSION

To define social science as a moral or a political science turns out to be a kind of tautology. Social science at its best *and* its worst cannot help but function as a moral science—that is to say, a political science. This is so, first, because society is a morally constituted entity and human beings are social animals. As Plato already observed, there must always be a correspondence between "subject" and "object." Second, social science as a science itself has social and cognitive characteristics. The explication of the immanent "nature" or "essence" of social science does not solve all methodological problems, but it makes it possible to pose and face the problems in a nonrepressive, nonmanipulative way. To put it another way, those who try to exclude the moral quality from social science as a whole lose the scientific quality also. There is no choice in the matter. The existence of much literature about the apolitical (amoral, value-free) quality of social science and the phenomenon that the main bulk of studies by social scientists concentrate on collecting data and analyzing scientific objects as though there is no dialectical relation between "subject" and "object" do not alter the moral imperative of social science. Just as the worldwide existence of domination and inequality does not prove the ontological status of domination and inequality, nor their historical inevitability, so the existence of an enormous and increasing amount of social science literature that pretends to analyze and produce results in an apolitical way does not support the assumption that social science is apolitical. Quite the contrary. Any apparent apolitical social science functions, in a hidden way, politically! In this sense it stands in opposition to the claims of science itself. The analytical understanding of social science as a moral science does not reduce or soften the scientific postulates: to argue distinctly and clearly, as Leibniz put it, to show evidence for assumptions, to prove hypotheses as well as possible, and to clarify the reach and the limit of the validity of statments. Again, quite the contrary. Now it is possible to show the relations among methodological premises, the discovery and constitution of data, the interpretation of relationships, etc.—in short, between the methodological constitution of reality (its "scientific" construction), on the one side, and the real interests and reasons behind a given methodological starting point, on the other. Scientific arguments do not become more arbitrary as a result. They lose the false priestlike pretension of God-like scientific security, but they gain in precision and in social mediation. Moral questions are not beyond methodical or systematic discourse; they are not parts of an irrational realm in which no "rational" foot can step. Moral decisions and moral status can be explained, their premises and consequences shown. Even questions as to whether this or that decision and measure should be taken on if this or that institution is more or less appropriate in regard to human freedom and happiness (which, again, are social terms to be defined according to social situations) can be tentatively and approximately answered by the social science analysis of human suffering, consciousness, and behavior patterns. The approximation improves as soon as social science begins to take its profession seriously, as soon as it gives up false pretensions. To be able to reorient itself in such a way, it would have to determine once again its own position in a world of power, domination, spheres of influences, war, and exploitation, and it would have to determine once again its own social (human) purposes.

As I have argued above, as soon as social science starts to reflect on its own moral, that is, scientific, obligation not as an additional job but as *the* job, it will have to draw some quite incisive conclusions about its patterns of perception, its methods of tackling problems, and, especially, its form of organization. Otherwise, its moral attitudes will remain abstract and become what Nietzsche aptly called a "double moral."[29]

There are many roads to Rome, but also many dead ends and one-way streets; and no mere social scientist knows the right one. Yet pluralism is only possible as long as one does not give up the orientation toward "Rome," the orientation toward a "good society" with free, equal, authentic human beings. This goal makes social science utopian in a realistic sense. This goal gives social science some coherence, some reliance, and by the way, much analytical power too. Otherwise, social science can only bark with different voices, as it was polemically said about the monks of the Order of Saint Dominicus during the late Middle Ages: as instruments of the dominant order.

NOTES

1. In this paper I shall speak of social science in the singular because the fundamental problems of all the social sciences are identical.

2. I have borrowed this term from Thomas Mann; in German it is *streitbare Einfalt.*

3. Jean-Jacques Rousseau, *Du Contrat Social* (Paris: Editions Garnier Frères, 1962), p. 243, cf. Ernst Bloch, *Das Prinzip Hoffnung* (Frankfurt: Suhrkamp, 1973), pp. 625–29.

4. Max Horkeheimer and Theodor W. Adorno, *Dialektik der Aufklärung* (Amsterdam, Querido Verl, 1947).

5. Jürgen Habermas, *Technik und Wissenschaft als "Ideologie"* (Frankfurt:Suhrkamp, 1968).

6. Leon Festinger, *A Theory of Cognitive Dissonance* (reissued, Stanford, Calif.: Stanford University Press, 1962).

7. Niklas Luhmann, "Systemtheoretische Argumentationen," in Jürgen Habermas and Niklas Luhmann, eds., *Theorie der Gesellschaft oder Sozialtechnologie* (Frankfurt: Suhrkamp, 1971).

8. See Robert K. Merton's famous remarks in the introduction to his influential work *Social Theory and Social Structure* (Glencoe, Illinois: Free Press, 1957), p. 4. There Merton expressed the hope that the social sciences would have their Galileo Galilei some day to make social science truly "scientific."

9. See William Buxton, "Social Science as a Strategic Vocation: Parsonian Theory, Political Sociology, and the American State" (Ph. D. diss., University of Berlin, 1980), passim.

10. See Gabriel A. Almond and G. Bingham Powell, *Comparative Politics* (Boston: Little, Brown, 1966); Gabriel A. Almond and Sidney Verva, *Political Culture* (Princeton, N.J.: Princeton University Press, 1963); Walt White Rostow, *The Stages of Economic Growth* (London: Cambridge University Press, 1960).

11. See Gunnar Myrdal, *Asian Drama* (New York: Pantheon, 1968), 3:1941–2005; Wolf-Dieter Narr, *Theoriebegriffe und Systemtheorie,* 4th ed. (Stuttgart: Kohlhammer, 1976), pp. 131–69.

12. I do not argue here against the so-called "basic human needs" approach. It is very valuable as long as the authors do not claim a kind of ontological security and do realize the political and historical implications of this approach. Notice the works of Abraham Maslow, such as *Motivation and Personality* (New York: Harper, 1954); consult especially numerous articles by Christian Bay, including "Needs, Wants, and Political Legitimacy," *Candian Journal of Political Science* (Sept. 1978), 1(3):241–60.

13. Gabriele Gutzmann, *Logik als Erfahrungswissenschaft: Der Kalkülismus und Wege zu seiner Überwindung* (Berlin; Duncker & Humblot, 1980); Werner Loh, *Kombinatorische Systemtheorie: Evolution, Geschichte und logischmathematischer Grundlagenstreit* (Frankfurt: Campus, 1980).

14. Alvin W. Gouldner, "Anti-Minotaur: The Myth of a Value-Free Sociology," in Irving Louis Horowitz, ed., *The New Sociology* (New York: Oxford University Press, 1965), pp. 196–217.

15. In regard to the important but not sufficient postulate of explication, see Arnold Brecht, *Politische Theorie* (Tubingen: Mohr & Siebek, 1963); and Gunnar Myrdal, *Objectivity in Social Research* (New York: Pantheon, 1969).

16. Gotthold Ephraim Lessing, "Die Erziehung des Menschengeschlechts," *Gesammelte Werke,* Otto Mann, ed. (Guetersloh: Mohn Verlag), pp. 720–39.

17. Georg Simmel, *Soziologie, Untersuchung über die Formen der Vergessellschaftung* (Berlin: Duncker & Humblot, 1958).

18. Rousseau, *Du Contrat Social,* p. 243; cf. Bloch, *Des Prinzip Hoffnung,* pp. 625–29.

19. Walter Schutz, *Philosophie in der veränderten Welt* (Pfullingen: Neske, 1972), p. 704 (my translation).

20. Thomas S. Szasz, *The Ethics of Psychoanalysis* (New York: Basic Books, 1974), p. 20.

21. This is the only argument of the fasionable "Nouveaux Philosophes" in Paris that has to be taken seriously.

22. Theodor W. Adorno, "Soziologie und empirische Forschung," *Sociologica II, Reden und Vortrage* (Frankfurt: Europäische Verlagsanstalt, 1962), pp. 205–22.

23. Max Horkheimer, *"Traditionelle und Kritische Theorie,"* *Zeitschrift für Sozial-forschung* (1937), 5:245.

24. Gero Lehnardt, *Berufliche Weiterbildung* (Frankfurt: Suhrkamp, 1978).

25. Ernst Bloch, *Gesammelte Werke* (Frankfurt: Suhrkamp, 1970), p. 37.

26. To avoid misunderstandings, the implicit criticism here does not mean that social science could "live" without statistical approaches and the like.

27. This statement is qualitative, in regard to goal attainment, and not quantitative, in regard to pattern of maintenance, to use Parson's terms (slightly altered).

28. Pierre Bourdieu and Jean-Claude Passeron, *Die Illusion der Chancengleichheit* (Stuttgart: Klett Verlag, 1971).

29. Friedrich Nietzsche, *Zur Genealogie der moral* (Frankfurt: Ullstein, 1972).

Thirteen

BEYOND POLICY SCIENCE: THE SOCIAL SCIENCES AS MORAL SCIENCES

William M. Sullivan

EXPERT KNOWLEDGE AND PUBLIC POLICY: A DEBATE

In the contemporary debate over the nature of social investigation, the continuing vogue which announces that the social sciences find their true vocation as contributors to a soon-to-be-established policy science is a case of old positivist wine in new casks. According to its advocates, the goal of policy science—or sciences, as there is no unanimity about whether we are discussing a heterogeneous or unified set of methods—is to provide a complete and expert understanding of societal problems. They see this as an essential step toward the rational formation of social policy, believing that "the solution of societal problems generally implies a rational model."[1] These advocates assert that the kind of expert knowledge which society needs can and should be produced by practitioners of a scientific form of social investigation. The general contours of their vision thus emerge clearly. "The distinctive quality of social policy is its aim for what might be called programmatic rationality; it seeks to achieve substantive goals through instrumental action programs that can be proven logically or empirically to achieve those goals."[2] But questions about where these "substantive goals" come from, who determines them, and how they are arrived at are not discussed within the program of the new policy science.

The hopes for a programmatic policy science can be construed as another manifestation of that widespread conception of social investigation according to which social inquiry is directly analogous to research in the natural sciences. That conception is identified with a long tradition of thought in modern Western culture, including Thomas Hobbes, Jeremy Bentham, and August Comte among its illustrious progenitors. It envisions society as a system of interactions which can be investigated and explained without the use of moral assumptions or the engagement of the investigator in the processes under study. Policy science envisions a knowledge about society that could be used to design appropriate technologies for controlling social development in a systematic way.

However, this ruling conception of social science has come increasingly under question and attack from within the professional disciplines, as well as from skeptical or hostile outsiders. Recently, David Cohen and Charles Lindblom, the latter a major contributor to discussions about the uses of social science, have addressed to their colleagues in "professional social investigation" a series of provocative questions and critiques. In *Usable Knowledge: Social Science and Social Problem Solving,* Lindblom and Cohen challenge, on the basis of decades of premature announcements of achievement, the pretensions of social scientists to realizing an authoritative status for their work comparable with that of the natural sciences.[3] Furthermore, they point out that the programmatic model of policy science is strongly wedded to a conception of social order, essentially administrative, which is anything but free of moral and political assumptions.

Lindblom and Cohen argue that the common conception of a policy science founded on expert knowledge identifies social rationality with instrumental and strategic thinking. It thereby ties the professional social investigator both theoretically and practically close to the wielders of established social power, the presumptive audience for such technical knowledge. Thus, a self-aware social science cannot avoid the questions, What audience does research address? What is the source of the goals it seeks to implement? Indeed, there is a particular irony here in that, from the side of "decision makers," there is much skepticism about the claims of "policy scientists" to expert knowlege, a knowledge secured by esoteric techniques superior to the everyday understandings of events shared by lay people, journalists, and, presumably, also by the decision makers and social scientists themselves.[4] Still, in practice, policy scientists gain a socially authoritative position which they cannot acquire for their work on cognitive grounds alone by means of their relation to decision makers. Reciprocally, their "clients" in government hope to further legitimate their own positions through an appeal to social scientific expertise.

The issue of the authoritativeness of social science is important. As Lindblom and Cohen point out, social science has not been able to achieve the independent authoritativeness of natural science. This is another way of saying that the language and theoretical explanations advanced by social investigators have not succeeded in supplanting the less formal understandings of ordinary language in practical social life. At best, social scientific knowledge seems to supplement and clarify practical understandings.[5] This failure is scandalous from the viewpoint of positivistic social scientists and creates a major difficulty for any argument to the effect that the ideal of a social scientific technology is a credible one. In simple terms, the history of professional social investigation ill accords with its pretensions to establishing itself as authoritative and so has created a potential crisis for the way proponents of policy science wish to view themselves and their enterprise.

In the face of the continued incongruity, or perhaps contradiction, between what proponents of an expert policy science proclaim their epistemological status to be, on the one hand, and the historical record of their achievements, on the other, it seems reasonable to become suspicious about the face value of those claims. The programmatic conception of policy science embodies, by virtue of its explicit assumptions about social life and social knowledge, the premise that human action is best conceived of as instrumental and strategic, with the corollary that society is, if not exhaustively then at least most importantly, a system of instrumental relationships.

The practical correlate to these theoretical assumptions is the ideal of the decision maker, the administrative director of the social system or subsystem. But this, too, is laden with assumptions about the nature of social life and, indeed, the nature of the good or—to remain within a consistent frame of discourse—the efficient society. The conception is at root a utilitarian one, in which social elements and actions are measured by their success in promoting either their individual strategic goals or the orderly functioning of the system, or both. The role of the policy maker is clear: it is to serve as guardian and crisis manager, as a sort of scientific shepherd of a highly rationalized flock.

However, none of these conceptions nor their internal linkages are new with the policy science debate, although, since policy science thinks in an essentially ahistorical way, it does not acknowledge its indebtedness to the past. Yet a reading of an early liberal thinker such as the Baron de Montesquieu helps us realize that the ideal of programmatic policy science has not sprung up de novo, without parent.[6] A programmatic policy science gains much of its authoritativeness not only from its practical alliance with social power but also culturally, through its "fit" with the scientific and instrumental ethos dominant in contemporary industrial society. Further, it can be argued that the belief in the power of analytic and instrumental rationality to know exhaustively and to transform the social world is itself a constituent part of this ethos.

But this is to suggest that there is a real linkage between the cognitive and theoretical stance of social thinking and the social position and practical orientation of this thinking. Although such a suggestion is not intelligible within the framework of positivistic social science, nonetheless it can be entertained by social investigators. Thus, an alternative or wider understanding appears at the limits of the policy science program. The exploration of this alternative increasingly suggests itself, if only to shed light on why the policy sciences remain confounded in their efforts to fulfill their own objective of scientific authoritativeness. Indeed, an examination of the conceptual issues involved in the debate over the epistemological status of social investigation directly suggests an alternative to policy science as now conceived. However, this alternative cannot be well articulated in the same kind of ahistorical, purely conceptual discourse used by policy scientists. Instead, it requires a self-reflection that is situated, and thus takes up a stance, within the social and cultural world of the present.

THE PRACTICAL CONTEXT OF INVESTIGATION IN THE HUMAN SCIENCES

More is at stake in the policy science debate than an epistemological or conceptual issue. In question is a vision of society, all human action, and ultimately, how life is to be lived and understood. Yet from a positivistic standpoint the issue is fundamentally one of epistemology; thus, problems in that area are critical for the credibility and viability of the enterprise of scientifically conceived social inquiry. The increased questioning of the approach now provides an opening for other modes of discourse formerly banished from respectability by the positivist orthodoxy.

From the orthodox position, a true science of society must be able to generate a theory which can explain meanings and motives, along with behavior, as variants of constant patterns of relationship among social elements. A formula expressing such relationships must be defined over elements whose specific value or content can vary without thereby changing the relationships described by the formula. Given this conception of social knowledge, a conception of social policy on the analogy of mathematical problem solving appears at least consistent if not convincing.

However, in the human sciences this goal is always problematical. Even were it attainable—and it is far from clear that it is—there is good reason to think that it would be of only small benefit for the kind of inquiry social scientists conduct and the kind of practical difficulty they confront. Thomas Kuhn's widely known work on the history of the natural sciences and his much-discussed notions of normal and revolutionary science are helpful in clarifying these difficulties.[7] The real and powerful achievement of science has been the ability of scientists as a community to settle upon univocal standards of measurement and techniques of research, constituting what Kuhn calls paradigms. These common standards and procedures have enabled the natural sciences to make steady incremental advances by subsuming events under lawlike patterns. Typically, in a period of "normal science," young scientists are trained in a paradigm and proceed to extend it into new, uncharted domains of experience.

There is, of course, irony here. The more imperially successful the paradigm in extending its domain, the more anomalous cases pile up. Eventually, the anomalies may receive explanation through a new scheme of order, and a new paradigm may be born. Kuhn calls the displacement of an established paradigm by a new one a revolution. It is a distinguishing mark of the natural as against the social sciences that they have been able to isolate events and transcribe them as patterns of lawlike regularity. However, as Kuhn points out, the concept of the explanatory theory which makes sense of the mathematical statements cannot usually be translated among paradigms. Before the development of a firmly agreed-on consensus on a paradigm, the world of investigation is marked by contention among a variety of incommensurable, competing paradigm candidates. For those who wish to see the coming of a paradigmatic age in the social sciences, all previous ages have been sadly preparadigmatic.

However, Kuhn has called attention to precisely the aspects of scientific work which have remained in the background, at least among philosophical commentators on the history of the sciences. The development of agreement about what the basic problems for research are, about exemplary models of explanation and classic experiments—these facets of science are social activities. Even more important, the education of a scientific researcher is a process of coming to accept and finally become a part of a way of doing research which penetrates more deeply into the personality of the student than mere assumptions or beliefs. In a way that recalls Charles Peirce, Kuhn has highlighted the fact that science is a social and cultural activity pursued in common and continued through shared activities and forms of cooperation. A large part of what Kuhn styles the "disciplinary matrix" of a normal science is actual know-how passed on in collaboration between generations of scientists, an apprenticeship, that cannot be made totally explicit in rules of procedure. It is a kind of "personal knowledge," as Michael Polanyi has dubbed it, but it is essentially a shared knowledge.[8] Normal science is a form of life. As scientific revolutions occur, more than concepts are changed. The cognitive, practical, even bodily skills of scientific research are being re-formed.[9]

The distinction between the "disciplinary matrix" of a science and its formalized measuring system and explanatory theory provides an insight into why the social sciences remain pre- or, better, nonparadigmatic. The complicated skills passed on through scientific apprenticeship serve to train the scientist in the difficult task of ignoring many of the everyday meanings and purposes of events. Scientists learn to view events within the specialized frameworks of scientific measurement. It is a task of relearning, of attending to the measurable "primary qualities" of things, in the seventeenth-century sense of that term. It means looking away from the human relevance of things to see them as detached, measurable "qualities" that can then be charted and interrelated by conceptual formulas. As Whitehead put it, the narrowness and artificiality of the concepts of science have proven precisely the keys to power, as Bacon had hoped.[10] Yet the skills of the scientists, like the scientists themselves, remain embedded in and guided by a matrix of cultural patterns and meanings, the scientific "subculture," which shares pervasive aspects of the wider cultural world it inhabits.

When we extend these considerations to the conduct of the human sciences, the central difficulty leaps immediately to view. The object of the human sciences is to gain insight into what human life is, what makes it specifically different from other aspects of the world, and so on. Human inquiry is embedded within the social matrix it seeks to understand. This suggests that there is a limit to the applicability of scientific techniques in human inquiry which does not obtain in natural science. This is because the final object of study is exactly this underlying social matrix, the forms of life which sustain the inquirers even as they are their object. The realization of the embedded quality of our inquiries is at once the realization of what it is to be human. It is the discovery that humanity is, as a species, living in a world of meaning that makes it necessary and possible to ask the question, What is human life? The answer is given by the way in which we in fact live out or try to live out our concrete situations.

Efforts to formalize this context, while they may be made for specific purposes, never achieve the power to compel assent in the way the paradigms of natural science do. The classical political economy of Adam Smith and David Ricardo, perhaps the first attempt at a precise "policy science," could serve as a case in point. Classical political economy proclaimed a formalized reduction of human culture to a measurable set of categories, such as labor, capital, and exchange. One intellectual response to this was Marxism, which attacked those categories for what they omitted or misread in human affairs. The omissions here proved crucial. What political economy thought it could take for granted, the social matrix in which it operated, was shown by Marx and later by Max Weber to have such critical importance that if a different "background," such as another society or historical period, were substituted for the background of nineteenth-century Britain, which the political economists took for granted, their "science" severely narrowed.

The work of contemporary economic thinkers such as Robert Heilbroner provides a powerful argument that formalized statements about elements and rules in the human sciences are bought at high cost, utterly unlike anything found in the natural sciences.[11] The "laws" of economics are statements about human activity which the policy makers, as well as individual entrepreneurs, have often accepted as truths. Now, while molecules do not noticeably alter their behavior because a new theory has been published about them, conceptions of human behavior can and do change the way human beings act. Part of the cruel irony of contemporary society is that by acting on certain notions of economic theory, modern governments have precipitated changes in the institutions of their societies, which have fatally weakened the matrix of social practices such as honesty and self-restraint, on which the apparent validity of those "laws" depends.[12]

Human investigation thus has an ineluctable moral, indeed political, as well as a philosophical dimension. This is because it not only takes place within the cultural matrix but has direct and indirect effects on the understanding of those living within the world it seeks to clarify. The objective of the human sciences is the deepening of our understanding of what it is to live a human life. That understanding conditions the whole matrix of questions and themes within which the investigation proceeds. Because of the peculiarly intimate and complex bond between the subject and the object of study, all efforts to render the significance of human action can become weapons of fanatical partisanship or mere apologies for the status quo. They may be subversive of deep elements of a culture. Indeed, theories of man may lead to a forgetfulness of the very question of what it is to be human. But the investigator's stance toward his subject is in part already formed by that subject. He takes up a position toward the question of what it is to be human regardless of conscious intention.

There is thus an urgency, a risk, and a responsibility embedded in the task of understanding human action that the disciplinary matrix of the natural sciences, pursuing quite different goals, is able to screen out without distorting the results of research. In human investigation, as economics powerfully illustrates, there is no way to attain a complete clarity of theoretical language because the epistemological question is actually derived from the practical or existential one. The epistemological question of the truth of a particular interpretation involves the quality of its penetration and the depth of its insight. This depth reveals itself as a kind of practical questioning of self, at its deepest point forcing the "knowers" to the realization that their knowing is actually a way of being, a part of their way of living as moral beings as well as of their work as scientists.

PAST AND PRESENT IN SELF-UNDERSTANDING: A CASE STUDY

These developments in the debate about the nature of the human sciences have refocused attention on the actual forms of life and thinking which underlie the highly abstract renderings of much contemporary social science. Attention to the "disciplinary matrix"—the actual practices, social locations, and practical understandings of social investigators—returns us to the old notion that practical activity involves a kind of reasoning and knowing which precedes and provides the basis for all theoretical statements about the human world. That realization has the effect of uncovering the connections, submerged by instrumental and analytical thinking, between the particular disciplinary matrix of social investigation, including its categories of analysis, and a tacit projection of the nature of society.

In the case of contemporary programmatic policy science, the complementarity among its theoretical understanding, the kind of bureaucratic audience to which it speaks, and its advocacy of an instrumental, social management approach becomes manifest once one inquires about the relationships of theory and practice among its practitioners. However, in contemporary society the dominance of a utilitarian, instrumental mode of thinking about social life inherited from classical liberalism has made the articulation of critical positions not so much impossible as professionally and often politically unacceptable and, therefore, often unheard. A social investigation that aims—in a critical sense, exemplified by the investigation of the disciplinary matrix of the social sciences—at insight and self-awareness runs the risk of cognitive illegitimacy. It cannot be readily fitted into the channels of communication or the practices of investigation established by existing professional social science. This is not surprising, since inquiry for insight and awareness implies another, indeed an opposing, image not only of rationality but of social processes.

Awareness of the limitations and pretensions of established social forms and social thinking becomes valuable and makes sense only in a context in which human beings live more than instrumental, strategic lives. An alternative kind of inquiry draws its legitimacy from an awareness that human beings live within language as well as use language, that they can understand their situation and take a stance toward that situation and, by so doing, help to organize and structure it. Persons are not simply counters in a systemic map or game, moved from without. Persons are moral agents in that they can question themselves and take responsibility for the stances they adopt.

But what kind of argument can we make for this understanding? How can a conception of human social life which acknowledges an intrinsic—indeed, a logically circular—relationship between awareness and moral commitment and between cognitive and practical positions present its case as in some sense authoritative? It is clearly impossible to establish such a case within the cognitivist criteria of modern science alone. In fact, an indispensable aspect of the alternative claim is its normative assertion that its truth requires a certain kind of practical experience to be comprehended and that its comprehension requires a kind of enactment. And this further entails an ineluctably social and finally political dimension.

Insight requires a disposition toward a certain kind of ethical relationship toward others, a notion of society as aiming for a consensual and shared realm characterized by reciprocity. This conception implies a political practice the opposite of that of the instrumental vision of policy science. Habermas has summed this up well by arguing that "the vindicating superiority of those who do the enlightening over those who are to be enlightened is theoretically unavoidable, but at the same time it is fictive and requires self-correction: in a process of enlightenment there can be only participants." [13]

It follows that the necessary condition for such social inquiry is a living practical context. In contemporary society the vitality of critical inquiry itself provides evidence that such contexts do exist. Furthermore, one important contribution of self-conscious social inquiry is to influence the general understandings of the social world we share. In particular, this linkage of practical and theoretical understanding is illustrated by developments in American historiography, ultimately an area of great influence on public interpretations of events. These historiographic developments have moved in close interrelationship with the debate over our utilitarian society, dominated by a market ethos which continues to have a heavy influence on American national life.

It has been common in American thinking to see the nation's growth as a majestic expansion of a unified liberal political culture. Louis Hartz's well-known work on American political thought proposed such a conception in the mid-1950s, and it resonated powerfully with the national mood of those cold war years.[14] According to that vision, America has always been an essentially Lockean society, dedicated to the advancement of individual interests. Lacking a feudal past of aristocratic privilege and peasant misery, America was also spared the bitterness of European-style social antagonism. Thus, Hartz interpreted the American Revolution as conducted in spiritual equanimity, the assertion of a native liberalism against a British version of the Old Regime. Aside from efforts by antebellum Southerners to conceive an ideology of caste privilege and paternalism, Americans never developed real class oppositions or ideologies. Hence the failure of socialism to strike root here and, Hartz argued, the mistake of progressive historians who sought to find in social conflict a significant dynamic in the United States.

While the mainstream of postwar orthodoxy, represented by Hartz's view of America as an almost purely liberal society, tended to banish social conflict from U.S. history, it also celebrated the dynamic, expanding character of the society. Indeed, the deepest motif of liberal culture and of the liberal conception of politics is the notion of dynamic expansion. In the idealized portrait of liberal society which was reasserted during the postwar years, the great superiority of liberalism over all earlier as well as contemporary nonliberal philosophies was said to lie in the tremendous capacity of liberal society to free the potentials for economic development slumbering through the night of centuries of feudalism. The superiority of "the American way of life" was alleged to lie in an unrivaled capacity to arouse and then organize the energies of individuals, energies aroused in the hope of fulfilling their material needs. The result of liberated energies, harnessed through work and commerce, was abundance, and this the proponents of liberalism declared to be the true goal of civilization— the definer of progress. Thus, the history of the liberal tradition in America became identical with national success defined as economic growth, and the venerable liberal ideal of personal freedom in the sense of security of person and ability to enter into contracts for personal advantage became identified with the successful expansion of the American economy.

The peculiar genius of America was said to lie, therefore, in its ability to transform potential social antagonisms into mutual enrichment. The instrument of this social alchemy was the competitive market, aided by the vast natural endowments of North America and the "cultural capital" of an Anglo-Saxon nation naturally given to enterprise and to the tradition of limited government. There was about that vision of the 1950s some quality of a caricature of liberal philosophy, but it was essentially faithful to the liberal spirit in its celebration of economic dynamism as the goal and result of a new kind of society.

Thus, utilitarian liberalism finds itself committed in principle to a program of economic expansion. Hence its close tie with commercial capitalism and the vision of material abundance. Liberal historians such as Hartz and Boorstin have accordingly tried to justify America's present commitment to capitalistic growth as, over the long run, the most effective and humane means of fulfilling the promise of a modern liberal society to "deliver the goods" and so provide the greatest happiness for the greatest number. This implies that human needs and their satisfaction can always be dealt with as individual preferences which have minimum impact on the preferences and fulfillment of other individuals. For this reason, the repeated recourse to government to regulate and sometimes restructure or even plan the distribution of resources and the kinds of production, especially pronounced since the New Deal, puts strains on the apparent coherence of this liberal scheme.

The reason for the increasing turn to political means of redressing economic imbalances has remained the negative social effects, the so-called externalities, of individual acquisitive behavior. Anxiety about economic security and the risks of entrepreneurship are all necessary side effects of the market's functioning. So the turn to government to resolve these problems not only demonstrates the failure of the Invisible Hand to balance commerce so that everyone's needs are fairly met; it also forces the liberal state to try to function in ways liberal political philosophy is ill suited to assume. The reason for this is the assumption that government's sole legitimate aim is the liberty of its citizens, by which liberal thinkers have meant security of person and property. The liberal theory of government is squarely founded on the premises of individual self-interest and the utilitarian conception of value. Society is conceived in fact, or at least in ideal terms, as an instrument created by autonomous individuals to further their desires and fulfill their needs. These needs are viewed in liberal theory as essentially private and not subject to rational discussion because human beings are conceived as creatures determined by passional wants. This makes self-interest in all cases the overwhelming and decisive motive that controls human affairs.

The ideal of a perfectly self-correcting market mechanism is essential to make this conception of human nature plausible, since it alone could ensure a harmonious outcome to the relations among many desire-driven individuals. This helps account for the tortured arguments of contemporary neoconservatives to prove the utopian possibilities of the real market, despite the overwhelming historical evidence to the contrary. But although each individual is moved by private desires, these desires in the aggregate threaten to overwhelm particular or peculiar wants. The social contract doctrine tries to provide a role for the state precisely as an institution that can guarantee individual autonomy, that is, that treats each individual in the same way, making sure the desires of one are not subordinated to those of another without consent. The general or universal rules of law are trusted to enable the state to do just that: to police the operations of the market.

Thus, there has long been an optimistic quality about mainstream liberal thinking, one still present after the trauma of the Great Depression and, indeed, not without voice today. However, in the American context there has also been a contrapuntal theme even among proponents of the instrumental vision of economic society. Indeed, James Madison's early optimism about the ability of the liberal system of constitutional checks and balances to disperse and regulate the struggle of interests was forcefully challenged by Alexander Hamilton. Hamilton argued that the inevitable result of unrestrained commercial development was—and he advocated this—the development of large economic organizations, sharp inequalities of wealth, and international competition for markets.[15] In such a case, Hamilton thought, the state necessarily became a leviathan, acting to uphold some and to flatten others and controlling all.

This Hamiltonian understanding of liberal capitalism and the modern state emphasized that competitive action is strategic, aiming at besting other competitors. Hamilton saw that once social relations become lived and conceived as instrumental to competitive success, as they do in liberal society, the public realm becomes the scene of power struggle. The benign vision of competitive society which liberal thinkers such as Hartz offer plays down the strategic aspects of utilitarianism and greatly deemphasizes conflict and domination. Hartz largely dismissed Hamilton and his party as "whigs" and would-be aristocrats radically out of synchrony with mainstream liberal thought and practice.[16] And of course the Hamiltonian conception does raise fundamental questions about the effectiveness of the institutions of market or constitutional government to transform the struggle for dominance into a dynamic equilibrium. Hartz has loaded into his notion of liberal society something more than the individualist, utilitarian, capitalist core of philosophic liberalism can carry. It is as though Hartz, fearing that the suffocating organic ties extolled by conservative thinkers of the Burkean stamp were the sole alternative to liberal individualism, felt compelled to ascribe any sense of moral solidarity among Americans to some kind of magically sublimated self-interest.[17] At the same time his interpretation rendered him oblivious to the connection Hamilton saw between market capitalism, administrative social control, and international military struggle. That unawareness, of course, was widespread in cold war America.

While some liberal intellectuals were celebrating the liberal consensus and others had declared an end of ideology in American politics, uneasiness with the individualistic, growth-oriented direction of American society aroused still others to question the adequacy of the liberal notion of the good life to the nation's own ideals. The political and cultural turmoil of the 1960s began with an awakening of moral idealism spurred by the nation's failure to achieve its ideal of human dignity and expressed itself in the political emergence of groups marginal in postwar society. The movement for the civil rights of black Americans embodied in its leadership and in its rhetoric the civic themes and criticisms of a complacent society which had been silent for at least a decade. The student movement of those days recalled ideals in the American tradition not readily assimilable to the liberal vision. After announcing that the United States was at a point of moral and political stalemate, dominated by a corporate leviathan, its citizens in private withdrawal from public life, the new movement proposed a counterimage of the good society—"participatory democracy."

In a participatory democracy, the political life would be based in several root principles: that decision-making of basic social consequences be carried on by public groups; that politics be seen positively, as the art of collectively creating an acceptable pattern of social relations; that politics has the function of bringing people out of isolation and into community, this being a necessary, though not sufficient, means of finding meaning in personal life.[18]

Particularly significant in this statement is the concern that politics be seen as a positive, indeed necessary, activity conceived not as the advancement of preformed, private interests but as a process of social construction shared in common. The notion that public action was positive affirmed the New Deal's brand of liberalism as well as the "direct action" politics which that era made a common feature of political life.

The practical concerns which led to this turn toward an explicitly positive, participatory, and egalitarian notion of politics stemmed from a negative appraisal of postwar society, especially the "permeating and victimizing fact of human degredation," the cold war orientation toward military needs, and the apparent cynicism and narrowness of political leadership.[19] In appealing for a mass social movement of reform, the students, civil rights activists, and other fledgling movement leaders found themselves invoking ideals they sensed to be part of their tradition but which clashed with the self-interested utilitarian language of the dominant interpreters of American politics. Some American intellectuals were able to respond to this clash by rediscovering an important dimension of American experience which postwar preoccupations had relegated to virtual silence. In various fields, but significantly in historical study, new conceptions of the national experience were stirring. A distinction between the liberal strands and a civic or republican constellation of thought in American democracy became apparent. This conceptual change has evolved along with a new configuring of American history, and as a crucial part of that development.[20] The rediscovery of a civic republican strand in the American tradition has thus proceeded hand in hand with new enunciations of civic activism as a political concept, and this intellectual development has occurred in interrelation with the political and moral aspirations of the reform movements themselves.

During the 1960s American historians were constructing a more complex understanding of national development, one which gave special attention to the political and religious cultural context out of which American society and, in particular, its political tradition emerged. Perry Miller's work on early New England provided a groundwork by giving a far broader and generally more sympathetic understanding of the Puritan impact on national culture than had been given.[21] The discovery that the Americans who made the Revolution and launched the new republic were not the straightforward Lockeans beloved of liberal legend suggested reassessments of many assumptions. Indeed, the effort to reconstruct the intellectual work of early America revealed a strong concern with individual character but a concern centered on the idea of virtue as the subordination of private wants to the common good, a preoccupation with self-development rather than self-advancement. The liberal theme of "pursuit of property" was certainly there, but it appeared in conjunction with a strongly egalitarian concern with the social conditions which must obtain for citizens to become full participants in republican government. Perhaps most surprising of all, the new historiography revealed that both Jeffersonians and Federalists shared these concerns to a high degree and that the liberal conception of government as an instrument for advancing interests emerged only gradually and in tense relationship to an older idea of republican politics as active community initiative.[22]

The new historiography revealed a more complex picture of the American founding, one full of tensions and conflicts. The inequalities generated by the pursuit of self-interest and an expanding market grew along with and often in opposition to the republican concern with civic initiative and the equal dignity of citizens. The rediscovery that Americans of the Revolutionary period thought of themselves as the inheritors of both the covenantal tradition of radical Protestantism and the republicanism of the Commonwealth of the seventeenth-century English revolution challenged the view of Hartz and Boorstin that Americans were acting from a native individualistic notion of liberty.[23] The civic republican tradition to which the colonial patriots were heir countered the individualistic emphasis of Hobbes and Locke with a social conception of human nature derived from classical, Christian, and Renaissance sources.

The Enlightenment liberals generally thought of individuals as morally preformed by their largely private needs and wants, so that government was a matter of regulations—the view that the Federalists used to structure the Constitution, though not without strong opposition. The "Real Whig" republicans, on the other hand, saw civic participation and the moral equality that made it possible as active achievements of a particular kind of social and political life. Their term for this kind of active social life in which politics was a positive culturing of individuals was the traditional one of civic virtue. It was the goal of republican statecraft. The untrammeled pursuit of self-interest, on the other hand, they saw as drawing men away from their full development as ethical persons and undermining the civic spirit on which liberty depended. The antiegalitarian tendencies of self-interest, which they associated with "empire," were called corruption.

Thus, the conflict of interpretations between the new historiography and the liberal one was responsible for the rediscovery of a conception of politics, expressed in the struggle for independence, which was not an instrumental politics of interest, indeed not a liberal vision of politics at all.[24] Rather, in that republican view politics was a positive art, a necessary expression and completion of social life. But neither could this view be called conservative in the modern philosophic sense. The patriots' republicanism contained little enthusiasm for social passivity. The language of civic virtue versus corruption and of republic versus empire suggests a highly active and engaged notion of the good society. In fact, allied with the strong resonances those terms held for members of the dissenting religious bodies so important in America, that republican moral-political language fired a revolution.

The recovery of the civic republican understanding of politics so powerful through the early years of the republic has enabled historical continuities to emerge which the liberal orthodoxy could not see. The key to this recovery has been grasping civic republicanism as a coherent moral and political vision which, while deeply interlocked with liberal individualism throughout American history, is a separate and in many ways opposed tradition. Neither liberal nor conservative, it must be understood in its own right. For civic thinkers the egalitarian spirit typical of a republic is a moral attitude involving self-restraint and mutual aid. Its foundation is the factual social interdependence among citizens, but its cultivation is a conscious process by which the individual citizens develop their own characters through a shared enthusiasm for the ideals of dignity and justice that the political community represents. The republican thinkers called this process of concomitant personal and collective development civic virtue and took it to be the primary concern of political life. In their view a self-governing society, a republic, exists only through the active initiative of its citizens. Hence the precarious quality of republican life; the vitality of the society depends on the virtue of its citizens.[25] Thus, the civic consciousness begins with a focus on the moral quality of active social relations, as opposed to economic enrichment, as in the liberal mind, or immemorial custom, as in the conservative mind. In this, above all else, citizens are interdependent. Virtue sustains the common good because without it the egalitarian spirit of sharing gives way to the contest for privilege and domination, the corruption and finally despotism so feared by the American republicans.

As contemporary theorists of republicanism have emphasized, a republican society is not founded on a social contract as the liberals understand that idea. The freely given consent of the liberal contract theory is a fiction that overlooks the most important point, that the moral willingness to bind oneself in mutual commitment is not given outside actual social relations. It cannot be realized apart from a certain kind of moral culture, which recognizes social differences and interdependency as well as individual dignity. The morally responsible personality is taken by civic thinkers as the goal of cultural and personal development and not as an explained given, as in much liberal thinking.

THE INTERPRETIVE TURN

The developing American republican historiography, which has so closely followed discontent with the liberal vision of progress, illustrates the circular pattern of practical and theoretical understanding characteristic of interpretive inquiry. But it is a conception alien to the tradition of analytical reason which is the epistemological root of liberalism. The notion of social science which seeks to know by objectifying its objects as elements in a rule-governed system has an affinity for a social and political practice of expert control by instrumental means. Critics of that conception of policy science have made strong arguments against the cognitive as well as the practical validity of that project. But an interpretive approach that seriously reflects on its own moral and political stance is committed by that reflection to a different understanding of the relation of social inquiry to public policy.

The first axiom of this understanding is that the investigator can understand the object of study, be that contemporary or historical, only to the degree to which he can see his own predicament as related to that of another. If we can now discern the role of a tradition of concern with moral solidarity in the American founding, that is part of a process of coming to understand in a new way what is important and what is possible in our own historical situation. The contribution of an interpretive social investigation is to enhance society's understanding of itself, however, disturbing that may be. In fact, it can hardly help being critical and disturbing as it brings hidden or half-ignored facets of our collective condition to light. But even in this, its premise is that it speaks within a consensus that affirms the equal right of each person to a moral existence and thus to a part in the common discussion about how we should live together.

The practical premise of a responsible interpretive social inquiry is thus a social and moral relation to the members of society within which one speaks. In one expression this is the republican understanding of mutual interdependency. However, this idea carries the implication that the achievement of social investigation as dialogue and consensus among citizens is a historically rare and difficult collective achievement. It is directly involved with and dependent on the moral culture of citizen equality and participation and thus is not possible anytime, under any circumstances. Its fate is tied to that of republican political life in the full sense.

The strongly defensive and individualistic ethos engendered by the declining growth in the consumption-oriented and bureaucratically managed capitalism of the present puts severe strains on that moral and political culture, and the institutional forms of contemporary American life often threaten the viability of democratic politics. Therefore the reconstruction of consensual understanding has become essential if an alternative to a technically managed but morally undeveloped civilization is to be realized, even in limited form.

Still, discontent with the prevailing instrumental, strategic forms of public conduct continues to arouse resistance. Philosophical critiques of instrumental society serve the important function of keeping us aware of the complexity of human life experience, even in a scientifically rationalized era. The spread of interest in ecological ways of thinking, which substitute interdependence and nurture for the instrumental emphasis on growth and control, is likewise suggestive of the continuance of forms of living which resist the pressures of instrumental control. Renewed interest in restructuring economic and social institutions has generated new political movements of citizen participation, of the disadvantaged along with the more affluent.[26] These are intimations that American society is not altogether one-dimensional.

The alternative to seeing the social sciences as policy sciences is recovering dimensions of knowledge which positivistic and instrumental modes of thought and action have obscured. Knowledge in the human sciences is finally more than the explanation of objects. It is always a knowing *with* the other. The tyranny of positivistic discourse has meant that knowledge came to be respectable only when the other could be exhaustively talked *about*. Not that insight disappeared. It simply ceased to be called knowledge in any respectable sense. The task of a new postpositivistic social science is thus considerable. It will have to develop its authoritativeness as it gathers a hearing, not just among specialists but among concerned citizens as well. But in seeking to persuade, it can also hope to arouse as well as to instill insight. It thereby can help create the moral grounds of its own possibility.

NOTES

1. Thomas Dye, *Understanding Public Policy*, 2nd ed. (Englewood Cliffs, N.J.: Prentice-Hall, 1975), p. 27. For other examples of this kind of thinking, see Yehezkel Dror, *Design for Policy Sciences* (New York: American Elsevier, 1971), and its antecedent Daniel Lerner and Harold D. Lasswell, eds., *The Policy Sciences: Recent Developments in Scope and Method* (Palo Alto: Stanford University Press, 1951).

2. Herbert J. Gans, "Social Science for Social Policy," in Irving Louis Horowitz, ed., *The Use and Abuse of Social Science*, 2nd ed. (New Brunswick, N.J.: Transaction Books, 1975), p. 4.

3. Charles E. Lindblom and David K. Cohen, *Usable Knowledge: Social Science and Social Problem Solving* (New Haven: Yale University Press, 1979).

4. *Ibid.*, pp. 12–17, 31–35.

5. Lindblom and Cohen cite a number of reasons for this failure, all traceable to social scientists' mistaken notion that natural scientific methods exhaust the possibilities of reasoned understandings. Consequently, social scientists have often become intent upon deriving ahistorical, neatly defined explanatory categories and theories which fail to take seriously into account the relation between knowledge about human

action and the social position of the investigator. These difficulties become acute in policy science debates, because policy science by definition seeks to influence as well as explain or understand social action. See *Usable Knowledge,* pp. 43–53.

6. It is interesting and instructive on this point that Montesquieu seems to have conceived *his* architectonic as genuinely new. See, for example, his preface to *The Spirit of the Laws,* Thomas Nugent, trans. (New York: Hafner's, 1949).

7. The now nearly classic work is Thomas S. Kuhn, *The Structure of Scientific Revolutions,* 2nd ed. (Chicago: University of Chicago Press, 1970).

8. See Michael Polanyi, *Personal Knowledge: Toward a Post-Critical Philosophy* (Chicago: University of Chicago Press, 1974).

9. Kuhn, *The Structure of Scientific Revolutions,* p. 192.

10. Whitehead's discussion of the relation of modern science to its background assumptions remains classic. See Alfred North Whitehead, *Science and the Modern World* (New York: Macmillan, 1927).

11. See Robert Heilbroner, ed., *Economic Means and Social Ends: Essays in Political Economics* (Englewood Cliffs, N.J.: Prentice-Hall, 1969).

12. For discussions of these unintended consequences of "applied policy science" in the mode of stimulating and "fine tuning" growth in market economies, see Fred Hirsch, *Social Limits to Growth* (Cambridge: Harvard University Press, 1976); and Robert Heilbroner, *Business Civilization in Decline* (New York: W. W. Norton, 1976).

13. Jürgen Habermas, introduction to *Theory and Practice* (Boston: Beacon Press, 1973), p. 44.

14. Louis Hartz, *The Liberal Tradition in America: An Interpretation of American Political Thought Since the Revolution* (New York: Harcourt, 1955). A similar argument forms the substance of Daniel Boorstin's *The Genius of American Politics* (Chicago: University of Chicago Press, 1953). Liberalism as a tradition of political, social, economic, and philosophical thought is characterized by an instrumental view of social and political relationships, an atomistic theory of human nature for which the individual naturally precedes social relations, a utilitarian theory of value according to which things derive worth from their function in fulfilling individual needs and wants, and a conception of knowledge as the reduction of complex wholes to their analytic components. This ideal of knowledge as applied to human affairs gives rise to hopes that social engineering can reorganize life so as to achieve a dynamic balance of mutual adjustment.

The major thinkers in this tradition who inherited the general form of these ideas from Thomas Hobbes and John Locke have been David Hume, Montesquieu, Adam Smith, and Jeremy Bentham, whose utilitarian philosophy represents a kind of pure logical view of the doctrine. John Stuart Mill's relation to Bentham was critical, and his position in regard to the entire construction of liberalism was ambiguous. (See Michael McPherson's paper in this book for a discussion of Mill.) The literature on liberal thought is vast, but the following works are especially useful in grasping the overall contours of the tradition: Louis Dumont, *From Mandeville to Marx: The Genesis and Triumph of Economic Ideology* (Chicago: University of Chicago Press, 1977); Élie Halévy, *The Growth of Philosophic Radicalism,* Mary Morris, trans. (Boston: Beacon, 1955); Albert O. Hirschman, *The Passions and the Interests: Political Arguments for Capitalism Before Its Triumph* (Princeton: Princeton University Press, 1977); Steven Lukes, *Individualism* (Oxford: Basil Backwell, 1973); C. B. MacPherson, *The Life and Times of Liberal Democracy* (New York: Oxford University Press, 1962); Leo Strauss, *Natural Right and History* (Chicago: University of Chicago Press, 1953); Roberto M. Unger, *Knowledge and Politics* (New York: Macmillan, Free Press, 1975); and Sheldon Wolin, *Politics and Vision* (Boston: Little, Brown, 1960).

15. See Gerald Stourzh, *Alexander Hamilton and the Idea of Republican Government* (Palto Alto: Stanford University Press, 1970), pp. 158–62.

16. Hartz, *Liberal Tradition*, pp. 15ff.

17. It might seem as though Hartz were following Alexis de Tocqueville's famous discussion of "self-interest rightly understood." However, a close reading of Tocqueville shows that he is not. Tocqueville's point is that although Americans often *interpret* their acts of public involvement as self-interested and although they may in fact begin as such, the importance of civic life is its transformative effect. It is an educative process in which self-interested motives become enlarged into genuinely altruistic ones. See Alexis de Tocqueville, *Democracy in America,* George Lawrence, trans. (Garden City, N.Y.: Doubleday Anchor Books, 1969), vol. 2, part 11, ch. 5.

18. From the Port Huron Statement of the Students for a Democratic Society, quoted in Kirkpatrick Sale, *SDS* (New York: Vintage Books, 1973), p. 52.

19. *Ibid.,* p. 72.

20. This development provides a vivid illustration of the procedure in human inquiry called interpretive or hermeneutical. Jürgen Habermas has described this approach, in his *Knowledge and Human Interests* (Boston: Beacon Press, 1971), pp. 309–10, as follows: "The world of traditional meaning discloses itself to the interpreter only to the extent that his own world becomes clarified at the same time. The subject of understanding establishes communication between both worlds. He comprehends the substantive content of tradition by *applying* tradition to himself and his situation."

21. See Perry Miller, *Errand into the Wilderness* (Cambridge: Harvard University Press, 1975).

22. The development of these themes is discussed in some detail by Robert E. Shalhope, "Toward a Republican Synthesis: The Emergence of an Understanding of Republicanism in American Historiography," *William and Mary Quarterly,* 3rd series (1972), 29:49–50; and Jack Green, *The Reinterpretation of the American Revolution* (New York: Harper & Row, 1968).

23. Bernard Bailyn's work has been a powerful catalyst in launching this direction in interpretation. See his *Ideological Origins of the American Revolution* (Cambridge, Mass.: Belknap Press, 1967), and his *Origins of American Politics* (New York: Knopf, 1968). See also Pauline Maier, *From Resistance to Revolution* (New York: Knopf, 1972). The importance of religious sentiments in the American revolutionary experience has been explored by Perry Miller, *Errand into the Wilderness;* and Alan Heimert, *Religion and the American Mind: The Great Awakening to the Revolution* (Cambridge: Harvard University Press, 1966).

24. Liberalism's overshadowing of the republican tradition in the development of the new nation is presented, though in perhaps too simple a scenario, by Gordon S. Wood, *The Creation of the American Republic: 1776–1787* (Chapel Hill: University of North Carolina Press, 1969). The complex interrelations between republicanism and philosophic liberalism are interestingly explored in the collection by Robert H. Horwitz, ed., *Moral Foundations of the American Republic* (Charlottesville: University of Virginia Press, 1976).

25. The best overall treatment of the history of republican thought is J. G. A. Pocock, *The Machiavellian Moment: Florentine Political Thought and the Atlantic Republican Tradition* (Princeton, N.J.: Princeton University Press, 1975). The Machiavellian elements emphasizing virtue as the ability to prevail against circumstances were joined with the Greek and Roman notion of virtue as devotion to the common good, as Pocock notes. To this must be added the long tradition of Christian Aristotelianism deriving from the Middle Ages and the Calvinist concern with civic order. See

Quentin Skinner, *The Foundations of Modern Political Thought,* 2 vols. (London: Cambridge University Press, 1978).

26. Current research is underway to bring to light the ways Americans are striving to make moral sense out of the strains and new possibilities in both private and public life. The research in which I am currently involved, a collective project on "The Moral Basis of Social Commitment," with Robert Bellah, Richard Madsen, Ann Swidler, and Steven Tipton, is seeking to understand the resources various Americans bring to thinking about social reality and the moral understandings they are using to maintain or to alter their notions of self and a meaningful life within both public and private contexts.

Fourteen

BELIEVING IN SOCIAL SCIENCE: THE ETHICS AND EPISTEMOLOGY OF PUBLIC OPINION RESEARCH

Bruce Sievers

The appeal to give our credence to scientific expertise, a constant theme in the modern world, has extended in recent years to include the fields of the social sciences. The systematic study of human behavior through the social sciences has become central to our understanding of daily life, our organization of work and play, and our participation in public activity. Most fundamentally, social science has become an accepted element of the definition of human action.

In this paper I will focus on the ethical implications of this growing interrelationship between the social sciences and public life, and in particular on the application of the social sciences to the practical and theoretical dimensions of public policy. No longer limited to academic observation of the field of policy, today the social sciences are systematically integrated into the formulation, implementation, and evaluation of public policy in the forms of applied economics, psychology, sociology, survey research, organization and communications theory, behavioral political science, and, in some instances, anthropology and quantitative history.

Four supposed characteristics of the social sciences have particular appeal to policy makers and have thus led to the rapid appropriation of these fields as applied tools in the policy process. The social sciences promise *objectivity*—clear determinations of factual situations before and after desired policy changes; *efficiency*—the maximization of accomplishments with minimal expenditures of resources; *effectiveness*—demonstrations that they "work," at least within certain limited areas of activity; and *credibility*—receptivity of the public to scientific explanations as justifications for action.

These four factors build a powerful case for the adoption of social science approaches in the policy arena. Research results and techniques of the various social sciences have often been adopted by those in the field of policy as quickly as they have been judged useful. Indeed, the assimilation of the social sciences into policy seems to have been limited primarily by the hesitancy and disputatiousness within the disciplines rather than by reluctance by policy makers to exploit whatever knowledge might be available.

Although the merits of widespread application of the social sciences to public policy matters can be and have been argued extensively (primarily on grounds of increased rationality, clarity, and responsibility in the policy process), its gifts are fraught with ambiguity, and they are the more problematic because of the subtle importation of conceptual structures into the very definition of policy issues and, further, into the self-understanding of human purpose and action. These problems, I suggest, embody the fundamental moral dilemmas of the application of the social sciences to public policy.

I will consider the issues separately on three levels: practical use and misuse of social scientific knowledge, normative assumptions, and epistemological foundations and moral consequences. I will consider the first two problem areas only briefly, since both have been treated extensively elsewhere; the third is, I suggest, the most complex and potentially the most far-reaching. All three may be illustrated in the many areas of social scientific research which are applied to policy. As an example, I will suggest how moral dilemmas involved in the application of social science to the policy process arise in the case of public opinion polling.

POLICY APPLICATIONS OF SOCIAL SCIENCE: USE AND MISUSE

Immediate moral questions arise in the application of social scientific research to the formulation and implementation of social policy. Regardless of the truth or utility of particular results of social scientific investigation, a first moral question arises concerning the application to be made of the knowledge.

The possibility of using particular observations about social behavior for calculated political purposes is a familiar moral issue in the political sphere, commonly acknowledged in the Western tradition at least since Machiavelli. The situation here is rather traditional and straightforward: social scientific knowledge, like natural scientific knowledge, may be used for good or ill, depending on the aims and motives of the user. Thus, just as the discovery of the properties of the laser beam may be used either to enhance communications or to develop weapons of destruction, so may studies of learning behavior be used either for improving school curricula (and ultimately for formulating improved educational policy) or for developing more effective techniques of mass manipulation and subtle forms of political legitimation.

A more complex case is that of psychological conditioning, particularly as applied in the criminal justice system. Methods of behavior modification, whether through psychotherapy, biofeedback, operant conditioning, or other psychological techniques, are capable of changing deep-seated patterns of behavior. On one level, both society and the individual have an interest in changing criminal behavior patterns. Yet, in a prison setting, the use of psychological techniques to induce changes in personality is morally ambiguous, suggesting system-conforming control at the deepest level of the human personality, substantially beyond the physical confinement prescribed in the legal code.

A long list of similar examples might demonstrate the moral questions raised in the use of social scientific information. Such a list is included in a study undertaken by the Congressional Subcommittee on Research and Technical Programs of the Committee on Government Operations in 1967.[1] The study documents exhaustively the wide-ranging application of the social sciences in federal governmental activity. Most cases examined in the study, whether rural sociology in the Department of Agriculture or research on human factors in traffic problems by the Bureau of Public Roads, raise unexamined moral dilemmas, although the study optimistically concludes with a recommendation for increased application of the social and behavioral sciences to the problems of government. The application of techniques of social science for the purpose of influencing the action of people without their direct knowledge and thereby of implementing predetermined governmental policies poses the same sorts of moral issues that have surrounded the use of scientific research throughout history.

NORMATIVE PRESUPPOSITIONS AND IMPLICATIONS OF SOCIAL SCIENCE

A second traditional debate in the philosophy of social science is the question of "value freedom" in scientific inquiry in general and in social scientific inquiry in particular. This debate is distinguished from the question of the moral and immoral use of social science research and raises fundamental implications of the nature of inquiry in the social sciences and the relationship between theory and practice. Max Weber posed the classic formulation of the problem of *Wertfreiheit* in an early essay, " 'Objectivity' in Social Science and Social Policy," and later in his celebrated twin lectures, "Politics as a Vocation" and "Science as a Vocation,"[2] delivered in Munich in 1918. In these works he strongly contrasts the "ethic of ultimate ends and ethic of responsibility" of the archetypal politician with the "intellectual integrity" of the scientist who pursues the lonely and rigorous path toward the acquisition of value-free scientific knowledge.

Wissenschaft (in German, science in the broadest sense), whether social or natural, is in Weber's view carried out with detachment and objectivity, separated from the interests and desires of political life, although scientific information is available to the political leader as a means of informing judgment or carrying out decisions through the administrative process. This concept surfaces in a contemporary form in Karl Popper's elaboration of the concept of "social engineering," in which empirical experiments are carried out in social policy by using the tentative results of social scientific inquiry.[3]

One might notice that Weber's formulation contains three separable elements: the normative presuppositions of science in general, the special normative presuppositions of a science of society, and the particular normative questions that arise in the application of social science to public policy. The first two will not be examined extensively here because they have been exhaustively treated elsewhere, but both bear strongly on the third.

The paradoxical nature of the normative presuppositions of an avowedly nonnormative form of inquiry reaches special heights in the application of the results of the "value-free" study of society to practical policy issues. Weber addressed these particular paradoxes in only a limited way, because he held that the two enterprises, scientific investigation and political action, could and should be kept separate, and he was concerned primarily with the normative presuppositions of the researcher rather than with those of the practitioner. But, as we shall see shortly, the very separation of fact and value presumed by the researcher constitutes part of a larger moral problem for the policy maker.

Weber's model predicated a strong division—"an unbridgeable distinction"—between the work of the scientific investigator and the work of the evaluating, acting person. On this model, scientists attempt to neutralize their values in the attempt to come to an objective analytical ordering of empirical reality, whereas policy makers may use these results to clarify, bring internal consistency to, and implement policy choices which are ultimately made on other grounds.

> To apply the results of this [scientific] analysis in the making of a decision is not a task which science can undertake; it is rather the task of the acting, willing person: he weighs and chooses from among the values involved according to his own conscience and his personal view of the world. Science can make him realize that all action, and naturally, according to the circumstances, inaction, imply in their consequences the espousal of certain values—and herewith—what is today so willingly overlooked—the rejection of certain others. The act of choice itself is his own responsibility.

The bases for such a choice, then, are the personal value scheme and the "sentiments" of the actor, who, although possibly informed by an analytical understanding, is under stringent obligation to retain an awareness of "exactly at which point the scientific investigator becomes silent and the evaluating and acting person begins to speak."[4]

All of this is a familiar part of the history of the philosophy of social science. The common thread in this traditional treatment has been the ethical questions faced by social scientists in considering the presuppositions and consequences of their work, and this discussion has formed a constant theme from the early development of the disciplines, for example, in the work of Weber and Durkheim, to the work of such contemporary writers as Bierstedt, Matson, Means, Roubiczek, and, recently, Miller, who argues for "going half way with Weber, admitting value freedom as a constraint on the content of social explanations but rejecting it as a constraint on the personal commitments influencing research."[5]

But the generation and application of value-free social science, as seen from the standpoint of contemporary policy makers, takes on a new ethical dimension. In addition to a commitment to a particular mode of rationality entailed in all scientific endeavor, there are also commitments specific to the concept of value-free social science vis-à-vis one's stance toward human interaction: nonpartisanship, neutrality with respect to ethical systems under investigation, and externalization to subjective meaning schemes. Thus, the social scientific attitude requires a break from ordinary interactive relationships shared among human beings and, for the purposes of scientific investigation, the treatment of subjects under investigation as objects to be analyzed. This situation immediately raises Kantian means-end questions, but more important to our interest here, it also poses the moral dilemma of the technical application of knowledge applied to ethical-social problems which lie at the heart of public policy.

When social science is applied to policy problems, policy makers, faced with the task of reaching specified goals, are encouraged and in fact impelled to make use of social scientific information at their disposal. They are induced to use social science in order to, as one text advises, "establish more clearly the constraints under which [they] operate and to clarify the consequences that are likely to follow when certain kinds of policies are adopted."[6] Judicious policy makers will thus wisely use all valid knowledge available to address their problems; indeed, they will be accused of willful ignorance or unprofessional conduct if they do not.

The nature of the social scientific information they use, however, is technical; that is, it is necessarily acquired and applied outside the interactive context of the persons under study or subject to the policy and in a manner which inherently circumvents self-images of action and motivation. Thus, the very structure of the situation undermines a basic premise of ethical competence on the part of those to whom the policy is applied: the presumption of knowledgeable and voluntary participation by the agent.

These particular dilemmas involved in the application of the results of social scientific research to policy making, as seen from the viewpoint of the larger public, have only begun to be explored. Here Roubiczek's list of tendencies in sociology which "infringe upon ethics" moves us closer to the frame of action of the policy maker. The tendencies in social science "(1) to see everything as relative; (2) to discredit, or 'unmask,' moral or ideal motives; (3) to 'informalize,' as psychology does, external demands; (4) to personify abstract concepts; and (5) to claim that the discipline is a pure science"[7] begin to color the world of social scientifically inclined policy makers as they attempt rationally to reach their goals. By adopting the use of seemingly unobjectionable social scientific data as an aid to making a decision or implementing a policy, political actors also accept a much more subtle set of presuppositions and a reformulated approach to problem solving derived from scientific-technical methodology. Ultimately the logically organized framework of science displaces a less rigorously held and therefore apparently less defensible pastiche of values, which include such arguably outmoded notions as those described by Weber: sentiments, conscience, will, feeling for practical and cultural forms, and metaphysical value judgments.

Thus, whether scientifically informed policy making has the intended results—for example, a lower recidivism rate in the criminal justice system through the application of psychological rehabilitation techniques—or unintended consequences—for example, a diminished sense of moral responsibility in those involved in the treatment—the overall moral situation is the same. The introduction of scientific methods has systematically altered the relationship among the policy makers, their decisions, and those affected by the policies; and in this relationship the policy choice has been infused with technically conceived and applied criteria.

The drive toward objectivity, rationality, efficiency, and credibility thus permeates and transforms the ethical context of decision making on public policy. The attempt to insulate the value choices of the policy makers from the analytical ordering of the scientific investigators cannot be sustained on either theoretical or practical grounds, and the two, in coming together, alter the structure of choice in the situation. What has changed, in addition, is the very definition of the policy situation and rational approaches to it. This brings us to the topic of epistemology.

THE EPISTEMOLOGY OF SOCIAL SCIENCE:
MORAL DIMENSIONS

The third and least discussed aspect of the relationship between social science and public policy concerns epistemological assumptions. In addition to the pragmatic uses of the social sciences and the normative presuppositions and consequences of the scientific attitude in research and practice there lie questions of the claims to knowledge made by the social sciences and the implications of these claims for public policy.

There has developed a considerable body of literature in recent years on the epistemology of the social sciences, including discussion of the sorts of claims which can be made for the validity of social scientific knowledge, the bases of these claims, and how they differ from the claims made for natural scientific knowledge. What is striking about this literature is the degree to which students of diverse traditions find themselves in agreement on several fundamental presuppositions about the nature of social knowledge. Neo-Kantians, phenomenologists, existentialists, pragmatists, ordinary language philosophers, adherents of the Frankfurt school—indeed, almost all those outside strict positivism or behaviorism—agree on the importance of meaning and interpretation to the explanation of social action.[8]

The fundamental division between positivists and their opponents on the nature of explanatory schemes of human action reflects a deeper underlying disagreement on what constitutes acceptable criteria for the validation of knowledge. Stated oversimply, the antipositivists argue that what count as the criteria for verifiable knowledge in the natural sciences, namely, the "empirical-analytic" circle of relationships as Habermas describes them,[9] are not adequate criteria for the acquisition of knowledge of human action. These questions are beyond the purely empirical questions of acquiring knowledge of human thinking and doing—problems of complexity, experimentation, self-fulfilling prophecy, and so on—which merely pose unusually difficult technical challenges to the researcher. The epistemological questions bring to light the unique relationships among knowledge, mind, action, and explanation, which are presupposed by attempts to provide definitive analyses of human actions. Stuart Hampshire summarizes this point:

The knowledge that I have of the origin or causes, and therefore of the true nature, of my own states of mind is knowledge of independent objects, whose nature is independent of any belief about what their nature is. Where an intentional state of mind is in question, the subject's belief about its cause and its nature is one element in the state of mind itself, and any change in the subject's belief about his state of mind will bring some change in the state of mind itself.[10]

Hampshire's *Thought and Action* explores criteria for validity in statements about human action predicated on consciousness and intentionality.[11] Philosophers from diverse traditions have developed similar lines of argument into thoroughgoing critiques of natural science epistemology as applied to the human sphere. Two recent treatments of this issue, Habermas' *Zur Logik der Sozialwissenschaften* and Louch's *Explanation and Human Action*, systematically analyze, from different perspectives but with common intent, false moves made in arguments attempting to justify the social sciences as comprehensive and verifiable sources of knowledge about human motivation and action.[12] Neither Habermas nor Louch disputes the ability of the social sciences to predict and control human behavior in certain situations. Their criticism is directed instead toward the degree to which the framework of logical and empirical relationships involved in prediction and control can be said to provide an adequate account of what it means to be engaged in human activity.

Although there are precedents for this critique in the notion of *Verstehen* in Dilthey and even in Weber, the contemporary argument in Habermas and in Louch rests primarily on the central role of language in the structure of human experiences. As Habermas demonstrates, one cannot construct a coherent account of an action which involves intentionality without reference to the linguistically modulated meaning scheme of the actor, because, in Habermas' words, "social action is constituted solely through ordinary communication."[13]

Once action is interpreted through the web of language, however, one is immediately enmeshed in a Wittgensteinian world of meanings and interpretations, in which, as Louch notes, multiple levels of seeing, defining, and justifying become prerequisite to understanding:

Mental events, such as mental images qualify as events, but inasmuch as they are human doings, intended as opposed to observed, they enter into relations with other items in the network of reasons and not that of causes. Or, if you like, we could admit them as causes in the sense that, unless a person thought them he would not have acted the way he did. But this should not require us to picture these causal relations on the interaction or regularity models. The temporal order is present, but the manner of joining these links in the chain is logical; it consists in seeing the image or the thought as the grounds for acting.[14]

The ascertainment, with any degree of certainty, of what is going on in a given situation involving human action, therefore, becomes a function of one's acceptance of a particular linguistic interpretation. Interpretations must have recourse to what is "warranted" (Louch's term) by the situation, and this involves judgments of appropriateness not, according to Louch, by "temporal antecedents or functional dependencies but by deciding that the situation entitles a man to act in the way he did or is likely to do."[15]

Epistemologically, then, we find ourselves closer to the philosopher (or even the novelist) than to the natural scientist. Knowing one's own or another's motives becomes at least in part an act of reflection, and a systematic study of action becomes dependent on a form of reflection:

The natural sciences merely extend in methodical form the technically exploitable knowledge that has accumulated prescientifically within the transcendental framework of instrumental action. The science of man, however, extends in methodical form the reflective knowledge that is already transmitted prescientifically within the same objective structure of the dialectic of the moral life in which this science finds itself situated.[16]

What does this mean for the realm of public policy? Initially a matter of philosophic reflection, epistemology becomes in this dimension a significant and even controlling feature of the public policy process. When certain modes of certifying knowledge and reality become accepted as valid by participants in the policy process, the entire process is transformed. Theories of the apprehension of reality exert a subtle and thorough influence on the way policy issues are viewed; indeed, they supply the ultimate legitimation for particular policy approaches.

This process has deep moral consequences. In "Technology and Science as Ideology," Habermas analyzes the transposition of a positivistic theory of scientific knowledge onto the social world:

It can also become a background ideology that penetrates into the consciousness of the depoliticized mass of the population, where it can take on legitimating power. It is a singular achievement of this ideology to detach society's self-understanding from the frame of reference of communicative action and from the concepts of symbolic interaction and replace it with a scientific model. Accordingly the culturally defined self-understanding of a social lifeworld is replaced by the self-reification of men under categories of purposive-rational action and adaptive behavior.[17]

Ultimately, he continues, the application of the scientific mindset to the political world results in "technocratic consciousness [which] reflects not the sundering of an ethical situation but the repression of 'ethics' as such as a category of life."[18]

The influence of a conceptual model based on a scientific understanding of human action affects public life in the most profound ways, altering the policy makers' concepts of rationality, the public's self-images, the idea of what counts as evidence, and, finally, the political process itself. Louch's description of the consequences is ominous:

Totalitarianism is too weak a word and too inefficient an instrument to describe the perfect scientific society. For in the totalitarian regimes known to us, one is still conscious of coercion and thus of alternatives, however disastrous to the individual such alternatives may be. In the engineers' society, perhaps unwittingly promoted by psychologists and sociologists bent on being scientists, we should have to give up the concept of an open or civil society which, however inefficiently, serves as the prop for a social order based on respect for men as persons or autonomous agents.[19]

Habermas and Louch describe the potentially controlling influence of general social science epistemology in the political process. I want to suggest that in one area of public life such a social scientific model has already been adopted and these moral questions arise in practice.

PUBLIC OPINION POLLING AND PUBLIC POLICY

Widespread public opinion polling has been a significant part of national political life for the past quarter century. Developed by George Gallup and others as a vehicle to "speed up the processes of democracy," polling has gained popularity during the past several decades to become widely seen as an essential part of the political process, as important to political campaigns as it is to media projections of the public's states of mind.

The fundamental logic of the poll is clear. If it is desirable to know what people are thinking as part of the operation of a democracy, it is argued, then it is even more desirable to ascertain that information on a systematic and reliable basis. The scientific public opinion poll makes possible for the first time in mass society what Gallup, quoting Lord Bryce, notes that earlier ages had only imagined—an era in which "the will of the majority of citizens were to become ascertainable at all times."[20]

On this theory, polling provides a more efficient and accurate means of attaining an essential element of the democratic process, the ability of the public to communicate views among citizens and leaders, than had been available before.[21] But the introduction of scientific polling techniques also induces changes in the structure of the situation, linking the systematic study of human behavior to the systematic alteration of human conduct.

The moral consequences of these changes may be viewed, for the purposes of analysis, through the same conceptual framework used earlier by examining the ethical implications of practical applications, normative presuppositions, and epistemological foundations of applied social science.

Practical Applications

The most immediate moral issue which arises in the case of polling is the potentially manipulative use of information on attitudes. Survey research, which began as a straightforward process of questioning persons on their beliefs and opinions, has now evolved into a highly sophisticated process of "attitudinal analysis," which probes underlying fears, concerns, behavioral responses, and motivations, which relate only partially to articulated beliefs.

Information gained from survey research can be easily translated into manipulative techniques designed to gain public acceptance for whatever is purveyed, whether products, television programs, or political candidates. The use of such techniques is an accepted fact of commercial and political life, and, indeed, merchandisers and candidates who ignore such techniques do so only at their own peril and to the advantage of their competitors. The president of a major commercial polling organization, for example, described his firm's success in creating a dramatic turnaround by voters in an initiative campaign.

We realized early on that it was a matter of fear versus anger. . . . If the fear was great—that police, fire, and school services would be cut back, for example—then we'd lose. But if we could get them going on anger—taxes going up, politicians withholding information, and so on—we'd win.[22]

In the subsequent campaign, the firm effectively used polling data and advertisements keyed to the anger theme to accomplish a lopsided victory for their client.

Although political persuasion itself is not a new phenomenon— rhetoric in ancient Greece had the same end—the techniques of persuasion have become so radically advanced that the notion of speakers acting in an equal environment to convince one another of opinions has become but a nostalgic memory. Current political contests have become highly financed, professionally managed advertising campaigns, borrowing the most effective techniques from research in commercial sales.

Thus, political campaign firms, which are typically commercial advertising firms with partial interests in political campaigns, apply their combined expertise in attitude research, polling, demography, computer analysis, and media packaging to the political sphere. An example of one such integrated approach is "Claritas," a system created by the combined efforts of a computer-demographer, a pollster, and a political consultant and called by one of the inventors "a new and magical tool that allows a body to spend money more wisely by targeting the people most likely to respond." Through the computerized analysis of precise census and polling data, the system contributed heavily to a reversal in one campaign, from 60 percent of the electorate favoring an issue to 60 percent ultimately voting against it.[23]

The logic of this approach is articulated by Tony Schwartz, a leader in the field of media advertising and consultant to many major political campaigns. Schwartz, following his mentor Joseph Napolitan, considers a political campaign like a drive toward a "one-day sale," that is, the election. The point is to "tie up the voter and deliver him to the candidate," so that "it is really the *voter* who is packaged by the media, not the candidate." To do this, Schwartz advises heavy reliance on polls and other forms of sophisticated attitudinal research.

Good political research seeks out attitudes in the environment and then judges a political spot by the way it affects these attitudes. . . . The political poll is a way to measure attitudes and concerns of people in the environment. It can provide raw data that are valuable only to someone who can analyze it honestly and critically. As an X-ray, it is a great tool if it is read correctly. For instance, we often deal with the LOP factor—that is, a favorable response on a poll often means that the candidate is the Least Objectionable Politician. . . . If one accepts this view, the logical task of the media specialist is to make his candidate the least objectionable politician in the race. Many presidential campaigns have been organized with this specific task as the major goal.[24]

Polling thus becomes an essential part of modern political campaigning, more to discern inner feelings and underlying concerns than to serve as a vehicle for the expression of specific beliefs and opinions. Such in-depth polling and attitudinal research were used effectively, for example, by a California campaign firm in 1978 in two successful efforts, one to elect a senator and the other to defeat a ballot initiative.[25] In both cases the firm used massive polling and survey research, and in the latter it used small-group attitude research conducted by a psychologist. From this research, which included the firm's extensive involvement in constructing the polls, the professionals developed "meta-messages" which played on themes ascertained in the surveys. In this way they were able to gain acceptance for their causes.

Moral questions arising from this kind of applied research are apparent. Although the use of such information and of associated techniques is rapidly becoming essential to political survival, the techniques show an increasing potential for use in manipulative ways. Indeed, the growing ability of attitude researchers, pollsters, and media specialists to uncover and exploit people's deepest fears, hopes, and other sensitivities gradually eradicates the demarcation between political persuasion and demogogic propaganda.

Normative Presuppositions

The concept that the acquisition of information about public attitudes should, in order to be objectively scientific, be segregated from the researchers' aims and the users' applications flows out of the Weberian normative stance on social science, described above. The consequences of this stance are immediately evident in the field of polling. From the premise that a poll is simply an extension of the normal human interaction in which one person questions another about opinions, scientific survey research immediately moves to a new level of inquiry which fractures that interaction. No longer does the situation constitute a dialogue in which both parties are engaged in a process of mutual inquiry, both asking questions and modifying each other's attitudes accordingly. Instead, the poll predicates a linear relationship in which the researcher solicits responses from the interviewee according to a predetermined analytical scheme and for prospective applications unknown to the participants. The normative requirements for good research thus come into direct conflict with the ethics of open human interaction.

Even in the most straightforward polling situations this distinction in roles takes place, with a resulting distortion noted by Nimmo: "The interview is a contrived situation in which the respondent plays an unfamiliar role. He expresses a single opinion when, in fact, he may have a variety."[26] The polling framework is structured by the pollster's aim of producing results which can be effectively implemented as tools of prediction and potential attitudinal change. The interpretation, analysis, and further application of polling data occur outside the assumptions and direct understandings of those questioned. What is ultimately important for the pollster are not specific opinions but the implications of responses for the analytical study.

It is but a short next step to the circumvention of the actual expressed views of the "respondent" and their interpretation and causal explanation in a manner dictated by the analytical needs of the user. Schwartz emphasizes this approach in a discussion of the use of his "resonance theory" in political advertising:

Political advertising involves tuning in on attitudes and beliefs of the voter and then affecting these attitudes with the proper auditory and visual stimuli. . . . In this way, you surface attitudes (held by many) that can produce the desired effect. Commercials that attempt to *tell* the listener something are inherently not as effective as those that attach to something that is already in him. We are not concerned with getting things *across* to people as much as *out* of people. Electronic media are particularly effective tools in this regard because they provide us with direct access to people's minds.[27]

The moral issues which arise in the circle of relationships involved in collecting information, analyzing it, and changing attitudes differ from those having to do with the unethical *use* of information (although the ethics of use may be involved as well) in that they focus essentially on the orientation toward control presupposed by the scientific collection of data. The analytical instruments employed in polling are designed to yield information suitable for the prediction and control of attitudes and choice behavior, such as voting, and are not, despite claims to the contrary, designed to extend the traditional mode of conversation about political views. In short, in the field of polling, the researchers' and users' aims are paramount, whereas traditional political conversation gives primacy to the discussants' aims.

Contemporary researchers in polling clearly accept this view of their own work as based on the model of scientific neutrality and a corresponding separation of the investigator from the normal interactive context. Berelson, for example, describes approvingly the scientific development of public opinion studies.

The field has become technical and quantitative, a-theoretical, segmental-ized, and particularized, specialized and institutionalized, "modernized" and "group-ized"—in short, *as a characteristic behavioral science*, Americanized. Twenty-five years ago and earlier, prominent writers, as part of their general concern with the nature and functioning of society, learnedly studied public opinion not "for itself" but in broad historical, theoretical, and philosophical terms and wrote treatises. Today, teams of technicians do research projects on specific subjects and report findings. Twenty years ago the study of public opinion was part of scholarship. Today it is part of science.[28]

With progressive refinement of interviewing and data collection techniques and correspondingly better success at prediction, social scientists and pollsters claim to be drawing closer to an accurate as-sessment of the reality of public opinion.

Political scientists have borrowed the in-depth interview from a number of other disciplines, including psychology, medicine, and market research, while tailoring it to the discipline's particular interests. . . . In an effort to improve the quality of information obtained by survey research, analysts have drawn from the field of psychotherapy, where psychiatrists, clinical psychologists, counselors, and social workers have spent years working out techniques for delving into the dynamics of people's attitudes. In short, the technique of the clinical interview has been adapted to the needs of large-scale sample sur-veys.[29]

More recently, psychologists and market research firms have con-ducted experiments with skin galvanometers and electroencephalo-graphs to refine further the objectivity and accuracy of their results.[30]

When policy makers become aware of the availability of such infor-mation, organizational imperatives make it highly probable that it will be applied. Motivated by competition and the desire for unbiased, ob-jective information about public attitudes and moods, those charged with policy responsibilities would seem to be acting irrationally if they ignored information and analyses available to them from modern so-cial science. Neither serious, unanswered moral questions about the instrumental orientation of the collection and use of data about hu-man beings nor the fundamental epistemological problems examined below pose sufficient obstacles to deter the systematic incorporation of polling data into the policy process.

Epistemological Foundations
The foregoing discussion has not raised questions about the ultimate validity of polling data, only questions concerning applications and

normative implications of polling research. But now we turn, regardless of the effectiveness of polling or the moral dilemmas of public opinion research, to the claims made for the descriptive power of polls and the impact of these claims on the policy process.

One should notice, first, the rather odd descriptions of what it means to hold the beliefs, opinions, and attitudes which the scientific researchers are forced by behavioral requirements to adopt. Here are a few examples.

The term *public opinion* is given its meaning with reference to a multi-individual situation in which individuals are expressing themselves, or can be called upon to express themselves, as favoring or supporting (or else disfavoring or opposing) some definite condition, person, or proposal of widespread importance, in such a proportion of number, intensity, and constancy as to give rise to the probability of affecting action, directly or indirectly, toward the object concerned.[31]

An opinion, we will say, is an "implicit verbal response" or "answer" that an individual gives in response to a particular stimulus situation in which some general "question" is raised.[32]

"Public opinion" . . . may simply be taken to mean those opinions held by private persons which governments find it prudent to heed.[33]

Our first theoretical definition equates political opinion with "an expressed attitude concerning political phenomena such as candidates, issues, and parties." We understand a political attitude to be a subjective internal predisposition toward some object in the individual's political world. In order to observe and measure the existence, direction, intensity, or stability of attitudes, they have to be expressed. Usually, they are expressed in response to questions asked by a trained opinion analyst. Our theoretical definition not only tells us what an opinion is but also specifies what makes it politically relevant and observable.[34]

The last example is particularly interesting because it illustrates most explicitly the epistemological presuppositions of public opinion polling. According to these definitions, knowledge of public opinion is that which can be validated in observable behavior, such as a "response to questions asked by a trained opinion analyst." This concept is embedded in the larger theoretical framework of controlled experimentation, which underlies the epistemology of positivistic social science described above.

But such an approach to perceiving and describing beliefs and attitudes is severely limited. "Holding an opinion" is taken in normal parlance as well as in philosophical analysis to mean clearly more than uttering specific responses to particular questions. Rather, to hold an opinion is to be engaged in thinking and believing in a particular way, taking a tentative stance in the ebb and flow of consciousness, and putting things together for further reflection and consideration. The notions of opinion and belief have been traditional sources of philosophical deliberation, and they raise larger philosophical issues.

Holding an opinion seems to be closely connected with the way one acquires one's meaning scheme, the way one applies shifting levels of interpretation to one's own and others' actions, the interaction of rational and emotional states of mind, and the degree of one's awareness about outside events and persons. In short, holding an opinion is interwoven with the malleable and constantly reinterpretable nature of thinking and, as such is subject to the same diverse interpretations and philosophical complexities as thinking about thinking. From Plato's notion that thinking is the soul conversing with itself to Ryle's suggestion that thinking is "trying out promissory tracks,"[35] philosophers have characterized thinking with a dynamic quality that is at once nonreductionist and elusive. Holding an opinion, as a pause in this dynamic process, resists easy depiction.

The perplexity grows when we try to specify the things that count as valid criteria for knowledge about thinking and having opinions. Ryle notes that "we cannot, apparently, answer the simplest concrete questions about it [thinking],"[36] and other philosophers have struggled inconclusively with the problem of establishing reference points for ascertaining what is and what is not being thought. The paradox that emerges in these formulations is that the establishment of *criteria* essentially predetermines the description of thinking itself, and so on into a problem of infinite regression. What is clear from such philosophical ruminations is that an arbitrary depiction of thinking as answers to interviewers' questions or behavioral responses amounts to a reduction of the polymorphous character of thinking into a formula that is technically manageable but misses the essence of what it is to think and opine.

The difficulties are magnified when the idea of holding an opinion is projected onto the public realm. Social forces which shape meaning schemes are overlaid onto the hermeneutics of individual thinking, yielding a kaleidoscopic pattern of meaning and interpretation. Beyond the difficulty of characterizing particular acts of thinking, we now have the additional problem of specifying the nature of thoughts and opinions as social phenomena. The assessment of a given depiction of public sentiment as a statement of class, occupational, generational, national, or political philosophical views depends centrally on one's theoretical vision of society and of the forces that shape it and through which it is articulated.

The attempt to distill from polls a "popular will," a "long-term trend," or a "public mood," as presumed by opinion research firms,[37] falters not on inadequate statistical data or insufficiently sophisticated research methods but rather on a misguided notion of what political thinking actually is and how it may be apprehended. Polling not only fosters a static image of opinion, which substitutes measurements for reality, as Bogart has warned,[38] but more important, it postulates a reified model of consciousness which contradicts the dialogic nature of private and public thinking. What began as a technique to predict election results has thus become a definer of the political process.

Public opinion polls, in this view, are the means by which the public articulates its identity and needs. Surveys portray the existence of a concrete entity called "public opinion," which takes on its own life and even, according to Ladd, has its own inertia: "It is slow to get started in a particular direction, and once on the move it is hard to stop."[39] An analysis of the elements of this entity is supposed to provide guidance in the political process.

> There is still an important place for polling in American affairs. In a democracy, it is vital for the elected leadership to recognize long-term, deep-seated trends in public opinion. Are people pessimistic or optimistic about the future? Are people confident or worried about our status as a world power? Are people satisfied or dissatisfied with their financial situation?[40]

But to pose these questions is to illustrate the limitations of the theoretical basis of survey research and its claims to apprehending intentional phenomena. An epistemology appropriate to the examination of meaning patterns, as Habermas has thoroughly demonstrated, is premised on the concept of *Interaktion,* which requires mutual interpretation, rather than on that of technical control, which presumes a unidirectional relationship between theory and empirical test.

Reduction of the concept of public opinion to that which can be validated through the epistemology of positivistic social science has immediate consequences for the public and the political process. Acceptance by policy makers and the public of the survey research model of public opinion subtly transforms the concept of the political community into that of an administrative circle of instrumentally rationalized action, as described by Habermas in an early work, *Strukturwandel der Öffentlichkeit*.

> The manufactured consensus does not of course have much in common with a final unanimous vote reached after an extended process of mutual enlightenment, because the 'general interest' which could serve as the sole basis for the free playing out of a rational agreement of competing opinions disappears precisely to the degree to which the publicized self-presentations of privileged private interests claim that concept for themselves. . . . A consensus generated through the symbols of a 'public interest' which has been developed through sophisticated opinion-molding services and captured by private interests lacks the basis for reasonableness in general.[41]

Because of the central role played by the notion of public opinion in the political process, this introduction of the scientific model of survey research and its application to policy making become for Habermas the prerequisites to the "scientization" of politics.[42] Ultimately, this has the most fundamental implications for democratic theory: reduction of the sphere of politics from the field of the interplay of ideas to the mechanism of rational administration.

This, then, is the crux of the problem of applied opinion research in the democratic polity. Neither the potential misuse of polling data nor the ethical quandaries of survey research pose as serious a challenge to the democratic ideal as does the impact of the operational definition of public opinion. Redefined as leaders prudently following (and shaping) the articulated sentiments of the people as conveyed to them by opinion researchers, democracy emerges as a managerial, not a political, phenomenon.

Policy makers, media professionals, and opinion researchers alike share in defining public opinion as the "input" to this process and in communicating this definition to the general public. The notion of democracy as a political response mechanism with a reified public opinion as the stimulus is gaining wide national, and more recently international, acceptance, as noted by the Yugoslav opinion researcher Firdus Džinić.

> Public opinion in a Socialist society is one of the essential factors in arriving at political decisions. . . . Systematic research into public opinion is essential for modern political decision making. . . . These investigations constitute the only exact means of collecting information on the attitudes and opinions

of large social groups, or of society as a whole. This conception has gradually been brought home, and is today adopted by most political leaders and forums.[43]

How far this notion of the democratic polity varies from older concepts of democracy is suggested by comparison with democratic theory in classical Athens. Central to that original model was the idea of dialogue among citizens, dialogue that would change and evolve the moral character of the *polis* by the very process of participation by the discussants. Indeed, as Finley points out, *isēgoria,* the universal right to speak in the Assembly, was used by some Greek writers as a term synonomous with democracy.[44] The *polis* was not only controlled but, much more important, *defined* by the citizens' exercise of their right to speak. This concept of democracy, based on interaction, stands in striking contrast to the notion of democracy as polling techniques reinforced by the mass media and in control of the management of campaigns and policy making. The difference illuminates one dimension of the fundamental moral dilemmas which arise in the application of the social sciences to the sphere of public policy.

NOTES

1. *The Use of Social Research in Federal Domestic Programs, Part 1: Federally Financed Social Research—Expenditures, Status, and Objectives,* Staff Study for the Subcommittee on Research and Technical Programs of the House Committee on Government Operations (Washington, D.C.: United States Government Printing Office, 1967), p. 106.

2. Max Weber, " 'Objectivity' in Social Science and Social Policy," in Maurice Natanson, ed., *Philosophy of the Social Sciences* (New York: Random House, 1963), pp. 355–418; Max Weber, "Politics as a Vocation," in H. H. Gerth and C. Wright Mills, eds., *From Max Weber* (New York: Oxford University Press, 1958), pp. 77–128; Max Weber, "Science as a Vocation," in *From Max Weber,* pp. 129–56.

3. Karl Popper, *The Poverty of Historicism,* 3rd ed. (New York: Harper and Row, 1961), p. 64.

4. Weber, " 'Objectivity,' " p. 359.

5. Emile Durkheim, *Sociology and Philosophy,* D. F. Pocock, trans. (New York: Free Press, 1974); Robert Bierstedt, *The Social Order* (New York: McGraw-Hill, 1957); Floyd W. Matson, *The Broken Image* (New York: George Braziller, 1964), Richard L. Means, *The Ethical Imperative: The Crisis in American Values* (New York: Doubleday, 1969); Paul Roubiczek, *Ethical Values in the Age of Science* (Cambridge: Cambridge University Press, 1969); and Richard W. Miller, "Reason and Commitment in the Social Sciences," *Philosophy and Public Affairs* (Spring 1979), 8:242.

6. Jerald Hage and J. Rogers Hollingsworth, "The First Steps Toward the Integra-

tion of Social Theory and Social Policy," *Annals of the American Academy of Political and Social Science* (November 1977), 434:1.

7. Roubiczek, *Ethical Values*, p. 46.

8. Philosophers from these diverse schools of thought whose works illustrate the essential inclusion of intentionality in nonreductionist theories of social action include, for example, Ernst Cassirer, Maurice Merleau-Ponty, Jean-Paul Sartre, John Dewey, Stuart Hampshire, and Max Horkheimer.

9. Jürgen Habermas, *Knowledge and Human Interests,* Jeremy Shapiro, trans. (Boston: Beacon Press, 1971), p. 176.

10. Stuart Hampshire, "Self-Consciousness and Society," in Conor Cruise O'Brien and William Dean Vanech, eds., *Power and Consciousness* (New York: New York University Press, 1969), p. 238.

11. Stuart Hampshire, *Thought and Action* (New York: Viking Press, 1960).

12. Jürgen Habermas, "Zur Logik der Sozialwissenschaften," *Philosophische Rundschau* (February 1967), Supplement 5; and A. R. Louch, *Explanation and Human Action* (Oxford: Basil Blackwell, 1966).

13. Habermas, *Zur Logik,* p. 177.

14. Louch, *Explanation and Human Action,* p. 157.

15. *Ibid.,* p. 51.

16. Habermas, *Knowledge and Human Interests,* p. 61.

17. Jürgen Habermas, "Technology and Science as Ideology," *Toward a Rational Society: Student Protest, Science, and Politics,* Jeremy J. Shapiro, trans. (Boston: Beacon Press, 1971), pp. 105–6.

18. *Ibid.,* p. 112.

19. Louch, *Explanation and Human Action,* p. 239.

20. George Gallup, *A Guide to Public Opinion Polls* (Princeton, N.J.: Princeton University Press, 1944), p. 3.

21. See, for example, Gallup's defense of the growing influence of polling in government and politics throughout his *Guide to Public Opinion Polls*. He describes the particular importance of polling to leaders: "Great leaders will seek information from every reliable source about the people whom they wish to lead. For this reason they will inevitably pay more attention to facts about the current state of public thinking and of public knowledge. The public opinion poll will be a useful tool in enabling them to reach their highest level of effectiveness as leaders" (p. 8).

22. Bill Butcher of Butcher-Forde, cited in Nora B. Jacob, "Butcher and Forde, Wizards of the Computer Letter," *California Journal* (May 1979), 10:163.

23. Duane Bradford, "See How They Run," *Sky,* November 1979, p. 15.

24. Tony Schwartz, *The Responsive Chord* (New York: Anchor Books, 1973), pp. 82, 100–1.

25. See Bob Korda, "Woodward and McDowell: Keepers of the Treasure Chest," *California Journal* (May 1979), 10:159–61.

26. Dan Nimmo, *The Political Persuaders* (Englewood Cliffs, N.J.: Prentice-Hall, 1970), p. 104.

27. Schwartz, *Responsive Chord,* p. 96.

28. Bernard Berelson, "The Study of Public Opinion," in Leonard D. White, ed., *The State of the Social Sciences* (Chicago: University of Chicago Press, 1956), pp. 504–5.

29. Edward Dreyer and Walter Rosenbaum, *Political Opinion and Behavior* (Belmont, Calif.: Wadsworth, 1970), p. 19.

30. One approach developed by research psychologist Sidney Weinstein uses electroencephalograph techniques to test "positive interest" and right and left brain hem-

isphere stimulation as indicated in brainwave patterns. His firm, Neuro-Communications Research Laboratories, tests audience reactions for television networks and advertising agencies. For a description, see Richard Saltus, "Ad Agencies' Direct Line to the Brain," *San Francisco Examiner*, August 27, 1978, p. 1.

31. Gallup, citing Floyd Allport, *A Guide to Public Opinion Polls*, p. 74.

32. Robert E. Lane and David O. Sears, *Public Opinion* (Englewood Cliffs, N.J.: Prentice-Hall, 1964), p. 6.

33. V. O. Key, Jr., *Public Opinion and American Democracy* (New York: Knopf, 1961), p. 14.

34. Dreyer and Rosenbaum, *Political Opinion*, pp. 10–11.

35. Gilbert Ryle, "Thinking and Self-Teaching," in Konstantin Kolenda, ed., *Rice University Studies, Studies in Philosophy: A Symposium on Gilbert Ryle* (Summer 1972), 58:121.

36. *Ibid.*, p. 111.

37. See, for example, the description of the operation of a major polling organization and its depiction of public attitudes in Stephen Chapman, "The Public Opinion Hustle," *New Republic*, November 25, 1978, pp. 12–16.

38. Leo Bogart, *Silent Politics* (New York: Wiley Interscience, 1972).

39. Everett Carll Ladd, Jr., "What the Polls Tell Us," *Wilson Quarterly* (Spring 1979), 3:83.

40. David Gergen and William Schambra, "Pollsters and Polling," *Wilson Quarterly* (Spring 1979), 3:72.

41. Jürgen Habermas, *Strukturwandel der Öffentlichkeit*, 2nd ed. (Neuwied am Rhein: Luchterhand Verlag, 1965), p. 213 (author's translation).

42. See Habermas' excellent discussion of this relationship in "The Scientization of Politics and Public Opinion," *Toward a Rational Society*, pp. 62–80.

43. Firdus Džinić, "Opinion Surveys in a Federal Republic," *Polls* (1968), 3:8.

44. M. I. Finley, *Democracy Ancient and Modern* (New Brunswick, N.J.: Rutgers University Press, 1973), p. 19.

Fifteen

MORAL COMMITMENT, PRIVATISM, AND ACTIVISM: NOTES ON A RESEARCH PROGRAM

Richard Flacks

Rather than discuss in general terms the relationship between morality and the social sciences, I assume here that certain forms of human action and orientation may be regarded as socially responsible, that social responsibility is worth promoting, and that social science offers means for substantially improving understanding of the conditions that both promote and retard social responsibility. Instead of systematically justifying this position, I will sketch a conceptual framework from which some researchable questions flow and describe some current research that bears on them.

MAKING HISTORY AND LIVING LIFE

We can usefully distinguish two realms of human experience and action.[1] Let us call these the realm of "everyday life" and the realm of "history." "Everyday life" consists of activities that the actors take for granted as necessary for survival, as obligatory in terms of commitments to specific, known others, or as needed for the maintenance of self. Everyday life is thus experienced as *primary reality*, since it occurs in relation to definite other people with whom one feels concretely interdependent. It is experienced as *required* in the sense that one feels that one's life and the life of others depends on carrying through the daily round. It is felt to be *right*, since these activities constitute one's most basic obligations to those (including oneself) that one cares about most.

Everyday life is governed by the roles, routines, and rules that structure work, household maintenance, and similar mundane responsibilities. Thus, large portions of the day are carried through that involve little individuality and self-expression. In addition to having the constraints of impersonal routines, a great deal of everyday activity is constraining because it involves meeting other people's needs and expectations and postponing and denying one's own.

It is, however, crucial to see that everyday life cannot be interpreted simply in terms of constraints and role conformity. Instead, analysis of everyday life must be sensitive to the dialectic of daily activity—the ways in which actors are continuously and simultaneously role-playing *and* individuating, conforming *and* resisting, free *and* subordinated as they move through the day. Indeed, everyday constraints could not be accepted were it not for the ability of people to find some means for self-expression and self-fulfillment in the midst of everyday activity and during free time. Moreover, in our society privacy, free time and space, and the opportunity to undertake self-chosen activity are increasingly taken as *rights* and provide much of the basis for the formation and development of personal identity. All cultures offer opportunities to pursue, in the everyday world, a variety of nonmundane activities, activities felt to be special, extraordinary, or ecstatic—forms of release, relief, and escape. In our society these have become extraordinarily differentiated and elaborated in a profusion of religious and mystical expression, communal festival, athletic participation and spectacle, and such personal activities as vacations, hobbies, the creation and consumption of works of art, etc. Increasingly, the doing of these activities not only serves to make everyday routine and constraint more tolerable but represents the main means of sustaining one's individual identity, since these activities, in our culture, represent an area of wide choice compared with the daily round of role conformity.

Thus, I am defining the realm of everyday activity as including experiences of constraint, necessity, and obligation and also experiences of freedom, self-expression, and personal choice that individuals view as integral to their well-being and identity and as part of what is due them because they have fulfilled the roles and obligations set by the terms of daily existence.

"History" is being made to the extent that decisions and actions are taken that affect the terms and conditions of daily life for a collectivity. "Power" may be defined as the capacity to make history—that is, the capacity to influence the conditions and terms of everyday life of a community or society. People have "authority" to the extent that they can make history as a normal feature of their daily lives and in ways that accord with their intentions. To the degree that change in social life occurs as a result of forces beyond human intention and control, power is absent. To the extent that society's daily life is organized by self-sufficient, autonomous household units, history and power are largely absent. More than twenty years ago, C. Wright Mills argued that we have come to a time in which technological advance and social organization have created such a high degree of interdependence and central control that history is in large measure the result of conscious activity and power is highly concentrated in the decisions and acts of a definite, small group of men. Such men are themselves relatively unbound by the constraints and terms of ordinary everyday life but make "making history" an integral feature of their daily roles and routines. Increasingly, those below the elite level find their daily lives structured by the projects, rules, and resource-allocating decisions made at the top and lack the capacity to influence or intervene in elite processes.[2]

Mills's diagnosis appears to capture our experience—namely, that there is a deep gap between daily life and history. This experience results not only from the established structures of authority that concentrate and centralize the history-making process but also from the fact that for those not in high positions of authority any capacity to intervene in history appears to require the disruption of daily life. Political participation appears to demand the diversion of time and energy away from the requirements of the personal sphere. It may result in taking stands and actions that risk the security and well-being that daily life would otherwise provide. In short, public involvement seems to require a degree of freedom from everyday constraint and obligation that people do not have or a degree of risk that people do not believe they can afford or wish to incur. Moreover, if power is defined as the capacity to influence the terms and conditions of daily life, then the power available to those without institutional authority rests largely on their capacity to directly disrupt, threaten, or alter the established pattern and flow of everyday life. For example, the paradigm of the power available to subordinated people is the strike by workers—a deliberate refusal to carry on with the routines of daily life that sustain a given institution. The strike has the additional, crucial effect of disrupting the daily lives of a significant portion of the surrounding society. There are numerous other forms of popular protest and intervention, but all have in common the fact that their efficacy rests on threatened or actual disruption of the daily routine of participants, of bystanders, and of those in authority whose plans depend on the implementation of such routines.[3] If the purpose of one's life is to live (rather than to make history), then the willingness to stop normal life or to undertake actions that threaten it is most likely to occur only when the accustomed modes of daily life have become fundamentally problematic. Conversely, if conditions permit most people to carry on their daily lives in such a way that psychological and moral coherence can be maintained, history and the capacity to make it are experienced as fundamentally separated from personal existence.

The morality of daily life is organized around the deep sense of obligation felt toward concrete, living others about whom one personally cares, or at least whom one personally encounters face to face. It is this level of morality and obligation that is experienced as most "natural" and most required. Thus, daily life is the central preoccupation of most people not only because it is the framework of survival and reward but also because it is the arena of primary moral commitment. "Privatism" (commitment to everyday life) may or may not be an expression of narcissism, but it is, for most, the primary mode in which responsibility, selflessness, and sacrifice are ordinarily exercised. Thus, appeals to Americans to shake off their apparent moral indifference and critiques of American moral callousness often miss the point that efforts to be concerned about "humanity" may be thought of as contradicting one's felt moral obligations to those whom one actually knows, loves, and must care for.

Moreover, "commitment to everyday life" is not to be understood as a phrase describing mass conformity, obedience, or quiescence. Despite the gap between history and everyday life, commitment to the latter may be interpreted as being grounded in a kind of social contract between the underlying population and those in power. This contract permits elites to make history as long as certain empirically identifiable popular expectations about what everyday life should consist of are met. This contract is fundamentally unstable because it depends on the growth of an economy and a productive apparatus not organized or planned in terms of universal needs for liberty and happiness. Thus, although popular expectations about the conditions of everyday life include expectations about full employment, rising living standards, and better material conditions for coming generations, the economy does not automatically fulfill such hopes. The social contract is unstable also because of manifold inequalities in life chances within each nation-state, and on a global level because of diverse scarcities. Inequality in life chances and access to resources means that even in times of relatively high economic growth parts of the underlying population will be less willing than others to accept the terms of daily life. Finally, the social contract is never fully stabilized because the needs and expectations that constitute everyday life are themselves subject to change and development.

Thus, mass readiness to maintain commitment to daily life is contingent on the degree to which the material conditions for coherent living are provided and on whether rights and benefits that the people expect are respected and protected by those in authority. What people expect in the way of conditions, rights, and benefits is a feature of established culture, but such expectations have developed out of the past historical struggles and political interventions of the underlying population and are always in flux. Moreover, popular expectations about rights and obligations and about authority are themselves a political force. These expectations constitute constraints on history-making and institutional elites in their efforts to mobilize populations for historical projects. In other words, the legitimacy of contemporary authority appears to depend on the degree to which people view the authority structure as guaranteeing and protecting their ability to make their lives according to an accustomed balance between obligation and freedom. Thus, despite the alienation of most Americans from historical processes, despite the emergence of a "power elite," and despite the prevalence of civic privatism, a certain kind of democratic struggle remains characteristic of the society. The effort to make lives within private free space represents a continuing claim to rights achieved through past struggles and constitutes the grounds for voiced and unvoiced popular resistance to those projects and adventures of national and corporate elites that threaten security, freedom, and coherence in everyday life.

These definitions and considerations constitute a useful framework for empirical inquiry into capacities for moral commitment and public responsibility. They rest on the assumption that the starting point for such an inquiry is to understand and interpret commitment to everyday life as it is lived and articulated in popular consciousness. Such research would test the perspective I have been outlining here, namely, that privatism is an expression of *both* subordination *and* self-expression, of political moral withdrawal *and* personal moral responsibility, of elite control *and* popular resistance. Among the many questions such a program of research might ask would be these: What demands and rights—to life, liberty, and the pursuit of happiness—are claimed by the people as necessary to sustain everyday commitments? How have such claims been asserted historically and how have they been treated so as to sustain structures of authority, domination, and inequality? What variations are there, across classes and strata, in such claims? How does the practical and moral need for everyday life constrain history-making and institutional elites in their efforts to mobilize populations for historical projects? What conditions foster mass intervention in history, mass abandonment of everyday commitment? If legitimation of established structures of authority requires guarantees of everyday opportunities for liberty and happiness, what are the contents of such guarantees and to what extent do these strain the capabilities of the system as a whole?

I have been arguing that commitment to everyday life constitutes the primary framework for moral responsibility in our society and the primary motivational basis for such public participation and political intervention as average people are currently willing to undertake. This state of affairs is, in many ways, integrated into our culture, and yet it is morally dubious in light of deeply embedded cultural values. Thus, we may, culturally speaking, recognize the practical necessity of everyday commitment and morality, but such a commitment is not a moral ideal. Clearly, a far "higher" value is placed on those who take responsibility and make sacrifices for the larger social welfare, who dedicate themselves to causes beyond their immediate private sphere, who are concerned with the consequences of their actions for the society and for the future. In addition to valuing such "idealism," we also recognize the higher morality of those who refuse to conform to everyday roles and rules in behalf of conscience, principle, or the public interest.

Contemporary privatism therefore encourages people to avoid living up to the highest moral standards of the culture. In addition, insofar as commitment to everyday life is primary, a socially destructive moral callousness is a likely outcome. The more effective the established social contract is at binding commitment, the more likely are long-range social disasters. For example, current problems of environmental pollution, resource depletion, and waste require the development of capacities to take account of the social costs and long-run consequences of existing patterns of individual consumption. Gross global disparities in the distribution of life chances similarly require fundamental changes in the organization of daily life within the United States and other developed countries if a relatively peaceful international transition is to be possible. The logic of organizational growth requires capacities for resistance to hierarchical authority if trends toward bureaucratic control, militarism, and technocracy are to be undermined. Yet insofar as commitment to everyday life is grounded in privatized material consumption and trade-offs between role conformity and leisure time freedom, capacities for social responsibility, altruism, and institutional dissent are undeveloped. In short, there is a need for systematic empirical inquiry into the social bases of such virtues as social responsibility, altruism, and moral courage. This need derives not only from an abstract desire to encourage people to be more moral but also from the practical requirements of social life in an increasingly interdependent world society.

Social scientists therefore have two social warrants for studying how people can be encouraged to be more socially responsible and nonconforming. One, relatively uncontroversial, derives from the culture itself and its high valuation of selflessness and dissent. Indeed, a good deal of what has been the mainstream of research in social psychology has been guided by a concern for finding the social and psychological bases of altruism, nonconformity, and democratic behavior. What may be more controversial, however, is recognition that the established structures of authority—of "democratic elitism" and "civil privatism"—by their inherent logic reproduce the kinds of social amorality I have been referring to. If this is so, then a morally guided social science must have the goal of enabling the people themselves to make their own history, of breaking down the structures and motivational frameworks that sustain elitism and privatism, of achieving social arrangements in which communities can engage in the formulation of the terms and conditions of daily life as an integral part of daily life itself. Such a vision of authentic democratization—which

I believe requires a society in which social initiative largely comes from relatively self-determining localities—goes beyond the conception of a good society established in our culture and goes against the apparent logic of contemporary social trends. In other words, social science efforts directed at inculcating social responsibility within the established institutional framework seem likely either to fail or to improve elite capacities for the engineering of consent. A more promising direction for systematic inquiry is to try to expand the capacities of popular movements to intervene democratically in the historical process. But such a direction is by its nature highly controversial and hence threatening to the status of the social sciences. It also implies a certain kind of partisanship in social conflict. However, insofar as democratization of society depends on systematic empirical inquiry— on scientific self-understanding on the part of democratic actors—I do not see any grounds for assuming that such partisanship is logically incompatible with the spirit or procedures of empirical social science. It is in that spirit that I want to describe some further research on the problem of social responsibility.

THE ACTIVIST AS SOCIAL TYPE

Between elites making history as a feature of their daily lives and masses making their daily lives but alienated from history stands another social type—those who may be thought of as seeking to make history as a feature of their daily lives but lacking the authority to do so. I am talking about "political activists"—that is, people who tend, over some period of time, to conceive of themselves as centrally concerned with the public interest at some sacrifice to their own private interests and in some conflict with established authority or conventional social patterns.

I assume that systematic study of political activists can shed light on the possibilities for, and barriers to, moral development in the population at large. Researchable questions can be formulated whose answers may provide important clues about the ways in which social responsibility, sacrifice of privatistic concerns, and capacities for dissent and nonconformity may in fact be developed, sustained, and undermined. Some of these follow: How is it that some people develop a commitment to political action, despite prevailing cultural and structural patterns that dispose most to privatism? (Comparison of the social origins and personal development of activists and nonactivists may provide us with deeper understanding of variations in processes of socialization and identity formation within the society and of how these, in turn, affect moral outcomes.) How and to what extent are activists' commitments and identities maintained in the face of political discouragement, defeat, risk, and repression? How and to what extent are activists' commitments and identities maintained throughout the life cycle? (What, for example, is the fate of "youthful idealism"?) How are such commitments maintained in the face of the constraints (and seductions) of everyday life?

These questions concerning the maintenance of commitment can be studied as aspects of individual life histories. But answers to them cannot be found solely by referring to the motivational resources of individuals. Understanding of the personal development of political activists must incorporate such factors as the material and occupational resources available to individuals, the kinds of social supports and obligations they have, the quality of "cadre organization," the availability of ideologically coherent frameworks for political action, the ways in which historical circumstance intersects with life history, and the ways in which activists' self-definitions are subject to reinterpretation as historical and personal circumstances change.

There are, in addition, other questions. How do activists interact with "elites" and "masses"? What are the political functions and dysfunctions of activist commitments? What has been (and can be) their cultural/moral impact? The activist's relation to everyday life differs rather sharply from the typical by definition. If this is so, then inherent in the situation of the activist is a fundamental barrier to smooth communication with ordinary members of society. The activist and the average person live, to some extent, in different realms. Yet the activist's primary interest is in mobilizing the nonactive—in "reaching," "organizing," and "awakening" or "leading," "representing," and "speaking for" them. How such communication is accomplished— and with what effects—demands further investigation. Of particular interest is the situation of leftist activists. I define the Left as that tradition of ideology, action, and cultural expression that envisions the integration of everyday life and history in terms of popular control over the direction of society and its institutions. Ironically, in the United States that tradition has been carried by only a minority of the people—most of whom have been self-conscious political activists. At first glance, then, the American Left is a failed tradition, because it has been unable to turn significant numbers away from commitment to everyday life when such a turning is a requisite of the Left's self-defined historical mission. On the other hand, a closer look at the history of American political and cultural development suggests that leftist activists and intellectuals may have a rather decisive *social* function, despite the Left's failure as a force for *political* leadership. Inquiry into the fate of the Left in the United States provides an important key to understanding popular consciousness and morality in this society.

In short, I am asking these questions on the assumption that activists (as I have here defined them) are of particular interest to those who want to understand the processes of moral development. They are of interest because their behavior and self-definitions express a willingness or readiness to subordinate privatistic concerns and everyday commitments to a sense of social responsibility, a readiness for sacrifice and risk on behalf of a better world. Such a characterization should not, however, be taken to imply that we are referring to people who are necessarily morally "superior" to ordinary people. For activists are, by self-definition and often by circumstance, to some degree alienated from the experience, the rationality, and sometimes the morality of everyday life. Such estrangement makes activists' commitment problematic, since it weakens their capacity to communicate with and stimulate the public participation of more privatized people.

Both the life history of individual activists and the collective history of activist traditions provide primary source material for understanding the ways in which people can be socialized for moral commitment that transcends the everyday. Put another way, if our model of moral development includes the notion that development entails the emergence of capacities for active citizenship and public responsibility, then biographical and historical studies of activists provide material for understanding the practical possibilities, dilemmas, and ambiguities of such development.

Further, we may view activists as socializing agents, experimenting with methods of fostering social responsibility and social ethics in the population at large. Systematic inquiry into the tradition of the Left (defined in the broad terms I have been employing) may help activists recover historical instances in which successful socialization has occurred and help them overcome the tendencies toward isolation that inhere in the situation of the Left in this country. Such inquiry may also help social scientists understand better the conditions under which a social ethic actually gets incorporated into the everyday activity of the populace.

THE LEFT AND DEMOCRATIC SOCIALIZATION

I ought to be somewhat less elliptical about my own commitments. They lie with the tradition of the Left as I have defined it. I think I understand the wisdom embodied in a morality based on rational self-interest and personal liberty—the kind of morality that is embodied in what I have called commitment to everyday life. But I cannot help feeling that at best such an ethic is limited. It is a limited view of what human beings are capable of, a truncated perspective on moral development. It has the ring of realism, since it does not require of individuals much more in the way of moral responsibility than what common sense deems possible or prudent; but, as I have already suggested, global interdependence combined with global inequality requires the fostering of more long-range rationality than the terms of "middle-class" daily life seem to demand. I am unable to identify very many social and cultural currents, other than the tradition of the Left, that seek consistently to draw ordinary people into responsible social action. Indeed, I would propose as a working proposition that were it not for the influence of socialism, anarchism, pacifism, radical democracy, and related ideological currents on activists, intellectuals, artists, preachers, and teachers, there would be precious little in American culture that socializes its members (below the elite level) for social responsibility. It is, therefore, the strengthening of such socialization and of the capacity for democratic social action that I want to contribute to as a social scientist. It should be clear, incidentally, that I am not trying in such a project to promote a particular political organization, ideology, or movement. When I speak of the Left, I am talking about a framework of thought and action much broader than the particular organized expressions that may fall within it.

SOCIALIZATION THROUGH ACTIVISM: RESEARCH IN PROGRESS

Several loosely related research projects that derive from the problems I have been posing here are now in progress. One concerns the fate of student activists. There has been very little research on the poststudent, postmovement careers of student activists of the sixties. The paucity of research is astonishing, given the enormous number of studies and writing done on the causes of the student revolt and the origins of the activists.[4] It is also astonishing given the frequency of the question "What happened to the sixties generation?" Jack Whalen and I have been exploring this question in a project that has involved the locating and in-depth interviewing of those who were indicted for burning the Bank of America and related protest activity in Isla Vista in 1970. We have so far interviewed ten of a potential group of about twenty-five such people (no one, incidentally, was convicted of burning the bank, but all who were indicted were, in varying degrees, well known as student activists—some as leaders, others at the rank-and-file level). I knew most of these people quite well when they were students, and for several of them we have some interview material gathered in 1974 as well as several hours of interview material gathered in 1979 and 1980. This material will provide some important clues about the pathways out of total commitment to a movement and the factors in young adulthood that reinforce and undermine continuing political engagement. Our interviews also include a good deal of new information about the circumstances that drew students in the late sixties into movement activism and into the experience of intense movement involvement itself.[5]

A second research project focuses on grassroots activism and daily life. The features of daily life that promote and limit activist commitment and the ways in which politically active people deal with the demands and the seductions of the everyday are being studied. We are interviewing a sample of about thirty people drawn from a pool of several hundred who are currently self-identified as involved in grassroots political action. This sample is being interviewed in depth, and our plan is to remain in regular contact with the sample over the next two years. Through this procedure, we hope to gain detailed information about the dilemmas and choices presented by political participation, the ways in which daily life may and may not be integrated with citizen action, and the attractions and repulsions of both spheres. This sample will be compared with a group of thirty "average citizens" interviewed several years ago about their relations to the political realm.

A third project centers on a history of the United States Left. For several years, I immersed myself in historical materials concerning the Left in the United States. The focus of this interest is to understand the Left as an agency of socialization both for its members and for broader, "mass" constituencies. To this end, the following questions are of utmost importance: What generalizations can be made about the historical role and personal fate of leftist activists over the last eighty years? What instances have there been where the Left as an organized force has successfully affected the ethical orientations of large numbers of people? What modes of organization and practical activity may serve as models of effective socialization? What organizational practices contribute to disillusionment, defection, and cynicism? Under what circumstances does commitment to active social responsibility foster authoritarian tendencies and moral dogmatism and when and how does activism promote antiauthoritarianism and free moral discourse? Analysis of historical cases, combined with my own first-hand experience as a left-wing activist, seems likely to provide some ways of treating these issues.[6]

SOME PRELIMINARY FINDINGS

It would be premature for me to report systematic "findings" from these recently begun investigations. But here, briefly, are some examples of the notions that our studies so far have generated or reinforced.

Activism and "Normal Adulthood"

Two broad moral orientations to which I have already alluded seem to constitute the core of a public morality: a capacity for autonomous moral judgment, antiauthoritarianism; and a capacity for taking responsibility for the social consequences of one's actions, or for giving priority to the collective over the personal. American culture, emphasizing individualism, nourishes the first a good deal more than the second. Indeed, to a considerable extent, commitment to everyday life may be viewed as an expression of antiauthoritarian drives for personal autonomy and liberty. Alienation from history making may often be a positive refusal to subordinate the self to nationalist or bureaucratic efforts to mobilize loyalty. Thus, as David DeLeon has suggested recently, anarchism is a far more powerful radical current in American consciousness than is socialism.[7] These considerations appear to be reflected in our effort to understand continuities and discontinuities in the postmovement careers of former student activists. A number of those we have interviewed are not now engaged in political activity, but all have refused to settle down into a conventional round of "adult" daily life. None works in a bureaucratic organization. None lives in a conventional nuclear family (and none has any children). The "refusal of adulthood" that characterized the youth movement of the sixties remains a continuing theme for these people, now in their late twenties and thirties. Most see themselves as continuing to uphold the core values of the youth revolt–namely, the right to autonomous self-development and to express oneself rather than submit to authority or conventional role-conformity. Only some find possibilities for this within frameworks of political action. In the sixties, antiauthoritarianism and collective action seemed to be intertwined (although it was then evident that there were marked differences and tensions between "politicos" and "hippies"). Our interviews provide a good deal of material suggesting the ways in which culture and historical circumstance enable activists to return to everyday life commitments (and withdraw from political commitments) without feeling that they have markedly betrayed their youthful idealism. They also suggest ways in which periods of historical activity may open space for a new privatism by legitimating rights to personal expression that enable daily life to be lived more freely.

Political Commitment and Personal Development

The informal friendship group is a primary locale for fostering of antiauthoritarian and collectivist moral orientations.[8] This is particularly true when the group is located within a situation of institutional subordination. Thus, for example, informal work groups are the framework for everyday solidarity and resistance among factory workers.[9] Our interviews provide strong reinforcement for the view that student friendship groups were similarly the ground for student activism and for sustaining and deepening commitment to radical action. In particular, the interviews indicate that the politicization of friendship groups—their evolution into self-conscious political "collectives"—helps account for the increasing militance and radicalization of the movement in the late sixties. But such settings may often become morally dogmatic and insular. Total commitment often precedes disillusionment and withdrawal. Groups that become self-consciously committed to the personal transformation of members—as was typically the case in the sixties movements—are powerful agencies of socialization and moral commitment. But our interviews show that such groups often, consciously or unconsciously, deny the legitimacy of individual needs and interests and hence deny members the right and opportunity to articulate such needs. As a result, many members withdrew from collectives and friendship circles because they were fearful or guilty about their needs for personal development. A framework that had been important to personal growth at one moment became, somewhat later, a constraint on further growth. This dynamic is a clue to the disintegration of the sixties New Left. It represents a fundamental problem for any movement that demands high levels of commitment from members, and it may be fatal for youth movements in particular, since their members must, inherently, deal with crucial issues of personal development.

The Continuing Social Effects of Activism

Everyday life and making history can be integrated. Both in the past and today, leftist currents have found ways of providing public, historical meanings for the activities of daily existence; have fostered institutional frameworks for politically relevant daily activity; and have promulgated codes for everyday activity that enhance the capacity of individuals to be socially responsible. It is instructive that the best single predictor of political activism is a family climate in childhood that is supportive of democratic values.[10] It is instructive that many former communists recall party politics with disgust but remain positive about the party as a framework for self-development and education.[11] The history of social movements is filled with examples of how such movements promulgate ethical codes that guide the everyday action of "mass" constituencies. For example, labor solidarity, consumer boycotts, ecological consciousness, black nationalism, feminist consciousness—all express such ethical codes, fused with the national culture or with particular subcultures, incorporated into the daily life of large numbers of people who do not themselves adopt activist identities but who are, as a result of such fusions, more oriented toward social responsibility and more involved in history.

PARTISANSHIP AND THE SOCIAL SCIENTIST

My intention has been to illustrate how moral development and public commitment may be studied in natural settings, as aspects of lived experience. In other words, my way of dealing with the theme "morality and the social sciences" has been to show that the methods of social science can be used to investigate the potentialities and conditions for "social responsibility" and related moral orientations. Such investigation appears necessarily to entail certain kinds of partisanship from the investigator—or at least in my case it does. But such partisanship does not invalidate the research enterprise. First, the data themselves are relatively independent and "neutral" with respect to the value judgments that may have motivated their collection. Second, I believe it is morally and scientifically incumbent on the investigators of such research projects to cultivate a deep empathy with their subjects. Since the goals of my work include the improvement of possibilities for communication between activists and the politically uninvolved, such empathy is mandatory. Such communication is possible only if it is grounded in deep appreciation of the position of the uninvolved and the privatized, an appreciation of the *rationality* of everyday commitment and of the *moral* critique the "apathetic" person is making of the "political." Such empathy and appreciation, it seems to me, constitute not only tools of empirical inquiry but a fundamental corrective of the biases one brings to the research enterprise. Social science aids moralists, not by improving their capacity to judge, praise, or blame, but by compelling them to face as fully as possible both the good news and the bad about human situations and possibilities at a given historical moment.[12]

NOTES

1. The following discussion is based on Richard Flacks, "Making History vs. Making Life: Dilemmas of an American Left," *Sociological Inquiry* (1976), 46:263–81.

2. C. Wright Mills, *The Power Elite* (New York: Oxford University Press, 1956).

3. Fran Piven and Richard Cloward, *Poor People's Movement* (New York: Pantheon, 1977).

4. Key studies on the social origins and social psychological characteristics of sixties activists include Richard Flacks, "The Liberated Generation," *Journal of Social Issues* (1967), 23:52–75; Norma Haan, Brewster Smith, and Jeanne Block, "Moral Reasoning of Young Adults," *Journal of Personality and Social Psychology* (1968), 10:183–201; Kenneth Keniston, *Young Radicals* (New York: Harcourt, Brace, 1968); and Lawrence Kerpelman, *Activists and Non-Activists: A Psychological Study of College Students* (New York: Behavioral Publications, 1972). Significant research following up student activities includes James Fendrich and A. T. Tarleau, "Marching to a Different Drummer: Occupational and Political Correlates of Former Student Activists," *Social Forces* (1973), 52:245–53; Alberta Nassi and Steven Abramowitz, "Transition or Transformation? Personal and Political Development of Former Berkeley Free Speech Movement Activists," *Journal of Youth and Adolescence* (1979), 8:21–35; and Daniel Foss and R. W. Larkin, "From the 'Gates of Eden' to 'Day of the Locust,' " *Theory and Society* (1976), 3:45–64.

5. Preliminary results of this study appear in Jack Whalen and Richard Flacks, "The Isla Vista 'Bank Burners' Ten Years Later: Notes on the Fate of Student Activists," *Sociological Focus* (1980), vol. 13.

6. For a preliminary analysis of these issues, see Richard Flacks, "Socialists as Socializers: Notes on the Purposes of Organization," *Socialist Review* (1979), 9:102–13.

7. David DeLeon, *The American as Anarchist* (Baltimore: Johns Hopkins University Press, 1978).

8. Robert Ross, "Primary Groups in Social Movements," *Journal of Voluntary Action Research* (1977), 6:139–52.

9. See, for example, Jeremy Brecher, *Strike!* (San Francisco: Straight Arrow Books, 1972).

10. See studies cited in note 4.

11. See, for example, Vivian Gornick, *The Romance of American Communism* (New York: Basic Books, 1977).

12. This position is strongly influenced by Alvin Gouldner, *For Sociology* (New York: Basic Books, 1973).

Sixteen

THE ETHICAL AIMS OF
SOCIAL INQUIRY

Robert N. Bellah

My argument is simple. In classical times social inquiry concerned itself with the effort to discern the best society. Modern social thought since Machiavelli and Hobbes has sought to understand the conditions for a good society, one that was understood to be independent, strong, expansive, and/or reasonably fair to its citizens. Nineteenth- and twentieth-century social science claimed at times to be a purely theoretical enterprise having no concern with either best or good societies. The great exemplars, however, have all been powerfully guided by ethical aims—Tocqueville and Marx obviously, but Durkheim and even Weber, as I will show. Even when ethical aims are eschewed and there is the conscious intention to construct an "explanatory science," as in the case of some contemporary sociologists, normative commitments are clearly present. If social inquiry is, as Aristotle said, a practical science, one indelibly linked to ethical reflection, then we might even use the term "moral sciences" interchangeably with "social sciences."

In support of this position, let us first look briefly at the natural sciences, which have served as models for the social sciences, before considering the history of the ethical direction that has always guided social inquiry. Physics, the archetypal case of a modern natural science, has served as a model both for philosophers of science and for sociologists; theoretical structures, paradigms in the Kuhnian sense, are well established, and well-conducted experiments can render determinate answers to theoretical questions. Yet it was in the physical

Previously published in *Teachers College Record* (1981), 83:1–18.

sciences that absolute objectivity was first brought into question. Heisenberg's uncertainty principle suggested that the observer is never entirely outside the system observed and will have a certain effect on it. In physics, however, things are tidy enough that the effects of the observer can themselves be calculated. The observer and the observed can be viewed mathematically as parts of a single system whose properties are understandable, and thus our knowledge of physical nature is not seriously undermined.

In biology things are not so neat. The observer is still not identical with the observed, but observer contamination can reach much less readily calculable levels than in physics. Research findings can even be credited or discounted in terms of informal gossip about the habits and personal character of the investigator, and experiments frequently come out differently when conducted in different laboratories. As a result, what biologists tend to trust is not so much the result of experimental predictions as the ability to take apart some bit of living matter and put it back together again. If one can analyze and synthesize something, then one may fairly well claim to understand it. That is both more and less than what physicists can usually do.

What happens when we take the same framework that we have just applied to physics and biology and use it to look at the social sciences? Actually, Hobbes used the model I have just described for biology as the basis for his claim for creating a social science. If we can take apart and put back together social things, said Hobbes, then it is pretty certain that we can understand them. And can't we do that with social things such as laws, relationships, and groups? Perhaps we can; but if so, the uncertainty principle reaches unmanageable proportions. We do not know whether what we have created, and so "understood," is the result of any natural necessity or the product of our own moral imagination. We cannot be sure whether we have really observed something or persuaded, cajoled, or forced it into existence.

That being the case, perhaps it would be best to admit that in the social sciences inquiry always has an ethical aim. Then we can be conscious of that aim and discipline our cognitive faculties to the practical task at hand. This notion of social science as practical reason is radically different from the conception of a theoretical social science that is then "applied." In the notion of applied or policy science, the ends of action are taken from outside the intellectual enterprise, for example, from policy makers or public opinion or consumer choice. The purpose of social science then is simply to provide the most effective means to predetermined ends. Social science as practical reason must, on the contrary, make ends as well as means the objects of rational reflection.

Platonic social science is more concerned with the ends than the means of action. The *Republic* opens with a discussion of justice and considers whether justice is the rule of the stronger or the willingness to suffer rather than commit evil; unless some clarity is gained about that issue, all else is secondary. Plato's central device for social reflection is the linkage between types of personal character and types of societies. What kind of society would it be, he asks implicitly throughout the *Republic*, in which a good person is also a good citizen? To that end Plato performs a series of what Weber would have called "thought experiments," in which he considers social arrangements that on the face of them might be thought bizarre or even comical, to see what light they might shed on his problem. The suggestions about the equality of women, the abolition of the family and private property, and the philosopher-king are all made with this end in view. Analysis of contemporary society goes hand in hand with a utopian critique. It would be hard to think of a text that tells us more about the mediations between personal ethical development and forms of social life. What we have is not a book of "philosophy," in the modern academic sense, but a profound analysis of social life that simultaneously illuminates as perhaps no other work does the ethical ends of human action.

Aristotle was more empirical than Plato. He does not indulge in Platonic thought experiments but gives us a much fuller record of what the variety of Greek social arrangements was actually like. Yet we know that his *Ethics* and *Politics* were written as a single unified treatise. Since it was clear to Aristotle that the end of society (*polis*) is the good life, it was essential that he undertake an analysis of virtue in the *Ethics* in order to specify what the good life is before turning to the actual variety of social arrangements in the *Politics*. It is, of course, in its analysis of virtue that the *Ethics* provides the principles of the typology of regimes in the *Politics*. Societies can be classified in terms of the ways they do indeed help or hinder the realization of the good life.

With Machiavelli we have entered a different world. He is quick to inform us that, unlike the ancient philosophers, he is not interested in telling us how the world should be but how it actually is. Yet his *Prince* and the *Discourses,* for all their apparent immorality, have passionate ethical ends in view. *The Prince* is not just a set of instructions to a new ruler about how to maintain and extend his power, though it is that also. The new prince that Machiavelli envisages exists for the purpose of unifying Italy and guaranteeing its independence from its powerful neighbors. The *Discourses* was written as a guidebook for free republics and their statesmen about how to maintain, expand, and revive their institutions in order to secure free citizenship within and independence or imperial rule without.

It is true that there is precious little ethical reflection in Machiavelli. He does not bring ethical aims—even the good he so obviously desires—within the sphere of rational consideration. He does develop an implicit anthropology that shows the human desire for strength, freedom, and independence to be "natural." It is that fundamental intentionality that he refers to as "virtue" (*virtù*), which for him is more a naturalistic motive than an ethical norm. That virtue in this sense is "natural" is suggested by the fact that Machiavelli finds it most often among "uncorrupted" peoples. But what is natural is not universal precisely because there are conditions that can corrupt men and divert them from their natural course. Of course, corruption too is "natural," which adds another level of complexity to Machiavelli's thought.

But whatever may be the implications of Machiavelli's fundamental anthropology, which had major consequences for all subsequent modern social thought, his work is clearly directed toward certain commonly shared social norms that provide the moral passion for the whole intellectual enterprise. Of course, his work is not an ethical injunction without cognitive analysis; it is the moral passion that opens the space for the cognitive analysis—the two are inseparable. Therefore, Machiavelli's work is at the same time a profound analysis of the nature of certain kinds of societies (in fact, more can be learned about the current problems of the American republic from his *Discourses* than from any contemporary work of American political science), a reflection (largely implicit) about the ends of man, and an effort at persuasion that the ends he desires are admirable and attainable (in that highest and truest sense, it is a work of rhetoric). However different its fundamental presuppositions, in its combination of the analytic, the ethical, and the rhetorical, Machiavelli resembles Plato and Aristotle.

Hobbes is a particularly good example for our purposes. More explicitly than Machiavelli, he rejects the classical model of practical reason. There is no point in talking about the good society because there is no point in talking about the good: there is no such thing. "Good" is only a word that people use to indicate what they desire. There are as many "goods" as there are desires. Hobbes's empiricism, unlike Machiavelli's, uses the newly prestigious model of natural science as an underpinning. Thus, *Leviathan* is a scientific work that replaces all previous metaphysical speculations on social and political things. Yet the way Hobbes goes about setting up the basic terms of his science through the thought experiment of the state of nature is profoundly revealing. If the truth of the human condition in the state of nature is that man is fundamentally individual, that tells us not only something about what is socially possible but about what is socially desirable.

"So that in the first place, I put for a generall inclination of all mankind, a perpetuall and restlesse desire of Power after power, that ceaseth onely in Death," says Hobbes. "And the cause of this, is not alwayes that a man hopes for a more intensive delight, than he has already attained to; or that he cannot be content with a moderate power: but because he cannot assure the power and means to live well, which he hath present, without the acquisition of more."[1] With such a creature it becomes the role of the state to assure a basic security so that the "desire of Power after power" can be restrained and the bloody consequences of that quest for power avoided. Hobbes's moral aim, then, is not the good, or even a good, so much as survival itself, the essential precondition for the pursuit of the multitude of private goods. Thus, it is clear that Hobbes's powerful and in some respects unsurpassed social psychology (foreshadowed by Augustine, elaborated by Freud) had a profound moral implication and purpose. And of course *Leviathan* is a masterpiece of rhetoric—it seeks to persuade its readers to act for social peace.

Alexis de Tocqueville, even compared with his great ancient and early modern predecessors on whom we have already touched, is a reticent writer. He hints that he is founding a new political science ("A new political science is needed for a world itself quite new."),[2] but he never quite spells it out. His idea of virtue is largely modern but at moments has classical overtones. Self-interest is obviously a profound reference point for his fundamental anthropology, yet Tocqueville believes that the passion for liberty, which is also indelibly human, is not just an expression of self-interest but can at moments override it. "In fact, those who prize freedom only for the material benefits it offers have never kept it long. . . . The man who asks of freedom other than itself is born to be a slave."[3]

What is explicit is the overriding moral purpose of his work. Providence ensures that equality will steadily advance as the dominant principle of social organization; it is up to us whether that equality will be despotic or free. *Democracy in America* is one long argument for the possibility and desirability of freedom, but it is also an extraordinarily ambitious example of what our contemporaries would call empirical social inquiry. Though some of his research can be faulted, what Tocqueville achieved remains quite staggering to all future investigators. The book is unrivaled as an analysis of a total society, culture, and modal personality and of how they fit together. But it is always ethical and political in its intent and a superb example of rhetoric.

One might dismiss those I have discussed so far as "literary," "humanistic," or "philosophical" precursors of the genuine social science, with its purely cognitive intent, which has emerged in the last century or so. That is peculiarly difficult to do in the case of Tocqueville (which is why I include him), because he is increasingly recognized as a master of modern social analysis in spite of his antique moralizing. I would like to show now that the ambiguities about the relation between the cognitive and the ethical aspects of social inquiry that are already present in early modern social thought continue in the work of those who have in fact defined modern social science. Marx is an interesting example but almost too easy, the tension as well as the unity between moral passion and analytic rigor being altogether clear. I would like to concentrate on the examples of Emile Durkheim, the very model of a positivist social scientist, and Max Weber, who explicitly eschewed value judgments in social investigation.

At first glance, Durkheim is an unpromising example for my argument. Deliberately rejecting the graceful literary tradition of humane moralizing about society so popular in France, he chose for his hero (disregarding Tocqueville quite deliberately) one of the worst stylists in the history of France, Auguste Comte. Though Durkheim never actually did much with the almost unreadable writings of the great positivist and inventor of the word "sociology," he used him to legitimate his own enterprise as indubitably scientific. Yet for Durkheim (as for Marx), "science" keeps oscillating between being a model of method and a symbol, a rhetorical device for moral persuasion. It is not so much that Durkheim only pretended to be scientific as that he saw science itself as one element in a set of moral ideals which he thought it possible to realize in the Third Republic.[4]

It is certainly not so that Durkheim first created scientific sociology and then placed it at the service of the Third Republic. The very concept that was the cornerstone of his sociology from the beginning had profound moral and political implications that determined the practical meaning of his science. That concept is, of course, "society" itself. By deliberately rejecting the entire tradition of early modern social thought that derived society from the individual (through some version of the social contract) and by making society prior to the individual, Durkheim returned, without admitting it, to the Aristotelian definition of man as a political (social) animal. Since Durkheim did not view society as a contrivance whereby individuals fulfilled their random desires, he could raise questions again in a new way about the good society and about the importance of shared moral beliefs.

Durkheim's practical activities, which were considerable, were not extraneous to his scientific enterprise but flowed directly from it. It was insight that he had to offer, insight that was simultaneously cognitive and moral, in part because it was the cognition of a fundamental morality. As scholars, Durkheim said, "above all, we must be *advisers, educators*. It is our function to help our contemporaries know themselves in their ideas and in their feelings, far more than to govern them."[5] As a student of Rousseau, Durkheim knew that who educates a people in a sense governs it. In any case, in holding up the mirror to his society, Durkheim did not hesitate to enter the struggle, to argue and persuade, to attempt to show what the true patrimony of modern France was. In his essay "Individualism and the Intellectuals," he argues that an ethical individualism is the true collective representation of modern society. It is that end toward which modern society tends and which defines its good. He rejects too negative a definition of that individualism that would see it defined exclusively in terms of freedom. Thus, Durkheim stunningly transcends the whole tradition of modern liberalism:

Now political freedom is a means, not an end; its worth lies in the manner in which it is used. If it does not serve some end which goes beyond itself, it is not simply useless; it becomes dangerous. It is a battle weapon; if those who wield it do not know how to use it in fruitful struggles, they soon end by turning it against themselves. . . .

Thus we cannot limit ourselves to this negative ideal. We must go beyond the results achieved, if only to preserve them. If we do not finally learn to put to work the means of action we have in our hands, they will inevitably lose their worth. Let us therefore make use of our liberties to seek out what we must do and to do it, to smooth the functioning of the social machine, still so harsh on individuals, to place within their reach all possible means of developing their abilities without hindrance, to work finally to make a reality of the famous precept: to each according to his labor![6]

For all the vigor with which he entered the fray, there remains something ambiguous about how Durkheim derived his ethical standards and political goals. Though differing profoundly in the content of his ideas from his early modern predecessors, he was tempted to follow their example in thinking about society "scientifically" by deriving the ethical ends of action from empirical investigation. This was in part a rhetorical device. It was an effective argument to turn the tables on the conservatives in the Dreyfus affair and to demonstrate that it is defending the rights of individuals that is really true to the French tradition. But it was more than that. Durkheim never wished to derive norms from existing society in a conformist way. He admired the great nonconformists who died for their unpopular views, such as Socrates and Jesus, but he tended to explain them as those who discerned better than others what the future course of society would be. They reflected, thus, not the present but the future social consensus. Durkheim was loath to say that they in part created that future consensus; that would have broken the facade of science too completely and revealed his enterprise as indeed an example of practical reason—which, as a matter of fact, in spite of his final hesitation, I believe it was. I will return to the question of how we do derive these norms after discussing the work of Max Weber.

Weber would seem to be, if anything, an even more unpromising example than Durkheim for the argument that social inquiry is always intrinsically linked to ethical aims. No one has ever argued more eloquently that the relation between scientifically discoverable means and ethical ends is extrinsic and that science has nothing whatever to say about ends. In his essay "Science as a Vocation" (published in 1919), Weber writes:

> *If* you take such and such a stand, then, according to scientific experience, you have to use such and such a *means* in order to carry out your conviction practically. Now, these means are perhaps such that you believe you must reject them. Then you simply must choose between the end and the inevitable means. Does the end "justify" the means? Or does it not? The teacher can confront you with the necessity of choice. He cannot do more, so long as he wishes to remain a teacher and not to become a demagogue.[7]

This is Weber's decisionism: with respect to the ends of action, science has nothing to say; we must simply find our own demon and obey it.[8] Those who would claim anything more are excoriated:

> Science today is a 'vocation' organized in special disciplines in the service of self-clarification and knowledge of interrelated facts. It is not the gift of grace of seers and prophets dispensing sacred values and revelations, nor does it partake of the contemplation of sages and philosophers about the meaning of the universe. This, to be sure, is the inescapable condition of our historical situation. We cannot evade it so long as we remain true to ourselves. And if Tolstoi's question recurs to you: as science does not, who is to answer the question: 'What shall we do, and, how shall we arrange our lives?' or, in the words used here tonight: 'Which of the warring gods should we serve? Or should we serve perhaps an entirely different god, and who is he?' then one can say that only a prophet or a savior can give the answers. If there is no such man, or if his message is no longer believed in, then you will certainly not compel him to appear on this earth by having thousands of professors, as privileged hirelings of the state, attempt as petty prophets in their lecture-rooms to take over his role.[9]

But after all, what is Weber? By not answering, he answers. The ominous image of Isaiah's watchman hovers over the end of the essay, and certainly meeting the "demands of the day" and obeying our demon is a kind of answer.

Still, it is an extrinsic answer. If we turn to Weber's "Politics as a Vocation" (published in 1919), the issue becomes somewhat clearer. At the very beginning of this essay, Weber makes what appears to be almost a definitional aside that has enormous implications for his whole sociological project and its ethical implications:

> But what is a "political" association from the sociological point of view? What is a "state"? Sociologically, the state cannot be defined in terms of its ends. . . . Ultimately, one can define the modern state sociologically only in

terms of the specific *means* peculiar to it, as to every political association, namely the use of physical force.[10]

In this almost casual way Weber makes it clear that he is rejecting Aristotle and following Hobbes. For Aristotle, the end of the state is the good life for the citizens; for Hobbes, the state monopolizes violence in order that anyone can survive. In making his choice, Weber is not merely stating a scientific truth; he is opting for a whole view of humanity, of person and society in interrelation. And making the choice he does also has profound intrinsic ethical implications. Indeed, it already determines the outcome of the central ethical conflict of the essay, that between the ethics of responsibility and the ethics of ultimate ends. Since the ethics of responsibility involves, above all, responsibility for the use of force, it is sociologically realistic. Since the ethics of ultimate ends, illustrated most often by Weber as the ethics of acosmic brotherly love, rejects the use of force, it is sociologically unrealistic. Weber's sociology, in this instance, is clearly not neutral between these two options, however torn Weber was personally.

Actually, Weber's polytheism, his conflict between the "warring gods," is less radical than it first appears. However numerous the spheres ("Religious Rejections of the World and Their Directions"[11] contains perhaps the most complete description), there are two options that seem especially to pull Weber over and over again, and they are precisely those contrasted in "Politics as a Vocation." One is political power and the other is salvation religion. It is, I believe, the conflict between these spheres that determines the whole structure of Weber's lifework and its unresolved tensions, including the tensions between science and ethics.

Before turning to that point, I want to remark on one brief moment when the two spheres came together because Weber seemed to know something that he could not know from the perspective of his own fundamental presuppositions. Suddenly, late in "Politics as a Vocation," he tells us that he knows what a *"mature* man" is. One is tempted to say, "If you know what a mature man is, then surely you know what a good society is, and that would imply a very different sociology." Let us listen to the words in which the warring spheres have been temporarily overcome and Weber sounds like Aristotle, who also used the mature man (*spoudaios*)[12] as a measure in ethical reflection:

However, it is immensely moving when a *mature* man—no matter whether old or young in years—is aware of a responsibility for the consequences of his conduct and really feels such responsibility with heart and soul. He then acts by following an ethic of responsibility and somewhere he reaches the point where he says: 'Here I stand; I can do no other.' That is genuinely human and moving. And every one of us who is not spiritually dead must realize the possibility of finding himself at some time in that position. In so far as this is true, an ethic of ultimate ends and an ethic of responsibility are not absolute contrasts but rather supplements, which only in unison constitute a genuine man—a man who *can* have the 'calling for politics.'[13]

But aside from this passage it is much more usual for Weber to emphasize the conflict than the reconciliation. Power, particularly the rationalized power of the modern state, and religion, particularly the ethical prophecy of brotherly love, seem to be on a total collision course. There can be no Buddha, Jesus, or Saint Francis, says Weber, in the streets of the modern city.[14] Because of the fundamental presuppositions of his sociology, power must be more important than brotherly love. Yet Weber's soul rebels against that conclusion. Some of his last essays include an extraordinary nostalgic idealization of acosmic mysticism.

The conflict seems to determine the main outlines of his lifework. For all his interest in economics, Weber produced primarily a sociology of politics and a sociology of religion. For all his yearnings for religion, his theoretical commitments told him that it is power that counts. That presupposition determined even his sociology of religion. For it is Calvinism, not Franciscan or Tolstoyan mysticism, that was his focus of attention, and Calvinism is important because of the contribution it made to rationalization, which is ultimately the rationalization of power. In "Religious Rejections of the World" (published in 1915), Weber shows his ambivalence by speaking of Calvinism as succumbing to "the world dominion of unbrotherliness"[15] and saying its spiritual elitism makes it no longer a genuine religion of salvation. It is thus only a religion that has ceased to be genuinely and fully religious that can have a powerful impact on the world.

This fundamental ambivalence runs through all his work, as Jeffrey Alexander makes clear.[16] In his major treatises on the non-Western religions, Weber gives an analysis of social and economic structures and of political and class interests that is complete in itself and sufficient to explain capitalism's failure to appear. The analysis of religion that follows has the same conclusion but is not really integrated with this more structural analysis. In "The Social Psychology of the World Religions" and elsewhere, Weber goes to great lengths to insist on the independent causal significance of religion and of ideas in general. Ideas are the "switchmen" of history.[17] And yet in practice this position is inconsistently carried through. The famous Protestant Ethic argument about the importance of religion in the emergence of modern rational capitalism comes into question when seen from the point of view of the massive effort in *Economy and Society*[18] to find many sources of the unique Western pattern of rationalization.

What I am suggesting is that the irresolution in Weber's work is in part a reflection of an irresolution in Weber's life. He made intellectual commitments that he clearly found attractive (his nationalism was, though not blind, intense) but that also had ethical implications that he found repugnant. The direction that he saw the development of the power state taking, and more generally the consequences of the rationalization of modern life, did not give him any comfort. "Not summer's bloom lies ahead of us, but rather a polar night of icy darkness and hardness. . . ."[19] The pathos of some of Weber's later writings cannot be explained away by the narrow problems of German society, though specifically German problems undoubtedly added to his gloom. I am not trying to say that Weber's pessimism was unjustified—perhaps it was not—but only that the lack of resolution of intellectual and ethical issues that led to his "polytheism" undoubtedly increased its intensity.

There is a consistency and wholeness, both as a person and in his conception of his social role, about Durkheim that puts him in sharp contrast with Weber and that is related to the more unified architecture of Durkheim's thought (though Durkheim too was not without his dark forebodings). Yet to take some of Weber's statements about the disjunction between means and ends literally and to believe that his sociology was a collection of neutral scientific truths that could be equally useful to policy makers of different persuasions would be a travesty of his accomplishment. Riven with inner tensions though it is, Weber's corpus is a profound commentary on the human condition in the twentieth century. It is at once intellectually and morally passionate and, in the final essays, extraordinarily intense rhetorically.

I would like now to use Weber's most famous typology for a pur-

pose he did not intend, namely, to attempt an answer to the question
I previously raised and deferred about the sources of the ethical aims
that guide social inquiry. We can use the categories of traditional,
charismatic, and rational for this end, particularly if we see that the
categories are not exclusive but deeply interrelated.

Tradition provides us with ethical aims in several important ways.
Social inquiry is always responsive to some extent to the problems of
the society where such inquiry arises. Thus, socially current notions
about what is a good society, a satisfactory marriage, an able person,
etc., will always affect the investigator. A profound ethical crisis in
society may impel the investigator to begin work in the first place, as
with most of the thinkers we have discussed, and clarifying existing
moral conflict may be one of his major motives. While taking moral
definitions current in his society as a major reference point for his
inquiry, the investigator will seldom do so uncritically, for he is the
inheritor not only of the general social tradition but of the particular
tradition of social inquiry itself. That tradition provides not only intellectual tools but, simultaneously, ethical interpretations of human action.

In modern societies, both the general social tradition and the tradition of social thought are multiple, diverse, and partially in conflict.
Though individuals will, through accidents of birth and education,
feel closer to some strands of tradition than to others, there will always also be an element of choice. That is why, even in drawing on
tradition for the sources of our ethical reflection, charisma (in a
somewhat extended sense) and reason are always involved. Of course,
charisma and reason are part of the substance of tradition itself. Traditions often form around individuals who embody and live out certain ethical intentions in a particularly vivid way. They make a certain ethical possibility real because of the sheer vitality of their
example, not because of argument. Such, for our present purposes,
we might call charismatic figures. Rational reflection too becomes
part of tradition; not only reason as a value but the tools of rational
thought have to be transmitted. But for the individual faced with an
ethical choice, reason and charisma are present realities that are to
some degree in tension with tradition. Tradition may be followed because it is familiar, because it belongs to oneself and one's group. But
the self-conscious individual is never wholly satisfied with that, but

wants to know the reason for the tradition, wants to examine it critically. And such an individual also wants to experience it, not as an outer form but as an inner conviction that gives meaning to life. Such experience is more apt to come from committed practice than from argument alone.

In actuality, all the elements are found together. No one of us is without tradition—indeed, a multiplicity of traditions. One finds oneself believing in and practicing several of them. One uses one tradition (for example, social inquiry) to criticize another (for example, the norms of society). One reflects on the logical coherence of and the empirical evidence for different traditional views. One experiences life as flowing from ethical commitments that one has made. In this process of reception, practice, and reflection it is quite arbitrary to decide what is cognitive and what normative, when we are being scientific and when ethical. Indeed, intellectual acuteness and ethical maturity in this area go hand in hand. Wisdom is the traditional word that includes both.

If this way of putting it is right, then it is not surprising that ethical reflection is not extrinsic to the work of the most significant social thinkers. To disjoin social inquiry from ethical concerns would impoverish it cognitively. Without a reference point in traditions of ethical reflection, the very categories of social thought would be empty. The construction of an entirely new abstract vocabulary would render the enterprise opaque, as some critics have argued is the case with the work of Talcott Parsons. While an arid formalism does on occasion diminish the usefulness of Parsons' work, even his more obscure vocabulary is usually easily traceable to sources in the tradition of modern social thought, and the ethical impetus of his work as a whole is reasonably clear.[20] Nonetheless, in Parsons even more than in Durkheim and Weber, the powerful ethical aim of his intellectual enterprise remained mute relative to the often repeated claim that he was establishing a genuinely scientific sociology. While adding to that string of unfulfilled declarations, extending over so many generations, that scientific sociology is about to begin, Parsons' work exemplifies a new element of professionalization that characterizes the middle and late twentieth century, which can be understood only in terms of some of the considerations discussed in Michel de Certeau's paper in this volume. It is science as profession (in an ironic development beyond Weber) that deprives much of Parsons' work of the rhetorical power of his great predecessors and that comes close to depriving it as well of the ethical force that it genuinely contains.

Yet even today we see the forlorn recurrence of proclamations about the establishment of a true social science. In some recent examples, while ideology is as difficult to banish as ever, ethical energy and intellectual vigor appear to be vanishing, not surprisingly, together. Randall Collins may serve as an example.

In the preface to his *Conflict Sociology*, Collins informs us that his pursuit of sociology is not for its practical benefits or for ideological justifications but as "a coherent, powerful, and verified set of explanatory ideas." He tells us that "there is a powerful science in the making." But the beginning of the third paragraph of the preface gives the game away:

> This book focuses on conflict because I am attempting to be realistic, not because I happen to think conflict is good or bad. After reading this book, anyone who still judges explanatory concepts in terms of their value biases will not have grasped what it is about. Past theorists who have done most to remove our thinking from the murk of artificially imposed realities that populate our everyday worlds have found a guiding thread for explanation in the existence of plurality and conflict. Their lead is worth special emphasis right now, when there is so much potential for getting our science straight, and so many vestiges of utopian unreality burdening our habitual modes of analysis.[21]

Collins would have us believe that his decision to focus on conflict has no moral dimension, that it is purely cognitive, motivated only by the desire to escape "the murk of artificially imposed realities" and the "vestiges of utopian unreality." By choosing to concentrate on plurality and conflict, however, Collins is hardly avoiding concepts that "populate our everyday worlds." These are among the commoner coin of contemporary American ideology. The real polemical intent lies elsewhere—not in a critique of the everyday world, but in opposition to another strand in the tradition of social inquiry, namely, functionalism or systems theory. This becomes clear in Collins' first chapter, which is entitled "Why Is Sociology Not a Science?" where, in a section on ideology, we come across the following stunning sentence: "Conflict theory is intrinsically more detached from value judgments than is systems theory."[22] Max Weber is then invoked as an authority for the idea that detachment is good and as an example of an archetypal "conflict theorist."

We must keep in mind the purpose of Collins' book. Its subtitle is "Toward an Explanatory Science," and the last paragraph of the preface begins with a familiar claim: "Looking back, historians will see a great intellectual revolution in the twentieth century—the establishment of a true social science."[23] What then are the first principles of this nonideological, value-free explanatory social science? The first of the "general principles of conflict analysis" that applies to "any empirical area" is, "Think of people as animals maneuvering for advantage, susceptible to emotional appeals, but steering a self-interested course toward satisfactions and away from dissatisfactions."[24] Principles two and three are rather prolix but have to do with the fact that people take advantage of inequalities in resources, but the fourth principle is quite clear: "Ideals and beliefs likewise are to be explained in terms of the interests which have the resources to make their viewpoint prevail."[25] It would seem that the fundamental principles of this revolutionary twentieth-century explanatory science are identical with those in Book 1 of *Leviathan,* published by Hobbes in 1651 (also with an announcement that social science had now begun), but what was indeed revolutionary in Hobbes has since become the common coin of Anglo-American popular ideology.

If Hobbes's effort to create a dispassionate social science was founded on the passionate moral concern to discover a basis for social peace in a world at war, what can we say about Collins' ethical concern, despite his denial of one? Or is Collins' book the great exception, a purely scientific endeavor with no ethical aim at all? I have been able to discover only one paragraph on ethics in his book of nearly 550 pages:

The field of ethics as well cannot but benefit from the development of a social science. This development, as I have demonstrated, cannot be carried out without a firm understanding of the distinction between value judgments and logical and descriptive statements. Ethics is always an area of the ultimately arbitrary, but concerns itself with drawing out the consequences from these choice points, or tracing courses of action back to them. With the aid of social science, ethics can move beyond its conventional middle-class Christian biases built into some notion of rationality, interest, or the concept of "good" itself, to a far more sophisticated view of the choices that confront us.[26]

At least we learn what Collins does not like: "conventional middle-class Christian biases." But, after all, what is the purpose of this profusion of words, postulates, propositions, and causal principles that repeat in antiseptic fashion a fair bit of received sociology (with significant omissions, reworkings, and waterings down)? In the final paragraphs, as we might expect, Collins finally allows himself to express some direct moral purpose.

Theoretical and explanatory developments in the social science, it seems to me, can have their greatest impact in making us aware of the plurality of realities, the multiplicity of interests, and the tricks used to impose one reality upon others. Here sociology may have a liberating effect. Illusions, after all, are primarily on the side of the oppressors. With new technological developments providing new resources for the ongoing conflict between man and man, this widespread sophistication could be of considerable importance.

Despite much romantic hankering after the past, and its use as an ideal with which to flay the trends of the present, has been [sic] a long slow progress, at least in the world of the intellect. For all its ups and downs, its effects over the last few centuries have been increasingly libertarian. The social science of the future thus may have something to contribute to free our minds still further from illusions, and to make it possible for all people to share the gifts that have hitherto been reserved for the very aggressive and the very lucky.[27]

This optimistic conclusion is something of a non sequitur, for it follows immediately after the assertion that "stratification" will somehow survive technological advance and the "have-nots" will continue to be exploited. At least the ethical purpose of social science is finally clear. It is to enlighten us and liberate us from our illusions, the "murk of artificially imposed realities" and the "vestiges of utopian unreality." Just possibly, though we cannot count on it, this mental liberation may have something to do with a better society. One could not accuse Collins of moral passion and certainly not of utopian dreaming.

If by dressing up current ideological commonplaces, deprived of any fervor, as explanatory science Collins has at least given us a full-scale example of how not to proceed, what are the alternatives? It seems to me there is only one. In the social sciences we study the same kinds of beings that we are. Unlike the natural scientists, we are not "outside" what we study and certainly not "above" it. To imagine that we are is to deprive those we study of their dignity by treating them as objects. It is also to imagine that we understand them better than they understand themselves because our heads are not filled with the muddled ideas, false consciousness, traditions, and superstitions (murk and vestiges) that theirs are. It is to imagine that we are enlightened and free of illusions. As a result, we are unable to see that we too have our unexamined presuppositions, that we are ourselves involved in promises and commitments, our thoughts and feelings partly molded by symbols we have been given by tradition and do not consciously fully understand. In the social sciences we are not outside what we study and not above it. We can undertake our inquiry only by continuing our dialogue with those we study and relative to whom we are as much students as teachers.

In all the sciences we are involved with what we study, and it is difficult to tell where what we study leaves off and we begin. But in the social sciences this involvement is inextricable. We are certainly fooling ourselves if we think we pass no judgments on those we study. For these reasons it is extremely unlikely that sociology can ever be a paradigmatic science in Kuhn's sense. The choice of fundamental categories in the social sciences cannot be other than ethical as well as cognitive. What we say human beings fundamentally are has inevitable implications about what they ought to be. We have noted above in the case of Weber how the choice of a fundamental anthropology made some ethical options "realistic" and others not. Just because our categories reveal a fundamental stance toward the world, there is not apt to be the consensus that occurs in the natural sciences. Like philosophy and literary criticism, social science is much less cumulative or progressive than is natural science.

What creates coherence and continuity in social science is not consensus around a theoretical paradigm but concern for practical problems in the world. Social science was itself the product of a particular kind of social crisis, the crisis of the transformation of traditional society into modern society. Part of this change was the transformation of traditional consciousness into critical consciousness, though that transformation is never completed but remains a permanent tension. Every one of the great theorists asked the questions, "Why is modern society so different from all other societies, and how can we understand its characteristics?" The question always contained the corollary, explicit or implicit, "What are we going to do about it?" If social science is a continuing reflection on the contradictions and paradoxes of modern society and the dilemmas for action that it creates, then, in the Aristotelian sense of the word, it is a practical science. That means, in the first place, that it is a reflection on what must be done.

But if social science is to be practical in this classical sense of the word, it means something very different from technological application on the model of the natural sciences. It means, above all, the participation of the social scientist in the process of social self-understanding. No one has seen better than Edward Shils the implication of this point of view for the definition of social science.

> The self-understanding of a society is not likely ever to be a wholly consensual affair; it is far more likely to be an act performed by only a few persons in that society. But those few persons to interpret their society correctly must see themselves as parts of it and not as isolated observers who have no affinity with it. This does not mean that they must approve of all that goes on in their society or that they must avoid reference to conflicts, exploitation, manipulation, and coercion. It does mean that the sociologist who interprets his society is also interpreting it to itself and that he is at the same time interpreting himself as a part of it.
>
> The sociological theory here under discussion—both on the level of relatively concrete middle principles and on that of more abstract analysis—is a discipline fundamentally alien to technological application; it is not capable of becoming a technological science. . . .
>
> . . . The real deficiency of technological sociology, which would remain despite its scientific rigor, its moral naiveté, and its harmlessness (hitherto) is its failure to grasp that the true calling of sociology is to contribute to the self-understanding of society rather than its manipulated improvement.[28]

In *The Last Half-Century,* Morris Janowitz gives us a good example of social science as practical because of its contribution to social self-understanding.[29] Janowitz takes as his central category "social control," a rather ambiguous concept. He argues persuasively that the idea of social control in the sociological tradition has primarily to do with the self-control of participating citizens and groups in a democratic republic rather than with the central control of bureaucratic administration. Political self-regulation in this sense is the key to the legitimacy and survival of democratic industrial societies. Thus, Janowitz speaks to his fellow citizens about the conditions for the very survival of citizenship.

In his epilogue, he deals rather subtly with the role of the social scientist in this situation. He wishes to avoid turning social science into a direct resource for ideological slogans, on the one hand, or a policy science to be used by decision makers, on the other. He suggests rather an indirect, clarifying educational role, similar to the one I have described for Durkheim and close to Shils's idea of social self-understanding. One need not agree with Janowitz in his choice of concepts or in his practical stance to see that he has seriously considered what kind of enterprise social science is. It is this kind of conscious, self-critical consideration that makes his book worth arguing with in a way that Collins' *Conflict Sociology* is not.

But a practical social science is not concerned only with the great problems that modern society presents to us. It is also concerned with the criteria by which one can judge whether an outcome is good or not. In asking, "What must we do?" one cannot take for granted the ends of action defined by any given group. One must inquire into the validity of the claims. One must ask, "What is a good society?" or perhaps even,"What is the best society?" This means keeping open the boundary that we now draw academically between social science on the one hand and philosophy on the other. A major social theorist at work today who keeps these doors open and asks the ultimate normative questions is Jürgen Habermas. In *Knowledge and Human Interests* [30] Habermas asks about the conditions for a good society today, and in his subsequent work he continues to refine the issue. Habermas ranges across many of the major resources of contemporary continental and Anglo-American philosophy and social science to shed light on these problems. Quite aside from his substantive achievements, he has succeeded through his intellectual seriousness and integrity in showing that the normative issue belongs at the head of our agenda, something social science for a long time has not wished to believe.

Because good social science is always morally serious, we can transpose Weber's saying that only a mature man can have the calling for politics into the statement that only a mature person can have the calling for sociology. Moral vacuity creates cognitively trivial work. The sterility of much sociological research is due to moral infantilism and not to the fact that "our science is still young." In particular, reductionism as an explanatory device is due to moral timidity or cowardice or—this is why reductionism and determinism are so attractive to the young—plain moral confusion. That people are "animals maneuvering for advantage" or that "ideals and beliefs . . . are to be explained in terms of . . . interests" are assertions that are often enough true. But in the interesting and decisive cases, these reductionistic statements are false, and as generalizations they are worthless, if not pernicious—pernicious because to the degree that they are rhetorically persuasive, they act as self-fulfilling prophecies. They help to create the moral cretinism they describe. No mature person, in Weber's terms, believes such things, and no viable social science can be built on them.[31] Power and meaning always go together in human action, and we forget it at our peril. But that solves no moral dilemmas. Indeed, it only heightens the moral stakes. The morally profound person who understands that is rare, and that person's works will be precious, no matter what the era. Perhaps that is another reason why social science is not cumulative and we still have much to learn from the ancients.

To listen, to reflect, to criticize, to respond—these are the tasks of social inquiry today, as they always have been. They are not tasks that will yield to cleverness. No child prodigy by dint of a phenomenal IQ has ever made much contribution to them. They require our full personhood. To accept these tasks is itself a form of moral discipline.

NOTES

1. Thomas Hobbes, *Leviathan,* ed. by C. B. Macpherson (Harmondsworth, England: Penguin Books, 1968), part 1, ch. 11, p. 161.

2. Alexis de Tocqueville, introduction to *Democracy in America,* George Lawrence, trans., J. P. Mayer, ed. (Garden City, N.Y.: Doubleday, Anchor Books, 1969), vol. 1, p. 12.

3. Alexis de Tocqueville, *The Old Regime and the French Revolution,* Stuart Gilbert, trans. (Garden City, N.Y.: Doubleday, Anchor Books, 1955), part 3, ch. 3, p. 168.

4. I have argued the case at length in the introduction to Robert N. Bellah, ed., *Emile Durkheim on Morality and Society* (Chicago: University of Chicago Press, 1973).

5. Emile Durkheim, "The Intellectual Elite and Democracy," in *ibid.,* p. 59.

6. Emile Durkheim, "Individualism and the Intellectuals," in *ibid.,* pp. 55–56.

7. H. H. Gerth and C. Wright Mills, eds., *From Max Weber* (New York: Oxford University Press, 1946), p. 151.

8. *Ibid.,* p. 156.

9. *Ibid.,* pp. 152–153.

10. *Ibid.,* pp. 77–78.

11. *Ibid.,* ch. 13, pp. 323–359.

12. Aristotle, *Nichomachean Ethics,* 1113a29–35.

13. Gerth and Mills, *From Max Weber,* p. 127.

14. *Ibid.,* p. 357.

15. *Ibid.*

16. Jeffrey Alexander, *Theoretical Logic in Sociology* (Berkeley: University of California Press, forthcoming), vol. 3.

17. Gerth and Mills, *From Max Weber,* p. 280.

18. Max Weber, *Economy and Society,* Guenther Roth and Claus Wittich, eds., 2 vols. (Berkeley: University of California Press, 1978).

19. Gerth and Mills, *From Max Weber,* p. 128.

20. These issues are discussed in Robert N. Bellah, "The World Is the World Through Its Theorists: In Memory of Talcott Parsons (1902–1979)," *Journal for the Scientific Study of Religion* (1979), 18:454–56, reprinted in *American Sociologist* (May 1980), 15:60–62; and in Jeffrey C. Alexander, "Sociology for Liberals," *New Republic,* June 2, 1979, pp. 10–12.

21. Randall Collins, *Conflict Sociology* (New York: Academic Press, 1975), pp. ix–x.

22. *Ibid.,* p. 21.

23. *Ibid.,* p. x.

24. *Ibid.,* p. 60.

25. *Ibid.,* p. 61.

26. *Ibid.,* p. 547.

27. *Ibid.,* pp. 548–49.

28. Edward Shils, *The Calling of Sociology: Essays on the Pursuit of Learning* (Chicago: University of Chicago Press, 1980), pp. 39, 76.

29. Morris Janowitz, *The Last Half-Century: Societal Change and Politics in America* (Chicago: University of Chicago Press, 1978).

30. Jürgen Habermas, *Knowledge and Human Interests* (Boston: Beacon Press, 1971; German ed., Frankfurt: Suhrkamp Verlag, 1968).

31. For similar reflections, see Edward Shils, *Calling of Sociology,* pp. 87–88.

INDEX